Reflections on Theoretical Issues in Argumentation Theory

Argumentation Library

VOLUME 28

More information about this series at http://www.springer.com/series/5642

Frans H. van Eemeren · Bart Garssen
Editors

Reflections on Theoretical Issues in Argumentation Theory

Springer

Editors
Frans H. van Eemeren
Faculty of Humanities, TAR
University of Amsterdam
Amsterdam
The Netherlands

Bart Garssen
Faculty of Humanities, TAR
University of Amsterdam
Amsterdam
The Netherlands

ISSN 1566-7650 ISSN 2215-1907 (electronic)
Argumentation Library
ISBN 978-3-319-21102-2 ISBN 978-3-319-21103-9 (eBook)
DOI 10.1007/978-3-319-21103-9

Library of Congress Control Number: 2015944150

Springer Cham Heidelberg New York Dordrecht London

Printed on acid-free paper

Springer International Publishing AG Switzerland is part of Springer Science+Business Media (www.springer.com)

Preface

Reflections on Theoretical Issues in Argumentation Theory contains a selection of papers reflecting upon theoretical issues in argumentation theory. The papers are selected from the contributions to the Proceedings of the 8th Conference of the International Society for the Study of Argumentation held in Amsterdam in 2014. After selection the papers have been reviewed and revised where this seemed useful.

The volume consists of six Parts: I. General Perspectives, II. Analysis of Argumentation, III. Evaluation of Argumentation, IV. Argument Schemes, V. Contextual Embedding of Argumentation, VI. Linguistic Approaches to Argumentation. Each part includes several papers dedicated to the specific theme concerned.

In Part I, *General Perspectives*, Frans H. van Eemeren identifies in "Bingo! Promising Developments in Argumentation Theory" three promising developments in the treatment of argumentation in argumentation theory: (1) the trend towards empiricalization, (2) the attention paid to the institutional macro-contexts in which argumentative discourse takes place, (3) the movement towards formalization. According to van Eemeren, if they are integrated with each other and comply with pertinent academic requirements, these developments will mean "bingo!" for the future of argumentation theory.

J. Anthony Blair describes in "What Is Informal Logic?" the emergence of two themes that are key to the constitution of informal logic: (1) the development of analytic tools for the recognition, identification and display of so-called "non-interactive" arguments, (2) the development of evaluative tools for assessing deductive, inductive, and other kinds of arguments. He also mentions current interests of informal logicians.

G.C. (Geoff) Goddu presents and analyzes in "Towards a Foundation for Argumentation Theory" principles that argumentation theorists agree upon and some closely related ones on which they do not agree. He argues that this set offers at best limited grounds for cross-theoretical evaluation.

Douglas Niño and Danny Marrero outline in "The Agentive Approach to Argumentation: A Proposal" an agent-centered theory of argumentation. Their working hypothesis is that the aim of argumentation depends on the purposes of the agents, their "agendas".

In part II, *Analysis of Argumentation*, Sharon Bailin and Mark Battersby argue in "Conductive Argumentation, Degrees of Confidence, and the Communication of Uncertainty" that there is an epistemic obligation to communicate the appropriate degree of confidence when asserting conclusions in conductive argumentation. They argue that such conclusions frequently are, and should be, expressed with appropriate qualifications.

David Hitchcock argues in "The Linked-Convergent Distinction" that this distinction, introduced by Stephen Thomas in 1977, is primarily a distinction between ways in which two or more reasons can directly support a claim, and only derivatively a distinction between types of structures, arguments, reasoning, reasons, or premises.

James B. Freeman summarizes in "Identifying the Warrant of an Argument" Hitchcock's procedure to extract the warrant from an argument and notes that applying it in specific cases may be problematic. He then extends the procedure by indicating how symbolization in a formal language addresses the problems.

Jens E. Kjeldsen observes in "Where Is Visual Argument?" that argumentation theory suffers from a lack of empirical studies of how audiences actually perceive and construct rhetorical argumentation from communicative stimuli. This is especially pertinent to the study of visual argumentation, because this argumentation is fundamentally enthymematic, leaving most of the reconstruction of premises to the viewer. Kjeldsen uses the method of audience analysis from communication studies to establish how viewers interpret instances of visual argumentation such as pictorially dominated advertisements.

In part III, *Evaluation of Argumentation,* Daniel H. Cohen explains in "Missed Opportunities in Argument Evaluation" why do we hold arguers culpable for missing obvious objections *against* their arguments but not for missing obvious lines of reasoning *for* their positions.

According to Maurice A. Finocchiaro in "Ubiquity, Ambiguity, and Metarationality: Searching for the Fallacy of Composition" "ubiquity" is the hypothesis that fallacies of composition are ubiquitous; "ambiguity" the hypothesis that "fallacy of composition" has at least three distinct and often confused meanings; "metarationality" the hypothesis that the best places to search for fallacies of composition are meta-arguments whose conclusions attribute this fallacy to ground-level arguments.

Scott Aikin and John Casey survey in "Don't Feed the Trolls: Straw Men and Iron Men" the three forms of straw men that are recognized in the literature: the straw, weak, and hollow man. The cases of inappropriately reconstructing stronger versions of the opposition's arguments they call *iron man* fallacies.

Paula Olmos proposes in "Story Credibility in Narrative Arguments" a multi-dimensional and explicit meta-argumentative approach to the assessment of arguments involving narratives.

In part IV, *Argument Schemes*, Manfred Kraus contributes in "Arguments by Analogy (and What We Can Learn about Them from Aristotle)" to the debate about arguments by analogy. He concentrates in particular on the distinction between 'deductive' and 'inductive' analogies and on the question of how such arguments can be 'deductive' yet nonetheless defeasible.

Fabrizio Macagno analyses in "A Means-End Classification of Argumentation Schemes" argument schemes as prototypical combinations of two distinct levels of abstraction.

In part V, *Contextual Embedding of Argumentation*, Harvey Siegel argues in "Argumentative Norms: How Contextual Can They Be? A Cautionary Tale" that, although argument quality sometimes depends upon criteria that are context-relative, the contextual dimension of argumentative norms depends upon a kind of context-independence.

A. Francisca Snoeck Henkemans and Jean Wagemans discuss in "Reasonableness in Context: Taking into Account Institutional Conventions in the Pragma-Dialectical Evaluation of Argumentative Discourse" the question of how to take institutional conventions into account in a pragma-dialectical evaluation of argumentative discourse.

Sally Jackson argues in "Deference, Distrust, and Delegation: Three Design Hypotheses" that in argumentation theory a design hypothesis is a broad notion about how argumentative practice can be shaped toward greater reasonableness. Different design hypotheses do not compete in the way empirical hypotheses do.

In part VI, *Linguistic Approaches to Argumentation*, Thierry Herman observes in "A Plea for a Linguistic Distinction Between Explanation and Argument" that there is no clear consensus about the difference between explanation and argument. After having explained why traditional points of view in informal logic raise a problem, he argues for a linguistic point of view and shows how rhetorical strategic moves can exploit the blurry frontier between explanation and argumentation.

Johanna Miecznikowski and Elena Musi examine in "Verbs of Appearance and Argument Schemes: Italian *Sembrare* as an Argumentative Indicator" the role of verbs of appearance as argumentative indicators. They analyze the uses of the Italian verb *sembrare* ('seem') in a sample of 40 texts chosen from a corpus of reviews, editorials and comment posts.

Pierre-Yves Raccah argues in "Linguistic Argumentation as a Shortcut for the Empirical Study of Argumentative Strategies" that discourses provide empirical hints that inform the observer about the institutional conventionalized practices involved in the study of strategic manoeuvring.

April 2015

Frans H. van Eemeren
Bart Garssen

Contents

Part III Evaluation of Argumentation

Part IV Argument Schemes

Part V Contextual Embedding of Argumentation

Contributors

Scott Aikin Department of Philosophy, Vanderbilt University, Nashville, TN, USA

J. Anthony Blair Centre for Research in Reasoning, Argumentation and Rhetoric, University of Windsor, Windsor, ON, Canada

Sharon Bailin Faculty of Education, Simon Fraser University, Vancouver, BC, Canada

Mark Battersby Capilano University (Retired), Critical Inquiry Group, Vancouver, BC, Canada

John Casey Department of Philosophy, Northeastern Illinois University, Chicago, IL, USA

Daniel H. Cohen Department of Philosophy, Colby College, Waterville, USA

Maurice A. Finocchiaro Department of Philosophy, University of Nevada-Las Vegas, Las Vegas, USA

James B. Freeman Department of Philosophy, Hunter College of the City University of New York, New York, NY, USA

G.C. Goddu Department of Philosophy, University of Richmond, Richmond, VA, USA

Thierry Herman EFLE and Institute of Language Sciences and Communication, Universities of Lausanne and Neuchâtel, Lausanne and Neuchâtel, Switzerland

David Hitchcock Department of Philosophy, McMaster University, Hamilton, Canada

Sally Jackson Department of Communication, University of Illinois at Urbana-Champaign, Champaign, USA

Jens E. Kjeldsen Department of Information Science and Media Studies, University of Bergen, Bergen, Norway

Manfred Kraus Philologisches Seminar, University of Tübingen, Tübingen, Germany

Fabrizio Macagno ArgLab, Instituto de Filosofia da Nova, Universidade Nova de Lisboa, Lisbon, Portugal

Danny Marrero Law School, Universidad Jorge Tadeo Lozano, Bogotá, Colombia

Johanna Miecznikowski Istituto di studi italiani, Università della Svizzera italiana, Lugano, Switzerland

Elena Musi Istituto di studi italiani, Università della Svizzera italiana, Lugano, Switzerland

Douglas Niño Department of Humanities, Universidad Jorge Tadeo Lozano, Bogotá, Colombia

Paula Olmos Departamento de Lingüística, Lenguas modernas, Lógica y filosofía de la ciencia, Teoría de la literatura y literatura comparada, Universidad Autónoma de Madrid, Madrid, Spain

Pierre-Yves Raccah CNRS LLL—UMR 7270, University of Orléans, Orléans, France

Harvey Siegel Department of Philosophy, University of Miami, Coral Gables, FL, USA

A.F. Snoeck Henkemans Department of Speech Communication, Argumentation Theory, and Rhetoric, University of Amsterdam, Amsterdam, The Netherlands

Frans H. van Eemeren ILIAS, University of Amsterdam and Leiden University, Leiden, The Netherlands

J.H.M. Wagemans Department of Speech Communication, Argumentation Theory, and Rhetoric, University of Amsterdam, Amsterdam, The Netherlands

Part I
General Perspectives

Bingo! Promising Developments in Argumentation Theory

Frans H. van Eemeren

1 Changes in the State of the Art of Argumentation Theory

Since the conference of the International Society for the Study of Argumentation held in Amsterdam in July 2014 was the eighth ISSA conference, argumentation theorists from various kinds of backgrounds have been exchanging views about argumentation for almost 30 years. My keynote speech at the start of this conference seemed to me the right occasion for making some general comments on the way in which the field is progressing.

I considered myself in a good position to strike a balance because during the past five years I have been preparing an overview of the state of the art in a new *Handbook of Argumentation Theory*. I have done so together with my co-authors, Bart Garssen, Erik C. W. Krabbe, A. Francisca Snoeck Henkemans, Bart Verheij, and Jean H. M. Wagemans. In this complicated endeavour we have been supported generously by a large group of knowledgeable reviewers and advisors from the field. On the 2 July reception of the ISSA conference the *Handbook* was presented to the community of argumentation scholars.

The *Handbook of Argumentation Theory* is the latest offshoot of a tradition of handbook writing that I started with Rob Grootendorst in the mid-1970s. We presented first several overviews of the state of the art in Dutch before publishing the handbook in English, the current lingua franca of scholarship (van Eemeren et al. 1978, 1981, 1984, 1986, 1987). The most recent version of the handbook was *Fundamentals of Argumentation Theory*, which appeared in 1996 and was co-authored by a group of prominent argumentation scholars (van Eemeren et al. 1996).

F.H. van Eemeren (✉)
ILIAS, University of Amsterdam and Leiden University, Leiden, The Netherlands
e-mail: f.h.vaneemeren@uva.nl

F.H. van Eemeren and B. Garssen (eds.), *Reflections on Theoretical Issues in Argumentation Theory*, Argumentation Library 28,
DOI 10.1007/978-3-319-21103-9_1

The overview offered by the newly-completed version of the handbook constitutes the basis for giving a judgment of recent developments in the discipline. It goes without saying that a short presentation does not allow me to pay attention to all developments that could be of interest; I limit myself to three major trends that I find promising. They involve innovations which are, in my view, vital for the future of the field.

Argumentation scholars are not in full harmony regarding the definition of the term *argumentation*.[1] There seems to be general agreement however that argumentation always involves trying to convince or persuade others by means of reasoned discourse.[2] Although I think that most argumentation scholars will agree that the study of argumentation has a descriptive as well as a normative dimension, their views on how in actual research the two dimensions are to be approached will diverge.[3] Unanimity comes almost certainly to an end when it has to be decided which theoretical perspective is to be favoured.[4]

The general theoretical perspectives that are dominant are the *dialectical*, which concentrates foremost on procedural reasonableness, and the *rhetorical*, focusing on aspired effectiveness. In modern argumentation theory both theoretical traditions are pervaded by insights from philosophy, logic, pragmatics, discourse analysis, communication, and other disciplines. Since the late 1990s, a tendency has developed to connect, or even integrate, the two traditions.[5] Taking only a dialectical perspective involves the risk that relevant contextual and situational factors

[1]See van Eemeren (2010, pp. 25–27) for the influence of being or not being a native speaker of English on the perception of argumentation and argumentation theory.

[2]In my view, instead of being a theory of proof or a general theory of reasoning or argument, argumentation theory concentrates on using argument to convince others by a reasonable discussion of the acceptability of the standpoints at issue. My view of argumentation theory is generally incorporated in more-encompassing views that have been advanced.

[3]As we observed in the new *Handbook*, "[s]ome argumentation theorists have a goal that is primarily (and sometimes even exclusively) descriptive, especially those theorists having a background in linguistics, discourse analysis, and rhetoric. They are interested, for instance, in finding out how in argumentative discourse speakers and writers try to convince or persuade others by making use of certain linguistic devices or by using other means to influence their audience or readership. Other argumentation theorists, often inspired by logic, philosophy, or insights from law, study argumentation primarily for normative purposes. They are interested in developing soundness criteria that argumentation must satisfy in order to qualify as rational or reasonable. They examine, for instance, the epistemic function argumentation fulfills or the fallacies that may occur in argumentative discourse" (van Eemeren et al. 2014, p. 29).

[4]According to the *Handbook of argumentation theory*, "The current state of the art in argumentation theory is characterized by the co-existence of a variety of theoretical perspectives and approaches, which differ considerably from each other in conceptualization, scope, and theoretical refinement" (van Eemeren et al. 2014, p. 29).

[5]See for various views on combining insights from dialectic and rhetoric van Eemeren and Houtlosser (2002a, b). Van Eemeren and Houtlosser (2002a, b) have proposed to integrate insights from rhetoric into the theoretical framework of pragma-dialectics. According to Tindale, who considers the rhetorical perspective as the most fundamental, the synthesis of the logical, dialectical and rhetorical perspectives should be grounded in the rhetorical perspective (1999, pp. 6–7).

are not taken into account, while taking a purely rhetorical perspective involves the risk that the critical dimension of argumentation is not explored to the full.[6]

Compared to some 30 years ago, both the number of participants and the number of publications in argumentation theory have increased strikingly. Another remarkable difference is that nowadays not only North-American and European scholars are involved, but also Latin Americans, Asians and Arabs. In addition, an important impetus to the progress of argumentation theory is given by related disciplines such as *critical discourse analysis* and *persuasion research*.[7]

Today I would like to concentrate on some recent changes in the way in which argumentation is examined. In my opinion, three major developments in the treatment of argumentation have begun to materialize that open up new avenues for research. Although they differ in shape, these developments can be observed across a broad spectrum of theoretical approaches. The three developments I have in mind can be designated as *empiricalization*, *contextualization*, and *formalization* of the treatment of argumentation.[8]

2 Empiricalization of the Treatment of Argumentation

Modern argumentation theory manifested itself initially by the articulation of theoretical proposals for concepts and models of argumentation based on new philosophical views of reasonableness. In 1958, Stephen Toulmin presented a model of the various procedural steps involved in putting forward argumentation—or "argument," as he used to call it (Toulmin 2003). He emphasized that, in order to deal adequately with the reasonableness of argumentation in the various "fields" of argumentative reality, an *empirical approach* to argumentation is needed. On their part, Chaïm Perelman and Lucie Olbrechts-Tyteca, who are among the co-founders of modern argumentation theory, claimed to have based the theoretical categories of their "new rhetoric" on empirical observations (Perelman and Olbrechts-Tyteca 1969).[9] Like Frege's theory of logic was founded upon a descriptive analysis of mathematical reasoning, they founded their argumentation theory on a descriptive analysis of

---

[6]In our new *Handbook* we take the position that argumentation theory can best be viewed as an interdisciplinary study with logical, dialectical, and rhetorical dimensions (van Eemeren et al. 2014, p. 29).

[7]According to van Eemeren et al. (2014), a great number of contributions to the study of argumentation are not part of the generally recognized research traditions; some of them stem from related disciplines: some of them have been developed in non-Anglophone parts of the world. See Chap. 12 of the *Handbook*.

[8]It goes without saying that, depending on one's theoretical position and preferences, other promising trends can be distinguished. A case in point may be the study of visual and other modalities of argumentation.

[9]In spite of various criticisms of the empirical adequacy of Perelman and Olbrechts-Tyteca's taxonomy of argument schemes (van Eemeren et al. 1996, pp. 122–124, 2014, p. 292), Warnick and Kline (1992) have made an effort to carry out empirical research based on this taxonomy

reasoning with value judgments in the fields of law, history, philosophy, and literature.[10]

In spite of their insistence on "empiricalization" of the treatment of argumentation, the empirical dimension of Perelman and Olbrechts-Tyteca's own contributions to argumentation theory remains rather sketchy. In fact, all prominent protagonists of modern argumentation theory in the 1950s, 60s and 70s concentrated in the first place on presenting theoretical proposals for dealing with argumentation and philosophical views in their support. This even applies to the Norwegian philosopher Arne Næss, however practical and empirical his orientation was.[11] The empirical research Næss wanted to be carried out with regard to argumentation was designed to lead to a more precise determination of the statements about which disagreement exists.[12] In his own work however he refrained from giving substance to the empirical dimension of argumentation theory.

Despite the strongly expressed preferences of the founding fathers, I conclude that the development of the empirical component of argumentation theory did not really take off until much later. Making such a sweeping statement however, forces you often to acknowledge exceptions immediately. In this case, I must admit that there is an old and rich tradition of empirically-oriented rhetorical scholarship in American communication studies.[13] The empirical research that is conducted in this tradition consists for the most part of *case studies*. One of its main branches, for instance, "rhetorical criticism," concentrates on analysing specific public speeches or texts that are meant to be persuasive. An excellent specimen is Michael Leff and Gerald Mohrmann's (1993) analysis of Abraham Lincoln's Cooper Union speech of February 27, 1860, designed to win nomination as spokesman for the Republican Party. Zarefsky (1986) offers another example of such empirical research of historical political discourse in *David President Johnson's War on Poverty*. His more encompassing central question is how Johnson's social program, put in the strategic perspective of a "war on poverty," and laid down in the Economic Opportunity Act, gained first such strong support and fell so far later on.

In my view, in argumentation theory argumentative reality is to be examined systematically, concentrating in particular on the influence of certain factors in

---

[10]The norms for rationality and reasonableness described in the new rhetoric have an "emic" basis: the criteria for the evaluation of argumentation that Perelman and Olbrechts-Tyteca provide are a description of various kinds of argumentation that can be successful in practice with the people for whom the argumentation is intended.

[11]In *Interpretation and Preciseness*, published in 1953, Næss revealed himself as a radical empirical semanticist, who liked questionnaires and personal interviews to be used for investigating what in particular circles is understood by particular expressions. However, he did not carry out such investigations himself.

[12]Although Næss's empirical ideas stimulated the coming into existence of the "Oslo School," a group of researchers investigating semantic relations, such as synonymy, by means of questionnaires, their influence in argumentation theory has been rather limited.

[13]Already since the 1950s, contemporary argumentative discourse in the political domain has been carefully studied by rhetoricians such as Newman (1961) and Schiappa (2002), to name just two outstanding examples from different periods.

argumentative reality on the production, interpretation, and assessment of argumentative discourse.[14] Two types of empirical research can be pertinent. First, *qualitative* research relying on introspection and observation by the researcher will usually be most appropriate when specific qualities, traits or conventions of particular specimens of argumentative discourse need to be depicted. Second, as a rule, *quantitative* research based on numerical data and statistics is required when generic "If X, then Y" claims regarding the production, interpretation or assessment of argumentative discourse must be tested. It is basically the nature of the claim at issue that determines which type of evidence is required—examples or frequencies—and which type of empirical research is therefore most appropriate. Although qualitative as well as quantitative empirical research has its own function in examining argumentative discourse, and the two types of research may complement each other in various ways, carrying out qualitative research is in my opinion always a necessary preparatory step in gaining a better understanding of argumentative reality.[15]

In France, Marianne Doury has recently carried out qualitative empirical research that is systematically connected with research questions of a more general kind (e.g., Doury 2006). Her research, which is strongly influenced by insights from discourse and conversation analysis, aims at highlighting "the discursive and interactional devices used by speakers who face conflicting standpoints and need to take a stand in such a way as to hold out against contention" (Doury 2009, p. 143). Doury focuses on the "spontaneous" argumentative norms revealed by the observation of argumentative exchanges in polemical contexts (Doury 1997, 2004a, 2005). Her "emic," i.e. theory-independent, descriptions contribute to a form of argumentative "ethnography" (Doury 2004b).

In contrast to theoretical research, in "informal logic" empirical research is rather thin on the ground. Nevertheless, Maurice Finocchiaro has carried out important qualitative research projects focusing on reasoning in scientific controversies (e.g., Finocchiaro 2005b). His approach, which is directed at theorizing, can be characterized as both *historical* and *empirical*. Finocchiaro states explicitly that the theory of reasoning he has in mind "has an empirical orientation and is not a purely formal or abstract discipline" (2005a, p. 22).[16] Rather than judging arguments in historical

---

[14]Because of its ambition to be an academic discipline which is of practical relevance in dealing with argumentative reality, argumentation theory needs to include empirical research relating to the philosophically motivated theoretical models that have been developed. To see to what extent argumentative reality agrees with the theory, the research programme of an argumentation theory such as pragma-dialectics therefore has an empirical component.

[15]Although in general quantitative research is only necessary with regard to more general claims, claims pertaining to a specific case can sometimes also be supported quantitatively. In any case, quantitative research is only relevant to argumentation theory if it increases our insight into argumentative reality.

[16]At the same time, Finocchiaro emphasizes that "the empirical is contrasted primarily to the a priori, and not, for example, to the normative or the theoretical" (2005a, p. 47).

controversies from an a priori perspective, as formal logicians do, Finocchiaro holds that the assessment criteria can and should be found empirically within the discourse.

The oldest and most well-known type of quantitative empirical research of argumentation takes place, mainly in the United States, in the related area of *persuasion research*. More often than not however persuasion research does not concentrate on argumentation. When it does, it deals with the persuasive effects of the way in which argumentation is presented (*message structure*) and the persuasive effects of the content of argumentation (*message content*). In the past years, both types of persuasion research have cumulated in large-scale "meta-analyses," carried out most elaborately by Daniel O'Keefe (2006).

Recently the connection between argumentation and persuasion has been examined more frequently, also outside the United States, in particular by communication scholars from the University of Nijmegen. Their research concentrates for the most part on message content. Hans Hoeken (2001) addressed the relationship between the perception of the quality of an argument and its actual persuasiveness. His initial research, which can be seen as an altered replication of research conducted earlier by Baesler and Burgoon (1994), examined the perceived and actual persuasiveness of three different types of evidence: anecdotal, statistical, and causal evidence. The experimental results indicate that the various types of evidence had a different effect on the acceptance of the claim. However, the differences only partly replicate the pattern of results obtained in other studies. Contrary to expectations, in Hoeken's study causal evidence proved not to be the most convincing evidence. It was in fact just as persuasive as anecdotal evidence, and less persuasive than statistical evidence.[17] Later research conducted in Nijmegen has focused on the relative persuasiveness of different types of arguments.

Since the 1980s, quantitative empirical research has also been carried out in argumentation theory, albeit not by a great many scholars. In order to establish to what extent in argumentative reality the recognition of argumentative moves is facilitated or hampered by factors in their presentation I conducted experimental research together with Grootendorst and Bert Meuffels (van Eemeren et al. 1984b).[18] Dale Hample and Judith Dallinger (1986, 1987, 1991) investigated in the same period the editorial standards people apply in designing their own arguments.[19] And

[17]Corresponding with its actual persuasiveness, statistical evidence is rated as stronger than anecdotal evidence. Ratings of the strength of the argument are in both cases strongly related to its actual persuasiveness. In contrast, causal evidence received higher ratings compared to its actual persuasiveness.

[18]See Garssen (2002) for experimental research into whether ordinary arguers have a pre-theoretical notion of argument schemes.

[19]More recently, Hample collaborated with Paglieri and Na (2011) in answering the question of when people are inclined to start a discussion.

Judith Sanders et al. (1991) compared the assessments given by different ethnic groups in evaluating the strength or quality of warrants used in argumentation with assessments given by experts in the field of argumentation and debate (p. 709).[20]

Several quantitative research projects have concentrated on ordinary arguers' pre-theoretical quality notions—or *norms of reasonableness*. Judith Bowker and Robert Trapp (1992), for example, studied laymen's norms for sound argumentation: Do ordinary arguers apply predictable, consistent criteria on the basis of which they distinguish between sound and unsound argumentation? Their conclusion is that the judgments of the respondents partially correlate with the reasonableness norms formulated by informal logicians such as Ralph Johnson and Anthony Blair, and Trudy Govier (p. 228).[21]

Together with Garssen and Meuffels I carried out a comprehensive research project, reported in 2009 in *Fallacies and Judgments of Reasonableness*, to test experimentally the intersubjective acceptability of the pragma-dialectical norms for judging the reasonableness of argumentative discourse (van Eemeren et al. 2009).[22] Rather than being "emic" standards of reasonableness, the pragma-dialectical norms are "etic" standards for resolving differences of opinion on the merits. They are designed to be "problem-valid"—or, in terms of Rupert Crawshay-Williams (1957), *methodologically necessary* for serving their purpose. Their "intersubjective"—or, in terms of Crawshay-Williams, "conventional"—validity for the arguers however is to be tested empirically. The general conclusion of our extended series of experimental tests is that all data that were obtained indicate that the norms ordinary arguers use when judging the reasonableness of contributions to a discussion correspond quite well with the pragma-dialectical norms for critical discussion. Based on this indirect evidence, the rules may be claimed to be *conventionally valid*—taken both individually and as a collective.[23]

[20]Another type of quantitative research focuses on cognitive processes. Voss et al. (1993), for instance, present a model of informal argument processing and describe experiments that provide support for the model.

[21]Making also use of an "empiricistic" method, Schreier et al. (1995) introduced the concept of *argumentational integrity* to develop ethical criteria for assessing contributions to argumentative discussions in daily life based on experimental findings.

[22]This research was, of course, not aimed at legitimizing the model of a critical discussion. All the same, by indicating which factors are worth investigating because of their significance for resolving a difference of opinion on the merits, the model gives direction to the research.

[23]Within the field of experimental psychology, Mercier and Sperber (2011) have recently proposed an "argumentative theory" which hypothesizes that the (main) function of reasoning is argumentative: "to produce arguments so we can convince others and to evaluate others' arguments so as to be convinced only when appropriate" (Mercier 2012, pp. 259–260). Putting forward this hypothesis on the function of reasoning enables them to (re)interpret many of the findings of tests conducted in experimental psychology. As to further research, Mercier (2012, p. 266) proposes to take typologies regarding argument schemes and their associated critical questions developed in argumentation theory as a starting point for experimental studies regarding the evaluation of arguments. In this way, it might become clear which cognitive mechanisms are at play when people evaluate certain types of argumentation.

3 Contextualization of the Treatment of Argumentation

A second striking development in argumentation theory is the greatly increased attention being paid to the context in which argumentation takes places. By taking explicitly account of contextual differentiation in dealing with the production, analysis and evaluation of argumentative discourse this development goes beyond mere empiricalization. All four levels of context I once proposed to distinguish play a part in this endeavour: the "linguistic," the "situational," the "institutional," and the "intertextual" level (van Eemeren 2010, pp. 17–19). Most prominent however is the inclusion of the institutional context I designated earlier the *macro*-context, which pertains to the kind of speech event in which the argumentation occurs. Paying attention to the macro-context is necessary to do justice to the fact that argumentative discourse is always situated in some more or less conventionalized institutional environment, which influences the way in which the argumentation takes shape.

Although in formal and informal logical approaches the macro-context has not very actively been taken into account,[24] in modern argumentation theory the contextual dimension has been emphasized from the beginning. In the rhetorical perspective in particular, contextual considerations have always been an integral part of the approach, starting in Antiquity with the distinction made in Aristotelian rhetoric between different "genres" of discourse. Characteristically, Perelman and Olbrechts-Tyteca see context in the first place as "audience," which is accorded a central role in their *new rhetoric*. Christopher Tindale (1999) insists that in a rhetorical perspective there are still other contextual components than audience that should be taken into account (p. 75).[25]

According to Lloyd Bitzer (1999), rhetoric is situational because rhetorical discourse obtains its character from the situation which generates it. By the latter he means that rhetorical texts derive their character from *the circumstances of the historic context in which they occur.*[26] The rhetorical situation should therefore be

[24]The exception is "natural logic," which studies arguments in a context of situated argumentative discourse in describing the "logic" of ordinary argumentative discourse in a non-normative, "naturalistic" way.

[25]A first contextual component Tindale (1999) distinguishes is *locality*, "the time and the place in which the argument is located" (p. 75); a second one is *background*, "those events that bear on the argumentation in question" (p. 76); a third one is the *arguer*, the source of the argumentation (p. 77); and a fourth component of context he distinguishes is *expression*, the way in which the argument is expressed (p. 80). Characteristically, Tindale defines audience relevance—an important element of contextual relevance which is a precondition for the acceptability of argumentation—as "the relation of the information-content of an argument, stated and assumed, to the framework of beliefs and commitments *that are likely to be held by the audience for which it is intended*" (1999, p. 102, my italics).

[26]In Bitzer's view, every rhetorical situation has three constituents: (1) the *exigence* that is the "imperfection" (problem, defect or obstacle) which should be changed by the discourse; (2) the *audience* that is required because rhetorical discourse produces change by influencing the decisions and actions of persons who function as a "mediator of change"; and (3) the *constraints* of the rhetorical situation which influence the rhetor and can be brought to bear upon the audience

regarded "as a natural context of persons, events, objects, relations, and an exigence which strongly invites utterance" (1999, p. 219). Thanks to Bitzer, more and more rhetorical theorists began to realize that their analyses should take the context of the discourse duly into account.

In the 1970s, in "contextualizing" the study of argumentation, American communication scholars picked up Toulmin's (2003) notion of *fields*. In 1958, Toulmin had maintained that two arguments are in the same field if their data and claims are of the same *logical type*. However, the difficulty is that he did not define the notion of "logical type" but only indicated its meaning by means of examples. Some features or characteristics of argument, Toulmin suggested, are field-invariant, while others are field-dependent. In 1972, in *Human Understanding*, Toulmin had already moved away from this notion of fields, and had come to regard them as akin to academic disciplines.[27]

Because, in Zarefsky's view, the concept of "fields" offers considerable promise for empirical and critical studies of argumentation, he thought it worthwhile to try to dispel the confusion about the idea of field without abandoning the concept altogether (1992, p. 417).[28] He noted an extensive discussion at conferences of the communication and rhetoric community in the United States on whether "fields" should be defined in terms of academic disciplines or in terms of broad-based world-views such as Marxism and behaviourism (2012, p. 211). It can be observed however that, varying from author to author, the term *argument fields* is generally used more broadly as a synonym for "rhetorical communities," "discourse communities," "conceptual ecologies," "collective mentalities," "disciplines," and "professions." The common core idea seems to be that claims imply "grounds," and that the grounds for knowledge claims lie in the epistemic practices and states of consensus in specific knowledge domains.[29]

(Footnote 26 continued)

(pp. 220–221). The rhetorical situation may therefore be defined as "a complex of persons, events, objects, and relations presenting an actual or potential exigence which can be completely or partially removed if discourse, introduced into the situation, can so constrain human decision or action as to bring about the significant modification of the exigence" (Bitzer 1999, p. 220).

[27]In spite of the confusion, some argumentation scholars still found the idea of argument fields useful for distinguishing between field-invariant aspects of argument and aspects of argument that vary from field to field.

[28]Zarefsky identifies and discusses three recurrent issues in theories about argument fields: the purpose of the concept of argument fields, the nature of argument fields, and the development of argument fields.

[29]The positions of the advocates of the various denominators can be interpreted by inferring the kinds of backgrounds they presuppose: the traditions, practices, ideas, texts, and methods of particular groups (Dunbar 1986; Sillars 1981). Willard, for one, advocated a sociological-rhetorical version of the field theory. For him, fields are "sociological entities whose unity stems from practices" (1982, p. 75). Consistent with the Chicago School, Willard defines fields as existing in the actions of the members of a field. These actions are in his view essentially rhetorical. Rowland (1992, p. 470) also addresses the meaning and the utility of argument fields. He argues for a purpose-centred approach. In his view, the essential characteristics of an argument field are best described by identifying the purpose shared by members of the field (p. 497).

Currently, in communication research in the United States the notion of "argument field" seems to be abandoned. Instead, a contextual notion has become prominent which is similar but not equal to argument field. This is the notion of *argument sphere*,[30] which was in 1982 introduced by Thomas Goodnight.[31] Each argument sphere comes with specific practices.[32] Goodnight offers some examples but does not present a complete list of such practices or an overview of their defining properties. For one thing, spheres of argument differ from each other in the norms for reasonable argument that prevail.[33] Members of "societies" and "historical cultures" participate, according to Goodnight, in vast, and not altogether coherent, superstructures, which invite them *to channel doubts through prevailing discourse practices*. In the democratic tradition, these channels can be recognized as the *personal*, the *technical*, and the *public* spheres, which operate through very different forms of invention and subject matter selection.[34] Inspired by Habermas and the Frankfurt School, Goodnight aims to show that the quality of public deliberation has atrophied since arguments drawn from the private and technical spheres have invaded, and perhaps even appropriated, the public sphere.[35]

A rather new development in the contextualization of the study of argumentation is instigated by Dougles Walton and Krabbe (1995), who take in their dialectical approach the contextual dimension of argumentative discourse into account by differentiating between different kinds of *dialogue types*: "normative framework[s] in which there is an exchange of arguments between two speech partners reasoning

[30]See Goodnight (1980, 1982, 1987a, b). For a collection of papers devoted to spheres of argument, see Gronbeck (1989).

[31]Although Goodnight does not reject the notion of argument field, he finds it "not a satisfactory umbrella for covering the grounding of all arguments" (2012, p. 209). In his view, the idea that all arguments are "grounded in fields, enterprises characterized by some degree of specialization and compactness, contravenes an essential distinction among groundings" (p. 209).

[32]Zarefsky (2012, pp. 212–213) proposes a taxonomical scheme for spheres which consists of the following distinguishing criteria: Who participates in the discourse? Who sets the rules of procedure? What kind of knowledge is required? How are the contributions to be evaluated? What is the end-result of the deliberation?

[33]While the notion of "argument field" seems to be abandoned, argumentation scholars still frequently use the notion of "sphere." Schiappa (2012), for instance, compares and contrasts in his research the arguments advanced in the technical sphere of legal and constitutional debate with those used in the public sphere.

[34]Hazen and Hynes (2011) focus on the functioning of argument in the public and private spheres of communication (or, as they call them, "domains") in different forms of society. While an extensive literature exists on the role of argument in democracy and the public sphere, there is no corresponding literature regarding non-democratic societies.

[35]Goodnight (2012) suggests that the grounds of argument may be altered over time: A way of arguing appropriate to a given sphere can be shifted to a new grounding. This means that spheres start to intermingle. It is important to realize that Goodnight combines in fact two ideas (the idea of the spheres and the idea of a threat to the public sphere), but that this is not necessary: One can find the "spheres" notion analytically useful without accepting the idea of a threat to the public sphere.

together in turn-taking sequence aimed at a collective goal" (Walton 1998, p. 30).[36] Walton and Krabbe's typology of dialogues consists of six main types: persuasion, negotiation, inquiry, deliberation, information-seeking, and eristics, and additionally some mixed types, such as debate, committee meeting, and Socratic dialogue (1995, p. 66).[37] The various types of dialogue are characterized by their initial situation, method and goal.[38]

Over the past decades the pragma-dialectical theorizing too has developed explicitly and systematically towards the inclusion of the contextual dimension of argumentative discourse, especially after Peter Houtlosser and I had introduced the notion of *strategic manoeuvring* (van Eemeren and Houtlosser 2002a, b). Strategic manoeuvring does not take part in an idealized critical discussion but in the multi-varied communicative practices that have developed in the various communicative domains. Because these practices have been established in specific *communicative activity types*, which are characterized by the way in which they are conventionalized, the communicative activity types constitute the institutional macro-contexts in which in "extended" pragma-dialectics argumentative discourse is examined (van Eemeren 2010, pp. 129–162). The primary aim of this research is to find out in what ways the possibilities for strategic manoeuvring are determined by the institutionally motivated extrinsic constraints, known as *institutional preconditions*, ensuing from the conventionalization of the communicative activity types concerned.

In order to identify the institutional preconditions for strategic manoeuvring in the communicative activity types they examined, the pragma-dialecticians first determined how these activity types can be characterized argumentatively. Next they tried to establish how the parties involved operate in conducting their argumentative discourse in accordance with the room for strategic manoeuvring available in the communicative activity type concerned. To mention just a few examples: in concentrating on the legal domain, they examined strategic manoeuvring by the judge in a court case (Feteris 2009); in concentrating on the political domain, strategic manoeuvring by Members of the European Parliament in a general debate (van Eemeren and Garssen 2011); and in concentrating on the medical domain, the doctor's strategic manoeuvring in doctor-patient consultation (Labrie 2012).

Meanwhile, at the University of Lugano, Eddo Rigotti and Andrea Rocci have started a related research program concentrating on argumentation in context. Characteristic of their approach is the combination of semantic and pragmatic

---

[36]Walton (1998) defines a dialogue as a "normative framework in which there is an exchange of arguments between two speech partners reasoning together in turn-taking sequence aimed at a collective goal" (p. 30). There is a main goal, which is the goal of the dialogue, and there are goals of the participants. The two kinds of goals may or may not correspond.

[37]In a recent version of the typology (Walton 2010), the list consists of seven types, since a dialogue type called *discovery*, attributed to McBurney and Parsons (2001), is added to the six types just mentioned.

[38]An *inquiry*, for instance, has a lack of proof as its initial situation, uses knowledge-based argumentation as a method, and has the establishment of proof as a goal.

insights from linguistics, and concepts from classical rhetoric and dialectic, with insights from argumentation theories such as pragma-dialectics. The communicative activity types they have tackled include mediation meetings from the domain of counseling (Greco Morasso 2011), negotiations about takeovers from the financial domain (Palmieri 2014), and editorial conferences from the domain of the media (Rocci and Zampa 2015).

Recently the pragma-dialectical research of argumentation in context has moved on to the next stage. It is currently aimed at detecting the *argumentative patterns* of constellations of argumentative moves that, as a consequence of the institutional preconditions for strategic manoeuvring, characteristically come into being in the various kinds of argumentative practices in the legal, political, medical, and academic domains.[39]

4 Formalization of the Treatment of Argumentation

The third development I would like to highlight is the "formalization" of the treatment of argumentation. When Toulmin and Perelman and Olbrechts-Tyteca, each in their own way, initiated modern argumentation theory, they agreed—unconsciously but emphatically—that the formal approach to argumentation taken in modern logic was inadequate. In spite of the strong impact of their ideas upon others, their depreciation did not discourage logicians and dialecticians from further developing such a formal approach.

It is important to note that in the various proposals "formality" enters in rather diverse ways and a borderline between approaches that are formal and those that are not is not always easy to draw. A theory of argumentation, whether logical or dialectical, can be "formal" in several senses—and can also be partially formal or formal to some degree.[40] Generally, in a "formal logical" or a "formal dialectical" argumentation theory "formal" refers to *being regimented* or *regulated*. Often, however, "formal" also means that the locutions dealt with in the formal system concerned are rigorously determined by grammatical rules, their *logical forms*

[39]The underlying assumption here is that in the argumentation stage protagonists may in principle be supposed to aim for making the strongest case in the macro-context concerned by trying to advance a combination of reasons that will satisfy the antagonist by leaving no critical doubts unanswered. In the process they may be expected to exploit the argument schemes they consider most effective in the situation at hand and to use all multiple, coordinative and subordinative argumentation that is necessary to respond to the critical reactions the antagonist may be expected to come up with.

[40]Of the three distinct senses of "formal" pointed out by Barth and Krabbe (1982, pp. 14–19), and the two added by Krabbe (1982, p. 3), only three are pertinent to argumentation theory. Krabbe's first sense refers to Platonic forms and need not be considered here. The same goes for the fifth sense, which refers to systems that are purely logical, i.e., that do not provide for any material rule or move.

being determined by their linguistic shapes. Additionally, an argumentation theory can be "formal" in the sense that its rules are wholly or partly *set up* a priori.

A formal theory of argumentation can be put to good use in different ways. The most familiar kind of use probably consists in its application in analyzing and evaluating arguments or an argumentative discussion. Formal systems often used for this purpose are propositional logic and first order predicate logic. Their application consists of "translating" each argument at issue into the language of one of these logics and then determining its validity by a truth table or some other available method.

Using a formal approach to analyse and evaluate real-life argumentative discourse leads to all kinds of problems. Four of them are mentioned in the *Handbook*. First, the process of translation is not straightforward. Second, a negative outcome does not mean that the argument is invalid—if an argument is not valid according to one system it could still be valid in some other system of logic. Third, by overlooking unexpressed premises and the argument schemes that are used the crux of the argumentation is missed. Fourth, as a consequence, the evaluation is reduced to an evaluation of the validity of the reasoning used in the argumentation, neglecting the appropriateness of premises and the adequacy of the modes of arguing that are employed in the given context. Formal logic can be of help in reconstructing and assessing argumentation, but an adequate argumentation theory needs to be more encompassing and more communication-oriented.

A second way of using formal systems consists in utilizing or constructing them to contribute to the theoretical development of argumentation theory by providing clarifications of certain theoretical concepts. In this way, John Woods and Walton (1989), for instance, show how formal techniques can be helpful in dealing with the fallacies. Employing formal systems to instigate theoretical developments is, in my view, more rewarding that just using them in analyzing and evaluating argumentative discourse.

From Aristotle's *Prior Analytics* onwards, logicians have been chiefly concerned with the formal validity of deductions, pushing the actual activity of arguing in discussions into the background. This has divorced logic as a discipline from the practice of argumentation. Paul Lorenzen (1960) and his Erlangen School have made it possible to counteract this development. They promoted the idea that logic, instead of being concerned with a rational mind's inferences or truth in all possible worlds, should focus on discussion between two disagreeing parties in the actual world. They thus helped to bridge the gap between formal logic and argumentation theory noted by Toulmin and the authors of *The New Rhetoric*.

Because Lorenzen did not present his insights as a contribution to argumentation theory, their important implications for this discipline were initially not evident. In fact, Lorenzen took not only the first step towards a *re-dialectification* of logic, but his insights concerning the dialogical definition of logical constants also signal the initiation of a *pragmatic* approach to logic. In *From Axiom to Dialogue*, Else Barth and Krabbe (1982) incorporated his insights in a formal dialectical theory of argumentation. Their primary purpose was "to develop acceptable rules for verbal resolution of conflicts of opinion" (p. 19). The rules of the dialectical systems they propose, which are "formal" in the regulative and sometimes also in the linguistic sense, standardize reasonable and critical discussions.

A third kind of use of formal systems consists in using them as a source of inspiration for developing a certain approach to argumentation. Such an approach may itself be informal or only partly formal.

In argumentation theory the approaches inspired by formal studies serve as a link between formal and informal approaches. The semi-formal method of "profiles of dialogue" is a case in point.[41] A profile of dialogue is typically written as an upside down tree diagram, consisting of nodes linked by line segments. Each branch of the tree displays a possible dialogue that may develop from the initial move. The nodes are associated with moves and the links between the nodes correspond to situations in the dialogue.

In pragma-dialectics, the method of profiles of dialogue inspired in its turn the use of "dialectical profiles" (van Eemeren et al. 2007, esp. Sect. 2.3), which are equally semi-formal as argument schemes and argumentation structures. A *dialectical profile* is "a sequential pattern of the moves the participants in a critical discussion are entitled to make—and in one way or another have to make—to realize a particular dialectical aim at a particular stage or sub-stage of the resolution process" (van Eemeren 2010, p. 98).

A fourth and last use of a formal approach proceeds into the opposite direction. This is, for instance, the case when insights from argumentation theory are employed for creating formal applications in Artificial Intelligence. In return, of course, Artificial Intelligence offers argumentation theory a laboratory for examining implementations of its rules and concepts. Formal applications of insights from argumentation theory in Artificial Intelligence vary from making such insights instrumental in the construction of "argumentation machines," or at any rate visualization systems, interactive dialogue systems, and analysis systems, to developing less comprehensive tools for automated analysis. Of preeminent importance in these endeavours is the philosophical notion of *defeasible reasoning*, referring to inferences that can be blocked or defeated (Nute 1994, p. 354). In 1987, John Pollock pointed out that "defeasible reasoning" is captured by what in Artificial Intelligence is called a *non-monotonic* logic. A logic is non-monotonic when a conclusion that, according to that logic, follows from certain premises need not always follow when more premises are added. In a non-monotonic logic, it is possible to draw tentative conclusions while keeping open the possibility that additional information may lead to their retraction.[42]

[41]Walton was probably the first to introduce profiles of dialogues by that name (1989a, pp. 37–38; b, pp. 68–69). Other relevant publications are Krabbe (2002) and van Laar (2003a, b).

[42]Dung (1995) initiated the study of argument attack as a (mathematical) directed graph, and showed formal connections between non-monotonic logic and argumentation. Just like Bondarenko et al. (1997), Verheij (2003a) developed an assumption-based model of defeasible argumentation. Prakken (1997) explored the connection between non-monotonic logic and legal argumentation.

Although in *The Uses of Argument* the term *defeasible* is rarely used, Toulmin (2003) is obviously an early adopter of the idea of defeasible reasoning. He acknowledges that his key distinctions of "claims," "data," "warrants," "modal qualifiers," "conditions of rebuttal," and his ideas about the applicability or inapplicability of warrants, "will not be particularly novel to those who have studied explicitly the logic of special types of practical argument" (p. 131). Toulmin notes that H. L. A. Hart has shown the relevance of the notion of defeasibility for jurisprudence, free will, and responsibility and that David Ross has applied it to ethics, recognizing that moral rules may hold *prima facie*, but can have exceptions. The idea of a *prima facie* reason is closely related to non-monotonic inference: Q can be concluded from P but not when there is additional information R.

In order to take the possibility of defeating circumstances into account, in Artificial Intelligence the notion from argumentation theory called *argument scheme* or *argumentation scheme* has been taken up.[43] The critical questions associated with argument schemes correspond to defeating circumstances. Floris Bex et al. (2003) have applied the concept of argumentation scheme, for instance, to the formalization of legal reasoning from evidence. One of the argument schemes they deal with is *argument from expert opinion*.

Viewed from the perspective of Artificial Intelligence, the work on argument schemes of Walton and his colleagues can be regarded as a contribution to the theory of knowledge representation. This knowledge representation point of view is further developed by Bart Verheij (2003b). Like Bex et al. (2003), he formalizes argument schemes as defeasible rules of inference.[44]

5 Bingo!

In my view, argumentation theory can only be a relevant discipline if it provides insights that enable a better understanding of argumentative reality. The empiricalization, contextualization, and formalization of the treatment of argumentation I have sketched are necessary preconditions for achieving this purpose. Without empiricalization, the connection with argumentative reality is not ensured. Without contextualization, there is no systematic differentiation of the various kinds of

---

[43]In the pragma-dialectical theory of argumentation, argument schemes are distinguished from the formal schemes of reasoning of logic. These argument schemes are defeasible. They play a vital role in the intersubjective testing procedure, which boils down to asking critical questions and reacting to them. By asking critical questions, the antagonist challenges the protagonist to make clear that, in the particular case at hand, there are no exceptions to the general rule invoked by the use of the argument scheme concerned (van Eemeren 2010, p. 206).

[44]Reed and Rowe (2004) have incorporated argument schemes in their Araucaria tool for the analysis of argumentative texts. Rahwan et al. (2007) have proposed formats for the integration of argument schemes in what is called the Semantic Web. Gordon et al. (2007) have integrated argument schemes in their Carneades model.

argumentative practices. Without formalization, the required precision and rigour of the theorizing are lacking.

Only if all three developments have come to full fruition, an understanding of argumentative reality can be achieved that constitutes a sound basis for practical intervention by proposing alternative formats and designs for argumentative practices, whether computerized or not, and developing methods for improving productive, analytic, and evaluative argumentative skills. In each case, however, there are certain prerequisites to the indispensable empiricalization, contextualization, and formalization of the treatment of argumentation.

Case studies, for instance, can play a constructive role in gaining insight into argumentative reality by means of empirical research, but, however illuminating they may be, they are not instrumental in the advancement of argumentation theory if they only enhance our understanding of a particular case. *Mutatis mutandis*, the same applies to other qualitative and quantitative empirical research that lacks theoretical relevance.[45] Some scholars think wrongly that qualitative research is superior because it "goes deeper" and leads to "real" insight, while other scholars, just as wrongly, consider quantitative research superior because it is "objective" and leads to "generalizable" results.[46] In my view, both types of research are necessary for a complete picture of argumentative reality, sometimes even in combination.[47] In all cases however it is a prerequisite that the research is systematically related to well-defined theoretical issues and relevant to the advancement of argumentation theory.

In gaining insight into the contextual constraints on argumentative discourse both analytical considerations concerning the rationale of a specific argumentative practice and a practical understanding of how this rationale is implemented in argumentative discourse play a part. In order to contribute to the advancement of argumentation theory as a discipline, the analytical considerations concerning the rationale of an argumentative practice should apply to all specimens of that particular communicative activity type—or dialogue type, if a different theoretical approach is favoured. To enable methodical comparisons between different types of communicative activities, and avoid arbitrary proliferation, the description of the implementation of the rationale must take place in functional and well-defined theoretical categories.

In the recent trend towards formalization, which has been strongly stimulated by the connection with computerization in the interdisciplinary field of artificial

[45]A great deal of the qualitative empirical research that has been carried out in argumentation theory is not only case-based but also very much ad hoc. In addition, a great deal of the quantitative persuasion research that is carried out suffers from a lack of theoretical relevance.

[46]An additional problem is that the distinction between qualitative and quantitative research is not always defined in the same way. Psychologists and sociologists, for instance, tend to consider interviews and introspection as qualitative research because the results are not reported in numerical terms and statistics does not play a role. There are also less restrictive views, in which numerical reporting and the use of statistics are not the only distinctive feature.

[47]In the pragma-dialectical empirical research concerning fallacies, for instance, qualitative and quantitative research are methodically combined—in this case by having a qualitative follow-up of the quantitative research, as reported in van Eemeren et al. (2009).

intelligence, not only logic-related approaches to argumentation are utilized, but also the Toulmin model and a variety of other theories of argumentation structure and argument schemes, such as Walton and Krabbe's (1995). However, responding to the need for formal adequacy so strongly felt in information science may go at the expense of material adequacy, that is, at the expense of the extent to which the formalized theorizing covers argumentative reality. Relying at any cost on the formal and formalizable theoretical designs that are available in argumentation theory, however weak their theoretical basis may sometimes be, can easily lead to premature or too drastic formalizations and half-baked results. Because of the eclecticism involved in randomly combining incompatible insights from different theoretical approaches, these results may even be incoherent.

Provided that the prerequisites just mentioned are given their due, empiricalizing, contextualizing, and formalizing the treatment of argumentation are crucial to the future of argumentation theory, and more particularly to its applications and computerization. As the title of my keynote speech indicates, succeeding in properly combining and integrating the three developments would, in my view, mean: "Bingo!".

Let me conclude by illustrating my point with the help of a research project I am presently involved in with a team of pragma-dialecticians. The project is devoted to what I have named *argumentative patterns* (van Eemeren 2012, p. 442). Argumentative patterns are structural regularities in argumentative discourse that can be observed empirically. These patterns can be characterized with the help of the theoretical tools provided by argumentation theory. Their occurrence can be explained by the institutional preconditions for strategic manoeuvring pertaining to a specific communicative activity type.

Dependent on the exigencies of a communicative domain, in the various communicative activity types different kinds of argumentative exchanges take place. The discrepancies are caused by the kind of difference of opinion to which in a particular communicative activity type the exchanges respond, the type of standpoint at issue, the procedural and material starting points, the specific requirements regarding the way in which the argumentative exchange is supposed to take place, and the kind of outcome allowed.[48]

Each argumentative pattern that can be distinguished in argumentative reality is characterized by a constellation of argumentative moves in which, in dealing with a particular kind of difference of opinion, in defence of a particular type of standpoint, a particular argument scheme or combination of argument schemes is used in a particular kind of argumentation structure (van Eemeren 2012).[49] The theoretical

[48]Viewed dialectically, argumentative patterns are generated by the protagonist's responding to, or anticipating, (possible) criticisms of the would-be antagonist, such as critical questions associated with the argument schemes that are used.

[49]If an argument in defence of a standpoint is expected not to be accepted immediately, then more, other, additional or supporting arguments (or a combination of those) need to be advanced, which leads to an argumentative pattern with a complex argumentation structure (cumulative coordinative, multiple, complementary coordinative or subordinative argumentation (or a combination of those), respectively).

instruments used by the pragma-dialecticians in their qualitative empirical research aimed at identifying argumentative patterns occurring in argumentative reality, such as the typologies of standpoints, differences of opinions, argument schemes, and argumentation structures,[50] are formalized to a certain degree.[51] Further formalization is required, in particular for computerization, which is nowadays a requirement for the various kinds of applications in actual argumentative practices instrumental in realizing the practical ambitions of argumentation theory.[52]

Certain argumentative patterns are characteristic of the way in which argumentative discourse is generally conducted in specific communicative activity types. In parliamentary policy debates, for example, a "prototypical" argumentative pattern that can be found consists of a prescriptive standpoint that a certain policy should be carried out, justified by pragmatic argumentation, supported by arguments from example. Such prototypical argumentative patterns are of particular interest to pragma-dialecticians because an identification of the argumentative patterns characteristically occurring in particular communicative activity types is more insightful than, for instance, just listing the types of standpoints at issue or the argument schemes that are frequently used.[53] Thus documenting the institutional diversification of argumentative practices paves the way for a systematic comparison and a theoretical account of context-independency and context-dependency in argumentative discourse that is more thorough, more refined, and better supported than Toulmin's account and other available accounts. In this way, our current research systematically tackles one of the fundamental problems of argumentation theory: universality versus particularity.

---

[50]We will make use of the qualitative method of analytic induction (see, for instance, Jackson 1986).

[51]To determine and compare the frequencies of occurrence of the various prototypical argumentative patterns that have been identified on analytical grounds while qualitative research has made clear how they occur, the qualitative empirical research will be followed by quantitative empirical research of representative corpuses of argumentative discourse to establish the frequency of occurrence of these pattern. This quantitative research needs to be based on the results of analytic and qualitative research in which it is established which argumentative patterns are functional in specific (clusters of) communicative activity types, so that theoretically motivated expectations (hypotheses) can be formulated about the circumstances in which specific argumentative patterns occur in particular communicative activity types and when they will occur.

[52]In view of the possibilities of computerization, other theories of argumentation that have been formalized only to a certain degree could in principle benefit equally from further formalization.

[53]An argumentative pattern becomes and to determine they are indeed stereotypical due to the way in which the institutional preconditions pertaining to a certain communicative activity type constrain the kinds of standpoints, the kinds of criticisms and the types of arguments that may be advanced.

References

Baesler, J. E., & Burgoon, J. K. (1994). The temporal effects of story and statistical evidence on belief change. *Communication Research, 21*, 582–602.

Barth, E. M., & Krabbe, E. C. W. (1982). *From axiom to dialogue. A philosophical study of logics and argumentation.* Berlin: Walter de Gruyter.

Bex, F. J., Prakken, H., Reed, C., & Walton, D. N. (2003). Towards a formal account of reasoning about evidence. Argumentation schemes and generalisations. *Artificial Intelligence and Law, 11*, 125–165.

Bitzer, L. F. (1999). The rhetorical situation. In J. L. Lucaites, C. M. Condit & S. Caudill (Eds.), *Contemporary rhetorical theory. A reader.* New York: Guilford Press.

Bondarenko, A., Dung, P. M., Kowalski, R. A., & Toni, F. (1997). An abstract, argumentation-theoretic approach to default reasoning. *Artificial Intelligence, 93*, 63–101.

Bowker, J. K., & Trapp, R. (1992). Personal and ideational dimensions of good and poor arguments in human interaction. In F. H. van Eemeren & R. Grootendorst (Eds.), *Argumentation illuminated* (pp. 220–230). Amsterdam: Sic Sat.

Crawshay-Williams, R. (1957). *Methods and criteria of reasoning. An inquiry into the structure of controversy.* London: Routledge & Kegan Paul.

Doury, M. (1997). *Le débat immobile. L'argumentation dans le débat médiatique sur les parasciences* [The immobile debate. Argumentation in the media debate on the parasciences]. Paris: Kimé.

Doury, M. (2004a). La classification des arguments dans les discours ordinaires [The classification of arguments in ordinary discourse]. *Langage, 154*, 59–73.

Doury, M. (2004b). La position de l'analyste de l'argumentation [The position of the argumentation analyst]. *Semen, 17*, 143–163.

Doury, M. (2005). The accusation of *amalgame* as a meta-argumentative refutation. In F. H. van Eemeren & P. Houtlosser (Eds.), *The practice of argumentation* (pp. 145–161). Amsterdam: John Benjamins.

Doury, M. (2006). Evaluating analogy. Toward a descriptive approach to argumentative norms. In P. Houtlosser & M. A. van Rees (Eds.), *Considering pragma-dialectics. A festschrift for Frans H. van Eemeren on the occasion of his 60th birthday* (pp. 35–49). Lawrence Erlbaum: London.

Doury, M. (2009). Argument schemes typologies in practice. The case of comparative arguments. In F. H. van Eemeren & B. Garssen (Eds.), *Pondering on problems of argumentation* (pp. 141–155). New York: Springer.

Dunbar, N. R. (1986). Laetrile. A case study of a public controversy. *Journal of the American Forensic Association, 22*, 196–211.

Dung, P. M. (1995). On the acceptability of arguments and its fundamental role in non-monotonic reasoning, logic programming and *n*-person games. *Artificial Intelligence, 77*, 321–357.

Feteris, E. T. (2009). Strategic maneuvering in the justification of judicial decisions. In F. H. van Eemeren (Ed.), *Examining argumentation in context. Fifteen studies on strategic maneuvering* (pp. 93–114). Amsterdam: John Benjamins.

Finocchiaro, M. A. (2005a). *Arguments about arguments. Systematic, critical and historical essays in logical theory.* Cambridge, NY: Cambridge University Press.

Finocchiaro, M. A. (2005b). *Retrying Galileo, 1633–1992.* Berkeley: University of California Press.

Garssen, B. J. (2002). Understanding argument schemes. In F. H. van Eemeren (Ed.), *Advances in pragma-dialectics* (pp. 93–104). Amsterdam-Newport News, VA: Sic Sat &Vale Press.

Goodnight, G. T. (1980). The liberal and the conservative presumptions. On political philosophy and the foundation of public argument. In J. Rhodes & S. Newell (Eds.), *Proceedings of the [first] summer conference on argumentation* (pp. 304–337). Annandale, VA: Speech Communication Association.

Goodnight, G. T. (1982). The personal, technical, and public spheres of argument. A speculative inquiry into the art of public deliberation. *Journal of the American Forensic Association, 18*, 214–227.

Goodnight, G. T. (1987a). Argumentation, criticism and rhetoric. A comparison of modern and post-modern stances in humanistic inquiry. In J. W. Wenzel (Ed.), *Argument and critical practices. Proceedings of the fifth SCA/AFA conference on argumentation* (pp. 61–67). Annandale, VA: Speech Communication Association.

Goodnight, G. T. (1987b). Generational argument. In F. H. van Eemeren, R. Grootendorst, J. A. Blair & C. A. Willard (Eds.), *Argumentation. Across the lines of discipline. Proceedings of the conference on argumentation 1986* (pp. 129–144). Dordrecht: Foris.

Goodnight, G. T. (2012). The personal, technical, and public spheres. A note on 21st century critical communication inquiry. *Argumentation and Advocacy, 48*(4), 258–267.

Gordon, T. F., Prakken, H., & Walton, D. N. (2007). The Carneades model of argument and burden of proof. *Artificial Intelligence, 171*, 875–896.

Greco Morasso, S. (2011). *Argumentation in dispute mediation. A reasonable way to handle conflict*. Amsterdam: John Benjamins.

Gronbeck, B. E. (Ed.). (1989). *Spheres of argument. Proceedings of the sixth SCA/AFA conference on argumentation*. Annandale, VA: Speech Communication Association.

Hample, D., & Dallinger J. M. (1991) Cognitive editing of arguments and interpersonal construct differentiation. Refining the relationship. In F. H. van Eemeren, R. Grootendorst, J. A. Blair & C. A. Willard (Eds.). *Proceedings of the second international conference on argumentation (organized by the International Society for the Study of Argumentation at the University of Amsterdam, June 19–22, 1990)* (pp. 567–574). Amsterdam: Sic Sat.

Hample, D., & Dallinger, J. (1986). The judgment phase of invention. In F. H. van Eemeren, R. Grootendorst, J. A. Blair & C. A. Willard (Eds.), *Argumentation. Across the lines of discipline. Proceedings of the conference on argumentation 1986* (pp. 225–234). Dordrecht: Foris.

Hample, D., & Dallinger, J. M. (1987). Cognitive editing of argument strategies. *Human Communication Research, 14*, 123–144

Hample, D., Paglieri, F., & Na, L. (2011). The costs and benefits of arguing. Predicting the decision whether to engage or not. In F. H. van Eemeren, B. J. Garssen, D. Godden & G. Mitchell (Eds.), *Proceedings of the 7th conference of the International Society for the Study of Argumentation* (pp. 718–732). Amsterdam: Rozenberg/Sic Sat. [CD ROM].

Hazen, M. D., & Hynes, T. J. (2011). An exploratory study of argument in the public and private domains of differing forms of societies. In F. H. van Eemeren, B. Garssen, D. Godden & G. Mitchell (Eds.) *Proceedings of the 7th conference of the International Society for the Study of Argumentation* (pp. 750–762). Amsterdam: Sic Sat.

Hoeken, H. (2001). Anecdotal, statistical, and causal evidence. Their perceived and actual persuasiveness. *Argumentation, 15*, 425–437.

Jackson, S. (1986). Building a case for claims about discourse structure. In D. G. Ellis & W. A. Donohane (Eds.), *Contemporary issues in language and discourse* (pp. 129–147). Hillsdale, NJ: Lawrence Erlbaum.

Krabbe, E. C. W. (1982). *Studies in dialogical logic*. Doctoral dissertation, University of Groningen.

Krabbe, E. C. W. (2002). Profiles of dialogue as a dialectical tool. In F. H. van Eemeren (Ed.), *Advances in pragma-dialectics* (pp. 153–167). Amsterdam: Sic Sat; Newport News, VA: Vale Press.

Labrie, N. (2012). Strategic maneuvering in treatment decision-making discussions. Two cases in point. *Argumentation, 26*(2), 171–199.

Leff, M. C., & Mohrmann, G. P. (1993). Lincoln at Cooper Union. A rhetorical analysis of the text. In T. W. Benson (Ed.), *Landmark essays on rhetorical criticism* (pp. 173–187).

Lorenzen, P. (1960). Logik und Agon [Logic and agon]. In *Atti del XII congresso internazionale di filosofia (Venezia, 12–18 settembre 1958), 4: Logica, linguaggio e comunicazione* [Proceedings of the 12th international conference of philosophy (Venice, 12–13 September 1958), 4: Logic, language and communication] (pp. 187–194). Florence: Sansoni. Reprinted in

Lorenzen, P., & Lorenz, K. (1978). *Dialogische Logik* [Dialogical logic] (pp. 1–8). Darmstadt: Wissenschaftliche Buchgesellschaft.
McBurney, P., & Parsons, S. (2001). Chance discovery using dialectical argumentation. In T. Terano, T. Nishida, A. Namatame, S. Tsumoto, Y. Ohsawa & T. Washio (Eds.), *New frontiers in artificial intelligence* (pp. 414–424). Berlin: Springer.
Mercier, H. (2012). Some clarifications about the argumentative theory of reasoning. A reply to Santibáñez Yáñez (2012). *Informal Logic, 32*(2), 259–268.
Mercier, H., & Sperber, D. (2011). Why do humans reason? Arguments for an argumentative theory. *Behavioral and Brain Sciences, 34*, 57–111.
Næss, A. (1953). *Interpretation and preciseness. A contribution to the theory of communication.* Oslo: Skrifter utgitt ar der norske videnskaps academie.
Newman, R. P. (1961). *Recognition of communist China? A study in argument.* New York: Macmillan.
Nute, D. (1994). Defeasible logic. In D. M. Gabbay, C. J. Hogger & J. A. Robinson (Eds.), *Handbook of logic in artificial intelligence and logic programming, 3. Non-monotonic reasoning and uncertain reasoning* (pp. 353–395). Oxford: Clarendon Press.
O'Keefe, D. J. (2006). Pragma-dialectics and persuasion effects research. In P. Houtlosser & M. A. van Rees (Eds.), *Considering pragma-dialectics. A festschrift for Frans H. van Eemeren on the occasion of his 60th birthday* (pp. 235–243). Mahwah: Lawrence Erlbaum.
Palmieri, R. (2014). *Corporate argumentation in takeover bids.* Amsterdam: John Benjamins.
Perelman, C., & Olbrechts-Tyteca, L. (1969). *The new rhetoric. A treatise on argumentation.* Notre Dame, IN: University of Notre Dame Press. (J. Wilkinson and P. Weaver of Ch. Perelman & L. Olbrechts-Tyteca (1958), English trans. *La nouvelle rhétorique. Traité de l'argumentation.* Paris: Presses Universitaires de France. (3rd ed. Brussels: Éditions de l'Université de Bruxelles)).
Pollock, J. L. (1987). Defeasible reasoning. *Cognitive Science, 11*, 481–518.
Prakken, H. (1997). *Logical tools for modelling legal argument. A study of defeasible reasoning in law.* Dordrecht: Kluwer.
Rahwan, I., Zablith, F., & Reed, C. (2007). Laying the foundations for a world wide argument web. *Artificial Intelligence, 171*(10–15), 897–921.
Reed, C. A., & Rowe, G. W. A. (2004). Araucaria. Software for argument analysis, diagramming and representation. *International Journal on Artificial Intelligence Tools, 13*(4), 961–979.
Rocci, A., & Zampa, M. (2015). Practical argumentation in news making: The editorial conference as a deliberative activity type. In F. H. van Eemeren, E. Rigotti, A. Rocci, J. Sàágua & D. Walton (Eds.), *Practical argumentation.* Dordrecht: Springer.
Rowland, R. C. (1992). Argument fields. In W. L. Benoit, D. Hample & P. J. Benoit (Eds.), *Readings in argumentation* (pp. 469–504). Berlin/New York: Foris.
Sanders, J. A., Gass, R. H., & Wiseman, R. L. (1991). The influence of type of warrant and receivers' ethnicity on perceptions of warrant strength. In F. H. van Eemeren, R. Grootendorst, J. A. Blair & C. A. Willard (Eds.), *Proceedings of the second international conference on argumentation (organized by the International Society for the Study of Argumentation at the University of Amsterdam, June 19–22, 1990), 1B* (pp. 709–718). Amsterdam: Sic Sat.
Schiappa, E. (2002). Evaluating argumentative discourse from a rhetorical perspective. Defining 'person' and 'human life' in constitutional disputes over abortion. In F. H. van Eemeren & P. Houtlosser (Eds.), *Dialectic and rhetoric. The warp and woof of argumentation analysis* (pp. 65–80). Dordrecht: Kluwer.
Schiappa, E. (2012). Defining marriage in California. An analysis of public and technical argument. *Argumentation and Advocacy, 48*(2), 211–215.
Schreier, M. N., Groeben, N., & Christmann, U. (1995). That's not fair! Argumentative integrity as an ethics of argumentative communication. *Argumentation, 9*(2), 267–289.
Sillars, M. O. (1981). Investigating religious argument as a field. In G. Ziegelmueller & J. Rhodes (Eds.), *Dimensions of argument. Proceedings of the second summer conference on argumentation* (pp. 143–151). Annandale, VA: Speech Communication Association.

Tindale, C. W. (1999). *Acts of arguing. A rhetorical model of argument*. Albany, NY: State University of New York Press.
Toulmin, S. E. (1958). *The uses of argument* (updated ed. 2003). Cambridge: Cambridge University Press.
Toulmin, S. E. (1972). *Human understanding*. Princeton, NJ: Princeton University Press.
Toulmin, S. E. (2003). *The uses of argument* (Updated ed). Cambridge: Cambridge University Press (1st ed. 1958; paperback ed. 1964).
van Eemeren F. H. (2010). *Strategic maneuvering in argumentative discourse. Extending the pragma-dialectical theory of argumentation*. (John Benjamins, Trans. into Chinese (in preparation), Italian (2014), Japanese (in preparation), Spanish (2013)). Amsterdam-Philadelphia.
van Eemeren, F. H. (2012). The pragma-dialectical theory of argumentation under discussion. *Argumentation, 26*(4), 439–457.
van Eemeren, F. H., & Garssen, B. (2011). Exploiting the room for strategic maneuvering in argumentative discourse. Dealing with audience demand in the European Parliament. In F. H. van Eemeren & B. Garssen (Eds.), *Exploring argumentative contexts*. Amsterdam-Philadelphia: John Benjamins.
van Eemeren, F. H., & Houtlosser, P. (2002a). Strategic maneuvering in argumentative discourse. Maintaining a delicate balance. In F. H. van Eemeren & P. Houtlosser (Eds.), *Dialectic and rhetoric. The warp and woof of argumentation analysis* (pp. 131–159). Dordrecht: Kluwer Academic.
van Eemeren, F. H., & Houtlosser, P. (Eds.). (2002b). *Dialectic and rhetoric. The warp and woof of argumentation analysis*. Dordrecht: Kluwer Academic.
van Eemeren, F. H., Grootendorst, R., & Kruiger, T. (1978). *Argumentatietheorie* [Argumentation theory]. Utrecht: Het Spectrum (2nd enlarged ed. 1981; 3rd ed. 1986), (English trans. (1984, 1987)).
van Eemeren, F. H., Grootendorst, R., & Kruiger, T. (1981). *Argumentatietheorie* [Argumentation theory] (2nd enlarged ed.). Utrecht: Het Spectrum (1st ed. 1978; 3rd ed. 1986), (English trans. (1984, 1987)).
van Eemeren, F. H., Grootendorst, R., & Kruiger, T. (1984). *The study of argumentation*. New York: Irvington. (H. Lake of F. H. van Eemeren, R. Grootendorst & T. Kruiger (1981), English trans.). *Argumentatietheorie* (2nd ed.). Utrecht: Het Spectrum. (1 st ed. 1978).
van Eemeren, F. H., Grootendorst, R., & Meuffels, B. (1984b). Het identificeren van enkelvoudige argumentatie [Identifying single argumentation]. *Tijdschrift voor Taalbeheersing, 6*(4), 297–310.
van Eemeren, F. H., Grootendorst, R., & Kruiger, T. (1986). *Argumentatietheorie* [Argumentation theory] (3rd ed.). Leiden: Martinus Nijhoff. (1st ed. 1978, Het Spectrum).
van Eemeren, F. H., Grootendorst, R., & Kruiger, T. (1987). *Handbook of argumentation theory. A critical survey of classical backgrounds and modern studies*. Dordrecht: Foris. (H. Lake of F. H. van Eemeren, R. Grootendorst & T. Kruiger (1981, English trans.). *Argumentatietheorie*. Utrecht: Het Spectrum).
van Eemeren, F. H., Grootendorst, R., & Snoeck Henkemans, A. F., with Blair, J. A., Johnson, R. H., Krabbe, E. C. W., Plantin, C., Walton, D. N., Willard, C. A., Woods, J., & Zarefsky, D. (1996). *Fundamentals of argumentation theory. Handbook of historical backgrounds and contemporary developments*. Mawhah: Lawrence Erlbaum. (trans. into Dutch (1997)).
van Eemeren, F. H., Houtlosser, P., & Snoeck Henkemans, A. F. (2007). *Argumentative indicators in discourse. A pragma-dialectical study*. Dordrecht: Springer.
van Eemeren, F. H., Garssen, B., & Meuffels, B. (2009). *Fallacies and judgments of reasonableness. Empirical research concerning the pragma-dialectical discussion rules*. Dordrecht: Springer.
van Eemeren, F. H., Garssen, B., Krabbe, E. C. W., Snoeck Henkemans, A. F., Verheij, B., & Wagemans, J. H. M. (2014). *Handbook of argumentation theory*. Dordrecht: Springer.
van Laar, J. A. (2003a). *The dialectic of ambiguity. A contribution to the study of argumentation*. Doctoral dissertation, University of Groningen.

van Laar, J. A. (2003b). The use of dialogue profiles for the study of ambiguity. In F. H. van Eemeren, J. A. Blair, C. A. Willard & A. F. Snoeck Henkemans (Eds.), *Proceedings of the fifth conference of the International Society for the Study of Argumentation* (pp. 659–663). Amsterdam: Sic Sat.

Verheij, B. (2003a). DefLog. On the logical interpretation of prima facie justified assumptions. *Journal of Logic and Computation, 13*(3), 319–346.

Verheij, B. (2003b). Dialectical argumentation with argumentation schemes. An approach to legal logic. *Artificial Intelligence and Law, 11*(1–2), 167–195.

Voss, J. F., Fincher-Kiefer, R., Wiley, J., & Ney Silfies, L. (1993). On the processing of arguments. *Argumentation, 7*(2), 165–181.

Walton, D. N. (1989a). *Informal logic. A handbook for critical argumentation*. Cambridge: Cambridge University Press.

Walton, D. N. (1989b). *Question-reply argumentation*. New York: Greenwood Press.

Walton, D. N. (1998). *The new dialectic. Conversational contexts of argument*. Toronto: University of Toronto Press.

Walton, D. N. (2010). Types of dialogue and burden of proof. In P. Baroni, F. Cerutti, M. Giacomin & G. R. Simari (Eds.), *Computational models of argument. Proceedings of COMMA 2010* (pp. 13–24). Amsterdam: IOS Press.

Walton, D. N., & Krabbe, E. C. W. (1995). *Commitment in dialogue. Basic concepts of interpersonal reasoning*. Albany, NY: State University of New York Press.

Warnick, B., & Kline, S. L. (1992). The new rhetoric's argument schemes. A rhetorical view of practical reasoning. *Argumentation and Advocacy, 29*, 1–15.

Willard, C. A. (1982). Argument fields. In J. R. Cox & C. A. Willard (Eds.), *Advances in argumentation theory and research* (pp. 24–77). Carbondale: Southern Illinois University Press.

Woods, J., & Walton, D. N. (1989). *Fallacies. Selected papers 1972–1982*. Berlin: de Gruyter/Foris.

Zarefsky, D. (1986). *President Johnson's war on poverty*. Tuscaloosa, AL: University of Alabama Press.

Zarefsky, D. (1992). Persistent questions in the theory of argument fields. In W. L. Benoit, D. Hample & P. J. Benoit (Eds.), *Readings in argumentation* (pp. 417–436). Berlin: Foris.

Zarefsky, D. (2012). Goodnight's "speculative inquiry" in its intellectual context. *Argumentation and Advocacy, 48*(2), 211–215.

What Is Informal Logic?

J. Anthony Blair

1 Introduction

Considering the 2014 ISSA conference keynote speakers, one gets the impression of a kind of Aristotelian trivium of argumentation theory—rhetoric, dialectic and logic. Professor Fahnestock represents rhetoric, Professor van Eemeren represents dialectic, and Professor Blair represents logic. However, since I am not a logician, I cannot fill that role. What I can and will do is represent informal logic, which is a somewhat different kettle of fish.

What motivated my topic—"What is Informal Logic?"—is my difficulty in coming up with a one or two sentence answer whenever someone asks me, "What IS informal logic, anyway?" or "What *exactly* is informal logic?"

It is not easy to say what informal logic is. I'm not entirely happy with the latest definition by Johnson and me that is quoted in the chapter on informal logic in the *Handbook of Argumentation Theory* (van Eemeren et al. 2014)[1]: "Informal logic designates that branch of logic whose task it is to develop non-formal$_2$ [i.e., not restricted to logical form] standards, criteria, procedures for the analysis, interpretation, evaluation, critique and construction of argumentation in everyday language" (van Eemeren et al. 2014, pp. 373–374). I would today drop 'standards,' and say "*arguments and* argumentation" and "*natural* language"; but the main point is that this is a very general definition, and so not very informative. Also, I'm quite unhappy with several features of the informal logic entries in the on-line *Stanford Encyclopedia of Philosophy* (Groarke 2013). It strikes me as over-emphasizing themes not central to informal logic, such as visual argument and the debate over

[1] *HAT* is the successor to *FAT*, *Fundamentals of Argumentation Theory* (van Eemeren et al. 1996).

J. Anthony Blair (✉)
Centre for Research in Reasoning, Argumentation and Rhetoric,
University of Windsor, Windsor, ON, Canada
e-mail: tblair@uwindsor.ca

F.H. van Eemeren and B. Garssen (eds.), *Reflections on Theoretical Issues in Argumentation Theory*, Argumentation Library 28,
DOI 10.1007/978-3-319-21103-9_2

so-called natural language deductivism[2] and underemphasizing the prominence of argument scheme theory and of non-deductive and non-inductive criteria; and it employs prominently and without explication the (to me) puzzling terms ‘informal reasoning’, ‘informal inference’ and ‘informal argument’ (—what would count as *formal* reasoning, inference or argument?). The accounts in *The Cambridge Dictionary of Philosophy* (Walton 1995) and *The Oxford Companion to Philosophy* (Tully 1995) are in my view subject to similar kinds of criticism, and in any case are now out of date. However, rather than defending my differences with these accounts, I will use this occasion to spell out what I take informal logic to be.

I will do this by telling the story of two themes that feature in its development and that I think are central to what constitutes informal logic.

A word of warning before I begin. You need to be wary of the notion that in the term “informal logic,” the word ‘informal’ means “informal” and the word ‘logic’ means “logic.” It is like the use of the term ‘football’ north of Mexico. In the USA and in Canada, the games called “football” don’t much call for the players to control a ball with their feet. Informal logicians use variables, and talk about argument schemes, which are quasi formal. So informal logic is not strictly-speaking informal. And if you understand by logic the study of axiomatized deductive systems, informal logic is not logic. No one seems to know for sure how the term originated. Perhaps it derived from the fact that the informal fallacies were a tool used for appraising arguments in natural languages. Some of us used it to signify that we were not studying the logical norms of argument from the perspective of formal (a.k.a. symbolic or mathematical) logic, that is, it meant “not formal logic.”

2 Background

Let me start with a bit of background.

Informal logic, from its beginnings in the 1970s and 1980s, has been motivated by goals of philosophy classroom instruction. Its subject matter was reasoning and arguments. And the enterprise was normative. The objective might be to improve reasoning or critical thinking skills, or to be able to assess the logic of everyday discourse. Reasoning and critical thinking skills were seen to be skills in judging the probative value of one’s own reasoning and of others’ arguments. Assessing logic was seen as recognizing, interpreting and evaluating the probative value of arguments. The telos of the enterprise was the formation of justifiable cognitive and affective attitudes such as beliefs or value judgments, and the assumption was that understanding the norms of cogent reasoning and arguments, and acquiring some skill in their application, will contribute to that end.

[2]“Natural language deductivism” is the thesis that all arguments [in natural languages] should be interpreted as attempts to create deductively valid arguments.

The value in question was and is epistemic or probative merit—not communicative or rhetorical merit. A logically good argument, on this view, contributes to justifying adopting the attitude in question—be it a belief, a judgement, a disposition to act, an emotion, or whatever. Whether such justification is in some cases—or always—relative to audiences or circumstances was and is an open question.

We focused, in the beginning, on the arguments found in the print media: in newspapers and magazines. We did so for several reasons. For one thing, these were not the artificial arguments of traditional logic textbooks—arguments that were designed to illustrate elementary valid argument forms or for practicing the use of truth tables—like this one from Irving Copi's *Symbolic Logic* (1954, p. 25):

> If I work then I earn money, and if I don't work then I enjoy myself. Therefore if I don't earn money then I enjoy myself.

Those examples sent the wrong message to the students, who wanted to improve their ability to understand and assess the arguments used in public life. So the arguments we used for teaching purposes were about the topical issues of the day. They thereby served to demonstrate that arguments are thought to make a difference. Their content might be expected to be familiar to students and of interest to them, and the course would not have to presuppose technical background knowledge. Short examples could be found in letters to the editor; slightly longer ones in editorials; and even longer ones in opinion columns. One wag said we were teaching "newspaper logic."

If you need a label for such writings, you might call them "non-interactive" (see Govier 1999). While targeting some set of readers, the writer is usually not engaged in a face-to-face dialogue with anyone in particular. The writer might be responding to previous comments and the arguments might anticipate and respond to various kinds of objections. So the text can be dialectical. However, any direct interplay is between the writer and that commentator or objector, not between the writer and every reader. In the early days, informal logicians did not think to take these non-interactive pieces to be conversations or dialogues. Later, some were attracted to the view that such texts might fruitfully be modeled as having the salient properties of two-party conversational interactions (e.g., Walton 1998). Others, however, resisted that model as misleading for non-interactive contexts (e.g., Govier 1999, Chap. 11; Blair 2012, Chap. 17).

As teachers of what we originally thought of as practical or applied logic, we were interested in guiding our students in assessing the logic of the reasoning employed in the arguments expressed in these non-interactive writings. To do so required recognizing the presence of arguments and getting at their features. Hence, the first task was to devise guidelines to aid in finding and extracting arguments, and then displaying them for critical examination. The second task was to assess their cogency, either from the point of view of an onlooker or from the point of view of the target audience.

3 Analysis

I first say a few words about what we came to see as required to "get at" the arguments. This is the first theme in informal logic's development. Later, I turn to the second theme, the question of the logical norms to be used in judging the arguments' cogency.

We quickly learned that sending students off to find examples of non-interactive arguments requires them to recognize that a communication might well be serving other purposes than arguing. Often it will consist of just a report or a description or a non-argumentative narrative. Sometimes the text is confused or confusing, so that it's unclear whether its author intends to be arguing. Sometimes the text makes some gestures in the direction of arguing, but on any interpretation the author's reasoning is muddled.

So it turns out that the interpretive tasks of argument recognition and identification, on the one hand, and argument assessment, on the other hand, while they're distinguishable, are not independent. That is because whether the author may be taken to be presenting an argument can depend on whether an at-least plausible argument can be attributed to what he or she has written. And that in turn can depend on whether there are sentences that may plausibly be taken to be functioning in probative support relationships with other sentences. So the recognition and identification of arguments in such writings can require the logical assessment of argument candidates.

To recognize the presence of argument in non-interactive texts, we found that it helps to identify what might be called the rhetorical situation of the text. Doing so includes, when possible, noting such features as the identity of the author, the author's ethos, the intended audience, the occasion, the venue, the surrounding circumstances, the author's objectives, any applicable institutional norms, and the function of the discourse. It also helps, we found, to identify what might be called the dialectical environment of the text. Here I have in mind such things as debates, disagreements, controversies and so on surrounding the author's topic; alternative positions to the author's view; and any particular opponent with whom the author has a history of dispute.

It also helps to have some knowledge of the habitats of arguments in general, such as locations of controversies or other contexts where burdens of proof arise. It requires knowing the signs of arguments, such as illation-indicator terms, qualifiers and hedging expressions, plus an appreciation of their fickleness. And it can help to have a sense for what counts as a reason in the subject-matter in question.

(By the way, speaking of fickle illative terms, notice the non-illative use of 'so' that has become widely used by experts interviewed in the media. They'll start off their explanations with a "so": "So, our study shows that … ." It seems to function like taking a breath before speaking.)

"So", having recognized the presence of argument, the next task is the identification of the argument. We've established that it's a bird making those noises in the bushes, but what kind of bird is it? Identifying the argument means identifying its parts and their functions, and identifying its structure. Here are to be set out the reasons, broken down into premises, and the claims, identified as their conclusions. Qualifications and hedging are to be noticed. We debated the distinctions among patterns of direct support such as linked, convergent, cumulative, and chained or serial.[3] Also, aside from direct support for the main conclusion, what various defensive supporting functions might be being served? We distinguished among defending a premise against an objection, defending a premise-conclusion link against an objection, arguing against alternatives to the conclusion, and defending the conclusion against arguments directly opposing it (see, e.g., Johnson 2000; Finocchiaro 2013). Many called for, or allowed for, the reformulation of parts of the author's original text so that the roles of given sentences in the argument can be made more evident. And many argued that unexpressed but assumed or needed components have to be identified and inserted. It also helps here to have some familiarity with the subject matter.[4]

Having developed guidelines to help understand the argument, we sought ways to portray that understanding so the argument could be methodically assessed. Many developed premise and conclusion numbering conventions that designate any sentence's place in the structure of the argument and/or its function in the argument. As well, many developed tree diagram conventions that do the same jobs. In my experience, students who can easily master the numbering conventions can have trouble working with tree diagrams, and vice versa, so having both seems pedagogically useful.[5]

These tasks of recognition, identification, and display lead up to the assessment of arguments in non-interactive texts. The guidelines help any assessor to gain an understanding of the arguments and so be in a position to judge their probative merits.

By the way, the need to formulate such guidelines does not belong to informal logic in particular. It belongs to any approach that undertakes to analyze the arguments in non-interactive texts. Still, one thread in informal logic is the generation of practical advice for the recognition, identification and display of arguments in non-interactive discourse. This thread was and is practice-driven; and workable and economically teachable guidelines were and are its objective.

---

[3]On these distinctions see, e.g., Govier (1985), Thomas (1986), Yanal (1991, 2003), Freeman (1993), Ennis (1996), LeBlanc (1998), Fisher (2001), Goddu (2003), Bailin and Battersby (2010), Vaughn and MacDonald (2010), Groarke and Tindale (2013), Hitchcock (2015).

[4]The developments described in this and the next paragraph are found in Thomas (1973), Scriven (1976), Johnson and Blair (1977) and Govier (1985), among many others.

[5]Some seem to conceptualize better visually, others, numerically. I don't know whether this difference has occurred to others and been investigated. The current fashion of developing computer-generated tree diagrams might be disadvantaging part of the student population.

4 Appraisal

I now turn to the second theme that I claim characterizes informal logic, namely the logical appraisal of these arguments.

To judge the logical merits of an argument, two kinds of decision are needed: (1) how acceptable are the reasons? And (2) how well justified are the inferences from the reasons to the claims?

Some informal logicians, me among them,[6] have thought that these questions can be asked from at least the following two perspectives. One perspective is that of an addressee or target of the argument. This can be a person or group to whom the author is directing his or her argument. Or it can be anyone who is interested in the argument because he or she wants to decide whether to accept its conclusion. An addressee could be someone trying to decide on a course of action, such as how to vote, whom the arguer is trying to win over, or she could be a scientist presented with evidence for a novel theory in her field, who wants to decide whether to give it credence. The other perspective is that of an onlooker. By an onlooker I mean someone not targeted by the arguer, who can detach himself or herself from interests or commitments touched by the argument, and who is in the position of judging how well the arguer makes his or her case to the audience in question. An onlooker would be a teacher grading a student's essay or a referee for a submission to an academic journal, each of whom has to decide how well the author has made his or her case relative to the burden of proof that is appropriate in the circumstances.

4.1 Premise Acceptability

Let me first say a word about the informal logic criterion for the appraisal of reasons.

Any inference made in reasoning, or invited in an argument, is clearly only as good as what it starts from: namely, its reasons, expressed through its premises. Now, you must understand that most nascent informal logicians had been trained in the analytic philosophy of the mid-twentieth century, according to which good premises are *true* premises. So it required a break with our upbringing to abandon this tradition and follow some of Charles Hamblin's arguments in his 1970 monograph, *Fallacies*. Hamblin proposed that, for cogency, the truth of premises alone is not sufficient, since premises would have to be not only true but also known to be true. And truth is not necessary, either, he said, since "reasonably probable" premises would be good enough (see Hamblin 1970, Chap. 7). However, not many informal logicians went all the way with Hamblin's dialectical conception.

[6]Among others I would include here Hitchcock (1983), Govier (1987), Biro and Siegel (1992), Johnson (2000), Pinto (2001), Freeman (2005), Allen (2013).

According to it, the appropriate criterion (both necessary and sufficient) for premises is that they be accepted, in the sense that they be commitments of the addressee of the argument. But there is a problem for non-interactive arguments addressed to a diverse or unknown audience: *whose* commitments are we talking about? Furthermore, in some cases there are propositions available for use as premises that are obviously true and known by all concerned to be true. But in the absence of obvious truth, many informal logicians opted instead for the criterion that the premises at least must be worthy of acceptance, that is, be acceptable. Of course, then the question is, "What counts as acceptability? That is, what makes claims that are used as premises in reasoning or arguments worthy of acceptance, and by whom?" Informal logicians have made serious, even book-length, attempts to answer that question (see Freeman 2005).

4.2 Logical Assessment: Deductive Validity and Inductive Strength

In addition to the assessment of the acceptability of the reasons, there is the assessment of the consequence relations—the premise-conclusion links—of reasoning and arguments to be considered.

Our thinking about premise-conclusion relations developed along the following lines. Our education in analytic philosophy meant that our basic training in logic, a training almost everyone shared, was in the symbolic logics of the day—at a minimum, formal propositional logic and predicate logic. These are logics of the deductive inference relation called "validity."[7] To use formal methods to test the inference relations of arguments in a natural language for deductive validity requires that the arguments be translated into standard logical form. However, doing so requires an understanding of standard logical form. We would have to teach our students some propositional and predicate logic before they could even begin to interpret these newspaper arguments. Moreover, we discovered that reformulating the newspaper texts into standard logical form usually required simplifying their sentences and thus changing the sense of the arguments. And, finally, when inspected for conformity to the established rules of inference of deductive logic, such arguments often proved to be deductively invalid, even when, independently, they seemed to be cogent.

One hypothesis suggested to explain this last anomaly was that the arguer was making unexpressed assumptions, which, once added to the stated argument as additional premises, would render it deductively valid (see Groarke 1995, 1999, 2002). The trouble is that, in many cases, the candidates for such needed missing

[7]Logicians gave their use of 'validity' a special, technical sense. In that sense, expressed in one of several possible ways, an inference from a set of premises to a conclusion is "valid" just in case the conclusion could not possibly be false if the premises were true.

premises are patently false (see Godden 2005). Often, a plausible argument's deductive validity could be saved only by adding problematic or false assumptions to it.

Of course many of these arguments were intended, not to be deductively valid, but instead, to be inductively strong. Thus arguments in support of causal explanations, statistical generalizations from samples to populations, inductive analogies, and so on, could have their conclusions well-supported by their premises even though they were deductively invalid. So the options became that an argument with acceptable premises would be logically cogent if it were either deductively valid or else, if deductively invalid, if it were inductively strong.

4.3 The Deductive/Inductive Dichotomy Challenged

An early question debated in the informal logic community was whether deductive validity and inductive strength are the only criteria for logically respectable inferences from reasons to claims. Put another way, it is the question whether all arguments are either deductive or inductive. Is the deductive-inductive dichotomy exhaustive—be it a dichotomy of criteria for inference adequacy or a dichotomy of inference types? (See Weddle 1979, 1980; Fohr 1979, 1980; Govier 1979, 1980a, b; Hitchcock 1980; Johnson 1980.)

To be sure, that dichotomy can be made exhaustive by definitional fiat. Inductive reasoning can be *defined* as any reasoning that is not deductive. But the plausibility of this dichotomy relies on assuming a very broad conception of induction. For logicians, however, inductive reasoning provides support for its conclusions in degrees of probability specifiable numerically, or it is reasoning that relies on the assumption that experienced regularities provide a guide to un-experienced regularities. Here, for instance, is a passage from the introduction of the article on inductive logic in the *Stanford Encyclopedia of Philosophy* (Hawthorne 2014):

> This article will focus on the kind of … approach to inductive logic most widely studied by philosophers and logicians in recent years. These logics employ conditional probability functions to represent measures of the degree to which evidence statements support hypotheses. This kind of approach usually draws on Bayes' theorem, which is a theorem of probability theory, to articulate how the implications of hypotheses about evidence claims influences the degree to which hypotheses are supported by those evidence claims.

The notion of induction that Hawthorne describes here is a not a broad conception of induction. It leaves out reasoning in which probability in the sense of plausibility or reasonableness is the appropriate qualifier or where it makes no sense to express the strength of support as a numerical probability. It leaves out reasoning that relies on reasons other than experienced regularities. Denying that the deductive-inductive dichotomy is exhaustive implies that there can be reasoning that both is deductively invalid and also to which the norms of induction narrowly defined do not apply, yet it is logically good reasoning.

Two examples were proposed early on in the informal logic community to show that some reasoning doesn't seem to fit either the deductive or the narrow inductive category. One example, due to Wisdom (1991), was the reasoning or the argument that Govier (1999) has called "a priori analogy." Here is an example:

> Ellen's essay merits a high grade by virtue of the lucid clarity of its organization and expression, the thoroughness of its argumentation and the cogency of its arguments. Jay's essay is similarly clearly organized and expressed, its argumentation is similarly thorough and its arguments similarly cogent. So Jay's essay merits a similarly high grade.

Generalized, this is the reasoning that, when a certain property belongs to something by virtue of that thing's satisfying certain criteria to a given extent, and another thing of the same sort as the first one is judged also to satisfy those criteria to a similar extent, then one may (i.e., is entitled to) infer that the property in question belongs to the second thing as well.

The premises of cogent reasoning or arguments from a priori analogy do not deductively entail their conclusions, because the second thing might have, besides the stated qualifying properties, others that disqualify it from having the feature in question. (Maybe Jay's essay was submitted well after the due date, and was not on the assigned topic.) Since it can't be known in advance what all the possible disqualifiers are, a list of them cannot be built into the criteria. Moreover, such reasoning or arguments are not narrowly inductive either, for there is no basis for assigning a numerical probability to their conclusions. Nor are they arguments from known regularities.

The other example, due to Wellman (1971), is what he called "conductive" reasoning. It is also known as balance-of-considerations reasoning. Here is an example.

> The blueberries for sale today are ripe, fresh and wild; blueberries are supposed to be good for you; and I adore wild blueberries. So I should buy them. On the other hand, they're outrageously over-priced and I don't really need them. So I shouldn't buy them. But I can afford them, and I need to indulge myself just now. So, everything considered, I should buy them.

In such reasoning, the reasoner takes one set of considerations to favour a claim, and at the same time takes another set of considerations to tell against that claim. The reasoner judges one set to outweigh the other, and on that basis judges the claim to be acceptable or unacceptable.

The premises of cogent balance-of-considerations reasoning or arguments don't entail their conclusions, because new information can tip the balance in the other direction, thereby affecting the legitimacy of the inference to the main conclusion. (For example, my wife tells me that there is no room in the refrigerator for the blueberries, or that she has already bought some.) But these are not narrowly inductive arguments either. There is no basis for assigning a numerical probability to the reasonableness of my decision to buy the blueberries. And again, there is no argument from known regularities here.

Based on examples like these two, many informal logicians concluded that it is false that all reasoning is either deductive or narrowly inductive. Some reasoning requires other criteria of inference appraisal than deductive validity and, for instance, statistical probability.

4.4 General Tools for Assessing Inference Strength

Most informal logicians did not address the question of what this other kind of reasoning is, beyond the judgment that it is not deductive and not narrowly inductive. Their motivation was classroom instruction, and the immediate need was useful teaching tools. So they adopted, adapted or invented various general methods of inference appraisal. These supposedly apply to reasoning and arguments of any sort, whether they are intended to be deductively valid, or inductively strong, or to belong to neither of these two categories.

At least five such methods turn up in the informal logic literature. I will describe each of them briefly.

4.4.1 Fallacy Theory

One early proposal was that an argument free of fallacies is probatively sound, and in particular, its consequence relation is fine so long as it is free of inferential fallacies. This answer leads straight to fallacy theory, and that was an early pre-occupation of informal logicians. That fact led some people, understandably but mistakenly, to identify informal logic with the study of informal fallacies. (For examples of early fallacy approaches, see Kahane 1971; Johnson and Blair 1977).

A broad consensus emerged that fallacies are not patterns of mistaken reasoning. Rather, they are errors in the sense of misfires or misuses of otherwise legitimate patterns of reasoning. What distinguishes the informal logic approach to fallacies is that not all fallacies are viewed as dialectical or rhetorical misdemeanors: many are seen as particular errors of reasoning. Some are confused deductions, some hasty inductions, and some other types of malfunctioning reasoning (e.g., Walton 1992, Chap. 7). I need to add that there are some informal logicians who seem to either question whether, or else deny that, the concept of fallacy has any legitimate application (see Finocchiaro 1981; Woods 2013).

4.4.2 Acceptability, Relevance, Sufficiency

Another general method of assessment is to use the triad of Acceptability, Relevance and Sufficiency—"ARS." Acceptability, as I have already noted, is a criterion for premises. Relevance and sufficiency are criteria for the adequacy of the link between premises and conclusion: the reasons offered must be probatively relevant to the conclusion, and they have to supply enough of the right kinds of evidence to justify accepting it.[8]

It's been argued that relevance is redundant, since sufficiency already presupposes it. You can't have enough evidence unless what you count as evidence is already relevant (Biro and Siegel 1992). That is true. However, people's arguments sometimes include irrelevant premises. Those have to be identified and set aside before judging the sufficiency of the relevant ones that remain.

Sufficiency has become seen to require not only reasons that directly support a claim but also those that support it indirectly, by way of refuting or weakening objections or criticisms of various kinds (see Johnson and Blair 1983, 1987; Johnson 1996, 2000). How far that indirect support should go is a matter that continues to be debated (e.g., see Govier 1999).

The ARS criteria are general, in that deductively valid and inductively strong reasoning and arguments, as well as those with other kinds of good consequence relations, all will pass their test. They, or variants of them, have been widely adopted as teaching tools (see, e.g., Johnson and Blair 1977; Govier 1985; Damer 1987; Freeman 1988; Seech 1988; Groarke and Tindale 2004) and their introduction has led to scholarly reflections on all three concepts.

Some people, again mistakenly, identify informal logic with the ARS method of argument assessment.

4.4.3 Inference Warrants

Some informal logicians have been attracted to Toulmin's (1958) concepts of warrant and backing as an account of what justifies reasoning and argument inferences in general. The idea is that any particular inference relies on a general rule or warrant that licenses inferences of that sort. An inference is justified provided that its warrant is itself defensible, that is, can be backed up if questioned. Although Toulmin did not emphasize this point, a warrant can be a deductive rule of inference, such as modus ponens, or an inductive principle, as well as such things as rules of practices. So warrant justification is general too. (On warrants entitling inferences, see, e.g., Freeman 2011.)

An obvious objection to this approach is that the backing of a warrant is itself an argument, thereby involving an inference that must rely on another warrant that can be backed up if questioned—and so there begins an infinite regress. A reply to this objection is that, while an infinite regress of warrants and backings is in principle possible, in practice, in short order one arrives at backing that is either clearly solid or obviously dubious.

---

[8]The terms 'acceptability,' 'relevance' and 'sufficiency' were originally introduced as names for the three criteria for logically good arguments by Johnson and Blair (1977).

4.4.4 Testing by Possible Counterexamples

A fourth general method that informal logicians have used for evaluating the inferences of reasoning and arguments is testing them by means of counterexamples.

The method is to think of considerations that are consistent with the given reasons but inconsistent with the claim being inferred or argued for. Depending on whether any such counterexamples are conceivable, and if so, either probable or plausible to some extent, the reasoning can be determined to be deductively valid, or invalid but with some degree of inductive strength, or invalid but more or less reasonable (see, e.g., Fisher 1988; Pinto et al. 1993).

This method is only as good as the assessors' ability to imagine possible counter-examples and the accuracy of their judgements of the possibility, probability, or plausibility or reasonableness of such counter-examples. This ability often depends on subject-specific knowledge about the topic of the reasoning or argument in question.

4.4.5 Reasoning Scheme/Argument Scheme Theory

I call the fifth method, "argument scheme theory." Douglas Walton is one theorist who has proposed an account of non-deductive, non-inductive kinds of reasoning. According to Walton (1996), such reasoning is presumptive. That is, it is reasoning that establishes, or shifts, a burden of proof. A general approach for assessing deductive, inductive and presumptive reasoning, according to Walton and others, is the use of reasoning or argument schemes.

A reasoning or argument scheme is a generalization of a token of reasoning or argument. I gave examples of two such schemes earlier—the schemes for reasoning by a priori analogy and the scheme for balance-of-considerations reasoning.

Such generalizations can be deductive, inductive or presumptive. Scheme theorists think it is reasonable to accept the conclusion of an instance of such a scheme as the consequence of its premises, so long as the use of that scheme in the situation is appropriate and the questions that test its vulnerable features—the so-called "critical questions"—are answered satisfactorily in the given case (see, e.g., Walton et al. 2008).

These five methods—freedom from inferential fallacy; the sufficiency of relevant offered reasons; justification by an adequately-backed warrant; passing the test of counter-examples; and being an acceptable instance of a reasoning scheme—are all general methods of assessing the inferences of reasoning or arguments. That is, they apply to reasoning or arguments with supposed deductive validity, or inductive strength, or other kinds of cogency. Whether these five initiatives are compatible, equivalent or otherwise related, whether they are correct, and whether the list is exhaustive, all remains to be seen.

5 Other Developments, and Conclusion

So far I have described two themes that have animated informal logic. One is the development of guidelines for the analysis of the reasoning in non-interactive arguments. The other is the articulation of generally applicable methods for evaluating the reasoning—that is, the reasons and the inferences—exhibited in arguments. My contention is that these are the principal defining threads of informal logic. I have omitted many details, some of which I want to acknowledge with a few closing notes.

One thing to note is that informal logicians came to realize that, although they had started out analyzing arguments in non-interactive texts for teaching purposes, what they are also interested in is the logic of the non-deductive, non-narrowly-inductive reasoning employed in any arguments, in whatever setting they are communicated (whether a dialogue, a group discussion, or a speech), by whatever mode they are communicated (whether orally or in writing, visually, or mixed-modally), for whatever purpose they are communicated (whether for persuasion, or disagreement resolution, or communication repair, or justification, or any other purpose), and with whatever subject-matter they are concerned.

A second thing to note is that at least some informal logicians (e.g., Tindal 1999, 2004), in some cases, belatedly (e.g., Blair 2012, Chaps. 18, 23), have come to appreciate the need to understand the rhetorical functions of communication in order to recognize and identify arguments, and in order to understand the nature and force of the reasoning expressed in them.

A third thing worth noting is that some informal logicians have taken up the study of historical exemplars of argument and argument analysis to both illustrate the reach of the informal logic approach to argument analysis and assessment and to find historical antecedents of this approach (e.g., Finocchiaro 2005; Hansen 2014a, b, c).

And a final note: I hope it is clear that informal logic does not aim to account for all the pragmatic and communicative properties of arguments. Nor is it a theory of argumentation, understanding by such a theory an account of the dynamics of, and the norms for, various kinds of exchanges of arguments for various purposes. It does not address the psychology, sociology, or politics of exchanges of arguments. If informal logicians happen to take up such topics, as some do, they do so flying other colours, such as "argumentation theorist."

By now I hope you can see why I have difficulty conveying an understanding of what informal logic is in a couple of sentences. If you will allow the above presentation to stand as a long footnote, my summary would run as follows. Informal logic is the combination of two related things. It is the development and justification of practical guidelines for recognizing, identifying and displaying the reasoning expressed and invited in arguments, especially arguments found in non-interactive discourse or other modes of non-interactive communication. And it is the development and justification of the probative norms applicable to the reasons, and applicable to the non-deductive, non-inductive inferential links, employed in the reasoning that is expressed or invited in any argument. The two are connected in that the tools for natural language argument recognition, identification and display are developed to enable and facilitate the assessment of the natural language arguments.

Acknowledgments My thanks to Fellows at the Centre for Research in Reasoning, Argumentation and Rhetoric at the University of Windsor for critical comments on, and suggestions for improvements of, earlier drafts of the keynote address, including Hans Hansen, Catherine Hundleby, Leo Groarke, Marcello Guarini, Bruno Leclercq, Christopher Tindale, and especially Ralph Johnson and Robert Pinto.

References

Allen, D. (2013). Trudy Govier and premise adequacy. *Informal Logic, 33*(2), 116–142.

Bailin, S., & Battersby, M. (2010). *Reason in the balance: An inquiry approach to critical thinking*. Toronto: McGraw-Hill Ryerson.

Biro, J., & Siegel, H. (1992). Normativity, argumentation and an epistemic theory of fallacies. In F. H. van Eemeren, et al. (Eds.), *Argumentation illuminated* (pp. 85–103). Amsterdam: SicSat.

Blair, J. A. (2012). *Groundwork in the theory of argumentation, Selected papers of J. Anthony Blair*. Dordrecht: Springer.

Blair, J. A., & Johnson, R. H. (1987). Argumentation as dialectical. *Argumentation, 1*(1), 41–56.

Copi, I. M. (1954). *Symbolic logic*. New York: The Macmillan Company.

Damer, T. E. (1987). *Attacking faulty reasoning* (2nd ed.). Belmont, CA: Wadsworth.

Ennis, R. H. (1996). *Critical thinking*. Upper Saddle River, NJ: Prentice-Hall.

Finocchiaro, M. A. (1981). Fallacies and the evaluation of reasoning. *American Philosophical Quarterly, 18*, 13–22.

Finocchiaro, M. A. (2005). *Arguments about arguments, systematic, critical and historical essays in logical theory*. Cambridge: Cambridge University Press.

Finocchiaro, M. A. (2013). *Meta-argumentation, an approach to logic and argumentation theory*. London: College Publications.

Fisher, A. (1988). *The logic of real arguments*. Cambridge: Cambridge University Press.

Fisher, A. (2001). *Critical thinking: An introduction*. Cambridge: Cambridge University Press.

Fohr, S. D. (1979). The deductive-inductive distinction. *Informal Logic Newsletter,* 2(2), 5–8.

Fohr, S. D. (1980). Deductive-inductive: Reply to criticisms. *Informal Logic Newsletter, 3*(1), 5–10.

Freeman, J. B. (1988). *Thinking logically: Basic concepts for reasoning*. Englewood Cliffs, NJ: Prentice Hall.

Freeman, J. B. (1993). *Thinking logically: Basic concepts for reasoning*. Englewood Cliffs, NJ: Prentice Hall.

Freeman, J. B. (2005). *Acceptable premises, an epistemic approach to an informal logic problem*. Cambridge: Cambridge University Press.

Freeman, J. B. (2011). Evaluating conductive arguments in light of the Toulmin model. In J. A. Blair & R. H. Johnson (Eds.), *Conductive argument, an overlooked type of defeasible reasoning* (pp. 127–144). London: College Publications.

Godden, D. (2005). Deductivism as an interpretive strategy, reply to Groarke's recent defense of reconstructive deductivism. *Argumentation and Advocacy, 41*, 168–183.

Goddu, G. (2003). Against the 'ordinary summing' test for convergence. *Informal Logic, 23*(3), 215–236.

Govier, T. (1979). Critical review of Carl Wellman's Challenge and response. *Informal Logic Newsletter,* 2(3), 10–15.

Govier, T. (1980a). More on deductive and inductive arguments. *Informal Logic Newsletter, 2*(3), 7–8.

Govier, T. (1980b). Assessing arguments, what range of standards? *Informal Logic Newsletter, 3* (1), 2–4.

Govier, T. (1985). *A practical study of argument* (1st ed.). Belmont, CA: Wadsworth.

Govier, T. (1987). *Problems in argument analysis and evaluation*. Dordrecht: Foris.

Govier, T. (1999). *The philosophy of argument*. Newport News, VA: Vale Press.

Groarke, L. (1995). What pragma-dialectics can learn from deductivism, and what deductivism can learn from pragma-dialectics. In F. H. van Eemeren, R. Grootendorst, J. A. Blair, & C. A. Willard (Eds.), *Proceedings of the third ISSA conference on argumentation* (Vol. 2, pp. 138–145). Analysis and evaluation Amsterdam: Sic Sat.

Groarke, L. (1999). Deductivism within pragma-dialectics. *Argumentation, 13*, 1–16.

Groarke, L. (2002). Johnson on the metaphysics of argument. *Argumentation, 16*, 277–286.

Groarke, L. (2013). Informal logic. In E. N. Zalta (Ed.), *The Stanford encyclopedia of philosophy*, Spring 2013 Ed. http://plato.stanford.edu/archives/spr2013/entries/logic-informal/.

Groarke, L. A., & Tindale, C. W. (2004). *Good reasoning matters: A constructive approach to critical thinking* (3rd ed.). Don Mills, ON: Oxford University Press.

Hamblin, C. L. (1970). *Fallacies*. London: Methuen.

Hansen, H.V. 2014a. Mill, informal logic and argumentation. In A. Loizides (Ed.), *John Stuart Mill's a system of logic: Critical appraisals* (pp. 192–217). Routledge.

Hansen, H. V. (Ed.). (2014b). *Riel's defence: Perspectives on his speeches*. Montreal: McGill-Queen's University Press.

Hansen, H. V. (2014c). Narrative and logical order in Riel's address to the jury. In H. V. Hansen (Ed.), *Riel's defence: Perspectives on his speeches* (pp. 135–164). Montreal: McGill-Queen's University Press.

Hawthorne, J. (2014). Indouctive logic. In E. N. Zalta (Ed.), *The Stanford encyclopedia of philosophy*, Summer 2014 Ed. (forthcoming). http://plato.stanfrd.edu/archives/sum2014/entries/logic-inductive/.

Hitchcock, D. (1980). Deductive and inductive: Types of validity, not types of argument. *Informal Logic Newsletter, 2*(3), 9–10.

Hitchcock, D. (1983). *Critical thinking: A guide to evaluating information*. Toronto: Methuen.

Hitchcock, D. (2015). Freeman's syntactic criterion for linkage. *Informal Logic, 35*(1), 1–31.

Johnson, F. (1980). *Deductively-inductively. Informal Logic Newsletter, 3*(1), 4–5.

Johnson, R. H. (1996). *The rise of informal logic*. Newport News, VA: Vale Press.

Johnson, R. H. (2000). *Manifest rationality, A pragmatic theory of argument*. Mahwah, NJ: Lawrence Erlbaum Associates.

Johnson, R. H., & Blair, J. A. (1977, 1983, 1993). *Logical self-defense*. Toronto: McGraw-Hill Ryerson.

Kahane, H. (1971). *Logic and contemporary rhetoric* (1st ed.). Belmont, CA: Wadsworth.

LeBlanc, J. (1998). *Thinking clearly: A guide to critical reasoning*. New York: W. W. Norton.

Pinto, R. C. (2001). *Argument, inference and dialectic, collected papers on informal logic*. Dordrecht: Kluwer.

Pinto, R. C., Blair, J. A., & Parr, K. E. (1993). *Reasoning, a practical guide for Canadian students*. Scarborough, ON: Prentice-Hall Canada.

Scriven, M. (1976). *Reasoning*. New York: McGraw-Hill.

Seech, Z. (1988). *Open minds and everyday reasoning*. Belmont, CA: Wadsworth.

Thomas, S. N. (1973, 1986). *Practical reasoning in natural language* (3rd ed. 1986) Englewood Cliffs, NJ: Prentice-Hall.

Tindale, C. W. (1999). *Acts of arguing, a rhetorical model of argument*. Albany: State University of New York Press.

Tindale, C. W. (2004). *Rhetorical argumentation*. Thousand Oaks, CA: Sage.

Toulmin, Stephen. (1958). *The uses of argument*. Cambridge: Cambridge University Press.

Tully, R. E. (1995). Logic, informal. In T. Honderich (Ed.), *The Oxford companion to philosophy* (p. 500). Oxford: Oxford University Press.

van Eemeren, F. H., et al. (Eds.). (1996). *Fundamentals of argumentation theory*. Mahwah, NJ: Lawrence Erlbaum Associates.
van Eemeren, F. H., et al. (Eds.). (2014). *Handbook of argumentation theory*. Dordrecht: Springer.
Vaughn, L., & MacDonald, C. (2010). *The power of critical thinking* (2nd Canadian ed.). Don Mills, ON: Oxford University Press.
Walton, D. N. (1992). *Plausible argument in everyday conversation*. Albany, NY: State University of New York Press.
Walton, D. N. (1995). Informal logic. In R. Audi (Ed.), *The Cambridge dictionary of philosophy* (p. 376). Cambridge: Cambridge University Press.
Walton, D. N. (1996). *Argument schemes for presumptive reasoning*. Mahwah, NJ: Lawrence Erlbaum Associates.
Walton, D. N. (1998). *The new dialectic*. Toronto: University of Toronto Press.
Walton, D., Reed, C., & Macagno, F. (2008). *Argumentation schemes*. Cambridge: Cambridge University Press.
Weddle, P. (1979). Inductive, deductive. *Informal Logic Newsletter, 2*(1), 1–5.
Weddle, P. (1980). Good grief! More on induction/deduction. *Informal Logic Newsletter, 3*(1), 10–13.
Wellman, C. (1971). *Challenge and response, justification in ethics*. Carbondale: Southern Illinois University Press.
Wisdom, J. (1991). *Proof and explanation, The Virginia lectures* (ed. by S. F. Barker). Lanham, MD: University Press of America (Originally delivered at the University of Virginia in spring 1957).
Woods, J. (2013). *Errors of reasoning, naturalizing the logic of inference*. London: College Publications.
Yanal, R. J. (1991). Dependent and independent reasons. *Informal Logic, 13*(3), 137–144.
Yanal, R. J. (2003). Linked and convergent reasons—again. In J. Anthony Blair, et al. (Eds.), *Informal logic at 25: Proceedings of the Windsor conference*, CD-ROM. Windsor, ON: OSSA.

Towards a Foundation for Argumentation Theory

G.C. Goddu

1 Introduction

Argumentation theorists disagree about many things. For example, is conductive reasoning distinct from deductive or inductive reasoning? Could a painting or a judo flip be an argument? How many types of fallacies are there? Are there any enthymemes? Is relevance an independent condition of a good argument? Can a non-virtuous arguer give a good argument? Are arguments better construed as acts or as propositions or as sentences? Are all arguments dialectical? Answering these sorts of questions are among the current challenges of argumentation theory.

One impediment to answering these questions is that differing answers are often grounded in different theoretical frameworks. Hence, the issue is not merely one of trying to marshal 'the best' reasons for a particular answer to one of these questions, but rather to produce 'the best' overall theory. But now a new problem emerges—how do we assess, across theories, whether theory X is right for saying an argument can have an infinite number of premises say, while theory Y is wrong for saying an argument cannot? We could of course try to adjudicate theories in the standard way in terms of simplicity, explanatory depth and breadth, etc., but such comparisons rarely generate a neat linear ordering. One theory may have advantages in one area of explanation, but do worse in another. Even worse, the theories may not agree on even the basic ontology of arguments, say, and so not agree on what sort of thing an argument is (or could be). Hence, one might doubt that it is possible to construct a fully adequate theory of argumentation—a theory that tries to understand and relate all the elements of the practice of argumentation: arguments, arguings, arguers, reasoning, etc.

My concern here is to at least begin to explore the possibility of adjudicating basic ontology issues in argumentation theory. What, if anything, are the constraints

G.C. Goddu (✉)
Department of Philosophy, University of Richmond, Richmond, VA 23173, USA
e-mail: ggoddu@richmond.edu

F.H. van Eemeren and B. Garssen (eds.), *Reflections on Theoretical Issues in Argumentation Theory*, Argumentation Library 28,
DOI 10.1007/978-3-319-21103-9_3

on an adequate theory of argumentation at the basic ontological level (at least from the perspective of argumentation theory)? Are there any substantive principles that are accepted by all theories that might serve as grounds for adjudicating amongst competing theories? In this paper I shall present and analyze numerous principles that argumentation theorists do agree upon (and some closely related ones which they do not) and argue that the set presented here offers at best limited grounds for cross-theoretical evaluation, though I shall also point to some possible paths forward.

2 Background Agreement

Argumentation theory does not take place in a vacuum. Indeed, for there to be a recognizable argumentation theory (as distinct from say particle physics or pre-Imperial Roman history or basket weaving or World Cup football) there must be much that is at least tacitly agreed upon, such as at least: there are thinking beings, there are material objects such as chairs, buildings, stars, etc. The thinking beings perform various kinds of actions and have various kinds of goals, beliefs, and desires. There are languages which thinking beings use to communicate information with each other. There are various academic disciplines that categorize this information, etc.

I am not claiming that these tacitly agreed upon items are definitely known or true or unchallenged. Churchland (1981) doubts there are beliefs. Merricks (2003) argues that there are no macro-sized non-conscious material objects while Turner (2011) argues there are no composite objects at all. All I am suggesting is that, as argumentation theorists, we presuppose that argumentation is a human activity that occurs within the context of human beliefs and desires and goals within a world of tables, chairs, buildings, etc.

So there is a vast swathe of propositions that I suspect we agree upon and take for granted when we are doing argumentation theory. But much of this that we presuppose does not itself impact or help us adjudicate disputes in argumentation theory since it is against this presupposed backdrop, when trying to understand the human activity of argumentation, that the disputes themselves arise. Hence, even if it turns out that Merricks is right that there are no baseballs (or any other non-conscious composite objects), but merely atoms arranged baseball-wise, then, while a part of our presupposed background is not quite accurate, the inaccuracy is not something that affects our argumentation theory. We can argue about whether baseballs were in the strike zone just as easily as whether atoms arranged baseball-wise were in the strike zone. So despite the existence of large-scale agreement, we have not necessarily made much progress in terms of helping adjudicate theory disputes in argumentation theory, since it is against the large-scale agreement that the disagreements arise.

3 Substantive Agreement

Is there anything substantively relevant to argumentation theory that all argumentation theorists agree upon? (or at least should agree upon?) At the very least it seems hard to be counted as doing argumentation theory if one does not accept:

(1) There are acts of arguing.

(Hard, though perhaps not impossible. Could there be a world in which people give/express arguments (and so there is a need for argumentation theory, and yet there is no arguing)? Perhaps they give arguments as a form of poetry or entertainment. The question of course is whether what the people give should in fact be called 'arguments' (or whether even if called 'arguments', the study of them should be called 'argumentation theory'). If we say 'yes' because historically they once used them to argue, but now do not, then the world is not a world in which there are no acts of arguing. If we say 'yes' because what they give/express correspond with what we give/express when we argue, then the matter is inconclusive since it may be that it is the usage of the giving/expression to argue that allows the giving/expression to be called an argument. So without the arguing, the giving/expressing in our hypothetical world would not be the giving/expressing of an argument. Regardless, even if it really were a possibility that one could do argumentation theory without there being acts of arguing, that possibility is quite remote from the situation in which we actually find ourselves—one in which there are acts of arguing.)

Given the plausible background assumption that action theory and argumentation theory are not the same thing, we should also accept:

(2) Not all acts are acts of arguing.

(2), unlike (1), is not a precondition for doing argumentation theory, but rather a fact about the background world that is presupposed and yet is relevant to argumentation theory. Given the world of agents with beliefs and desires, and goals and wants and needs who act on those beliefs and desires to achieve their goals in a world of tables and chairs and money, etc., there are in fact acts that agents perform that are not acts of arguing. My sitting down before turning on the computer was not an act of arguing. Your eating of breakfast this morning (assuming you ate breakfast this morning) was not an act of arguing. In general acts of poetry reading, prophesying, walking, etc., are, most of the time anyway, not acts of arguing. This of course leaves open where the line is between acts of arguing and acts that are not acts of arguing. For example, are acts of persuading (or attempted persuasion) all acts of arguing or not. Are at least some acts of explaining also acts of arguing? Is proving a type of arguing or not?

While we may disagree on where the line is, we agree that there is a line to be drawn. For the notion of arguing to be a relevant sub-class of action, then there need to be examples of action that do not fall into the sub-class—otherwise arguing and acting start to look like two different names for the same thing. Hence, any theory that ultimately claimed that all acts (or none) are acts of arguing is to be rejected.[1] So what to make of the critical thinking textbook—*Everything's an Argument?* Despite the title, the actual claim of the book is that every instance of language or symbol use is a form of argument, which, even if stronger than most argumentation theorists are willing to accept, is still much weaker than the claim that all acts are acts of arguing.

(2) is not to be confused with the related:

(Z) Not all acts could be acts of arguing.

Put another way (Z) is: there is some act that could not be an act of arguing, or there is some act for which it is impossible that it be an act of arguing. While I suspect that many argumentation theorists agree with (Z)—there just are some acts that could never be acts of arguing, I am not sure that such agreement is justified. Indeed, if exemplifying, providing an example to show a certain kind of object, act, or state of affairs is possible, is a kind of arguing and any action could, in the right circumstances, be an act of exemplifying, then every act could be an act of arguing.[2] (This does not mean that there is a possible world in which every single act in that world is an act of arguing—it merely means that for every act x, there is some possible world in which x is an act of arguing.)

Some argumentation theorists hold that there must be a linguistic component for an act to count as an act of arguing. Others disagree—consider for example, Gilbert's (2003) judo flip example. Nevertheless, if it is true that an act of arguing must involve a linguistic component, then any act with no linguistic component is not and (assuming it could not be the same act if it had a linguistic component) could not be an act of arguing. But since argumentation theorists do not universally agree on whether an act of arguing must involve a linguistic, or even symbolic, component, we cannot use such an appeal to ground accepting (Z).

While argumentation theorists disagree about what is and is not an act of arguing and disagree about whether there are boundaries to what acts could be arguings, theorists at least agree that:

(3) At least some acts of arguing involve the expression of reasons.

Stipulate that to express reasons it to give a symbolic representation of the reason. For many those expressions are limited to linguistic expressions—for others, pictorial expressions with no linguistic component will also count as expressions of reasons. But given the stipulation, Gilbert's judo flip may be the giving of a reason, but not the expressing of one. Hence, I cannot say that argumentation theorists agree that all acts of arguing involve the expression of reasons.

But what of:

[1] Woods (1992) appeals to a similar principle with regards to relevance—any theory of relevance that makes everything relevant to everything or nothing relevant to anything is to be rejected.

[2] The issue is made more complicated by the problem of trying to type acts or identify the identity conditions of an act—could act x have happened 2 min later and still be the same act? On some theories of the nature of acts the answer is 'no', but on others it is 'yes'.

(A) All acts of arguing involve the giving of reasons.

According to Blair (2003), "[e]ven the broadest definitions of argument, such as those of Willard (1989) and Gilbert (1997), presupposes some element of reason-using."[3] Is there then no arguing if one is just giving the conclusion without reasons for it? While plausible, I am not sure that all argumentation theorists agree. Finocchiaro (2003), argues that in at least some instances an argument is merely a defense of its conclusion from objections even if no reasons are given for that conclusion. Others allow the possibility of zero-premise arguments. (See Goddu 2012) In both cases, if one thinks that for every argument there is a corresponding potential arguing, then again it seems one is committed to the possibility of an act of arguing that does not involve the giving of reasons.

While resolving these issues is quite possible, the issue is that potential resolutions are themselves controversial. Finocchiaro (2013) himself argues in subsequent work that rebutting objections to X do constitute reasons for X. But anyone who hesitates to accept that discovering a pink sock, it not being a non-black crow, rebuts (minimally?) the claim that there are non-black crows may also hesitate to admit that rebutting objections to X are themselves reasons for X. Argumentation theorists do not have an uncontroversial account of what is or could be a reason. Nor do argumentation theorists agree on whether for every argument there is a corresponding potential arguing. Hence, as plausible as (A) is, I hold off from adding it to list of agreed upon principles.

Could you have an expression of reasons that was not part of an act of arguing? I suspect so. When I give an example of a reason, I express it, even if I do not argue. If I merely repeat someone else's reasons, I express them without arguing with them. A computer that generates complexes of sentences in the form: "A, B so C" may express reasons without any act of arguing happening. So I suspect we have evidence for:

(B) Not every expression of reasons is part of an act of arguing.

But I put (B) aside on the grounds that there may be some dispute about what counts as the expressing of a reason.

Finally, it is part of our background presuppositions about language and symbols and representations in general that they have meaning or content. Hence, all argumentation theorists should agree that:

(4) Expressions of reasons have informational content.

Of course we may disagree about how to capture the notion of informational content—say in terms of propositions, or some primitive 'same content as' property, or something else. Regardless of this potential disagreement, we still agree that there is informational content that is distinct from the expression—"x is a bachelor" and

[3]The subtleties of the distinction between 'giving' and 'using' reasons in the context of arguing, if there is one, is not relevant here. Gilbert's judo flip example is apparently an example of the giving or using of a reason, but still not the expressing of one.

"x is an unmarried male of marriageable age", or "x = 25" and "x = 5 squared" may have the same informational content, but are definitely not the same expressions.

Argumentation theorists, as far as I can tell, agree on (1)–(4). At the very least they act and write as if they do even if they have never explicitly uttered or written them. I suspect most would assent to (A) and (B) as well, but for the moment I am putting those aside. (Though what follows does not change if (A) and (B) are put in the mix.) If I am wrong and argumentation theorists do not even agree on (1)–(4), then the prospects for moving forward are quite limited. If we cannot even agree on the basic constituents out of which the data we are trying to explain are constructed, then we will certainly never agree on any attempt to explain and organize that data. But is agreement on (1)–(4) enough for any progress? I turn to that question in the next section.

4 Any Payoff?

Does (1)–(4) provide us enough agreement to make progress on our disputes? I suspect not, since the background presuppositions and (1)–(4) are currently consistent with:

(Y) There are no arguments.

Proof: Suppose the word 'argument' were stricken from our language as a myth, say on the par of 'subluminous ether' or 'phlogiston'. Could one still do argumentation theory with the ontology presupposed in (1)–(4)? Yes. There would be acts of arguing which we would try to distinguish from acts that were not acts of arguing. At least some of those acts of arguing would involve the use of expressions that had informational content. One could still debate whether the act or the expression or the informational content was the most important aspect of what was going on. One could still distinguish combinations of actions and expressions that in a certain context for a certain audience would be more likely to achieve assent than other combinations of actions and expressions in that context. One could talk of the logical properties holding between different pieces of informational content. One could ask whether the actions or the expressions or the informational content could be partitioned into various categories such as good, bad, rational, irrational, deductive, inductive, conductive, abductive, enthymeme, fallacy, convergent, divergent, virtuous, etc. One could, in short, I suspect, recapitulate much of argumentation theory without the word 'argument' referring to anything at all.

One might claim that all this shows is that the word 'argument' is ambiguous—sometimes it is used to refer to the acts of arguing, sometimes to reason/claim expressions, sometimes to the informational content of those expressions. Granted. But I was not trying to show that (1)–(4) *entail* that there are no arguments—I was merely trying to show that (1)–(4) are consistent with there being no arguments. The fact that (1)–(4) would also be consistent with 'argument' being a disjunctive ontological category, i.e. x is an argument iff x is an act of arguing or a reason/claim expression or the informational content of a reason/claim expression is beside the point. Put another way, (1)–(4) is consistent with none of the three contenders being arguments and with all of them being types of arguments. Nothing in (1)–(4) privileges one possibility over another. But note that even if one accepts that the word ‘argument’ is ambiguous, the word could still be excised for clarity’s sake with no ontological loss—in other words, at the very least one could be a reductionist about arguments—they are nothing over and above acts of arguing or reason/claim expressions or the informational content of reason/claim expressions (and if the ambiguity was causing theoretical problems, then for the sake of accurate theory we might decide to excise the word anyway.)

But if (1)–(4) are consistent with there being no arguments, or with just acts being arguments or with all three ontological categories including types of arguments, then agreement on (1)–(4) alone will not help us adjudicate disputes concerning the nature and types of arguments. We cannot resolve disputes concerning enthymemes or fallacies or whether there are deductive, inductive, conductive, and abductive types of arguments if we cannot agree whether there are arguments at all, or if there, are what ontological category they fall into.

Suppose, however, that, in addition to ~(Y), i.e. there are arguments, we add:

(C) Arguments are repeatable

to our list of agreed upon principles. Roughly speaking, repeatable entities can happen, exist, or be instantiated more than once. On most views, material objects are repeatable, but the temporal slices of material objects are not. Your desk chair is probably the same chair as yesterday. Even if the person in the next office is sitting in the same type of chair as you—they are not sitting in the very same chair. Similarly, on most views properties are taken to be repeatable even if the particular instantiations of them are not.

Argumentation theorists write and act as if arguments are repeatable. We worry about how to correctly extract the arguments from given texts, we expect our students to give us Anselm’s argument and not their own muddled version of it, we speculate about how an argument would fare when given in different situations or to different audiences, and so on. This is not to say that we agree on the identity conditions of arguments—by no means. But argumentation theorists do not take the identity conditions to be so stringent that arguments are not repeatable.

But holding to (1)–(4), ~(Y), and (C) has significant consequences for argumentation theory. Assume that the only three plausible candidates for arguments are some sort of act, expression, or abstract object. I know of no attempt to define argument that does not fall into one of these three categories (though I can find you various works where a given definition in one place puts arguments in one ontological category, but in another place puts arguments in a different ontological category—oops!). But given (C) we should also accept, what I take is a controversial claim in argumentation theory, viz.:

(*) Arguments are abstract objects.

The reason is simple. Neither acts nor expressions are repeatable. I raise my hand. I raise my hand again. While I performed two acts of the same type, I did not perform just one act—one act happened before the other and temporal location is one of the identity conditions of acts. Similarly for expressions: the first 'the' on this page may be the same type of symbol as the second 'the', but the two 'the's are not one and the same expression—they are located in different places and composed of different molecules of ink. Abstract objects of various stripes, on the other hand, are repeatable—informational content construed as propositions say, or act types or expression types which are properties. Hence, adding (C) to our list of agreed upon principles brings with it a commitment to arguments being a kind of abstract object.

Note that it does not commit us to a particular type of abstract object. Hence, those who favour act talk might opt for act types over propositions. I suspect that such solace will be short lived, for though I will not argue it here, I strongly suspect that any appeal to act types, to get the typing correct, will ultimately appeal to the informational content. For example, my giving Anselm's argument in a high falsetto in English while someone else presented Anselm's argument in booming Danish will count as instances of the same act type, for the purposes of identifying arguments, in virtue of the informational content presented since most of the other act types these two particular acts fall under do not overlap.

Regardless, I am not here trying to argue for the truth of (*), but merely to show that given (1)–(4), commitment to $\sim$(Y) and (C), short of finding another ontological option for arguments beyond the three standard ones used in argumentation theory, commits one to (*). If arguments as abstract objects cannot be tolerated, one is free to reject that arguments are repeatable (and live with the consequences) or even to reject $\sim$(Y) and just give up on arguments altogether and focus, in one prefers, on, say, arguings and types of arguings instead.

5 Conclusion

On the one hand I have made no progress on the list of issues I used as examples at the beginning of this paper. The principles we, as argumentation theorists, agree upon so far, are too minimal to help us resolve these issues. But I do hope that I have at least provided four possible avenues for moving forward. Firstly, we could try to find more principles that argumentation theorists agree upon. (Perhaps one might try to appeal to the principles offered in George Boger's "Some Axioms Underlying Argumentation Theory"? I suspect however that the tenets he gives are not generally agreed upon or non-contentious, even if widely accepted within one strain of argumentation theory.) For example, I strongly suspect that argumentation theorists also agree on some principles roughly like the following:

(D) All arguings involve the expressing/giving of a claim.
(E) All arguers have some goal to be achieved by arguing.
(F) Some arguings happen for the purpose of changing belief, promoting action, convincing, persuading, demonstrating, ...

One can hope that finding more agreed upon principles will generate a better basis for adjudicating disputes. Note however, that even adding (D)–(F) to our list of agreed upon principles does not change the results of Sect. 4.

Secondly, we could deny that there are arguments and focus instead on arguings, reason/claim expressions, and the informational content of such expressions (and the relationships and uses and types) of each and see if dissolving talk of arguments also dissolves the original problems. Thirdly, we could deny that arguments are repeatable and trace out the consequences for argumentation theory. Fourthly we could accept that arguments are repeatable and focus on arguments as abstract objects and trace out the consequences of that. For example, it is not at all clear that arguments as abstract objects can have missing premises—perhaps the expressions of the arguments in texts can have missing components (given the arguments we take those expressions to express), but the arguments themselves cannot. Hence, commitment to (*) might also commit one to 'enthymeme' not being a property of arguments at all. I leave it up to you which path you shall follow.

References

Blair, J. A. (2003). Towards a philosophy of argument. In J. A. Blair, et al. (Eds.), *Informal logic @25: Proceedings of the Windsor conference (CD-ROM)*. OSSA: Windsor, ON.

Boger, G. (2005). Some axioms underlying argumentation theory. In D. Hitchcock (Ed.), *The uses of argument: Proceedings of a conference at McMaster University, 18–21 May 2005* (pp. 40–47). St. Catherine's, ON: OSSA.

Churchland, P. M. (1981). Eliminative materialism and the propositional attitudes. *Journal of Philosophy, 78*, 67–90.

Finocchiaro, M. (2003). Dialectics, evaluation, and argument. In J. A. Blair, et al. (Eds.), *Informal logic @25: Proceedings of the Windsor conference (CD-ROM)*. OSSA: Windsor, ON.

Finocchiaro, M. (2013). *Meta-argumentation*. London: College Publications.

Gilbert, M. A. (1997). *Coalescent argumentation*. Mahwah, NJ: Lawrence Erlbaum Associates.

Gilbert, M. A. (2003). But why call it an argument?: In defense of the linguistically inexplicable. In J. A. Blair, etal. (Eds.), *Informal logic @25: Proceedings of the Windsor conference* (CD-ROM). Windsor, ON: OSSA.

Goddu, G. C. (2012). How many premises can an argument have? In F. Zenker (Ed.), *Argumentation: cognition & community* (CD-ROM). Windsor, ON: OSSA.

Lunsford, A., Ruszkiewicz, J., & Walters, K. (2013). *Everything's an argument* (6th ed.). New York: Bedford/St. Martin's.

Merricks, T. (2003). *Objects and persons*. Oxford: Oxford University Press.

Turner, J. (2011). Ontological nihilism. *Oxford studies in metaphysics* (Vol. 6). Oxford: Oxford University Press.

Willard, C. A. (1989). *A theory of argumentation*. Tuscaloosa: University of Alabama Press.

Woods, J. (1992). Apocalyptic relevance. *Argumentation, 6*, 189–202.

The Agentive Approach to Argumentation: A Proposal

Douglas Niño and Danny Marrero

1 Introduction

The main goal of this paper is to outline an agent-centered theory of argumentation. Our working hypothesis is that the aim of argumentation depends upon the agenda agents are disposed to close or advance. The novelty of this idea is that our theory, unlike the main accounts of argumentation (i.e., rhetorical, dialogical and epistemological theories of argumentation), does not establish an a priori function that agents are expected to achieve when arguing. Instead, we believe that the aims of argumentation depend upon the purposes agents are disposed to achieve (i.e., their agendas).

We borrow the concept of *function of argumentation* from the instrumentalist view of argumentation by Christoph Lumer (1990, pp. 43–51, 1991, p. 99–101, 2005, p. 219–220). The main principle of this view is that arguments are instruments, which fulfill a certain function. Lumer's terminology clarifies this tenet. An *instrument* is a system with a certain function. A *function*, respectively, is a relationship of an input producing certain output. Thus, instruments are systems aimed to produce certain outputs provided an appropriate input. For instance, the output of a screwdriver is to turn by driving or removing screws, and its input is the appropriate force applied to its handle, which is connected to the shaft with a tip that the user inserts into the head of the screw to turn it.

With this instrumentalist terminology in mind, Lumer interprets the main theories of argumentation as accounts fixing the function of argumentation, as follows:

D. Niño (✉)
Department of Humanities, Universidad Jorge Tadeo Lozano, Bogotá, Colombia
e-mail: edison.nino@utadeo.edu.co

D. Marrero
Law School, Universidad Jorge Tadeo Lozano, Bogotá, Colombia
e-mail: danny.marreroa@utadeo.edu.co

F.H. van Eemeren and B. Garssen (eds.), *Reflections on Theoretical Issues in Argumentation Theory*, Argumentation Library 28,
DOI 10.1007/978-3-319-21103-9_4

Rhetorical Theories:	The goal of argumentation is to persuade (e.g., Perelman and Olbrechts-Tyteca 1969; Hamblin 1970; Tindale 2004)
Dialogical Theories:	The goal of argumentation is to achieve a consensus resolving a difference of opinion (e.g., van Eemeren and Grootendorst 1984, 2004; van Eemeren 2010)
Epistemological Theories:	The goal of argumentation is to establish truth and justified belief (e.g., Biro and Siegel 1992; Feldman 1994; Goldman 1999; Johnson 2000; Lumer 1990, 1991, 2005; Siegel and Biro 1997).

From our perspective, the problem with fixing an a priori function for argumentation is that some argumentative practices do not fit into the proposed end. Our concern is that when an agent does not aim for the fixed function of argumentation, his/her argumentative practice could be misunderstood or overlooked. That is why our agentive theory suggests that the agendas agents are disposed to close or advance by means of argumentation determining the goal of such communicative activity. If our intuitions are right, our account shows a broader understanding of the diversity of argumentative practices than each of the main theories of argumentation individually considered.

Given the formal constraints of this paper, we are not going to do a thorough reconstruction of each of the aforementioned theories of argumentation. Instead, we are going to do cautious generalizations. First, we will use a counter-example showing that the methodology of fixing an a priori and unique function for argumentation is wrong. Second, we will present the main concepts of our approach and show how it deals with the proposed counter-example. Finally, we will present a potential objection for our account and provide a response for it.

2 A Counter-Example

As we already mentioned, the problem with fixing the aim of argumentation beforehand, is that some argumentative practices do not adjust to the fixed goal, and, consequently, the theorists analyzing and evaluating argumentation tend to misunderstand or overcome such argumentative practices. Justifying this claim, we are going to use one fragment of the following counter-example proposed by Marianne Doury in the paper "Preaching to the Converted. Why Argue When Everyone Agrees?" (2012). For future reference, we will refer to Doury's case as CAR RESTRICTION.

In Doury's words, this case is meant to show that "the goal of persuasion is but one goal among others that can be assigned to argumentation, and that, as a result, persuasion cannot be considered as the central element in the definition of argumentation" (2012, p. 100). To contextualize, CAR RESTRICTION is a transcription of a conversation between a vendor and two clients. All of them have seen each other before, but they know very little about each other.

CAR RESTRICTION

Vendor: Actually, what do you think of the law, er … we were actually talking about er… this law, there, that was just voted, that is in effect, you know, the law about traffic restriction for odd-even numbered license plates for the cars.

Client 1: Listen, I will tell you what I think, for Paris, we should be doing this all the time.

Vendor: All the time.

Client 2: Exactly. We all agree then.

Client 1: I find this a great idea. First of all because at last, every day, there is already a maximum number of people who could find a way to organize their transportation… People do not need their cars all the days!

Vendor: The opposition parties, actually, were against it at the beginning and we do not hear them speak anymore, now.

Client 2: They showed women who…who were actually commuting in the car of their friends, of a friend who came to pick them up; they can do this all the time.

Client 1: Of course! There are people…well, the problem is, that there need to be jobs or… or certain obligations that allow one to leave at a fixed time and to return at a fixed time. For example, in my case, this is not possible. But, ninety-nine percent of the time, I do not take the car!

Vendor: Yes, you are all the time using public transportation.

Client 1: Exactly. …(Doury 2012, p. 101).

According to Doury, CAR RESTRICTION is just an example of argumentative situations in which a debatable issue is proposed, and even though all the arguers agree on one same view, they provide arguments for their own positions (p. 103). To be sure, the debatable issue is posed by the vendor when asking "what do you think of the law … about traffic restriction for odd-even numbered license plates for the cars?" Doury interprets this as an *argumentative question*, which is a question inviting one to express positions for and against the proposed topic (p. 101). In CAR RESTRICTION, it is the restriction for odd-even numbered license plates. The agreement between the arguers becomes explicit when *Client 1* states "… we should [impose the restriction for odd-even numbered license plates for cars] all the time," *Vendor* assents saying "All the time," and *Client 2* responds claiming, "Exactly. We all agree then." Finally, without a detailed reconstruction, some of the arguments put forward are the following. *Client 1* "finds [the idea of imposing restriction for odd-even numbered license plates for the cars all the time] great" because, in her words, "at last, every day, there is already a maximum number of people who could find a way to organize their transportation". Additionally, from her perspective "People do not need their cars all the days." *Client 2* agrees with [the idea of imposing restriction for odd-even numbered license plates for cars all the time] because [with this restriction "[t]hey showed women who … were actually commuting in the car of their friends [that] they can do this all the time."

For Doury, CAR RESTRICTION is a counter-example against the idea that the aim of argumentation is persuasion. Shortly, if "to persuade" is defined by the Merriam-Webster dictionary as "to move by argument, entreaty, or expostulation to a belief, position, or course of action," then persuasion is not the goal of argumentation in CAR RESTRICTION. The reason for this is that one cannot "move" someone to believe something that he/she already believes (pp. 104–105). To illustrate, for Perelman and Olbrechts-Tyteca (1969), "[i]t is evident that the aim of oratory, the adherence of the minds addressed, is that of all argumentation" (p. 6). However, to look for the adherence of the participants of the conversation is not the goal of argumentation in CAR RESTRICTION because, in it, all the arguers adhere to the issue under discussion before any argument is provided. To clarify, the point is not that persuasion is never the end of argumentation, but to provide a negative instance for the claim that all argumentation aims to persuade.

We believe that CAR RESTRICTION is also a counter-example for the claims that all argumentation aims to resolve a difference of opinion, and that all argumentation aims to establish justified true belief. To recall, from the pragma-dialectical approach, "[a]rgumentation is basically aimed at resolving a difference of opinion about the acceptability of a standpoint by making an appeal to the other party's reasonableness" (van Eemeren and Grootendorst 2004, pp. 11–18; van Eemeren 2010, p. 1). In this sense, argumentation arises from a disagreement and ends with the dissolution of the difference of opinions. Yet, in CAR RESTRICTION the argumentation does not finish with agreement. Instead, even though the arguers recognize the agreement on the issue under consideration, they put forward arguments. Therefore, the aim of argumentation is not only to resolve a difference of opinion. Similarly, CAR RESTRICTION presents a counter-example for the epistemological theories of argumentation. For instance, Biro and Siegel (1992) claim that "[a]n argument aims at, and a good one succeeds in, leading an inquirer or an audience from some proposition(s) whose truth or justifiedness they accept, to others whose truth or justifiedness they will see themselves as having good reasons to accept *on its basis*" (p. 92). Yet, in CAR RESTRICTION the arguments provided do not seem to aim at a further epistemic support for a proposition. Better yet, they justify a belief that the arguers already have. Therefore, the goal of argumentation is not the achievement of justified truth belief.

3 The Agentive Proposal

Our proposal is that the problems posed by CAR RESTRICTION are explicated if we understand argumentation as a type of sub-agenda an agent has. We distinguish *argumentation*, as an activity, from an *argument*, as a set of bounded propositions. Shortly, such propositions are subdivided in two groups: the *premises* from which the *conclusion* would follow given an illative relation, identifiable by linguistic marks known as *premise* and *conclusion-indicators*, and having different degrees of conclusiveness, force or warrant. In contrast with other approaches mentioned above, we believe the purposes of arguing vary accordingly with the agendas and sub-agendas advanced by the agents. This implies that arguing is an activity performed by agents (as so far as argument-users) embedded in other activities and as a part of the requirements of the fulfillment of other agendas. The theoretical background of our account comes from two sources: the multivolume of Practical Logic of Cognitive Systems by Gabbay and Woods (2003, 2005), Woods (2013), and Agentive Semiotics by Niño (2015). Given the specific goal of this paper, we are not going to provide a systematic reconstruction of these accounts; better yet, we will use some of their central concepts to illuminate the issue under account.

In our theoretical background, an *agent* is an entity with capacity for acting and the objective he/she is trying to do is his/her *agenda* (Gabbay and Woods 2003, pp. 183–185, 195–219; Niño 2015, p. 39).[1] This objective is a type (in the sense of something that comprises variation) of outcome for which something is selected (Short 2007, p. 92–93). In the English language, the word *agentive* is used as an adjective referring to the performer, or agent, of an action, and we will follow this use. Additionally, we are going to use the word *agendive* to refer to the agenda or sub-agendas to be closed or advanced.

When an agent acts, he/she tries to achieve, fulfill or close his/her agenda. The conditions by which an agent would attain his/her agenda are the *agendive resolution conditions* (Niño 2015, p. 94–95). For instance, if the agenda is to put a 1000 piece jigsaw puzzle together, the resolution conditions involve the things that should happen for the puzzle to be properly assembled; the final product should look exactly like the picture of the puzzle—usually found on the front of its box. Each of its pieces should fit together smoothly; there should not be leftover or missing pieces, and so on. Notice that the agendive resolution conditions are determinable before the agent starts the jigsaw puzzle. In this sense, agendive resolution conditions are not merely capricious of the agent, but are conditions that the agent subdues himself/herself to in order to accomplish his/her agenda. These

[1]There is a remarkable difference between Gabbay and Woods's and Niño's approaches. While in Gabbay and Woods's proposal, the agenda is understood as the aim plus the plan for its realization, in Niño's account, the agenda is just the objective, and it is distinguished from its conditions of resolution. As a consequence, while in the former, if something is not planned, it is not an agenda, in the latter, everything that appears as an aim for an agent, either deliberately planned or not, is recognized as an agenda.

conditions, then, are like a reference point by which the agentive performance can be evaluated.

The *agentive performance* consists of the set of actual actions an agent performs in order to obtain the agendive resolution conditions of his/her agenda (Niño 2015, p. 104). To illustrate, an agent wanting to put a 1000 piece jigsaw puzzle together could perform activities such as selecting a working area (e.g., a table or a desk) large enough to facilitate the total number of pieces laid out individually, turning all the pieces up at the same time, selecting the edge pieces and putting them to one side, arranging the other pieces by color group, and the like. It is in relation to the previous agendive conditions of resolution that the actual agentive performances are contrasted and evaluated. In our example, it is in relation to the agendive resolution conditions of assembling a jigsaw puzzle that the agentive performance is evaluated. If the agent meets the resolution conditions, then he/she can expect to *close* his/her agenda. If those conditions are met partially, the agenda is *advanced*, but not closed. The agendive resolution conditions include constrictions concerning the degree of accuracy and precision required for the closure of the agenda. This demands precision in elements such as the time required for the closure of the agenda, the type of information needed, and the capacity of processing and enacting it (Gabbay and Woods 2005, p. 11). For instance, one thing is to try to resolve a practical problem under the pressure of time, such as the problems an internist has to deal with in an emergency room, and another thing is to try to resolve a purely theoretical problem, as in a laboratory of immunology.

These constrictions demand a *standard of precision* for the fulfillment of the agendive resolution conditions. This is the degree of accuracy, fluency, and exigency with which the agent expects to close his/her own agenda (Niño 2015, p. 108). Imagine that *X* and *Y* are contestants in a reality television singing competition and they are about to perform their song. While *X* would be satisfied just singing one time because this allows him/her to meet the judges of the competition who are very famous people in the music industry, *Y* would be frustrated if he/she does not win the whole competition. Thus, *X*'s agenda of meeting famous musicians has a lesser standard of precision than *Y*'s agenda of winning the competition. The *standard of precision* contrasts with the standard socially imposed on the agents in the resolution of their agendas because what counts as "good enough" for the agent does not necessarily coincide with what it is socially expected for someone like him/her to do. This is why one expects major accuracy, fluency, and exigency in the performance by a professional singer contrary to that of the performance by an amateur. We refer to this socially imposed standard as *standard of strictness* (Niño 2015, p. 128). An agent can align or not align his/her own standard of precision with the socially imposed standard of strictness. Thus, the standard of precision is the standard an agent him/herself adopts. The standard of strictness is a standard socially assigned to an agent. The *degree of precision* is the actual level of specificity to which an agent advances his/her agendas in relation to his/her standard of precision (Niño 2015, p. 131). The *degree of strictness* is the actual level of his/her performance according to the social standard of strictness (Niño 2015, p. 128). To illustrate, the degree of precision is the level of preciseness with which

X and *Y* perform their songs in relation to their own expectations. In this sense, the degree of strictness is the socially expected level of accuracy of a professional singer who is the participant in the reality TV singing competition.

Different societies establish different kinds of standards of strictness for clusters of agendas associated to social roles. This is what we call *agendive roles* (Niño 2015, p. 125–126). Examples of agendive roles are actors, doctors, scientists, musicians, teachers, lawyers and parents. Each role is composed of different activities having their own purposes. For instance, it is expected that doctors perform an anamnesis and physical examination in order to get a diagnosis, prescribe tests in order to verify it, supervise and control collateral effects, and so on. Another example is that teachers are expected to prepare their classes in order to facilitate learning, select relevant information to discuss in class, grade students in order to evaluate their level of learning, and the like. In this sense, activities have sub-agenda-like purposes, and agendive roles can be considered as clusters of activities. Agendive roles do not emerge *in vacuum*. They are socio-historic products. Because of their intersubjective nature, they behave in tandem: we have judges, juries, defendants, and prosecutors; scientists, laboratory auxiliary, experimental subjects; professors, teacher assistants, monitors, students, etc. We claim that a *context* is something where agendive roles are intersected (Niño 2015, p. 146–147), and we call *topic* the crosslinking of these role purposes. Practically, the topic of the context where the roles of student and teacher interact would be the interest for learning (Niño 2015, p. 150–151). In the case of patient and doctor, the topic would be the interest in the preservation of health or healing from a disease.

When an agent accepts the purposes, enacts the activities or assumes the responsibility of carrying an agendive role, he/she endorses an *agentive role* (Niño 2015, p. 146–147). As before, agentive roles are evaluated by contrast with the corresponding agendive roles. Therefore, the activities an agent carries out should be assessed in the frame of the activities attributed to its agendive role. Therefore, the actual performance of the lines that Hamlet says to Ofelia can be differently evaluated if the standard of strictness is that required from an amateur, or the one required from a professional actor. Finally, the topic in which the performance is embedded can change depending on the role the performer is playing. To illustrate, the topic changes if the actor is interacting with the director of the play, or with his/her theatre-audience.

The following T-chart will ideally help facilitate the grasping and recollection of the concepts presented until now (Table 1).

Agendas can be classified in several ways. For our actual interests, two distinctions are important. On one hand, with regards to the agents required for the closure of an agenda, there are agendas whose resolution conditions only demand the performance of the agent trying to close or advance them. Alternatively, there are agendas whose resolution conditions demand the participation of another agent who is not the one trying to close or advance the agenda in course. On the other hand, taking into account the actions required for the closure of the agenda, there are agendas that are closed at the very moment the actions required by its resolution conditions are performed. Differently, other agendas, are closed by the ulterior

Table 1 Agendive and agentive conceptual background

Agendive concepts	Agentive concepts
Agenda: the objective an agent has	*Agent*: entity with capacity for acting
Standard of precision: level of accuracy and exigency with which an agent expects to accomplish his/her own agenda	*Degree of precision*: actual degree of performance an agent does, in the frame of a standard of precision
Standard of strictness: socio-historic level of exigency and accuracy attributed to an agenda for its accomplishment	*Degree of strictness*: actual degree of performance an agent does, in the frame of a standard of strictness
Agendive role: cluster of activities socio-historically bounded to fulfill a social role	*Agentive role*: agendive role an agent endorses by assuming or accepting its agendas, as well as the responsibilities derived from that acceptance
Context: intersection of several agendive roles	
Topic: issues that the agendas of contextual agendive roles have in common	

effects those actions bring about. If these elements are combined, four types of agendas are obtained. Given the limited scope of this paper, we will mention only the two of them most useful to grasp the practice of argumentation. First, we will mention agendas whose resolution conditions only demand the performance of the agent trying to close them, and those which are closed directly by the proper performance of the actions required by their resolution conditions. Second, we move to agendas whose resolution conditions demand the participation of an agent different from the one trying to close them, and which are closed by the consequences of the actions required by their resolution conditions. Concerning the first type, if one's agenda is to raise his/her own hand, there is no need of another agent for closing this agenda, and one's agenda will be closed at the very moment he/she raises his/her own hand. A case of the second type appears when one wants Jones to raise his hand. Here there are at least three sub-agendas: to pronounce the words "Jones, raise your hand", and to do so in a sensible way so Jones understands, and to make Jones to move his hand in the requested way. In this case, although there is only one speech act, the agenda would be obtained as an effect on the other agent's agency through the proper closing of the first two sub-agendas. We refer to this as *per-agendas* (from the Latin "per" which means "action carried out until its end"). Their resolution conditions involve agency-modifications of another agent as effects of some previously performed action (Niño, pp. 120–121). These modifications can be actual, as in face-to-face communication, or idealized, as when a writer makes a cognitive model of his/her possible readers (cf. Lakoff 1987, pp. 68–76, 118–135).

With this terminology in mind, we claim that argumentation is an activity an agent performs in order to rationally modify other agent's agency. Therefore, argumentation is a kind of per-agenda. Among the multiple per-agendas an agent can pursue, argumentation has to do with *doxastic agendas* (i.e., agendas concerned with belief formation, maintenance, and defensibility). The resolution conditions of these agendas could vary enormously. Broadly speaking, the most stringent extreme of the spectrum only authorizes belief formation when most possibilities of error are scrutinized and/or complete information is achieved, while the other extreme allows for fallibilist belief formation with incomplete information. To illustrate, when argumentation takes place in scientific discovery, its aim can be taken to be the fixation of a justified belief triggered by scientific doubt. Yet, such a demanding goal is not a requirement for argumentation that is directed towards practical purposes, such as putting a hypothesis under probation or justifying a practical decision against a background of incomplete information. The practice of arguing should be understood as part of an activity associated with different social roles, but it does not constitute an agendive or agentive role by itself. In consequence, the standard and degree of strictness of argumentation are relative to the role or roles to which it belongs. This is why the practice of arguing is very different for a scientist, a medical doctor, a prosecutor or an educator. Therefore, a complete account of what argumentation is should involve the kind of agendive role and standard of strictness in which that practice is supposed to be embedded.

One thing is good argumentation, and another is a good argument. *Good argumentation* is one in which the agenda in course is properly closed, i.e., the argumentation causing the expected agency modification and using the arguments according to the soundness they are supposed have for the advancement of the agenda in course. Just as in the jigsaw example, the agendive resolution conditions demand the accurate assembling of the jigsaw pieces, in argumentation the agendive resolution conditions are not merely agent-dependent, but it demands normative standards for its resolution. We distinguish three kinds of agendas in which the act of arguing can intervene. These agendas are not presented in the spirit of showing an exhaustive list, but only as an example of the fruitfulness of our approach.[2]

The first type of agenda served by argumentation is the *agendas of doxastic arrival*. In these agendas, agents aim at forming a particular belief. A paradigmatic case of this kind of agenda is the verification of a scientific hypothesis. Typically, a scientific hypothesis is advanced where some fact, f_1, is expected and appears either a $\neg f_1$, which is an *anomaly*, or some new f_2, that is a *novelty* (Aliseda 2006, pp. 184–185). The purpose of a scientific hypothesis is to pose an explanation of the surprise coming from anomalies or novelties. In this sense, at the moment of putting forward a hypothesis, an agent gives reasons to someone or to him/herself for accepting, or at least for taking into consideration, the hypothesis. If the hypothesis were true, it would explain the anomalous or novel facts (Peirce 1903, p. 231).

To give scientific hypothesis as a reason is an activity with a very high standard of strictness. That is why, a scientific hypothesis, *prima facie*, should not create the expectation of forming a new belief, but a mere suggestion or suspicion about it. The inductive work, common in scientific contexts, consists of drawing some consequences of the hypothesis and putting them to the test through experience. If

[2]A previous version of these types of agendas was proposed in Niño (2013, pp. 233–236).

these tests falsify those consequences, it is necessary to pose another hypothesis. Yet, if the consequences are confirmed, the hypothesis is verified, and it could be accepted as more than a mere suspicion. When verification is considered good enough, the hypothesis has gained its right to be believed. In this sense, each instance of verification can count as a reason for accepting "more and more", and for the time being, the truth of the hypothesis under study.

Let us illustrate these ideas with the case of Kepler, as he reported himself in *Astronomia Nova* (Voelkel 2001). At that time, a circle was considered a paragon of perfection and the orbit of planets was understood as circular. However, taking Tycho Brahe's observations into account, Kepler realized that Mars' orbit could not be circular. This was his doxastic reason for doubting, insofar as it was a doxastic surprise. After a series of hypotheses, Kepler put forward the hypothesis that Mars' orbit was elliptical. Then, he calculated, from that hypothesis, different apparent positions of Mars, and the observations were in accordance with the predictions. This was the doxastic reason for belief formation. Notice that if Kepler had given the hypothesis the status of a belief at the moment of suggesting it, and before his observations, this would have been a doxastic irresponsibility, given the standard of strictness required in scientific contexts. Fortunately, Kepler's standard of precision was as high as the context demanded.

Normative epistemological approaches provide an account of these kinds of examples (cf. Blair 2004, pp. 139–141; Lumer 2005, p. 219). However, not all agendas of doxastic arrival are as strict as the verification of a scientific hypothesis. Some cases call for reasons in the absence of complete information in order to take an immediate course of action, for instance, the reasons given by an internist taking care of a patient in an emergency room. If we maintain the standard of strictness of a scientific agenda of epistemic arrival, it would demand more time and, accordingly, the delay would turn out to be fatal, literally. There are times when, given the risks at hand, aiming at an immediate educated guess is better than waiting for a warranted but temporally mediated truth.

A second type of agenda to reflect on is the *agenda of epistemic defensibility*. These agendas intend to present and defend a belief previously fixed by an agenda of epistemic arrival. This includes examples such as political harangues, prosecutor accusations, and attorney's allegations. This being so, the resolution of agendas of epistemic defensibility function as a means for an ulterior practical agenda, such as making a decision, endorsing a position, taking a course of action, among others. Notice that these agendas do not seek the formation of the arguer's beliefs, but the fixations of others' beliefs. Therefore, the admissibility conditions change in respect to the agendas of epistemic arrival. Cases of persuasion are paradigmatic examples of agendas of epistemic defensibility. There are at least three sub-agendas here: to assert that so and so is the case, to communicate this to someone, and the belief-formation in someone that so and so is the case (i.e., to gain his/her adherence of opinion). Persuasion is not a homogeneous phenomenon because the persuasive activity can vary along the spectrum of different standards and degrees of strictness as well as multiple admissibility conditions for a variety of audiences. Imagine that the arguer is a scientist who previously has formed the belief that a certain medication is a promising cure for a disease. He/she could confront a standard of strictness if he tries to convince a group of colleagues about his findings, and face another standard of strictness if he/she tries to convince a non-expert or possible sponsors for further research. The challenge faced by this scientist would also be different if his/her colleagues previously have formed the belief that the medication is useless than if they have not formed a distinct belief about it. Furthermore, this scenario would be different if the scientist is not aware of the doxastic position of his/her colleagues. In that sense, the resolution conditions of the agendas of doxastic defensibility take into account the admissibility doxastic system of the arguments-receiver.

The admissibility of reasons includes the plausibility of the facts and the acceptability of the values presented in the arguments. In empirical science, ideally, a high standard in methodology rules the factual plausibility: an arguer can give arguments to accept his/her conclusions because of the rigorous performance of the scientific method. In another context, such as politics, in so far as there can be different axiological positions, this would be not the case, and the acceptability would be as important as plausibility. In consequence, it would be useful for the arguer to anticipate if the addressee's doxastic system is more conservative or more liberal. Besides, it is not the same to present arguments to a hostile audience as to a sympathetic one. Of course, the belief system of any interlocutor may not be equally conservative or liberal. Some *topics* are more sensitive and more debatable than others. To illustrate, it is not the same to give reasons either for or against the acceptability of abortion or euthanasia as it is to give reasons for or against the acceptability of dining at a certain place for a dinner in a foreign country.

The third type of agenda is the *agendas of doxastic maintenance*. These agendas aim at ratifying a belief previously fixed by the agenda of epistemic arrival. This is clearly the case in CAR RESTRICTION. In this example, the arguers advance their arguments in order to have a surplus of reasons for maintaining and preserving a particular doxastic position. The peculiarity of this scenario is due to the fact that multiple agents carry out the agenda in a joint manner. But there are no obstacles for an agenda of doxastic maintenance to be an individual agenda (as in Peirce's 'tenacity' method for fixing belief) or a collective one. In any event, the collective case can become a mechanism of ideology preservation.

Let us observe that all these agendas are actually sub-agendas, that is, agendas that are carried out as a means with respect to an ulterior end. In this sense, their role is primarily 'methodological' (in the etymological sense of the word). Indeed, in the examples discussed above, *agendas of doxastic arrival* serve as a means for determining truth, saving a life, or arriving at some place. In the *agendas of doxastic defensibility* examples, persuasion is pursued in order to obtain votes or to make a decision about the innocence or culpability of someone. In *agendas of doxastic maintenance,* arguing serves the self-assertion of the arguers' belief system. In this sense, the agentive approach to argumentation explains why arguing is not an end in itself most of the time. Although it can be imagined of as an immediate agenda, as when agents argue as a way of training in argumentation,

argumentation is an activity agents engage in, in order to obtain things different than more arguments.

4 An Objection

A possible objection to our account comes from the notion of the standard, or proper function of argumentation.[3] From Lumer's perspective, the result an instrument is expected to produce is its *standard output* and its correlative terms are *standard input* and *standard function*. A case in point is a drill. "The standard output of a drill are holes of a certain size in solid material; the standard input consists of: supplying the drill with a bit, pressure against the solid material and electric current; and the standard function is: to drill holes" (Lumer 1991, p. 99). A drill satisfying its standard function is a *functioning* drill. That is, a functioning drill makes the expected hole when provided with a bit, pressure against a solid material, electric current, and so on. In a general way, an instrument is a functioning one if when provided with the standard input, it produces the standard output. However, things can go wrong: "[o]ne can use a good instrument in the wrong situation or for the wrong purpose" (p. 99), such as when a drill is expected to make a hole in concrete, but it is supplied with a bit made for drilling into wood. Additionally, instruments have *non-standard functions*, which are results that can be achieved by an instrument, but that are not the outputs the instruments are expected to produce, such as when a drill is used to whip cream. In Lumer's words: "the input, in this case, is to supply the drill with a whisk, to put this into the cream and to supply the machine with electric current; the output is whipped cream or butter" (p. 99).

With this instrumentalist approach, Lumer builds his epistemic account of argumentation. For him, "arguments as such are functional entities, instruments that shall be useful for some aim. The way here to conceptualize this is to say that they have a standard (or proper) function" (2005, p. 219). In this sense, although arguments have different functions, they have a proper function to meet. On one hand, the standard input of arguments is that they are presented to a linguistically proficient, open-minded, attentive, discriminating addressee who has certain knowledge, but does not have sufficiently founded knowledge of the argument's conclusion. On the other hand, the standard output of arguments is a justified belief that the thesis is true or acceptable (Lumer 1990, pp. 43–44, 1991, p. 100, 2005, p. 219). If this is right, the agentive approach to argumentation is wrong because it includes non-standard functions of argumentation such as the ones contemplated by the agendas of doxastic defensibility and doxastic maintenance. This is tantamount

[3]Here we are paraphrasing one of the main concerns that Lumer had about our proposal at the ISSA conference in 2014. We strongly appreciate his insightful ideas.

to say that a drill is expected to make whipped cream, but this is wrong because this is not the proper function of a drill.

From our perspective, the core of this criticism is in the analogy between arguments and instruments. Let us make explicit such an argument:

Premise 1: Instruments are systems designed to produce a specific output in a controlled manner by providing the structure with a certain input.

Premise 2: Arguments are like instruments

Conclusion: Arguments are systems designed to produce a specific output in a controlled manner by providing the structure with a certain input

From our perspective, this analogy is not sound. First, Lumer only takes into account instruments with one function, as in the drill example. This could be misleading because it may suggest that arguments just have one standard function. What happens with instruments that have more than one function? Think about an item like an aspirin: for certain purposes, it can be used as a painkiller and for others as prevention for heart attacks or stokes. In Lumer's account, there is not standardly multifunctional items, and this does not seem right.

Second, if for the sake of argument, we were to accept that instruments have standard, or proper, functions, how are they assigned and by whom? How is it to be decided that a certain function has been *well* assigned, and under which warrants or grounds? Notice that in the case of instruments, their functions are dependent on the agendas in course. Think of expressions as instruments, as in that "red pencil". This expression can be used to signify a pencil that leaves red marks when used or just as a pencil that is colored red on the outside. Thus, different meanings are at the service of different purposes. And, there is nothing in the expression itself that can tell us which one of those underspecified meanings are appropriated to use when the occasion comes. On the contrary, it is in the contextualized occasion—with its roles, standards, activities, and agendas—where the agents specify those possible uses. This happens with arguments, too. The inference that "from *C* and if *A* then *C*, hence *A*" is commonly interpreted as a fallacy of deductive logic. However, this is the standard logical form of abduction (Peirce 1903, p. 231). In this sense, the deductive and abductive uses of the conclusion-indicator "hence" are different. On one hand, its purpose is truth-preserving and authorizes classical consequence (with the properties monotonicity, reflexivity, cut, and compactness). On the other hand, its purpose is to get a possible solution to an ignorance problem (Woods 2013, p. 367). This abductive use only allows for the possibility of the conclusion in order to put it to the empirical test. This does not mean that the aforementioned argumentative scheme has two standard functions. Instead, it means that agents can use it of different manners according to their agendas in course. Just as the expression "red pencil" underspecifies its use conditions, the schema in question underspecifies its argumentative conditions. The agents are who specify those conditions in each context. It is not the case, however, that agents are allowed to use arguments at will. As we already mentioned, when using an argument, an agent is usually engaged in an argumentation activity that has its own agendive resolution conditions, with a certain standard of precision and strictness. This puts a normative bearing beyond the caprices of the agent who is trying to advance and close a specific agenda. It is in relation to these purposes that argumentation should be evaluated. If an agent uses an argument deductively when the agendive resolution conditions impose that the force of the argument should be non-deductive, he/she is advancing *bad* argumentation. By the same token, the use of a good argument in argumentation does not imply by itself that it is going to be good argumentation. This is so because a perfectly valid and sound argument can be irrelevant. Now, something is relevant insofar as it contributes positively to the fulfillment of its purpose (Gabbay and Woods 2003, pp. 158–163). In the case of argumentation, this implies the contribution the argument has in the modification of the addressee's doxastic system. Finally, what distinguishes argumentation from other kinds of activities with per-agendas as their aims, such as telling a story or making a joke is that argumentation modifies the addressee's agency as an effect of the arguments, and not as an effect of other things such as coercion, drugs, or even good luck.

References

Aliseda, A. (2006). *Abductive reasoning. Logical investigations into discovery and explanation.* Dordrecht: Springer.

Biro, J., & Siegel, H. (1992). Normativity, argumentation and an epistemic theory of fallacies. In F. van Eemeren, R. Grootendorst, J. Blair, & C. Willard (Eds.), *Argumentation illuminated* (pp. 85–103). Amsterdam: SicSat.

Blair, A. (2004). Arguments and its uses. *Informal Logic, 24*(2), 137–151.

Doury. M. (2012). Preaching to the converted. Why argue when everyone agrees? *Argumentation, 26*(1), 99–114.

Feldman, R. (1994). Good arguments. In: F. Schmitt (Ed.), *Socializing epistemology. The social dimensions of knowledge* (pp. 159–188). Lanham: Rowman & Littlefield.

Gabbay, D. & Woods, J. (2005). *The reach of abduction: Insight and trial. A practical logic of cognitive systems* (Vol. 2). Elsevier, Amsterdam.

Gabbay, D. & Woods, J. (2003). *Agenda relevance: A study of formal pragmatics. A practical logic of cognitive systems* (Vol. 1). Elsevier, Amsterdam.

Goldman, A. (1999). *Knowledge in a social world.* Oxford: Clarendon.

Hamblin, C. (1970). *Fallacies.* London: Methuen.

Johnson, R. (2000). *Manifest rationality. A pragmatic theory of argument.* Mahwah: Erlbaum.

Lakoff, G. (1987). *Women, fire, and other dangerous things.* Chicago: The University of Chicago Press.

Lumer, C. (1990). *Praktische Argumentationstheorie. Theoretische Grundlagen, Praktische Begründung und Regeln Wichtiger Argumentlonsarten.* Braunscheweig: Viewe.

Lumer, C. (1991). Structure and function of argumentations. An epistemological approach to determining criteria for the validity and adequacy of argumentations. In F. van Eemeren, R. Grootendorst, A. Blair & C. Willard (Eds.), *Proceedings of the Second International Conference on Argumentation. Organized by the International Society for the Study of Argumentation (ISSA)* (pp. 98–107). Amsterdam: Sicsat.

Lumer, C. (2005). The epistemological theory of argument—how and why? *Informal Logic, 25*(3), 213–243.

Niño, D. (2013). Agentes y circunstancias. Consideraciones en torno a factores epistémicos y fiduciarios en la argumentación intercultural. In C. Martinez (Ed.), *Cuatro aproximaciones al dialogo argumentativo intercultural* (pp. 187–246). Bogotá, Universidad Jorge Tadeo Lozano.
Niño, D. (2015). *Elementos de semiótica agentiva*. Bogotá: Universidad Jorge Tadeo Lozano.
Peirce, C. S. (1903). The logic of abduction. In The Peirce Edition Project (Eds.) *The essential Peirce* (Vol. 2, pp. 226–241). Bloomington: Indiana University Press.
Perleman, C., & Olbrecht-Tyteca, L. (1969). *The new rhetoric. A treatise on argumentation*. Notre Dame: University of Notre Dame Press.
Short, T. (2007). *Peirce's theory of signs*. Cambridge: Cambridge University Press.
Siegel, H., & Biro, J. (1997). Epistemic normativity, argumentation, and fallacies. *Argumentation, 11*, 277–292.
Voelkel, J. (2001). *The composition of Kepler's Astronomia nova*. Princeton: Princeton University Press.
Tindale, C. (2004). *Rhetorical argumentation. Principles of theory and practice*. Thousand Oaks: SAGE Publications.
van Eemeren, F., & Grootendorst, R. (1984). *Speech acts in argumentative discussions*. Dordrecht: Foris Publications.
van Eemeren, F., & Grootendorst, R. (2004). *A systematic theory of argumentation. The Pragma-Dialectical approach.*. Cambridge: Cambridge University Press.
van Eemeren, F. (2010). *Strategic maneuvering in argumentative discourse: Extending the Pragma-Dialectical theory of argumentation*. Amsterdam: John Benjamins Publishing Company.
Woods, J. (2013). *Errors of reasoning: Naturalizing the logic inference*. Milton Keynes: College Publications.

Part II
Analysis of Argumentation

Conductive Argumentation, Degrees of Confidence, and the Communication of Uncertainty

Sharon Bailin and Mark Battersby

1 Prologue

On April 6, 2009, a magnitude 6.3 earthquake struck L'Aquila, Abruzzo, resulting in considerable devastation and the death of 300 people. Seven Italian officials and scientists were subsequently put on trial for manslaughter. The accusation was that scientists presented incomplete, inconsistent information which falsely assured the public and caused the deaths of 30 residents. The usual practice when an earthquake was likely was for residents to sleep outside, but it was alleged that because of the assurance, these individuals remained in their houses and were killed in the quake (Ashcroft 2012). The prosecution argued that the assessment of risk communicated to the public was unjustifiably optimistic and that lives could have been saved had people not been persuaded by the assurances to remain in their houses (Hooper 2012). In 2012, the scientists were found guilty of manslaughter and sentenced to 6 years in prison (Six of the convictions were overturned on appeal in 2014).

We will return to this case later. We have no intention to try to evaluate its merits, but we shall examine the issues it raises regarding the obligation to communicate an appropriate degree of certainty or uncertainty in one's judgments.

S. Bailin (✉)
Faculty of Education, Simon Fraser University, 2568 W. 1st Avenue,
Vancouver, BC V6K 1G7, Canada
e-mail: bailin@sfu.ca

M. Battersby
Capilano University (Retired), Critical Inquiry Group,
2416 W. 14th Avenue, Vancouver, BC V6K 2W5, Canada
e-mail: mbattersby@criticalinquirygroup.com

F.H. van Eemeren and B. Garssen (eds.), *Reflections on Theoretical Issues in Argumentation Theory*, Argumentation Library 28,
DOI 10.1007/978-3-319-21103-9_5

2 Introduction

This paper begins by making the argument that a degree of uncertainty is an unavoidable aspect of conductive argumentation. The arguments which comprise instances of conductive argumentation vary in terms of the degree of support that they provide for their conclusions; for this reason the strength of the judgments warranted by particular instances of conductive argumentation will vary as well. We argue, further, that this variability imposes an epistemic requirement on arguers to apportion the confidence of their judgment to the strength of the reasons. Moreover, because of the dialectical nature of argumentation, there is the additional requirement for arguers to communicate the appropriate degree of certainty or uncertainty when making judgments in the context of an argumentative exchange.

3 Argumentation and Uncertainty

The traditional focus for the philosophical study of argumentation has been individual arguments, in terms of both their structure and their evaluation. The model of argument which has been dominant has been deductive argument, i.e., an argument whose premises entail the conclusion. Provided that the premises are true, the conclusion follows with certainty. Uncertainty may, of course, still arise with respect to the truth of the premises.

This requirement of inference certainty does not, however, fit a great deal of actual argumentation, as has been pointed out by theorists since the inception of the Informal Logic movement. In probable reasoning, for example, the conclusion does not follow necessarily but only with some degree of probability (Blair and Johnson 1987, p. 42). The situation is similar for inductive reasoning: "Inductive inferences vary from weak to strong; there is no all-or-nothing critique such as 'valid-or invalid' available" (Blair and Johnson 1987, p. 42).

Theorists have, however, been increasingly broadening their focus from exclusively individual arguments to the entire enterprise of argumentation. Argumentation can be conceptualized as a socio-cultural activity (Hitchcock 2002, p. 291) which is dialectical in the sense that it involves an interaction between the arguers and between the arguments (Blair and Johnson 1987). This focus is much broader than the making of individual arguments. Rather, arguments are put forward, criticisms and objections offered, responses proposed, and, frequently, revisions made to initial positions (Bailin and Battersby 2009). It is this practice of argumentation that is our focus here, and in particular the practice of conductive argumentation (or conductive reasoning). By conductive reasoning we are referring to the process of comparative evaluation of a variety of contending positions and arguments with the goal of reaching a reasoned judgment on an issue (Battersby and Bailin 2011). Such judgments are generally based on the weighing of both pro and con considerations.

The focus of many theorists working in the area is, however, on individual conductive arguments rather than on conductive reasoning. Conductive arguments are, as Govier puts it, "arguments in which premises are put forward as separately and non-conclusively relevant to support a conclusion, against which negatively relevant considerations may also be acknowledged" (Govier 2011, p. 262). In our view, however, viewing conductive reasoning in terms of individual arguments fails to due justice to the dialectical nature of argumentation (Battersby and Bailin 2011). In addition, attempting to make conductive reasoning fit into the traditional model of argument structure has resulted in unnecessary conundrums, for example how to analyze counter-considerations (are they premises? counter-premises?) or how to diagram these anomalous types of arguments. Our focus, in contrast, is on conductive reasoning more broadly. According to this perspective, the structure of conductive argumentation is viewed in terms of a balancing of competing arguments and claims rather than as a single argument.

4 Uncertainty in Conductive Argumentation

There are a number of reasons why conductive argumentation does not lead to conclusions which can be asserted with epistemic certainty. These include inferential uncertainty, the inherent uncertainty of particular claims and judgments, the open-endedness of the reason-giving process, and variability in the weighing of pro and con considerations. Because of these factors, the degree of certainty with which conclusions of conductive argumentation can justifiably be held will vary.

Inferential uncertainty is a feature of conductive reasoning just as it is with inductive reasoning. Given that particular claims are true, there is still the question of how much support they give to the conclusion.

The uncertainty has also to do with the inherent uncertainty of particular claims and judgments which go into the reasoning process. The likelihood of factual claims is an important factor in evaluating their weight as the greater the likelihood of the claim, the more weight it can add to the conclusion. Likelihood is, however, often difficult to determine. To compound the difficulty, any argument leading to a judgment about what to do must also take into account future states of affairs which are usually even less certain than judgments about current states of affairs. What one can do in both these cases is to use the available information, history, contextual factors, and statistical tools to make reasoned judgments. And in the area of moral issues, while there are some widely accepted general moral principles, their application in particular cases inevitably creates some degree of uncertainty, the degree depending on the strength of the supporting arguments (Battersby and Bailin 2011).

The uncertainty arises also from the nature of conductive reasoning itself. One important factor is the open-endedness of the reason-giving process. Competent conductive reasoning requires laying out the dialectic—the arguments on various sides of the debate, as well as objections to the arguments and responses to the objections. No survey of arguments will be exhaustive, however. The possibility always exists that additional reasons and arguments will be put forward which might affect the outcome of the reasoning (Battersby and Bailin 2011). This being said, the more extensive the review of the available evidence and argumentation, the stronger the support for the resultant judgment.

Uncertainty also comes in due to the process of weighing the various reasons pro and con. There is sometimes variability amongst arguers in the evaluation of the comparative strength of evidence and arguments on different sides of an issue and disagreement about the appropriate weight to be apportioned to various considerations. This is not to say that weightings are (primarily) subjective. Weightings can be justified (or criticized) by appeal to objective factors and considerations (e.g., the likelihood of claims, appeal to widely shared values and principles). Nonetheless, there may not be consensus on how some considerations should be weighted and there may be more than one judgment which is defensible given the context (Battersby and Bailin 2011).

Because of the uncertainty of particular claims, the variability in the evaluation of the comparative strength of evidence and arguments, the different weightings given to various considerations, and the open-endedness of the reason-giving process, an instance of conductive reasoning can, at best, offer good reasons and strong support for a conclusion but not certainty.

This does not mean, however, that it is not possible to make warranted judgments in instances of conductive reasoning. Guidelines exist for making reasoned judgments and criteria exist for their evaluation (Battersby and Bailin 2011). What it does mean is that there will always be some uncertainty with respect to the judgments emerging from the process of conductive argumentation and that the strength of the judgments warranted by particular instances of conductive argumentation will vary.

5 Confidence in Judgment

The strength of the evidence and argumentation in support of conclusions in conductive argumentation will vary from case to case (Battersby and Bailin 2011). In some cases the evidence for a particular judgment may be overwhelming. There are, for example, very strong reasons to believe that smoking causes cancer or that the enslavement of human beings is morally unjustifiable. In other cases the weight of reasons may favour a particular judgment but not without significant opposing reasons or counter considerations. Claims about the causes of climate change might fall into this category. In still other cases, the reasons may be insufficient for reaching a judgment, for example in debates about life on other planets. Thus, in robust argumentation, warrant is usually a matter of degree.

Engaging in the process of argumentation imposes certain epistemic requirements on arguers: that they present arguments justified by the available evidence, address appropriate objections and provide reasonable responses, and revise their initial position when warranted. But the variability in the degree of support for different judgments also imposes an additional requirement on arguers: that they apportion the confidence of their judgment to the strength of the reasons. Not all judgments warrant an equal level of confidence. It is important to be clear that we are not referring to subjective confidence—how confident an individual may happen to feel about a judgment, but rather rational or warranted confidence—the level of confidence that is justified by the reasons and evidence.

The following is a schema which we have developed to represent the level of confidence warranted by different weights of reasons:

- A *very confident judgment* is warranted when the weight of reasons clearly supports the judgment.
- A *reasonably confident judgment* is warranted when the weight of reasons strongly supports the judgment but there are still strong countervailing considerations.
- A *tentative judgment* is warranted when the weight of reasons is not overwhelming but is supportive of one position, and we can make a judgment *on balance*.
- A *suspended judgment* is warranted when the reasons for different positions are closely balanced or when there is insufficient evidence to make a judgment.

This schema has similarities to the categorization used for classifying the strength of causal inferences in science (US Department of Health 2006).

These four levels of judgment confidence are not discrete but can be seen as marking positions along a continuum. The categorization allows for a range of possibilities in between.

Apportioning one's confidence in a judgment to the strength of the reasons is always epistemologically significant. It is when there is a need to act on the basis of our judgments, however, that the issue of how justified our confidence is in our judgments becomes crucial. The greater the consequences of action (or inaction), the greater the need for a level of argumentative support that warrants a confident judgment. A useful comparison can be made to legal judgments. In criminal cases, where there is a great deal at stake (freedom versus imprisonment, or even life versus death), the standard of proof is beyond a reasonable doubt, which requires a level of evidence sufficient to warrant a very confident judgment. In civil matters, where there is usually less at stake, the standard of proof is usually balance of probabilities, which clearly requires only an on balance judgment.

6 Degrees of Certainty or Uncertainty

The fact that argumentation is dialectical imposes yet a further requirement on arguers. It is not just a matter of apportioning one's confidence in a judgment to the strength of the reasons. There is also a requirement to communicate the appropriate degree of certainty or uncertainty when making judgments in the context of an argumentative exchange.

There are many ways in which one's confidence in a judgment and hence the degree of certainty or uncertainty may be expressed:

- A very confident judgment implies a high level of certainty and would be marked linguistically by such phrases as "I am very confident that," "it is clear that," "there's little doubt that," "the evidence strongly indicates that."
- A reasonably confident judgment implies a moderately high level of certainty and might be indicated by such phrases as "I am reasonably sure that," "it seems very likely that," "the evidence by and large indicates that."
- A tentative judgment implies some degree of uncertainty, although not enough to preclude making a judgment. A tentative judgment may be indicated by such phrases as "it appears on balance that," "the weight of evidence tips somewhat in favour of," "my tentative conclusion is that."
- A suspended judgment implies a high level of uncertainty and would be indicated by such phrases as "there is not enough evidence to make a judgment," "the reasons on both sides seem equally balanced," "the judgment will have to be deferred until more evidence is available," "the jury's still out on this."

7 An Objection

Before going on to defend our claim regarding the requirement to communicate an appropriate degree of certainty, we need, first, to deal with an objection to the underlying claim, that conductive arguments can have a conclusion that expresses uncertainty. In a recent posthumous publication, Adler argues against the claim that countervailing considerations detract from the support for the conclusion in a conductive argument:

> The claim that I dispute is that once the conclusion is drawn, the counter-considerations continue to diminish its support (Adler 2013, p. 4).

As a consequence:

> … the conclusion of a Conductive Argument is characteristically detached and accepted without (epistemic) qualification (Adler 2013, p. 6).

And further:

> Let me summarize my reasons for taking Conductive Argument to characteristically lead to unqualified conclusions that are accepted and asserted (Adler 2013, p. 6).

If we understand him correctly, he is arguing that if we are asking an interlocutor to accept our conclusion, then we are always asking him to accept the conclusion without the modifiers of "all things considered," "on balance," "it is very likely that" etc.

It is significant that Adler's objection is framed in terms of conductive arguments while we frame the issue in terms of conductive argumentation. The difference in framing is important in terms of the consideration of his objection, a point to which we shall return.

We would maintain that qualified conclusions are common in conductive argumentation. In arguments for factual claims, expressing uncertainty is not unusual, e.g., "The forecast notwithstanding, it looks like it might rain." "Even though he doesn't like parties, Tom is a good friend so he'll likely come to my birthday party." "There are many fine contemporary authors, but she is probably the best of her generation." The communication of the degree of certainty of findings is also a common practice in the kind of argument to the best explanation exhibited in scientific reasoning and scientific reports. The following excerpt from an IPCC assessment report on climate change explains the confidence levels used in the report:

> The degree of certainty in key findings in this assessment is based on the author teams' evaluations of underlying scientific understanding and is expressed as a qualitative level of confidence (from *very low* to *very high*) and, when possible, probabilistically with a quantified likelihood (from *exceptionally unlikely* to *virtually certain*). Confidence in the validity of a finding is based on the type, amount, quality, and consistency of evidence (e.g., data, mechanistic understanding, theory, models, expert judgment) and the degree of agreement. SPM-2

The following examples from the report illustrate the use of these confidence levels:

(1) It is *virtually certain* that globally the troposphere has warmed since the mid-20th century. More complete observations allow greater confidence in estimates of tropospheric temperature changes in the extratropical Northern Hemisphere than elsewhere. There is *medium confidence* in the rate of warming and its vertical structure in the Northern Hemisphere extra-tropical troposphere and *low confidence* elsewhere {2.4} PSM-4.

(2) It is *likely* that anthropogenic influences have affected the global water cycle since 1960. Anthropogenic influences have contributed to observed increases in atmospheric moisture content in the atmosphere (*medium confidence*), to global-scale changes in precipitation patterns over land (*medium confidence*), to intensification of heavy precipitation over land regions where data are sufficient (*medium confidence*), and to changes in surface and sub-surface ocean salinity (*very likely*) {2.5, 2.6, 3.3, 7.6, 10.3, 10.4} SPM-13.

Although Adler's argument seems to be directed toward conductive arguments in general ("the conclusion of a Conductive Argument is *characteristically* detached …"), many of his examples involve practical reasoning, where the conclusion is a decision or recommendation about whether to act. Apparently, he would reject a conclusion that "we should probably do X." Yet, in practice, we do often qualify a recommendation by "we should probably," "on balance the best thing to do seems to be," "there are good reasons to" etc.

Given the frequency of qualified conclusions in conductive argumentation, one might wonder what Adler's reasons are for denying their possibility. The basis of his argument is a logical one—that in order for a conductive argument to be cogent, i.e., in order for its conclusion to be correctly accepted as true, the conclusion must stand on its own.[1] His focus is on cogent arguments, that is arguments that end inquiry. The alternative for Adler is not qualified conclusions but rather suspended judgment.

It is here that the problem of viewing conductive argumentation in terms of individual arguments becomes manifest. Adler's analysis has some plausibility when applied to examples such as the classic argument offered by Wellman: Although your lawn needs cutting, you ought to take your son to the movies because the picture is ideal for children and will be gone by tomorrow (Wellman 1971, p. 67). Most of the examples offered by Adler, however, (e.g., mandated health care insurance, stricter rules to restrict immigration, building nuclear power plants) are instances of complex, dialectical argumentation. (Indeed, the distinction between conductive arguments and conductive argumentation is one that Adler himself appears, in places, to acknowledge: Adler, p. 2, footnote 1). In such cases, it is inappropriate to expect certainty (for all the reasons outlined above). It is inappropriate to expect conclusions that are "true". What we can expect, instead, are judgments that have varying degrees of support.

Adler's argument does have some prima facie plausibility in that for practical arguments, either we should act, we should not act, or we simply do not know what to do. Indeed, it does seem that when we decide to do something, we have "detached" the decision from the reasoning through our commitment to action. But the detachment is in effect a pragmatic detachment which does not necessarily indicate unqualified confidence, nor will it necessarily end inquiry. On fairly straightforward practical issues, for example which camera to buy, making a decision will likely mark the end of the inquiry. But this may simply be because the action is a *fait accompli* and does not necessarily indicate a high level of confidence that we have made the right choice. With more complex issues, however, even once an action has been taken, inquiry does not necessarily end, e.g., the U.S. government has made a decision with respect to mandated health care insurance, but the debate has certainly not ended.

It seems to be Adler's view that it is only detached, unqualified conclusions that "discern or advance and settle new or interesting or important truths, that are worth believing for ourselves or for our audience. They increase our information and expand our corpus of beliefs" (Adler 2013, p. 6). We would argue, on the contrary, that it is appropriately qualified conclusions that really add to our justified beliefs. We are justified in holding our beliefs on such issues with varying degree of

[1]Surprisingly given his thesis, Adler does acknowledge that "there are loads of arguments that end with qualified conclusions, including, 'plausible' or, more equivocally, 'the best explanation is'" (p. 7). But the rest of his argumentation leads us to believe that he would reconcile this apparent contradiction by asserting that such arguments are not cogent, i.e., they are not arguments which can be put forward for acceptance.

confidence commensurate with the strength of the support. Jane's belief that there should be government mandated health care insurance is one she may hold with considerable confidence given the strength of the reasons in favor and the weakness of the reasons against. She may hold the belief that we should not build nuclear power plants with considerably less confidence given the force of the reasons for as well as against. Adler seems to hold that only unqualified conclusions put "arguers and inquirers in a position that is appropriate to guide further judgments and action" (Adler 2013, p. 6). We would argue, on the contrary, that appropriately qualified conclusions are, in fact, more reasonable guides to action. The conclusions of conductive argumentation are judgments and it is a requirement of reasonableness that such judgments should reflect the degree of support provided by our reasons.

8 Communicating Confidence and Certainty

We have been arguing, then, that there is a requirement to apportion one's confidence in a judgment to the strength of the reasons in support of the judgment. We would argue, further, there is also an epistemic and moral responsibility to communicate the appropriate degree of certainty or uncertainty when making judgments in the context of an argumentative exchange. This responsibility arises from the dialectical and interactive nature of conductive argumentation. According to Johnson, that an exchange is dialectical means that "as a result of the intervention of the Other, one's own logos (discourse, reasoning, or thinking) has the potential of being affected in some way" (Johnson 2000, p. 161). In other words, the reasoning and judgments made by others can and often should affect my reasoning and judgments and form part of the basis for my actions. Just as offering well justified judgments in the context of an argumentative exchange can contribute to others holding better justified beliefs and undertaking better justified actions, so also can communicating one's judgments at the appropriate level of confidence. Acknowledging uncertainty or confidence as part of one's judgment or decision to act can inform others of how much confidence you or they should have in the judgment. Communicating a judgment at an inappropriate level of confidence, for example with more confidence than is warranted by the evidence, may contribute to other interlocutors holding beliefs or acting in ways that are poorly grounded.

This responsibility is especially significant when one is in a position of epistemic authority. Experts have an obligation to provide reasons for their judgments, however in contexts requiring expertise, recipients of the judgment are often not in a position to assess the reasoning in any detail. These judgments are generally accepted largely on the basis of trust in the expertise and reliability of the authority. Thus the level of confidence that is expressed in the judgment is an important aspect of the information communicated in the judgment. Returning to the IPCC report, it would be have been misleading if the report had omitted the confidence levels in their various finding. This is especially important as such judgments often form the basis for decisions regarding action, or may themselves be recommendations for action. Compare the following judgments by a physician: (1) "I have carefully evaluated all the evidence and would not recommend surgery. It is my judgment that it would not help." (2) "I have carefully evaluated all the evidence and would not recommend surgery. It is my judgment that surgery is very unlikely to help and the surgical procedure is very risky. But I cannot be 100 % confident because there have been a few similar cases where it appears that a surgical invention may have helped to prolong life." To offer the same conclusion without an indication of the confidence level would be a misleading way of putting forth one's conclusion. In cases where the argument leads to a somewhat uncertain conclusion based on a balancing of conflicting considerations, failure to indicate the presence of these considerations is an epistemic failure. Given that the purpose of conductive argumentation is to consider countervailing considerations and yet come to a reasonable conclusion, failure to communicate the degree of justification or certainty that the arguments provide also violates basic norms of communication.

9 The L'aquila Case

The trial of the Italian scientists and officials in the L'Aquila earthquake case is a pertinent one to examine with respect to the issue of the communication of certainty or uncertainty. The earthquake had been preceded by a swarm of small quakes, and the charge against the defendants was that they did not do their duty in communicating the likelihood of a major earthquake to the citizens of L'Aquila.

One of the scientists tried, Enzo Boschi, the then-president of Italy's National Institute of Geophysics and Volcanology, is said to have compared the situation to a large quake that struck L'Aquila in 1703. Boschi is alleged to have said at a meeting in L'Aquila on March 31, 2009, "It is unlikely that an earthquake like the one in 1703 could occur in the short term, but the possibility cannot be totally excluded." In a press conference after the meeting, Department of Civil Protection official Bernardo De Bernardinis, also a defendant, is quoted (and on video record) as saying that the situation was normal given the context, posing "no danger," and urging residents to relax (Pappas 2012).

The details of the case are complex and include allegations of political pressure, and of misrepresentation of material. We have no intention to try to evaluate the merits of the case, nor are we in a position to do so. Nonetheless some of the issues raised are pertinent to our discussion. The statements of both Boschi and De Bernardinis would have been grounded in the knowledge that earthquake swarms are very common in seismically active regions such as Abruzzo but only a very small percentage are precursors to major quakes. In fact, seismologists claim that it is virtually impossible to predict major earthquakes. Yet we can note a difference in the level of certainty communicated in the two judgments. Boschi's judgment that a major earthquake was unlikely could be characterized as a reasonably confident judgment, but in alluding to the possibility of such a quake, it communicated a degree of uncertainty in the judgment. De Bernardinis, in contrast, seemed to be making a very confident judgment that there was no danger of a major quake. His judgment made no reference to the possibility, slight though it may have been. The risk was indeed very low, but not non-existent. Thus his pronouncement, communicated to the public, that there was "no danger" was epistemically overly confident, expressing an unreasonable degree of certainty.

The scientists and officials in question were considered epistemic authorities and the level of certainty communicated by them to members of the public appears to have affected the public's actions. A local investigator, Inspector Lorenzo Cavallo, is quoted as saying: "The Commission calmed the local population down following a number of earth tremors. After the quake, we heard people's accounts and they told us they changed their behaviour following the advice of the commission" (Watt 2011). This account is corroborated repeatedly by witnesses testifying at the trial (Billi 2013).

The specifics of this particular case are complex and contested, and it would be inappropriate and imprudent to attempt to pass any judgments. One thing that we do think that the case demonstrates, however, is a strong recognition of the responsibility to communicate the epistemically appropriate degree of certainty or uncertainty in our judgments. It is unreasonable, (epistemically inappropriate) to make or hold a judgment without the appropriate degree of uncertainty given the evidence. It is, in addition, a communicative and perhaps a moral failure to communicate a judgment without the appropriate expression of epistemic uncertainty.

Acknowledgments We would like to thank Monica Bhattacharjee for her contribution to the preparation of this paper.

References

Adler, J. E. (2013). Are conductive arguments possible? *Argumentation, 13*(1).

Ashcroft, H. (2012, November 20). *L'Aquila earthquake—shaking the scientific community*. Retrieved from http://www.bangscience.org/2012/11/laquila-earthquake-shaking-the-scientific-community/.

Bailin, S., & Battersby, M. (2010). *Reason in the balance: An inquiry approach to critical thinking*. Whitby, ON: McGraw-Hill.

Bailin, S., & Battersby, M. (2009). Inquiry: A dialectical approach to teaching critical thinking. In J. Ritola (Ed.), *Argument cultures: Proceedings of OSSA 8 CD-ROM*. OSSA: Windsor, ON.

Battersby, M., & Bailin, S. (2011). Guidelines for reaching a reasoned judgment. In J. A. Blair & R. H. Johnson (Eds.), *Conductive argument: An overlooked type of defeasible reasoning* (pp. 145–157). London: College Publications.

Billi, M. (2013). *Sentenza. Tribunale di L'Aquila. Sezione Penale. N.253/2010 R.G.N.R.* Retrieved from http://processoaquila.files.wordpress.com/2013/01/sentenza-grandi-rischi-completa-1.pdf.

Blair, J. A.., & Johnson, R. H. (1987). Argumentation as dialectical. *Argumentation, 1*(1), 41–56.

Blair, J. A., & Johnson, R. H. (Eds.). (2011). *Conductive argument: An overlooked type of defeasible reasoning*. London: College Publications.

Govier, T. (2011). Conductive arguments: Overview of the symposium. In J. A. Blair & R. H. Johnson (Eds.), *Conductive argument: An overlooked type of defeasible reasoning* (pp. 262–276). London: College Publications.

Hitchcock, D. (2002). The practice of argumentative discussion. *Argumentation, 6*(3), 287–298.

Hooper, J. (2012, October 22). *Italian scientists convicted for false assurances before earthquake*. Retrieved from http://www.theguardian.com/world/2012/oct/22/italian-scientists-jailed-earthquake-aquila.

Johnson, R. H. (2000). *Manifest rationality: A pragmatic theory of argument*. Mahwah, NJ: Erlbaum.

Pappas, S. (2012). *Scientists on trial for failing to predict Italian quake*. Retrieved from http://www.nbcnews.com/id/44596501/ns/technology_and_science-science/t/scientists-trial-failing-predict-italian-quake/#.U3J_LF69zw2.

US Department of Health and Human Services. (2006). *The health consequences of involuntary exposure to tobacco smoke: A report of the surgeon general*. Retrieved from http://www.ncbi.nlm.nih.gov/books/NBK44324/.

Watt, S. (2011, September 16). *Scientists in the dock over L'Aquila earthquake*. Retrieved from http://news.bbc.co.uk/2/hi/programmes/newsnight/9593123.stm.

Wellman, C. (1971). *Challenge and response: Justification in ethics*. Carbondale: Southern Illinois University Press.

The Linked-Convergent Distinction

David Hitchcock

1 Introduction

Once upon a time introductory logic textbooks did not mention the linked-convergent distinction. See for example Cohen and Nagel (1934), Black (1946), and Copi (1978). Stephen Thomas was the first one to draw it, in 1977.[1] Thomas took the term 'convergent' from Monroe Beardsley's earlier textbook, from which come also the terms 'divergent argument' and 'serial argument' (Beardsley, 1950, p. 19). A contrast concept was already implicit in Beardsley's recognition that a reason that "converges" along with one or more other reasons on a conclusion might itself consist internally of more than one coordinate premiss. Thomas refined Beardsley's concept of convergence, made the contrast concept explicit, coined the term 'linked' for it, and supplemented Beardsley's convention for diagramming convergent reasons with a convention for diagramming the linkage among the coordinate premisses of a multi-premiss reason. Independently of Thomas's innovation, Scriven (1976, p. 42) introduced a similar distinction, with a different diagramming convention, but used the term 'balance of considerations' to describe an argument with a convergent support structure. Johnson and Blair (1977, p. 177) and Hitchcock (1983, pp. 49–52) appropriate Scriven's way of making the distinction.

The distinction appears with Thomas's labels and diagramming conventions as a topic in many introductory textbooks. See for example Freeman (1993, pp. 86–106), Ennis (1996, p. 39), LeBlanc (1998, pp. 32–36), Fisher (2001, pp. 32–38),

[1] He claims (1986, p. 457) to have introduced it in the 1973 edition of his *Practical Reasoning in Natural Language*, but I have been unable to find a copy of this textbook published before 1977, despite the claim (Thomas 1977, p. ii) of copyright in 1973, 1974 and 1975.

D. Hitchcock (✉)
Department of Philosophy, McMaster University, Hamilton L8S 4K1, Canada
e-mail: hitchckd@mcmaster.ca

F.H. van Eemeren and B. Garssen (eds.), *Reflections on Theoretical Issues in Argumentation Theory*, Argumentation Library 28,
DOI 10.1007/978-3-319-21103-9_6

Bailin and Battersby (2010, pp. 42–44), Govier (2010, pp. 37–39), Vaughn and MacDonald (2010, pp. 95–96), and Groarke and Tindale (2013, 115–119). Many of these textbooks explain the distinction in one short section, with exercises on applying it, but neither mention nor use the distinction elsewhere–a sign that its inclusion has become a piece of scholasticism.

The distinction is intuitively clear. Where more than one premiss is offered in direct support of a conclusion, the premisses sometimes work together to support it and are in this sense linked, whereas at other times distinct subsets of them offer independently relevant reasons that "converge" on the conclusion. A paradigm case of linked support would be a deductively valid two-premiss argument where neither premiss by itself entails the conclusion, such as the argument:

(1) There is no life on Mars, because its atmosphere is in a stable equilibrium, which would not be the case if there were life on that planet.

A paradigm case of convergent support would be an appeal to disparate considerations or criteria in support of the attribution of some supervenient status to their common subject, such as the following argument:

(2) There should be no capital punishment. The death penalty violates human rights codes that forbid cruel and unusual punishment, cannot be reversed or compensated for if it is discovered that a person was innocent of the crime for which they were executed, is no less effective as a deterrent than the likely alternative of a long prison term, and is not needed to prevent a person convicted of a capital crime from repeating that crime.

Despite this intuitive clarity, it has turned out to be difficult to spell out theoretically when premisses are linked and when they "converge". This difficulty has given rise to several scholarly treatments of the distinction, among which Walton (1996) and Freeman (2011) stand out for making it a major focus of their books on argument structure.

In this paper I wish to make one main point: that the distinction is primarily a distinction among types of support, not among arguments, premisses, reasons or structures. Only derivatively can we apply the distinction to arguments, premisses, reasons and structures. This point seems to me to be obvious once one is made aware of it, but it seems not to have been made in the literature. It implies that it is futile to look for a criterion of linkage in the consequences for the strength of support of finding a premiss questionable or false (e.g. no support upon falsification, diminished type of support upon elimination, etc.). Nevertheless, I shall argue, the distinction is useful.

2 Convergence: Not Multiplicity of Arguments

Initially we should be clear that the linked-convergent distinction is not a distinction between a single multi-premiss argument and multiple independent arguments. There is nothing particularly problematic about the concept of distinct arguments for a single conclusion. We have clear examples of such "piling on" of arguments, as in Aristotle's 21 arguments in his *Metaphysics* against Plato's theory of forms (Aristotle 1984 [4th century BCE], 988a1-8 and 990a34-993a10), Thomas Aquinas's five ways of proving the existence of God (Aquinas 1913 [1269], I, Q. 2, Art. 3), and the 367 different ways of proving the Pythagorean theorem (http://www.wikihow.com/Prove-the-Pythagorean-Theorem; accessed 2014 05 24). The appropriate response to such texts is to treat each argument by itself: identifying, analyzing, interpreting and evaluating it as if no other argument for the conclusion were in the offing.

There is however some controversy over how to combine the results of such evaluations. Pollock (1995, pp. 101–102) doubts that there is accrual of independent reasons, and assumes that the degree of justification for a conclusion supported by separate undefeated arguments is simply the maximum of the strengths of those arguments. He argues that cases adduced as evidence of accrual of independent reasons, such as the greater reliability of testimony when given independently by two witnesses than when given by just one of them, are in fact cases where the separate pieces of information function as premisses of a single argument. Selinger (2014) on the other hand takes a new argument to reduce the uncertainty left by any preceding arguments for the same conclusion, provided that the premisses of the new argument are independent of the premisses of its predecessors. On the basis of this intuition, he provides a formula for calculating the degree of acceptability conferred on a conclusion by a set of such independent arguments. The inputs to this formula are provided by a valuation function which assigns to each premiss and each inference (but not to the conclusion) degrees of acceptability ranging from 0 for complete unacceptability via ½ for being neither acceptable nor unacceptable to 1 for complete acceptability. Let $v(\alpha_{ij})$ be the degree of acceptability of a premiss α_{ij} of an argument j with conclusion α, and $w(\alpha|\alpha_{1j}, \ldots, \alpha_{nj})$ be the degree of conditional acceptability in this argument of its conclusion α given total acceptability of its premisses $\alpha_{1j}, \ldots, \alpha_{nj}$. If the premisses of this argument are independent and the product of their degrees of acceptability is greater than ½ (meaning that the conjunction of the premisses is more acceptable than not), then the degree of acceptability $v_j(\alpha)$ conferred on the conclusion α by the argument is the product $v(\alpha_{1j}) \cdot \ldots \cdot v(\alpha_{nj}) \cdot w(\alpha_j|\alpha_{1j}, \ldots, \alpha_{nj})$. (This formula can be adjusted to accommodate cases where the premisses of an argument are not independent of one another.) The degree of acceptability conferred on α by m such arguments (m > 1) with independent premisses is given by the formula $v_1(\alpha) \oplus \ldots \oplus v_m(\alpha)$, where $x \oplus y = 2x + 2y - 2xy - 1$. Selinger's formula appears to give intuitively acceptable results. For example, according to the formula two independent proofs that each confer separately a total acceptability of 1 on a theorem confer together the same acceptability of 1, whereas two independent arguments that each confer an acceptability of 3/4 on a claim together confer an acceptability of 7/8 and a new independent argument that confers an acceptability on a claim only slightly greater than ½ raises the acceptability of this claim by a very small amount. Thus the conflict between Pollock's rejection of accrual of independent reasons and Selinger's acceptance of this sort of accrual comes down to a conflict of intuitions.

It is an open question whether there is any compelling argument that would resolve the conflict.

There is also an interpretive difficulty in determining whether an additional supporting reason introduced by a bridging term like 'besides' or 'moreover' or 'further' is a new argument or merely an independently relevant part of a single argument. This difficulty is best resolved by applying a moderate principle of charity, according to which an ambiguous text or discourse is to be disambiguated in the way that makes it more plausible.

The difference between independently relevant reasons in a single argument and multiple arguments for the same conclusion implies, as Freeman (2011, pp. 108–113) has pointed out, that the pragma-dialectical distinction between coordinatively compound argumentation and multiple argumentation is not the same as the linked-convergent distinction. Multiple argumentation involves distinct speech act complexes, in each of which one or more arguments are advanced in an attempt to justify a point of view–as it happens, the same one in each case. Coordinatively compound argumentation involves a single complex of speech acts in which more than one premiss is used in direct support of a point of view. From the pragma-dialectical perspective, the linked-convergent distinction is a distinction within the class of coordinatively compound argumentation. Snoeck Henkemans (1992, pp. 96–99), for example, recognizes two types of coordinatively compound argumentation, cumulative and complementary, which stand to each other roughly (but not exactly) as convergent arguments stand to linked arguments.

Beardsley and Thomas may have contributed to confusion between multiple arguments for a single conclusion and multiple independently relevant reasons in a single argument. Indeed, they may themselves have conflated these two concepts. They diagram convergent reasoning with a separate arrow from each independently relevant reason to the conclusion, thus giving the visual impression that there are distinct inferences to be evaluated but no need for a comprehensive assessment of how well the reasons taken together support the conclusion. Further, Beardsley refers to convergent reasoning as involving "independent reasons"–a phrase that could easily be read to cover independent arguments as well as independently relevant reasons in a single argument. Further, since Beardsley gives only two examples of convergent structures (one an argument from sign [1950, p. 18] and the other an [intuitively linked] argument for an evaluation [p. 21]) and makes nothing of the concept in his approach to evaluating arguments, it is hard to flesh out his ambiguous definition of a convergent argument as one in which "several independent reasons support the same conclusion" (p. 19). Beardsley in fact made less and less use of the concept of convergence in subsequent editions of his textbook; in the second (1956) edition it is merely mentioned at the beginning of a check-up quiz, and it is missing from the third (1966) and fourth (1975) editions. It seems then that users of the first edition did not find its concept of convergence particularly useful. For his part, Thomas (1977, p. 39) conflates independently relevant reasons in a single argument with distinct arguments sharing a conclusion by counting as convergent reasoning not only independent reasons for some action but also separate alleged proofs of a single claim, such as different arguments for the existence of God.[2]

3 The Primary Sphere of the Distinction

To get a sense of the primary field of application of the linked-convergent distinction, we need to go beyond the intuitive distinction between premisses that work together and premiss-sets that constitute independently relevant reasons. We need to look at how the distinction is used, and in particular how the concept of convergent reasoning is applied. For this purpose, our most extensive and therefore best sources are the treatment of practical decision-making in the various editions of Thomas's textbook (1977, 1981, 1986, 1997) and the treatment of conductive reasoning in the various editions of Trudy Govier's textbook (Govier 1985, 1988, 1992, 1997, 2001, 2005, 2010).

In the last edition of his textbook (Thomas 1977), which presumably incorporates his most developed thinking on the topic, Thomas devotes 57 pages (385–441) to practical decision-making. He recommends a five-component approach to important personal decision-making situations:

1. Identify mutually exclusive options.
2. For each option, articulate whatever possible reasons pro and con one can think of.
3. Evaluate separately the acceptability and relevance of each such reason.
4. Consider reasons bearing on the acceptability or relevance of each reason (and reasons bearing on the acceptability or relevance of those reasons, and so on).
5. Pick the option that is best supported by its undefeated pro reasons and least opposed by its undefeated con reasons.

Diagramming these components is helpful, and perhaps even essential, for keeping track of one's reasoning. In diagramming the reasoning concerning each option, Thomas uses separate arrows for each reason–solid if it is a pro reason, dashed if it is a con reason (including a reason against the acceptability or relevance of another reason). He illustrates his recommended procedure with reference to two personal decision-making situations, described initially in the words of the decision-maker: a choice of living accommodation (pp. 395–404) and a choice of whether to move cities in order to get a better job in one's company (pp. 414–430).

We find a similar approach in Trudy Govier's treatment of what she calls "conductive arguments" (Govier 2010, p. 353), which she characterizes as

---

[2]This example disappears from the fourth (1997) edition of his textbook. A third type of example, in which a claim is supported both by evidence and by testimony, occurs only in the first two editions (1977, 1981) of his textbook.

"arguments in which premises are put forward as separately and non-conclusively relevant to support a conclusion, against which negatively relevant considerations may also be acknowledged" (2011, p. 262) and whose structure she describes as "always convergent" (2010, p. 352). Like Thomas, she proposes that one evaluate such arguments by considering for each premiss separately not only whether it is rationally acceptable but also whether it is relevant, positively or negatively, to the conclusion. After having done so, one should judge the strength of support given by each positively relevant rationally acceptable reason separately and by these reasons cumulatively, the strength of opposition given by each negatively relevant rationally acceptable counter-consideration separately and by these counter-considerations cumulatively, and the size of the difference between the cumulative support and the cumulative opposition (Govier 1999, p. 170; 2010, pp. 365–366). Govier illustrates this complex procedure with reference to an invented argument for legalizing voluntary euthanasia (Govier 2010, pp. 360–363).

Thomas and Govier have developed more extensively than any other authors a procedure for evaluating convergent reasoning and argument. Although their procedures differ and are illustrated by application to different types of arguments, they have an important commonality: separate judgment of the relevance to some conclusion of each of a number of diverse considerations, criteria, or signs. The point of distinguishing independently relevant, or putatively relevant, reasons pro and con in a convergent structure is thus to isolate them for separate consideration. If a given reason turns out to be unacceptable, questionable or irrelevant, it is still possible to estimate the strength of support that the remaining acceptable and relevant reasons give to the conclusion. The partitioning into distinct reasons is a necessary preliminary to this evaluative approach, but would generally not be helpful for evaluating other types of arguments, i.e. those that do not involve appeal to distinct considerations, criteria or signs.

The appropriate criterion for convergence, then, is the independent relevance to a conclusion of distinct sub-sets of an argument's premisses. Relevance in this sense is an ontic property, that of counting in context for or against the conclusion drawn. It is not a mental property of the person putting forward the argument, such as the arguer's intention or belief. Nor is it a property of the argumentative text, such as a claim or textual indication that the supporting reasons are being put forward as independently relevant. Convergence is thus primarily a feature of the way in which multiple coordinate premisses of a piece of reasoning or argument in fact work to support the conclusion. They do so convergently when and only when distinct sub sets of the premisses adduce distinct considerations or criteria or signs that are in fact relevant, positively or negatively, to the conclusion drawn.

Although convergence is primarily a property of the support that multiple coordinate premisses provide to a conclusion, one can apply the concept derivatively to reasoning, arguments, premisses, reasons and argument structures. Reasoning and argument are convergent when they have multiple coordinate premisses that can be partitioned into distinct sub-sets that it is plausible to interpret as put forward as independently relevant to the conclusion. In that case, the reasoning or argument can be said to have a convergent structure. The reasons constituted by such distinct sub-sets should then be treated as being put forward as convergent, i.e. as independently relevant to the conclusion, even if on evaluation not all of them turn out to be both rationally acceptable and relevant. If any such reason consists of a single premiss, then one can take that premiss to be put forward as convergent; otherwise, the concept of convergence should not be applied to the individual premisses.

Since convergence is primarily a way that a claim can be supported, there is judgment involved in deciding to treat a piece of reasoning or argument by the procedure appropriate to a convergent support structure. In cases where the reasons into which one partitions multiple coordinate premisses are not all rationally acceptable and relevant, the decision to partition may rest on syntactical considerations (e.g. a number of premisses attributing various characteristics to a common subject to which the conclusion attributes some further characteristic), semantic considerations (e.g. the status of the conclusion as a policy decision and the corresponding status of the distinct premiss-sets as diverse consequences or rules or deontic principles, or the status of the conclusion as a diagnosis and the corresponding status of the distinct premiss-sets as diverse signs or symptoms), textual considerations (e.g. the introduction of a subsequent premiss-set by the word 'besides'), and perhaps other sorts of considerations. Decisions to partition premisses based on such considerations are not correct or incorrect, but only more or less reasonable. Thus there may be no fact of the matter about whether a particular piece of reasoning or argument with multiple coordinate premisses is convergent, since the case for partitioning the premisses may be about as strong as the case against partitioning them. In this respect, the situation is exactly like that of deciding whether a piece of reasoning or argument is deductive, i.e. appropriately evaluated by the standard of deductive validity. The claim of the present paper that convergence is primarily a way in which a claim can be supported rather than primarily a type of argument is exactly parallel to my claim long ago that deduction is primarily a type of validity rather than a type of argument (Hitchcock 1979).

What about the concept of linkage? If we take linkage to be the complement of convergence, we can define it as support by multiple coordinate premisses in some way other than by distinct considerations or criteria or signs that are separately relevant, positively or negatively, to the conclusion drawn. As with convergence, we can derivatively define linked reasoning, arguments, premisses, and argument structures as those that it is appropriate to treat for evaluative purposes as linked. Judgment will be involved in making the decision about appropriateness.

This conception of linkage is purely negative. It implies nothing about the effect on the strength of support of finding that a premiss of an argument with linked support is questionable or unacceptable. And *a fortiori* it implies nothing about this effect in the case of an argument or reasoning that one decides, appropriately or not, to treat as linked for evaluative purposes. Thus, if we accept this conception of linkage, we should regard as exercises in futility the many attempts in the literature to find a criterion for linkage in the consequences of "suspending" a premiss or finding it false: diminished support upon falsification (Thomas 1977, p. 38), no support upon falsification (Copi 1982, p. 21), insufficient support upon elimination

(Snoeck Henkemans 1992), type reduction upon elimination (Vorobej 1994), and so forth. In any case, there is a useless spinning of wheels in applying any such test if the point of classifying an argument as linked is to facilitate evaluation, since one has to do the evaluation first in order to classify the argument in a way that indicates how one is to do the evaluation. Better just to do the evaluation and forget about the classification.

How then should we evaluate an argument that we decide to treat as if its support were linked? A straightforward way is to judge first the status of each premiss separately, in terms for example of whether it is acceptable, questionable or unacceptable. Then determine how strongly the premisses with their attributed statuses collectively support the conclusion and whether in context that degree of support is enough.

4 Conclusion

The linked-convergent distinction introduced by Thomas (1977) is not the same as the distinction between a single argument for a claim and multiple arguments for a claim. It is a distinction to be applied within the class of single arguments for a claim, specifically to such arguments with more than one premiss. It is primarily a distinction between ways in which two or more premisses in such an argument can directly support a claim. Support is convergent if the premisses can be partitioned into independently relevant reasons. Support is linked if the premisses cannot be partitioned into independently relevant reasons that each consist of rationally acceptable premisses. One can classify arguments, reasoning, premisses, or structures as linked or convergent only in a secondary or derivative sense, where what is involved is a judgment call on what type of support the author is most plausibly interpreted as attempting to provide by means of the argument, reasoning or component. Hence, as with the deductive-inductive distinction, there may be no fact of the matter as to whether a given multi-premiss argument is linked or convergent.

The value of the distinction lies in the consequences of treating an argument component as having convergent structure. Such a decision introduces into the evaluation of the premisses a consideration of the independent relevance of each premiss-set that is partitioned as a reason–a step that makes no sense if one is treating it as having linked structure.

References

Aquinas, T. (1913). *Summa theologica, Part I, QQ. 1-XXVI.* London: Burns, Oates & Washbourne. Latin original first published in 1269.

Aristotle. (1984). Metaphysics. In J. Barnes (Ed.), *The complete works of Aristotle: The revised Oxford translation* (pp. 1552–1728). Bollingen Series 71. Princeton: Princeton University Press. Greek original written in the 4th century BCE.

Bailin, S., & Battersby, M. (2010). *Reason in the balance: An inquiry approach to critical thinking*. Toronto: McGraw-Hill Ryerson.

Beardsley, M. C. (1950). *Practical logic*. Englewood Cliffs, New Jersey: Prentice-Hall.

Beardsley, M. C. (1956, 1966, 1975). *Thinking straight: Principles of reasoning for readers and writers*. 2nd, 3rd and 4th editions of (Beardsley, 1950). Englewood Cliffs, New Jersey: Prentice-Hall.

Black, M. (1946). *Critical thinking*. New York: Prentice-Hall.

Cohen, M. R., & Nagel, E. (1934). *An introduction to logic and scientific method*. New York: Harcourt, Brace.

Copi, I. M. (1978). *Introduction to logic* (5th ed.). New York: Macmillan.

Copi, I. M. (1982). *Introduction to logic* (6th ed.). New York: Macmillan.

Ennis, R. H. (1996). *Critical thinking*. Upper Saddle River, New Jersey: Prentice-Hall.

Fisher, A. (2001). *Critical thinking: An introduction*. Cambridge: Cambridge University Press.

Freeman, J. B. (1993). *Thinking logically: Basic concepts for reasoning* (2nd ed.). Englewood Cliffs, New Jersey: Prentice Hall.

Freeman, J. B. (2011). *Argument structure: Representation and theory*. Argumentation Library Volume 18. Dordrecht: Springer.

Govier, T. (1985, 1988, 1992, 1997, 2001, 2005, 2010). *A practical study of argument*, 1st through 7th editions. Belmont, California: Wadsworth.

Govier, T. (1999). Reasoning with pros and cons: Conductive argument revisited. In T. Govier (Ed.), *The Philosophy of Argument* (pp. 155–180). Newport News, VA: Vale Press.

Govier, T. (2011). Conductive arguments: overview of the symposium. In J. A. Blair & R. H. Johnson (Eds.), *Conductive argument: An overlooked type of defeasible reasoning* (pp. 262–276). London: College Publications.

Groarke, L. A., & Tindale, C. W. (2013). *Good reasoning matters: A constructive approach to critical thinking* (5th ed.). Don Mills, ON: Oxford University Press.

Hitchcock, D. (1979). Deductive and inductive: Types of validity, not types of argument. *Informal Logic, 3*(2), 9–10.

Hitchcock, D. (1983). *Critical thinking: A guide to evaluating information*. Toronto: Methuen.

Johnson, R. H., & Blair, J. A. (1977). *Logical self-defense*. Toronto: McGraw-Hill Ryerson.

LeBlanc, J. (1998). *Thinking clearly: A guide to critical reasoning*. New York: W. W. Norton.

Pollock, J. (1995). *Cognitive carpentry: How to build a person*. Cambridge: MIT Press.

Scriven, M. (1976). *Reasoning*. New York: McGraw-Hill.

Selinger, M. (2014). Towards formal representation and evaluation of arguments. *Argumentation, 28*(3), 379–393.

Snoeck Henkemans, A. F. (1992). *Analyzing complex argumentation: The reconstruction of multiple and coordinatively compound argumentation in a critical discussion*. Dissertation, University of Amsterdam.

Thomas, S. N. (1977, 1981, 1986, 1997). *Practical reasoning in natural language*. 1st through 4th editions. Englewood Cliffs, New Jersey: Prentice-Hall.

Vaughn, L., & MacDonald, C. (2010). *The power of critical thinking* (2nd Canadian ed.). Don Mills, Ontario: Oxford University Press.

Vorobej, M. (1994). The TRUE test of linkage. *Informal Logic, 16*(3), 147–157.

Walton, D. (1996). *Argument structure: A pragmatic theory*. Toronto: University of Toronto Press.

Identifying the Warrant of an Argument

James B. Freeman

Abstract Hitchcock has presented a way to extract the warrant from an argument. We summarize his procedure and note that applying it in specific cases may be problematic. We then extend his procedure by indicating how symbolization in a formal language addresses the problems. We indicate the richness required of such a language and then present an expanded procedure for identifying the warrant of an argument.

Keywords Conclusive · Defeasible · Formal language · Hitchcock · Identification procedure · Symbolization key · Warrant

By a warrant we understand an inference licence, an instance of a general pattern:

From	$P_1, \ldots, P_n$
To infer (universally/*ceteris paribus*)	Q

where for some m ≥ 1, $P_1, \ldots, P_n$, Q contain free occurrences of m variables or schematic letters of some sorts (individual, k-ary operation symbol, k-ary predicate, for some k ≥ 1, propositional). Since we understand that any expression contains itself as an instance, our characterization allows propositional variables or schematic letters themselves as instances. Hence our formulation accommodates straightforwardly

From	P, Q
To infer	P & Q

J.B. Freeman (✉)
Department of Philosophy, Hunter College of the City University of New York, New York, NY 10065, USA
e-mail: jfreeman@hunter.cuny.edu

F.H. van Eemeren and B. Garssen (eds.), *Reflections on Theoretical Issues in Argumentation Theory*, Argumentation Library 28,
DOI 10.1007/978-3-319-21103-9_7

Characterizing warrants explicitly is important, since we find confusion in the literature over this concept. Warrants have been characterized as universally generalized conditionals, either unqualified or *ceteris paribus*, as opposed to inference licences. These two however are distinct. Every argument assumes that we can step from the premises to the conclusion, and as Hitchcock (1985) has argued, this step involves generality. That we may infer 'Socrates is mortal' from 'Socrates is human' is not something specific to Socrates. The warrant permits us to step from any instance of the premises to the corresponding instance of the conclusion. The warrant, then, is not part of the argument, the way premises and conclusions are. Formulating the warrant as a generalized conditional statement tempts us to regard it as an unstated premise, and thus a part of the argument. Different types of warrants raise different connection adequacy considerations. Hence identifying the warrant of an argument is an essential first step in evaluating its connection adequacy. In (1985), Hitchcock has proposed a generic way of extracting the warrant from an argument. We turn to summarizing that method first.

1 Hitchcock's Generic Proposal For Identifying Warrants

This procedure has two central steps. Let us agree that we are setting aside, in this paper, arguments properly analyzed as involving unstated premises, which would need to be stated explicitly and added to the explicit premises for a proper analysis. We may state Hitchcock's procedure this way:

1. Identify the repeated content expressions in the argument.
2. Uniformly replace repeated content expressions with variables of the appropriate category, i.e. replace proper names with individual variables, predicate expressions with predicate variables, repeated whole propositions with propositional variables, repeated content expressions of other types with variables of those types.[1]

Two problems may arise when faced with a particular argument. First, repeated content expressions may occur as constituents of wider repeated content expressions. Consider

If President Obama says that Hunter College is one of the best colleges in the United States, then Ima should go to Hunter College.
President Obama says that Hunter College is one of the best colleges in the United States. So Ima should go to Hunter College.

Here the repeated content expressions include 'President Obama,' 'says that,' 'Hunter College,' 'one,' 'best,' 'colleges,' 'United States,' 'Ima,' 'should,' 'go.'

[1]Hitchcock formulates this procedure not explicitly for warrants as we have characterized them, but for the associated generalization of the argument. See (1985, p. 89).

But also the entire sentence 'President Obama says that Hunter College is one of the best colleges in the United States' together with 'Ima should go to Hunter College' are repeated. But obviously this is a *modus ponens* argument and no more fine-grained analysis is needed to recognize its validity. We abstract the warrant

From:	If *P* then *Q*
	P
To infer:	*Q*

rather than, for example

From:	If *x* says that *y* is one of the best colleges in *z*, then *w* should go to *y*
	x says that *y* is one of the best colleges in *z*
To infer:	*w* should go to *y*

This example motivates Hitchcock's directive to replace the widest repeated content expression unless the resulting associated generalization is implausible (1985, p. 92).

An argument may contain a number of repeated content expressions which do not nest within one another. For example,

President Obama is the husband of Michele Obama. So Michele Obama is the wife of President Obama.

Intuitively, we should replace both repeated content expressions, the warrant being

From:	*x* is the husband of *y*
To infer:	*y* is the wife of *x*

This example motivates Hitchcock's second directive "to generalize over each of the repeated content expressions–unless it would be implausible to do so (1985, p. 92)

2 Applying the Procedure: Some Challenging Examples

Applying Hitchcock's proposal to identify the warrant of a given argument may involve two judgment calls:

(1) What are the widest repeated content expressions which should be replaced by variables of the appropriate type?
(2) If a sentence contains multiple repeated content expressions, which should be replaced by variables?

When confronted with actual examples of arguments, including textbook examples for analysis, applying Hitchcock's procedure may very well not be a trivial exercise. Let's examine several examples taken from Govier's text (2010):

(1) Most people take seriously what they have to pay for and take less seriously and are less dedicated to something that other people pay for. Adult students of music pay for their own lessons, whereas children who study music typically have their lessons paid for by their parents. For this reason, in the context of music lessons, we can expect adult students to be more serious and dedicated than children. (Govier 2010, p. 153)

What should strike us immediately with this example is that what you see is *not* what you get. That is, there is a distinct difference between the surface vocabulary of this passage and its depth vocabulary. On the surface, the repeated content expressions are 'people,' 'take,' 'seriously,' 'pay for,' 'music,' 'lessons.' But 'students of music' and '[those] who study music' express the same content, at least in this context, and so should be paraphrased by the same expression.

The first sentence is asserting something about comparative degrees of seriousness. So 'take' and 'seriously' are constituents of a complex expression 'takes seriously to degree.' Again, the sentence asserts that this degree of seriousness depends on who pays for what thing is to be taken seriously or less seriously. So the shared content expression is not 'pays for' but 'pays for by.' We also see that our paraphrase must include an expression to the effect that something is greater than something else. So upon paraphrase, the first sentence may become

(1.1) Most people who pay for one item where someone else pays for another, take the first item to a certain degree of seriousness and the second to a degree of seriousness less that the first.

The second sentence actually expresses two statements. Seeking to paraphrase brings out that 'lessons' is implicitly relational in the context of this argument: 'x is a lesson for y in (subject) z.' Stating the paraphrase of the second premise requires a further judgment call. The statement appears to be a conjunction of two straightforward A-categoricals. The universal quantifier is unrestricted. But is that interpretation fair? Would the statement really be refuted if one could cite a small number (i.e. greater than 0) of adult music students who did not pay for their lessons? Clearly this first conjunct makes a claim about most adult music students, or adult music students *ceteris paribus*. So the first conjunct of the sentence becomes

(1.2a) *Ceteris paribus* adult students of music pay for their own lessons in music.

The paraphrase of the second conjunct becomes

(1.2b) *Ceteris paribus* students of music who are children have a parent pay for their lessons in music.

In light of these paraphrases, the third sentence requires paraphrasing also. A qualified generalization is intended, witness 'we can expect.' For simplicity, let us omit the phrase 'with a certain degree of dedication:'

(1.3) *Ceteris paribus*, adult students of music will take seriously their music lessons to a certain degree and students of music who are children will take seriously their music lessons to a certain degree, and the first degree of seriousness is greater than the second.

By now, it should be obvious that in this exercise, we have been doing half of what is required in symbolic logic in setting up a symbolization key. Recall that such a key will match simple expressions in a formal language with English expressions. As Bergmann, Moor, Nelson point out in their text (2014), to represent an English sentence in a symbolic formal language, one must first paraphrase it to recognize how the symbols fit the sentence (or the sentence the symbols given the key). As with formal deductive logic, in seeking the warrant, we are seeking a formal (or at least quasi-formal) feature of the argument. Formal deductive logic concerns the special case where the warrant is completely formal, retaining no content expressions. Our reflection on this example shows we are seeking to generalize the procedure. We must then go the whole way–set up a symbolization key, symbolize the argument through that key, and then inspect the symbolization for repeated content expressions which should be replaced by variables of a certain sort. Our symbolization key will include not only formal expressions corresponding to the recognized shared content expressions in our paraphrase, but to all the non-logical expressions in the argument as paraphrased. This may lead us to recognize that some content expressions occurring only once in the argument as originally stated are actually repeated content expressions. For example, 'people' appears only once, but is implicitly repeated in the argument. Adult students of music are people; so are children. So not all repeated content expressions will be evident on the surface or upon first inspection of an argument text.

So what is our argument going to look like when symbolized? Let us set up the following symbolization key:

UD	$\{x\text{: } x \text{ is a thing}\}$
Hx	x is a human being
Sxy	x is a student of y
Txyz	x takes y seriously to degree z
Pxyz	x pays for y's z
$x < y$	x is less than y
$x > y$	x is greater than y
Lxyz	x is a lesson for y in (subject) z
Ax	x is an adult
Cx	x is a child
m	music
Rxy	x is a parent of y

This symbolization key reflects a prodigal attitude toward what is to count as a thing. The class includes far more than physical objects. Hence units of service such as lessons are things. Degrees are units of measure and so things. Areas of activity may be rather abstract objects, but ‘music’ refers to one of them. In general, then, anything which may be the designation of some referring expression may count for us as a thing for the purpose of analyzing an argument containing such a referring expression and may be included in the universe of discourse of the symbolization key for that argument.

Our symbolization key has not taken us beyond the resources of first-order predicate logic. (For the purists, we could have used ‘G*xy*’ instead of ‘$x > y$.’) But clearly we can not yet proceed to a symbolic representation of the first sentence as paraphrased and preserve the force of ‘most.’ Fortunately our work has already been done for us by the scholastics with the @-qualifier read as ‘other things being equal,’ which for our purposes can be taken as having the same function as ‘most.’ (See Rescher 1977, pp. 13–14. As pointed out there, the @-qualifier is treated in Oesterle 1961, pp. 27–38.)

(1.1′) $@(\forall x_1)(\forall x_2)(\forall y_1)(\forall y_2)(([(\mathrm{H}x_1 \;\&\; \mathrm{H}x_2) \;\&\; x_1 \neq x_2] \;\&\; [\mathrm{P}x_1x_1y_1 \;\&\mathrm{P}x_2x_1y_2]) \supset (\exists z_1)(\exists z_2)[(\mathrm{T}x_1y_1z_1 \& \;\mathrm{T}x_1y_2z_2) \;\&\; z_2 < z_1])$

(1.2a′) $@(\forall x)(\forall y)[([\mathrm{S}x\mathrm{m} \;\&\; \mathrm{A}x] \;\&\; \mathrm{L}yx\mathrm{m}) \supset \mathrm{P}xxy]$

(1.2b′) $@(\forall x)(\forall y)[([\mathrm{S}x\mathrm{m} \;\&\; \mathrm{C}x] \;\&\; \mathrm{L}yx\mathrm{m}) \supset (\exists z)(\mathrm{R}zx \;\&\; \mathrm{P}zxy)]$

(1.3′) $@(\forall x)(\forall y)(\forall z1)(\forall z2)[(([\mathrm{S}x\mathrm{m} \;\&\; \mathrm{A}x] \;\&\; [\mathrm{S}y\mathrm{m} \;\&\; \mathrm{C}y] \;\&\; ([\mathrm{L}z_1x\mathrm{m} \;\&\; \mathrm{L}z_2y\mathrm{m}])) \supset (\exists w_1)(\exists w_2)([\mathrm{T}xz_1w_1 \;\&\; \mathrm{T}yz_2w_2] \;\&\; w_1 > w_2)]$

Are we now in a position to extract a warrant from this argument as symbolized? Simplification before proceeding is desirable. If this simplification accords with the intent expressed by the argument, we should regard it as legitimate. Already our symbolization should suggest how that simplification should proceed. To be justified in asserting (1.3′), one must be justified in accepting the claimed connection between the subject (antecedent clause) and the predicate (consequent clause). The subject concerns adults and children who are students of music together with their music lessons. The predicate concerns the one valuing their music lessons more than the other. Premises (1.2a′) and (1.2b′) connect the subject with the concept of paying for something oneself (1.2a′) versus a parent, i.e. someone else, paying for something (1.2b′). Does (1.1′) serve to connect one’s paying for something oneself versus someone else paying for it with the difference in valuing that thing, i.e. do we in effect have a defeasible syllogism in Barbara here? At the propositional core of both a syllogism in Barbara and this argument, we may see a hypothetical syllogism, if we interpret (1.1′) properly. What is needed then is connecting one person’s paying for something himself or herself and valuing that thing to a certain degree versus someone else not paying for a thing and valuing it to less of a degree. Now (1.1′) concerns a single person, not a comparison between two persons. But does not (1.1′) suggest that people in general give a higher value to what they pay for and in general a lower value to what someone else has paid for? If this is fair, we have justification in revising (1.1′) as

(1.1″) $@(\forall x_1)(\forall x_2)(\forall y_1)(\forall y_2)(([(\mathrm{H}x_1 \,\&\, \mathrm{H}x_2) \,\&\, x_1 \neq x_2] \,\&\, [\mathrm{P}x_1x_1y_1\&(\exists w)(\mathrm{H}w \,\&\, [w \neq \mathrm{x}_2 \,\&\, \mathrm{P}wx_2y_2]) \supset (\exists z_1)(\exists z_2)[(\mathrm{T}x_1y_1z_1 \,\&\, \mathrm{T}x_2y_2z_2) \,\&\, z_2 < z_1])$

Look at premise (1.2b′). The point is not that the child's *parents* pay for the music lessons but that someone other than the child pays for them. So substituting '$z \neq x$' for '$\mathrm{R}zx$' in (1.2b′) is consonant with the intent of the argument.

Now we are nearly in a position to see how this argument involves the reasoning pattern of hypothetical syllogism. Elide (1.2a′) and (1.2b′). The result, which is logically equivalent to the conjunction of (1.2a′) and (1.2b′), is

(1.2″) $@(\forall x_1)(\forall x_2)(\forall y_1)(\forall y_2)[[([\mathrm{S}x_1\mathrm{m} \,\&\, \mathrm{A}x_1] \,\&\mathrm{L}y_1x_1\mathrm{m}) \,\&\, ([\mathrm{S}x_2\mathrm{m} \,\&\, \mathrm{C}x_2] \,\&\, \mathrm{L}y_2x_2\mathrm{m})] \supset [\mathrm{P}x_1x_1y_1 \,\&\, (\exists z)(z \neq x_2 \,\&\, \mathrm{P}zx_2\mathrm{y}_2)]])$

Now clearly it is a semantic truth, at least in the context of this argument, that adults are human beings, children are human beings, and adults and children are distinct human beings. So adding the conjuncts '(Hx1 & Hx2) & x1 ≠ x2' to the consequent of (1.2′) yields a symbolization of a semantically equivalent statement in this context. Also we may exchange the bound variable 'z' for 'w' in (1.2′) via alphabetic variance. The result is

(1.2′) $@(\forall x_1)(\forall x_2)(\forall y_1)(\forall y_2)([([\mathrm{S}x_1\mathrm{m} \,\&\, \mathrm{A}x_1] \,\&\, \mathrm{L}y_1x_1\mathrm{m}) \,\&\, ([\mathrm{S}x_2\mathrm{m} \,\&\, \mathrm{C}x_2] \,\&\, \mathrm{L}y_2x_2\mathrm{m})] \supset [[(\mathrm{H}x_1 \,\&\, \mathrm{H}x_2) \,\&\, x_1 \neq x_2] \,\&\, [\mathrm{P}x_1x_1y_1 \,\&\, (\exists w)(w \neq x_2 \,\&\, \mathrm{P}zx_2y_2)]]])$

Both the antecedent and the consequent of the conditional subformula of (1.2″) express quaternary relations. Likewise, antecedent and consequent of (1.1″) express quaternary relations and the consequent of (1.2″) and antecedent of (1.1″) express the same relation. Likewise both antecedent and consequent of (1.3′) express quaternary relations, and the antecedent of (1.3′) is logically equivalent to the antecedent of (1.2″) (via commutation and alphabetic variance), while the consequent of (1.3′) is the same as the consequent of (1.1″). We have in effect a hypothetical syllogism. Recall Hitchcock's directive to generalize over the widest repeated content expressions. We have now identified what they are. The warrant of this argument is

From:	$@(\forall x_1)(\forall x_2)(\forall y_1)(\forall y_2)[\varphi x_1x_2y_1y_2 \supset \psi x_1x_2y_1y_2]$
	$@(\forall x_1)(\forall x_2)(\forall y_1)(\forall y_2)(\psi x_1x_2y_1y_2 \supset \chi x_1x_2y_1y_2]$
To infer *ceteris paribus:*	$@(\forall x_1)(\forall x_2)(\forall y_1)(\forall y_2)[\varphi x_1x_2y_1y_2 \supset \chi x_1x_2y_1y_2]$

In going from English to a formalization of this argument, we needed a formal language whose vocabulary includes predicate letters, individual variables, individual constants, sentential connectives, and quantifiers together with punctuation symbols. A standard formal language for full first-order predicate logic will also include sentence letters together with the identity sign and operator symbols. We have also seen that symbolizing defeasible universal generalizations requires adding the *ceteris paribus* qualifier '@' to our vocabulary. We shall need more. To analyze certain arguments properly, we shall need modal concepts. Consider the following:

(2) There are idiots among students who have taken my courses and I have given them passing grades. There are bigger idiots among government officials and the electorate has put them in office. Am I required to be more rigorous than the electorate?

Clearly this argument has an unstated conclusion:

My giving passing grades to students who are idiots is acceptable.

From the informal logic point of view, this argument appears to be a classic example of the Two Wrongs Make a Right fallacy. (See Govier 2010, pp. 341–342). From the fact that behavior of a certain type has been accepted, one infers that some further behavior similar to that type is acceptable. Looking at the argument as stated, we may formulate the following symbolization key:

I*x*	*x* is an idiot
S*xy*	*x* is a student in a course of *y*
P*xy*	*x* gives a passing grade to *y*
G*x*	*x* is a government official
B*xy*	*x* is a bigger idiot than *y*
Oxy	*x* has put *y* in office
i	I myself
e	the electorate

Symbolizing the premise is straightforward:

(2.1′) $(\exists x)(\exists y)[([\mathrm{I}x \mathbin{\&} \mathrm{S}x\mathrm{i}] \mathbin{\&} \mathrm{Pi}x) \mathbin{\&} ([(\mathrm{G}y \mathbin{\&} [\mathrm{I}y \mathbin{\&} \mathrm{B}yx]) \mathbin{\&} \mathrm{Oe}y]]$

How shall we symbolize the conclusion as we have formulated it, including the concept of 'acceptable'? One way to approach this problem uses deontic logic, We may construe 'being acceptable' as a deontic modal operator equivalent with 'permissible.' Should '$\Box_{\text{deontic}}$' represent 'it ought to be the case that,' then '$\Diamond_{\text{deontic}}$' represents 'it is permissible that,' i.e. '$\sim\Box_{\text{deontic}}\sim$.' On this analysis, we symbolize the conclusion as

(2.2′) $\Diamond_{\text{deontic}}(\exists x)(\mathrm{I}x \mathbin{\&} \mathrm{Pi}x)$

As our previous example illustrates how symbolization may help to identify what are the widest repeated content expressions in an argument, so this example illustrates how we may identify which of several non-overlapping content expressions we should generalize over. Our symbolization identifies 'idiots,' 'gave a passing grade to,' and 'I myself' as the shared content expressions. But we cannot generalize over either 'idiots' or 'gave a passing grade to.' The resulting inference rule is clearly unacceptable. Keeping in mind that 'P*xy*' and 'O*xy*' share the meaning of accepting or approving, and 'B*xy*' presents a comparative form of 'I*x*,' we can straightforwardly construct a refutation by logical analogy:

> There are highly competent students of mine whom I have failed unfairly and there are highly competent government officials, even more competent than the students, whom the electorate has thrown out of office. Therefore my unfairly failing those highly competent students is acceptable.

This argument is obviously fallacious. On the other had, the fact that I myself, i.e. the argument's proponent, as opposed to some other instructor gave the passing grades seems of no importance. We may then replace 'I' with an individual variable to identify the warrant:

From:	(∃*x*)(∃*y*)[([I*x* & S*xz*] & P*zx*) & ([(G*y* & [I*y* & B*yx*]) & O*ey*]]
To infer *ceteris paribus*:	$\Diamond_{\text{deontic}}$(∃*x*)(I*x* & P*zx*)

Let us consider one further instructive example:

(3) Charred rhinoceros bones, thought to be about 300,000 years old, were found in an archeological site in France. Therefore the rhinoceros species lived in Europe about 300,000 years ago. (Example adapted from Govier 2010, p. 152. She credits the example to a report in the *Globe and Mail*, June 21, 1995.)

Although seemingly very simple, this argument has some interesting features. First, the shared content expressions, at least on the surface, are 'rhinoceros,' '300,000' and 'years.' But 'years' is embedded in two different contexts, 'years old' and 'years ago.' The first is adjectival while the second is adverbial. These units, rather than 'years,' should count as content expressions (or elements in content expressions), rather than 'years' as an independent expression. Next, although 'rhinoceros' is a content expression shared between premise and conclusion, in each case the word is embedded in a context referring to completely different things–charred rhinoceros bones versus members of the rhinoceros species.

C*x*	*x* is charred
B*xy*	*x* is a bone of *y*
R*x*	*x* is a rhinoceros
Y*xy*	*x* is *y* years old
F*xy*	*x* was found in *y*
L*xyz*	*x* lived in *y z* years ago
t	300,000
f	France
e	Europe

Given this key, we may symbolize the argument this way:

(3.1′) (∃*x*)(∃*y*)([([C*x* & B*xy*] & R*y*) & Y*x*t] & F*x*f)
(3.2′) (∃*y*(R*y* & L*y*et)

It is now straightforward to see how the shared content expressions enter into this argument. By replacing 'R' with a schematic monadic predicate letter or monadic predicate variable ‘φ’ and ‘t’ with an individual variable, ‘z,’ extracting the warrant of the argument is totally straightforward:

From:	$(\exists x)(\exists y)([([Cx \& Bxy] \& \varphi y) \& Yxz] \& Fxf)$
To infer *ceteris paribus:*	$(\exists y(\varphi y \& Lyez)$

Hence analyzing beyond surface vocabulary is necessary to identifying the depth content expressions of the passage and in some cases their grammatical category. The analysis involves symbolizing the component statements of the argument in a formal language. This point, however, immediately raises another question. What categories must a formal language include to be rich enough to handle the different categories of expressions arguments in general may involve? Answering that question is the subject of the next section of this paper.

3 A Comprehensive Language for Analyzing Ordinary Language Arguments

It is easy to see that we shall need more categories of expressions in our language than the vocabulary of first-order predicate logic with identity and operator symbols, supplemented by modal operators for various types of modality, will allow. The argument

(4) Tom vouches that he saw the accused leaving the house at 3:00 am. Therefore *ceteris paribus* the accused left the house at 3:00 am

indicates a further needed expansion. The expression ‘vouches that’ is a propositional attitude, to be classed with ‘knows that’ and ‘believes that.’ Understanding the expression as building a statement operator from a name or other referring expression, e.g. ‘Tom vouches that,’ ‘Mary believes that,’ ‘Larry knows that,’ we have a category of expression which functions as the modal operators we have already seen. We understand them this way and refer to them as attitudinal modalities. Our example makes the point that our formal language must include them. We may have more than one-place modalities, both attitudinal and non-attitudinal. ‘Karen believes more strongly that the cosmological argument is fallacious than she believes that the teleological argument is fallacious’ instances a two-place attitudinal modality. The counterfactual conditional and the implication sign in relevance logic are two-place non-attitudinal modalities. Attitudinal modalities may be represented in our language by expressions parallel to non-attitudinal modalities, already familiar, for example, from epistemic or doxastic logic–a capital letter subscripted with an expression referring to whomever has this attitude toward some proposition. Thus ‘V_t’ may symbolize ‘Tom vouches that.’

We must expand the vocabulary of our language even further. Consider the argument

(5) The Secretary of State spoke forcefully about the Syrian President's crimes against humanity. Therefore the Secretary of State spoke about the Syrian President's crimes against humanity.

It seems intuitively clear that if a verb adverbially modified holds of some instance, the verb without modification holds also.

(6) Socrates runs quickly. So Socrates runs

to give a much simpler example. Hence, we need a category of adverbial modifiers in our symbolic language. A convention uses a lower-case letter followed by a dash attaching it to the representation of the verbal expression.

(6′) q-Rs
Therefore Rs

Let's summarize this exposition of the categories of expressions in our vocabulary by specifying the vocabulary systematically, including both content and logical expressions. In this exposition, we are supplementing the formal language for first-order predicate logic with identity and operator symbols presented by Bergmann, Moor, Nelson (2014):

Content Symbols

i. Sentence letters: A–Z, with our without positive integer subscripts
ii. Predicate letters: A^k–Z^k, with our without positive integer superscripts, $k \geq 1$. The integer superscript indicates the degree of the predicate and does not appear in a symbolization, degree being indicated by the number of terms following the predicate letter.
iii. Constants: a–v, with or without positive integer subscripts
iv. Individual variables: *w*, *x*, *y*, *z*, with our without positive integer subscripts
v. Operation symbols: $a^k(\,)$–$z^k(\,)$, with our without positive integer subscripts. As with predicate letters, the superscripts indicate the degree of the operation symbol. Omitted in practice, the degree is indicated by the number of terms within the following parentheses.
vi. Adverbial symbols: a-–z-, with or without positive integer subscripts

Logical Symbols

i. Sentential connectives: $\sim$, &, $\vee$, $\supset$, $\equiv$
ii. Quantifier symbols: $\forall$, $\exists$
iii. Qualifier symbol: @
iv. Identity sign: =
v. Modal connectives:

$\Box$ it is logically necessary that
$\Diamond$ it is logically possible that

$\Box_C$	it is causally necessary that
$\Diamond_C$	it is causally possible that
$\Box_F$	it always will be the case that
$\Diamond_F$	it sometimes will be the case that
$\Box_P$	it always was the case that
$\Diamond_P$	it sometimes was the case that
O	it ought to be the case that
P	it is permissible that
$\Box\!\!\rightarrow$	would conditional
$\Diamond\!\!\rightarrow$	might conditional

vi. Attitudinal modalities: A_t-Z_t, where ‘t’ is some term

Punctuation Symbols (,)

Given these vocabulary categories, the grammar of our language consists of the well-formedness rules of first-order logic supplemented by rules for incorporating the additional vocabulary elements. Such rules are totally straightforward, but require noting two points. First, for forming atomic sentences, the class of predicate letters must be widened to the class of predicate expressions. Besides predicate letters, this class includes predicate expressions formed by prefixing an adverbial symbol to a predicate expression. An atomic formula then, will be either a sentence letter, a k-ary predicate expression followed by k terms, or the identity sign flanked by two terms. Second, a quantifier may be immediately preceded by an @-qualifier.

The richness of this language should aid in seeking to identify the warrant of an argument. Does our language deliver on its promise?. We shall answer that by proposing an overall procedure for identifying the warrant of an argument which incorporates symbolizing the argument in a formal language.[2] That is our topic in the next section.

4 A Comprehensive Procedure for Identifying Warrants

Step I. Identify any merely background statements. Disregard further.

Step II. Construct a symbolization key and proceed to symbolize the statements of the argument.

Step III. Decide whether the argument is conclusive or defeasible.

Step IV. “Reduction Step”

[2]This procedure is a first approximation. We must address the warrant’s being unacceptable but the inference step intuitively acceptable.

A. Identify the repeated complex expressions in the symbolization.
B. If a repeated complex expression is a complete sentence not a sentential component of another repeated complex expression, replace it with a propositional schematic letter.
C. In the resulting set of expressions, if a repeated complex expression is an n-ary relation expression, not a subformula of some wider repeated n-ary relation expression, replace with an n-ary predicate schematic letter applied to the n-individual terms in the symbolization.
D. In the resulting set of expressions, if an expression is a complex term (i.e. an n-ary operation symbol applied to n-terms), not a component of some more complex term, replace with an individual variable.

The resulting symbolic sequence represents a reduction in complexity of the symbolization of the argument. The sequence may still contain repeated expressions. We do not generalize over any logical constants. Also, we do not generalize over modal connectives or attitudinal modalities, regarding them as logical as opposed to content symbols. Neither do we generalize over adverbial symbols. The principle governing all these cases is that we do not generalize over syncategoremata, i.e. expressions which do not have an independent meaning of their own but modify the meaning of expressions to which they are attached.

Simple repeated content expressions, i.e. constants, operators, predicate, and propositional expressions, may remain.

Step V. Replace repeated remaining content expressions by individual variables, and operator symbols, predicates, and propositional expressions by schematic letters of the appropriate sort.

The resulting sequence may still contain content expressions, but not repeated content expressions.

Step VI.

(A) If the argument is deemed conclusive, determine whether the conclusiveness rests solely on formal considerations or on some connection between some of the remaining content expressions. If the conclusiveness rests solely on formal considerations, replace the remaining content expressions with individual variables or schematic letters of the appropriate sort. If the conclusiveness rests on some connection, leave the expressions involved in that connection and replace only the other content expressions by individual variables or schematic letters of the appropriate sort.
(B) If the argument is deemed defeasible, no further replacement is appropriate.

Step VII. Take the resulting sequence of statement schemata as the warrant of the argument.

Does our procedure effectively make Hitchcock's judgment calls for identifying the warrant? After symbolizing the argument, identifying the repeated content expressions which are not contained as components or subformulas within other repeated content expressions is a matter of inspecting the symbolization. This allows us easily to make the first judgment call. Our method then calls for replacing these widest repeated content expressions with individual variables or schematic letters of the appropriate type. Where there are multiple repeated content expressions, again inspecting the symbolization identifies them. This lets us straightforwardly make the second judgment call.

What is the relation between identifying the warrant of an argument and determining the argument's connection adequacy? We hold that connection adequacy depends on the acceptability of the associated generalization of the warrant or, if the warrant contains schematic letters, of the associated generalization schemata. Hence, identifying the warrant is a significant early step in the evaluation process. How can we present an argument either that such an associated generalization is acceptable or unacceptable? Answering such a question lies beyond the scope of this paper. We intend top address that question in future inquiry.

References

Bergmann, M., Moor, J., & Nelson, J. (2014). *The logic book.* New York, NY: McGraw-Hill.

Govier, T. (2010). *A practical study of argument* (7th ed.). Belmont, CA: Wadsworth, Cengage Learning.

Hitchcock, D. (1985). Enthymematic arguments. *Informal Logic, 7*, 83–97.

Oesterle, J. (1961). The significance of the universal *ut nunc.* In J. A. Weisheipl (ed). *The Dignity of Science,* Washington, DC, pp. 27–38.

Rescher, N. (1977). *Dialectics: A controversy-oriented approach to the theory of knowledge.* Albany, NY: State University of New York Press.

Where Is Visual Argument?

Jens E. Kjeldsen

1 Audiences and the Reconstruction of Pictorial Argumentation

It has been argued that the reconstruction of pictorial and visual argumentation is especially problematic since pictures contain neither words nor precise reference to premises, nor do they have syntax or explicit conjunctions that coordinate premise and conclusions. Researchers have been critical of the speculative reconstruction of visual premises and arguments that are—they claim—absent, or cannot be known for sure to be present. So a central question becomes: Where is argument? Or rather, where is visual argument?

I propose that we should turn to the study of audience reception because if an audience actually perceives an argument when encountering an instance of visual communication, then surely an argument has been provided.

The first audience analysis is surely Aristotle's description of the various types of human character in the Rhetoric. However, in rhetorical research, qualitative empirical audience analyses are rare, and appear to be completely absent in argumentation studies. In the field of argumentation studies, some quantitatively empirical research has been performed; at the University of Amsterdam, for instance, researchers have conducted experimental research concerning the pragma-dialectical rules. These studies (van Eemeren et al. 2009, cf. van Eemeren et al. 2012) attempt to go beyond theorising about fallacies by examining how ordinary arguers actually view fallacious argumentative moves. Nonetheless, rhetorical argumentation research is, above all, text focused.

When rhetoricians actually discuss the audience, they are mostly concerned with the audience as theoretical or textual constructions. They examine the universal

J.E. Kjeldsen (✉)
Department of Information Science and Media Studies, University of Bergen,
5073 Bergen, Norway
e-mail: jens.kjeldsen@uib.no

F.H. van Eemeren and B. Garssen (eds.), *Reflections on Theoretical Issues in Argumentation Theory*, Argumentation Library 28,
DOI 10.1007/978-3-319-21103-9_8

audience (Perelman and Olbrechts-Tyteca 1971), the second persona (Black 1998), the audience constituted by the text (e.g. Charland 1987), the ignored or alienated audience (e.g. Wander 2013), or they theorise about the audience's cognitive processing of messages (Benoit and Smythe 2003).

Instead of limiting ourselves to such textual and theoretical approaches, I propose that research into rhetorical argumentation should more often examine the understandings and conceptualisation of the rhetorical audience. From mainly approaching audience as a theoretical construction to be examined textually and speculatively, we should pay more attention to qualitative exploration of actual audiences and users.

When discussing the audience, argumentation theorists mostly engage in discussions about the identity of the audience and the (im)possibility of determining its identity (Govier 1999, p. 183 ff.; Johnson 2013; Tindale 1992, 1999, 2013). Because it is difficult to define or locate the audience, aspirations to examine audiences are sometimes countered with the argument that such studies are futile because we cannot really know who the audience is.

Trudy Govier, for instance, in her book *The Philosophy of Argument*, questions the importance of the audience for the "understanding and evaluation of an argument". She introduces the concept of the "Noninteractive Audience—the audience that cannot interact with the arguer, and whose views are not known to him" (Govier 1999, p. 183).

The mass audience, which is probably the most typical audience in contemporary media society, is "the most common and pervasive example of a Noninteractive Audience". The views of this noninteractive and heterogeneous audience, Govier says, are unknown and unpredictable (Govier 1999, p. 187). This means that "trying to understand an audience's beliefs in order to tailor one's argument accordingly is fruitless" (Tindale 2013, p. 511). Consequently, "Govier suggests, it is not useful for informal logicians to appeal to audiences to resolve issues like whether premises are acceptable and theorists should fall back on other criteria to decide such things" (Tindale 2013, p. 511).

Ralph Johnson continues this line of reasoning, and proposes that a Noninteractive Audience is not only a problem for pragma-dialectics, as Govier suggests, but also for rhetorical approaches because it is not possible to know this type of audience. Johnson criticises the views of Chaim Perelman and Christopher Tindale, who hold that "the goal of argumentation is to gain the acceptance of the audience" (Johnson 2013, p. 544). Advising a speaker to adapt to the audience when constructing arguments, says Johnson, "is either mundane or unrealistic" (Johnson 2013, p. 544). It is unrealistic because we cannot truly grasp the concept of an audience as an objective reality.

Johnson is right in saying that grasping the concept of an audience, understanding and defining its identity, is a difficult matter. However, while this issue of the audience might be a problem for the speaker, it need not be so problematic for the researcher because the desire to determine the identity of the audience is, I think, not the most fruitful way toward an understanding of how rhetorical argumentation works. Desperately seeking the audience (cf. Ang 1991) is not the way forward.

I am *not* arguing that researchers should cease speculation about what an audience is, nor do I claim that speakers should refrain from defining their audience, and adapt their messages accordingly. But, I *am* arguing that the primary concern for scholars of rhetoric and argumentation should not be to determine the exact identity of the audience or to conclude whether or not an argument, or indeed any other instance of rhetoric, creates adherence.

What we should be more concerned with is *how* an argument or any rhetorical appeal is constructed, *how* it is audience-oriented, and—which is the main point of this paper—*how* it is received, interpreted, and processed—that is: how audiences actually respond to instances of rhetorical argumentation.

As pointed out by Schiappa (2008, p. 26): "We need to find out what people are doing with representations rather than being limited to making claims about what we think representations are doing to people." This requires a combination of close readings of rhetorical utterances, contextual analyses of the situation, and empirical studies of audience reception and response. This is why I have conducted reception studies of ads exploring the responses of focus groups to pictures and pictorially dominated ads.

2 Focus Group Studies

Through focus groups, I have attempted to establish if respondents perceive arguments in the advertisements, how they perceive them, and thereby explore the characteristics of visual argumentation. The three focus group interviews carried out for this essay were conducted in Norway in June 2014. The three groups consisted of six pensioners in their 70s, five young women aged 18–19, and four university students who did not know each other. The groups were selected in order to allow for variation in and breadth of knowledge and life situation.

The respondents were first introduced to each other and the focus group situation, and then asked to fill out a short survey with relevant personal information. It was then explained that I, as a researcher, was interested in hearing what they thought about the images I was about to show them. They were not told that I was particularly interested in visual argumentation. I explained that I would first show them five pictures, each for less than one minute, and requested that during this time they write five words or short sentences to describe the first thoughts that came to mind when they viewed each picture.

When this activity was completed, I instigated focus group conversations with open questions such as "What do you think when you see this picture", and then posed open follow-up questions such as "why?" or "how?" Pictures other than the one mentioned in this paper were shown to the respondents and discussed within

Fig. 1 Steimatzky book chain "Read more". Courtesy of: Shalmor Avnon Amichay/Y&R Interactive Tel Aviv

the focus groups. One of the advertisements I examined was this one, for the Israeli bookstore Steimatzky (see Fig. 1).[1]

When I asked a young group of women of the age of 18–19 what we could say about this ad, the first respondent immediately said:

> You lose intelligence by watching television, because your head becomes smaller by doing so (MI/AN 5:33).[2]

Another respondent followed up:

> I think that you become more focussed on watching television than on building knowledge by reading. So, according to the advertisement, the head will become smaller and smaller when watching television. However, it will become larger and larger by reading books. (MI/AN 05:55)

---

[1]I have previously written about several of these pictures (including the Steimatzky ad) shown to the respondents (cf. Kjeldsen 2012). This afforded the possibility to assess my previous interpretations of the visual argumentation in relation to the actual interpretation in the focus group situation.

[2]This code marks the focus group (MI), the identity of respondent (AN), and the timeslot in the tape and the transcription of the utterance.

When asked what the ad proposed, most of the young women answered: "Read instead of watching TV" (MI/AN: 07:21). When I asked *why* one should read, the young women generally responded something along the lines of either: "Because reading makes you smarter" (MI/MA 06:52), or "Because watching television makes you stupid" (MI/JA: 05.55). The first response of a group of pensioners in their 70s to my question "What can we say about this picture" was: "That you should read instead of watching television" (BR/UN 09:37).

When a respondent from a group of university students saw the ad, a male respondent immediately said, "it implies that if you don't read you will become stupid" (MA/BJ 08.32). I asked him why, and he answered: "Because he has such a little head compared to his body, it implies that if you do not read you will become stupid" (MA/BJ 10:25). When asked how one could infer that, he explained: "There is (only) room for a small brain inside, and a small brain figuratively means stupid" (MA/BJ 12:29). A young woman in the same focus group added to this explanation that she read the message of the ad: "more as *instead of watching television*, because he is sitting there with the remote control" (MA/XX11:55, my emphasis).

So, it is clear that the respondents actually decode an argument from the ad.

And it is clear that without the visuals the argument would not be constructed. Almost all respondents created the argument: "Read more, because if you don't, you will become stupid". Several, as we saw, added the circumstance: "Read more *instead of* watching television".

We should also note that the formulations of the argument do not say that *the person in the picture* should read more. In general, the respondents do not talk specifically about him, when reconstructing the argument. Instead they use general pronouns such as "*one* should read more", or "*you* should read more". They thus move from the specifics of the picture to a general level expressing a moral claim.

In general, then, in spite of the variation in and breadth of knowledge and life situation of the three groups, the respondents made the same kind of cognitive moves, and there was no obvious difference in the processing between the young girls, the students, or the pensioners.

3 Pragmatic Decoding

It is obvious that the respondents construct the term "stupid" from the visual representation of the little head. In general, it seems possible to visually evoke adjectives such as big, small, stupid, and the like. At the same time, we would probably be inclined to say that, because of their lack of syntax and grammar, images are incapable of evoking conjunctions that connect premises in an argument to create the necessary causal movements for an argument to be established. What do conjunctions such as "therefore", "hence", and "then" look like?

As we have seen, respondents do actually use conjunctions such as "then" and "therefore" both explicitly and implicitly. They also use formulations saying the visual elements "imply" certain conclusions. Furthermore, the respondents explicitly mention the adversative conjunction "instead of". Like the other conjunctions, the term "instead of", and the way it is used to connect premises, is neither in the caption "read more", nor represented directly in the picture.

So, where do the conjunctions come from? In making sense of the three central elements in the ad—the caption "read more", the little head, and the person's sitting position with the remote—a connection has to be made. In light of the advertising genre, the most relevant and plausible connection would be argumentative conjunctions.

This kind of search for argumentative meaning is clear in several of the respondents' interpretations. Take the pensioner, who commented on the Steimatzky ad: "That you should read instead of watching television" (BR/UN 09:37). When I asked her to elaborate, the woman continued:

> Well, if it is an advertisement for a bookstore, then they obviously want to give a message saying that he needs to read more, right? And then, where is the message in that picture? That's got to mean that his head is so small, that he needs to fill it up" (BR/UN, 09:37)

It is clear from this that she is not only searching to make sense of the ad by connecting verbal, visual, and contextual elements. She is also presupposing that the message has a persuasive character. Because of the imperative mood in the caption, she immediately assumes that "read more" is the claim, and she naturally proceeds by looking for the reason. Her brief elaboration illustrates two things.

Firstly, the reasoning of the pensioner illustrates that she, as an audience member, is active in an exploratory kind of mental labour while looking for the meaning and assumed argument in an image. This mental exploring is not incidental, but is generally performed in accordance with pragmatic rules of speech acts (Austin 1973; Searle 1969), relevance (Wilson and Sperber 2012), and implicature (Grice 1989)—all theories that we know have been successfully applied to the study of argumentation in, for instance, pragma-dialectics (e.g. Eemeren and Grootendorst 1983; Henkemans 2014). People obviously make inferences, and are consciously aware that the ads are trying to convey messages, even arguments. And they clearly try to reconstruct these arguments. This is also in accordance with the cognitive response approach to persuasion, which emphasises that people are active information processors who generate cognitive responses to messages (Greenwald 1968; Petty and Cacioppo 1996, p. 225 ff.). Cognitive response theory argues that when people encounter a persuasive message, such as the ads analysed in this paper, they will relate the information in the message to their pre-existing knowledge about the topic. This means, as I will illustrate below, that a person engaging with a rhetorical utterance will "consider a substantial amount of information that is *not found in the communication itself*" (Petty and Cacioppo 1996, p. 225, my emphasis).

One of the reasons that pictures in general are able to elicit similar arguments in different viewers is the shared cultural knowledge and common awareness of specific situations or contexts of these viewers that allow them to (re)construct similar arguments (cf. Kjeldsen 2007, 2012). Generally, this requires a particular kind of situation that leads the viewer to perceive the image as a piece of argumentation, and that it provides enough cues to let the viewer construct the argument. Situations or circumstances that help the viewer evoke the arguments must entail a context of opposition (cf. van Eemeren et al. 2002, p. 8 ff.). Establishing claims, premises and their connection through such contextual knowledge is more readily done in ongoing debates and in specific, well-defined situations. In such circumstances, the visual will be able to tap into existing and already proposed arguments.

This kind of contextual decoding, however, is more difficult in commercial advertising, where the viewer is usually unable to connect the particular text to any specific circumstances, debates or discourses. Instead, as we have seen in the example of the Steimatzky ad, the viewers of advertisements will primarily base their reconstruction of the argument on their knowledge of the general genre and its aim: to sell products and to promote brands (cf. Kjeldsen 2012).

In the Steimatzky ad, as in many other commercial advertisements, the use of conspicuous visual tropes (e.g. the small head) attracts attention through visual strangeness, and guides the viewer towards the intended inference. Tropes and figures are constituted by certain recognisable patterns: a metaphor requires viewing something in light of something else; a contrast requires opposites. Thus, the figurative presentation controls the interpretation by letting the viewer notice "an artful deviation in form that adheres to an identifiable template" (McQuarrie and Mick 1996). This kind of augmented control is possible (Philips and McQuarrie 2004, p. 114)

> because the number of templates is limited, and because consumers encounter the same template over and over again, they have the opportunity to learn a response to that figure. That is, through repeated exposure over time consumers learn the sorts of inference operations a communicator desires the recipients to undertake [...]. Because of this learning, rhetorical figures are able to channel inferences.

Rhetorical figures may thus function argumentatively by directing the viewer's attention towards certain elements in the advertisement and offering patterns of reasoning. This guides the viewer towards an interpretation with certain premises that support a particular conclusion (cf. Kjeldsen 2012, p. 243 f).

Secondly, and in accordance with cognitive response theory, the reasoning of the pensioner illustrates that much more is going on in the reception of this kind of visual argumentation than can be expressed by stating only the premises and conclusion of the argument. The picture, so to speak, has a thickness and condensation that holds much more than the content of these brief assertions.

4 Thickness and Condensation

It is an important characteristic of predominantly visual argumentation that it allows for a symbolic condensation that prompts emotions and reasoning in the beholder. In the focus group of students, for instance, a young woman commented on the ad in this way:

Fig. 2 Ad for the tram in Oslo: "Unngå pinlige øyeblikk" ("Avoid embarrassing moments")

> If you do not read, you will become a narrow-minded couch potato—non-thoughtful. He is not exactly sitting in a position, which is considered very flattering, intellectual, positive. The whole position is connected with a sick person (MA/SI 11:34).

The basic argument: "Read more, because if you do not read, you will become stupid" is clearly present in this comment, but the interpretation involves much more. Let me illustrate the significance of this visual surplus-meaning with a Norwegian ad for the tram system in Oslo (see below, Fig. 2). The ad shows a scene from the tram. The light blue box in the upper left has the same appearance as a ticket for the tram; however, the text reads: "Avoid embarrassing moments. Buy a ticket". At the bottom of the ad the text reads: "There are no excuses for dodging the fare (We are intensifying our controls)".

Most respondents summed up the argument of this ad something like this: "Buy a ticket, and you will avoid an unpleasant situation" (MV/MA 48:43). We could state the argument like this: "You should buy a ticket, *because* it will let you avoid an unpleasant situation" However, if we reduce visual arguments to only these kind of context-less, thin premises, we also limit ourselves to putting forward only the skeleton of the rhetorical utterance instead of the full body. We reconstruct, in a sense, a lifeless argument.

In contrast to this, it quickly became obvious, when I interviewed people about the ads that much more was going on. We see that the stating of the premises and the reconstruction of the argument is embedded in a much thicker understanding of the depicted situation, and of similar situations and emotions evoked by the ad.

We discover that one of the benefits of visual or multimodal argumentation is that they provide what I call *thick representations*, a full sense of the situation, making an integrated, simultaneous appeal to both the emotional and the rational (Kjeldsen 2012, 2015). One respondent said:

> Well, they are obviously playing on the embarrassment of getting caught when not having a ticket. The way you shrivel up when the inspector comes (MV/BJ 48:43).

He later continued, saying: "You try to hide a little, you want to sink into the ground; because it is so embarrassing to get caught, you make yourself as little as possible" (MV/BJ 48:43). Another respondent elaborated even more on what she felt the ad represented (MI/AN 31:15):

> I am thinking that the person, the little man, has sneaked on. And when there is a ticket inspection, you always end up with those embarrassing situations, those looks, and you become embarrassed. Because it says, the text, "Avoid embarrassing moments. Buy tickets". And then you would avoid being tense and getting caught. And there are a lot of other people around that might think "Oh well, he got caught now"; and then you begin to think strange thoughts about the person that got caught.

The image clearly evokes imagined or previous experiences of embarrassment connected with fare-dodging on public transport. One person recounted that she herself had witnessed a "grown man" seemingly well enough off to pay the fare, but he still got caught without a ticket (MA/SI 48:43). Another vividly told about his fear and shame when he himself almost got caught without a ticket. All these descriptions and evoked emotions are, in fact, relevant parts of the argument. The more you feel the embarrassment, the more persuasive the argument will be. This, however, does not mean that the contribution of the image—or the ad as such—is just psychological and irrational persuasion.

It is true in this case that the argument is more or less fully expressed by words in the text in the upper-left corner, which reads "Avoid embarrassing moments. Buy a ticket". However, the premises created by these words alone lack the full sense of situation and embarrassment experienced by the respondents, and expressed when they talk about the ad.

So, if we limit ourselves to reconstructions of the argument with short premise-conclusion assertions found only in textual analyses, we will only get part of the argument expressed multimodally in the ad. Because the more I feel the embarrassment, the more forceful the argument is, and the more correct the argument actually is because the feeling of embarrassment is an important part of the argument. If you do not really feel the embarrassment, then you have not really understood the argument, since the good reason offered to buy a ticket is the possibility of avoiding an unpleasant feeling. Of course one could attempt to express this in writing by saying something like: “You should buy a ticket, because it will allow you to avoid a *very* unpleasant situation”. However, adding modal modifiers to the premises does not truly capture the sense of embarrassment offered by the visual parts of the ad, and it is not likely to evoke the same kind of memories and full descriptions that the image clearly evoked in the respondents.

5 Conclusion

The point of the focus group analysis was neither to claim that the respondents’ interpretations are “the correct interpretations”, nor to claim that other audiences will necessarily interpret the ads in the exact same way—even though this is what the focus group interviews clearly suggest. The point is simply to show that the ads invite the construction of a specific argument, and that the respondents generally inferred the intended meaning (cf. Hall 1993).

Much more could be said about the ads and reception analyses of visual argumentation. My studies of these and other ads, for instance, also suggest that the active interpretation of respondents evolves to an active form of arguing back, when images are seen to claim something about which the respondents disagree. However, even though this has only been a very brief account of a small part of the focus group studies carried out, hopefully a few things have become clear:

Firstly, it is clear that audiences are cognitively involved in interpreting the meaning of pictures and multimodal utterances. In this rhetorical involvement, audiences actively reconstruct arguments from pictures. They not only reconstruct the premises of an argument, but also the conjunctions that connect these premises.

Secondly, it is also clear that audiences can and do move argumentatively from the specific content in a picture to more general moral assertions.

Thirdly, the audiences’ reconstructions of the arguments as (thin) premises are generally embedded in a condensed, thick understanding of situations, experiences, and emotions that is invoked by the picture and influence the character and force of the argument.

So, where is visual argument? It is obviously present. It is found in argumentative situations, and we can locate it not only in images, but also in the minds of audiences. A place I believe we should look into more frequently.

References

Ang, I. (1991). *Desperately seeking the audience*. New York: Routledge.

Austin, J. L. (1973 [1962]). *How to do things with words*. Oxford: Oxford University Press.

Black, E. 1998. The second persona. In J. Lucaites, C. M. Condit, & S. Caudill (Eds.), *Contemporary rhetorical theory: A reader* (pp. 331–340). New York: Guilford.

Benoit, W. L., & Smythe, M. J. (2003). Rhetorical theory as message reception. A cognitive response approach to rhetorical theory and criticism. *Communication Studies, 54*(1), 9–114.

Charland, M. (1987). Constitutive rhetoric: The case of the *Peuple Québécois*. *Quarterly Journal of Speech, 73*(2), 133–150.
Eemeren, F. V, Garssen, G., & Meuffels, B. (2012). The Extended Pragma-Dialectical Argumentation Theory Empirically Interpreted. In F. H. van Eemeren, & B. Garssen (Eds.), *Topical themes in argumentation theory. Twenty exploratory studies* (pp. 239–255). Dordrecht: Springer.
Eemeren, F. V., Grootendorst, R., & Snoeck Henkemans, F. (2002). *Argumentation: Analysis, evaluation, presentation*. Mahwah: L. Erlbaum.
Eemeren, F. V., Garssen, G., & Meuffels, B. (2009). *Fallacies and Judgments of Reasonableness. Empirical research concerning the pragma-dialectical rules*. Amsterdam: Springer.
Eemeren, F. V., & Grootendorst, R. (1983). *Speech acts in argumentative discussions*. Dordrecth: Foris publications.
Govier, T. (1999). *The philosophy of Argument*. Newport News, VA: Vale Press.
Greenwald, A. G. (1968). Cognitive learning, cognitive response to persuasion, and attitude change. In A. G. Greenwald, T. C. Brock, & T. M. Ostrom (Eds.), *Psychological foundation s of attitudes*. New York: Academic Press.
Grice, H. P. (1989 [1975]). Logic and conversation. In H. P. Grice (Ed.), *Studies in the Way of Words* (pp. 22–40). Cambridge: Harvard University Press.
Hall, S. (1993). Encoding/decoding. In S. During (Ed.), *The cultural studies reader*. London and New York: Routledge.
Henkemans, A. F. S. (2014). Speech act theory and the study of argumentation. *Studies in Logic, Grammar and Rhetoric, 36*(49), 41–58.
Johnson, R. (2013). The role of audience in argumentation from the perspective of informal logic. *Philosophy and Rhetoric, 46*(4), 533–549.
Kjeldsen, J. E. (2015). The rhetoric of thick representation: How pictures render the importance and strength of an argument salient. *Argumentation*. doi:10.1007/s10503-014-9342-2.
Kjeldsen, J. E. (2012). Pictorial argumentation in advertising: Visual tropes and figures as a way of creating visual argumentation. In F. H. van Eemeren, & B. Garssen (Eds.), *Topical themes in argumentation theory. Twenty exploratory studies* (pp. 239–255). Dordrecht: Springer.
Kjeldsen, J. E. (2007). Visual argumentation in Scandinavian political advertising: A cognitive, contextual, and reception oriented approach. *Argumentation and Advocacy, 43*, 124–132.
McQuarrie, E. F., & Mick, D. G. (1996). Figures of rhetoric in advertising language. *Journal of Consumer Research, 22*, 424–437.
Petty, R. E., & Cacippo, J. T. (1996). *Attitudes and persuasion. Classic and contemporary approaches*. Boulder, Colorado: Westview Press.
Perelman, C. & L. Olbrechts-Tyteca. (1971 [1969/1958]). *The new rhetoric. A treatise on argumentation*. Paris: University of Notre Dame Press.
Philips, B. J., & McQuarrie, E. F. (2004). Beyond visual metaphor: A new typology of visual rhetoric in advertising. *Marketing theory, 4*, 113–136.
Schiappa, E. (2008). *Beyond representational correctness. Rethinking criticism of popular media*. Albany: State University Press.
Searle, J. (1969). *Speech acts. An essay in the philosophy of language*. Cambridge: Cambridge University Press.
Wander, P. (2013). The third persona: An ideological turn in rhetorical theory. In B. L. Ott & G. Dickinson (Eds) (red.), *The Routledge Reader in Rhetorical Criticism* (pp. 604–623). New York: Routledge.
Wilson, D., & Sperber, D. (2012). *Meaning and relevance*. Cambridge: Cambridge University Press.
Tindale, C. (2013). Rhetorical argumentation and the nature of audience: Toward an understanding of audience—Issues in argumentation. *Philosophy and Rhetoric, 46*(4), 508–532.
Tindale, C. (1999). *Acts of arguing: A rhetorical model of argument*. Albany: SUNY Press.
Tindale, C. (1992). Audiences, relevance, and cognitive environments. *Argumentation, 6*, 177–188.

Part III
Evaluation of Argumentation

Missed Opportunities in Argument Evaluation

Daniel H. Cohen

1 Introduction: An Odd Asymmetry

There is a curious asymmetry in how we evaluate arguments. On the one hand, it is taken as fair game to point out obvious objections to a line of reasoning that have not been anticipated. Arguments that fail to do this are not as strong as they could be and should be. Elementary critical thinking textbooks and advanced argumentation theorists all agree that the failure to criticize an argument for failing to take relevant and available negative information into account would be critically culpable. Of course, arguments that fail to take relevant and available *positive* information into account are also not as strong as they could be and should be, but those same voices are curiously silent on this omission. The failure to criticize arguments this way is so routine that it largely goes unnoticed, and when it is noticed, it is apparently regarded as acceptably strategic. Following Finocchiaro 2013 (p. 136), the question can be put very simply: Why are unanticipated objections culpable omissions but missed opportunities are not?

In the first part of this paper I propose an explanation for the presence of this odd asymmetry, including how it arises, why it can seem natural and comfortable from one perspective, why it can seem artificial and discordant from another perspective, and why the difference has not even registered on other perspectives. In the next sections, I offer a partial justification for this asymmetry by reference to arguers' dialectical roles and obligations which put significant roadblocks in the way of offering positive and constructive criticism. Strategies are then proposed for overcoming them, leading, first, to the conclusion that the virtues approach to argumentation evaluation is especially well suited to accommodating and explaining the phenomena in question. However, those same considerations also lead to the conclusion that the fundamental insight of virtue argumentation—that a good

D.H. Cohen (✉)
Department of Philosophy, Colby College, Waterville, USA
e-mail: dhcohen@colby.edu

F.H. van Eemeren and B. Garssen (eds.), *Reflections on Theoretical Issues in Argumentation Theory*, Argumentation Library 28,
DOI 10.1007/978-3-319-21103-9_9

argument is one in which the arguers argue well—has to be qualified in two substantial ways. The crucial analytic element for understanding this largely invisible problem about evaluating arguments is recognizing that the critical evaluation of *arguments* cannot be independent of the critical evaluation of *arguers*—all the arguers, not just the proponents and opponents. And, in addition, the value of an argument is not simply the sum of the values contributed by its arguers, so virtuous arguers can be only a necessary but not sufficient condition for good arguments. Finally, the entire exercise forces us to rethink what we mean be a good argument.

2 The Curious Incident of the Missed Gambit

Let me begin with a parable about a noble chess player.

> It is the final match of a chess tournament between two intensely competitive grandmasters. One is an older, distinguished player who has devoted his whole life to the game of chess and the pursuit of the championship. He has risen to the highest ranks in the world, but he has fallen just shy of the top on several previous occasions. This may be his last chance. His opponent is much younger, but the defending champion. She is brilliant, even audacious, but sometimes erratic – a daredevil of a player who managed to control her bold style of play long enough in the previous tournament to take the crown. The series of games leading up to this one has included some epic games that will be studied and analyzed for years to come. It has also included some stinkers, games marred by rash attacks, sloppy defenses, and failed gambits. Now, at a crucial juncture in play, the young champion is about to make a daring but in fact very flawed move. The older player sees, leans forward, and whispers, "Don't do it." He pauses, then whispers again, this time through tears in his eyes because he realizes what he is doing. "Don't do it. You have a much stronger move over there. It will be a better game, a more interesting game, a *worthy* game."

I am afraid for how the story must end, but what are we to say of this chess master? That he was very, very good at chess, of course, but also that he knew chess intimately, and had an immense respect for the game, and perhaps, in the end, he may have loved chess too nobly. His love of chess got in the way of his skill at chess. A noble chess master, certainly; a great chess player, perhaps; but not a champion.

And now imagine the same scenario between two arguers, rather than two chess players: two eminent philosophers in debate, perhaps, or two heavyweight politicians arguing in a public forum. What are we to say of noble arguers who respect argumentation so much that they strengthen their opponents' hands? Would we really want to say that they are not good arguers *on that account*?

I will assume that we do *not* want to say that, so we are left with this question: why isn't the argumentative counterpart to "missing the good move" on any of the standard lists of fallacies? Part of the reason may be that it does not fit neatly into the standard conception of a fallacy: it is not an "error in reasoning" (both Kelley 2013 and Copi et al. 2011, the two best-selling introductory logic textbooks are among the many texts that use this exact phrase to define a fallacy). Neither is it a "procedural violation", a "mistake" in reasoning, nor a "form of argument that gains assent without justification" (van Eemeren and Grootendoorst 1984, 1992; Govier 1987, 2010). However, it arguably does qualify as a "discussion move which damages the quality of an argument" (van Eemeren et al. 1996) and it certainly counts as "a common mistake… that people tend not to notice" (Govier 2010).

I think we have something like the case of "Silver Blaze," the one that Sherlock Homes solved because of the curious incident of the dog in the night, namely that the dog didn't bark: it was an inside job. And just to be clear: we argumentation theorists are the dog that didn't bark here.

3 Explaining the Asymmetry: The "D.A.M. Model"

The most important and most easily identifiable factor at work in establishing and sustaining this asymmetry is the "Dominant Adversarial Model"—the DAM account—for arguments. When we conceptualize arguments as *essentially* agonistic, we cast our fellow interlocutors as opponents and enemies rather than as colleagues or partners in argumentation. Often they are in fact just that, of course, because some arguments really are zero-sum scenarios, so your gain is my loss, but since not all arguments are like that, the agonistic element is not in fact an essential element.

If an argument is conceptualized as essentially adversarial and elevated to something like verbal warfare, then two principles of action take hold. First, no holds are barred in all-out war. All is fair, so withholding suggestions for improving your opponent's argument is completely justified from a strategic point of view. Second, pointing out favorable but missed lines of thought would be giving aid and comfort to the enemy. It is not simply that withholding that information is advisable and permitted, but that providing that information is all but forbidden because it would be tantamount to treason! We may not have to think of arguments as wars but it can be very hard to escape the ways of thinking imposed by that DAM account.

I think that goes a long way to explaining why we do not expect arguers to offer that kind of helpful criticism of their fellow arguers' arguments, but it does not explain why the topic has been so consistently ignored by the textbooks and literature of critical thinking and argumentation theory. We also need to explain this curious incident of the theorists who have not barked at the failure to offer constructive criticism.

Part of an answer comes from the tension between trying to respect critical neutrality and offering constructive, i.e., *helpful,* criticism. Outside critics who suggest better lines of attack transgress in two ways: they become part of the argument rather than remaining safely on the level of meta-argumentation and in so doing, they violate the principle of critical impartiality. In addition, strengthening can distort an argument in dialectically unjustified ways (Aikin and Casey 2014). That lands us in a dilemma:

Q: If neither the proponents nor the opponents in arguments, nor impartial critics observing it from outside, are in an appropriate position to give that kind of positive criticism, who is?

The best way to analyze and understand this phenomenon is through the different roles in arguments and the different expectations that accompany those roles.

4 The Roles Roles Play

Arguing is not a single, homogenous activity. There are many different ways to participate in an argument. Arguing for a standpoint is not the same as arguing against it, which is not the same as raising objections to its supporting line of reasoning. The different roles have different goals, they require different skill-sets, and they follow different rules which generate different expectations.

The roles we assume in an argument are fluid, which makes separating them difficult. They often overlap in messy ways practically, functionally, and temporally. We may start out in the proponent's primary logical task of arguing for a position but then find ourselves in the subsidiary, dialectical task of *defending* it against objections or *revising* it in light of those objections, and then we might end up as an opponent arguing *against* a contrary position. Similarly, objecting to a pro-argument, another opposition role, presupposes argument evaluation, a critic's activity. As van Radziewsky 2013 notes, the transitions are continual, effortless, and seamless. Still, no matter how intertwined the roles may be in practice, they are conceptually distinguishable in theory, and making those distinctions has payoffs for analyzing arguments.

Judges, third parties arbiters, audiences, and kibitzers should also be counted as participants in an argument if only because biased judges, incompetent referees, meddlesome kibitzers, and bad audiences are all quite capable of ruining an argument. Since they do contribute to fully satisfying, optimally successful arguments (in the sense of Cohen 2008, 2013), they have some stake in the outcome of the argument. Consonant with the DAM account, these roles can be referred to collectively as the "non-combatants" in an argument, and there is some merit in that terminology: it highlights their subsidiary roles and secondary involvement, and insightfully imports from the cluster of concepts surrounding wars the idea that there could be "collateral damage" from arguments. For the present purposes, however, it will be better to think of them as more like a supporting cast: extras who have their own parts to play and their own contributions to make (following Cohen 2013).

One of the roles that arguers routinely fill is that of being a critic, an argument evaluator. As a first pass, we might say that arguers engage *in* the argument while argument evaluators make judgments *about* the argument, and thus are actually operating at the level of meta-argumentation. This is not a distinction that will stand up to close critical scrutiny, but it serves as a start for the purposes at hand.

The transitions between argument roles include transitions into and out of each and every one these non-combatant or supporting roles. Arguers can and do assume the roles of interested audiences, disinterested judges and juries, and even uninterested spectators. Above all else, arguers inevitably and routinely become argument critics. What makes this so important is that argument evaluation is supposed to be a neutral activity, so stepping into that role involves assuming an air of critical detachment attachment and impartiality, even for the most partisan participants. More often than not, of course, it is a hollow pretense, but the presumption is still there. The problem is that even the assumption of impartiality seems incompatible with aiding either side in a dispute while pointing out missed opportunities is *constructive* criticism. It helps its target. It appears to be at odds with the role of argument evaluator. "*I'm the judge. It's not my job to provide the arguers with their arguments.*"

5 Rules for Roles

That brings us to the duties and principles governing argument roles and the expectations that they generate.

Missed opportunities are failures on the part of proponents, the arguers constructing positive arguments for some conclusion. They are sins of omission, as it were, rather than sins of commission, and so they may be less noticeable, but since they are ways that arguments fall short, it is incumbent on argument evaluators to identify them. The failure to point them out is a critical failure, not a partisan arguer's failure. What emerges, then, is a more or less natural division of labor and division of expectations for the participants in arguments:

- *Proponents* are expected to find good reasons for their positions, so they can be criticized when they do not.
- *Opponents* are not expected to point those reasons out for the proponents when they don't present such reasons, so they cannot be criticized for remaining silent.

If neither the proponents nor the opponents in arguments can be expected to point out this argumentative failure, who can? This is a problem:

- *Critics* are expected to note missed opportunities, so they should be open to criticism for their silence on that score.
- *Judges, juries,* and *audiences* do have critical roles, so they can be expected to take note of missed opportunities, but they are not expected to point them out and, in many cases, expected to remain neutral, i.e., not to interfere and to refrain from pointing them out.

For most observers and non-principals in arguments, there are either no expectations for positive contributions or else positive expectations for no-contributions. They are like referees in a sporting event: the only time they get much attention is for unwanted contributions to the action.

Unfortunately, a workable schema of expectations for proponents, opponents, observers, and critics cannot be that simple. On the one hand, the expectations of those engaged in the critical assessment of arguments conflict with imperatives of impartiality and non-interference. Critics are supposed to be above the fray rather than active participants in the argument. On the other hand, the argument roles are fluid and everyone involved in arguments is constantly moving in and out of the critic's role.

We have reached an impasse. Were it not for the expectations of impartiality and non-interference, critics could be held responsible for failing to note missed opportunities, but there *are* those expectations of impartiality. Since critics are the *only* ones from whom we can positively expect that criticism, there is no place from which that kind of assessment can be made. And yet there are occasions when that kind of critical assessment really does need to be made. What we need to address, then, is the question of when the imperative for impartial but thorough critical assessment can outweigh the prohibitions against partisan non-interference.

One final complication further muddies the waters of the proposed schema of expectations: arguers are critics. The line between argumentation and meta-argumentation is so permeable as to virtually disappear: an argument for a position is simultaneously a meta-theoretic endorsement of that argument; the same is true for simply accepting that argument; on the other hand, *not* accepting an argument, whether by raising an objection or offering a counterargument, also implicates a meta-theoretic judgment, namely that the argument fails or that there is a stronger argument against it; conversely, most meta-argumentation evaluations can, and often ought, be included in the object-level argumentation (The inter-changeability of dialectical, rhetorical, and meta-argumentative approaches to argumentation is the over-arching thesis developed in Finocchiaro 2013). No matter their primary roles, all parties involved in any way in an argument also have the standing to be argument evaluators. Whether or not all critics are participants in arguments—and for the record, I do think there are good reasons to count them as such—all arguers are critics. That is a role participants cannot avoid.

Thus, arguers are subject to the impossible imperatives imposed by the contradictory expectations that arise from the complication of having to fill different roles in arguments.

It will prove helpful to look at this problem through the lens provided by virtue argumentation theory.

6 Overcoming Obstacles

The problem comes down to finding space from which to provide positive and constructive critical engagement. Positive and constructive critical engagement is a complex concept whose constituents do not fit together easily. On the one hand, constructive critical engagement is easy enough: pointing out fallacies, missteps, and other errors qualifies, but those common critical moves are not positive, in the relevant sense. They can be constructive insofar as they strengthen the critiqued argument by pointing out its weaknesses, but not by pointing out greater alternative strengths. On the other hand, positive and constructive critical evaluation is also conceptually unproblematic: it is the kind of criticism that can be safely offered from a distance without worrying about violating neutrality, rather than as a real-time, on-site engagement. The challenge is to combine them.

The main culprit is the DAM account of argumentation. It creates the asymmetry in allowable and expected criticism by making adversariality the essential, defining feature of argumentation and defining all of the roles within arguments accordingly, viz., by their role in the *conflict*. Even within that framework, however, arguers are constantly moving in and out of the different argumentative roles and occupying several roles at the same time. An arguer is a very "divided self." Because of that, proponents, opponents, and neutral third-parties all have possibilities for *positive and constructive critical engagement*, but they all have significant obstacles to overcome.

The obstacle for proponents is practical: critical self-evaluation is just plain hard. It is always more difficult to spot weaknesses in arguments with which one agrees, and apart from some special circumstances (e.g., lawyers representing clients, insincerity, and *reductio* argumentation), proponents tend to agree with their own arguments. The epistemic and cognitive blind-spots that prevented an arguer from seeing the missed opportunity in the first place may well still be in place, so, to use Wittgenstein's example, self-critique is often no better than checking a news-story about which one is skeptical by buying another copy of the same newspaper (Wittgenstein 1953, §265). Moreover, we can be undone by our own skills in argumentation here because the better we are at giving reasons for our beliefs—a skill that encompasses both prior deliberation and its often indistinguishable counterpart, *post facto* rationalization—the harder it will be to detect some flaws in our reasoning, especially the difference between reasoning and rationalization (Kornblith 1999, pp. 277, 278).

There are a couple of strategies for proponents to get around the obstacle to noting when they themselves miss an opportunity. Critical self-reflection may work to some extent. We exercise different skills-sets in constructing arguments than we do in evaluating arguments, so if we engage in the salutary but difficult task of turning a critical eye to our own arguments, the new perspective might help us notice things about our argument that were not as visible in constructing the argument. That is, we can take advantage of our ability to transition between argumentative roles. Of course, merely exchanging a proponent's hat for a critic's hat will do nothing to ameliorate any of the problems with personal bias, skewed data selection, cognitive blind spots, or rationalization that may have caused the omission in the first place. Critical self-reflection does not come with any guarantees of success.

Despite the limitations of this particular attempt at argumentative multi-tasking, the strategy to try a new perspective on one's reasoning is well grounded. So, if there are limits to what we as proponents can do with our own arguments, call for re-enforcements: fellow proponents—teammates in argument, as it were—to provide a more detached critical perspective on our reasoning. Professionally, we all know this: it is the reason why we might ask friends to read drafts of our manuscripts. There may be more to be gained from more hostile criticism, but missed opportunities are more likely to be noted by allies. Again, there are limits to how well this can work, as well as to its real-time availability in specific arguments, but even the possibility does mean that the obstacle is not insuperable.

The apparent obstacle for critics to overcome is the principle of neutrality and non-interference, but there are actually two principles here: neutrality and non-interference are different critical values. They ground different imperatives and those imperatives apply to distinguishable roles in arguments. The principles are easily separated in the context of team sports. Spectators may be as partisan as they like but cannot interfere, During intra-squad scrimmages, coaches will interfere for training and pedagogical purposes but they will properly remain neutral. It is referees during actual games who must abide by both neutrality and non-interference. All those possibilities have counterparts in arguments.

The first category encompasses interested but not-directly involved spectators. The second is a little trickier but the obstacles to neutral critical involvement are more real than imagined. Any constructive contribution that helps one side will be resented by the other side and taken as a violation of neutrality. The asymmetry comes into especially high relief here because pointing out stronger lines of reasoning that are not presented rather than fallacious or mistaken parts of the existing, presented argument is pro-active, giving the appearance of partisanship. The appearance is deceiving. The distinct imperatives of neutrality and non-interference are not contradictory. After all, pointing out missed opportunities is one of the great joys of kibitzing (see Cohen 2014). Kibitzers are the back-seat drivers of arguments, those observers who offer unsolicited, unwanted, and, in the common conception, *unhelpful* advice. *Good* kibitzers, however, will offer good advice. Kibitzers who do not point out missed opportunities are not doing their jobs. Kibitzers are quite capable of being completely impartial, at least insofar as they can be equally annoying to everyone.

The obstacle for opponents is the hardest to overcome: the adversarial element in DAM argumentation. In zero-sum contests, opponents cannot reasonably be expected to help out their adversaries. Therefore, to do so is above and beyond the call of any of the imperatives deriving from one's role as an opponent – or any of the ancillary roles one assumes along the way in pursuing the opponent's primary goals. And yet, thinking back to the noble chess player, there is certainly something praiseworthy in helping out one's opponents. Johnson (2007) distinguishes "dialectical excellence" from the simple "dialectical adequacy" that comes with fulfilling one's duties; Finocchiaro (2013, p. 175) glosses this as a distinction between "dialectical virtues" and "dialectical obligations." What they are getting at is the idea of an action that is very good to do but not something that we are expected or required to do. Actions that have value independent of any imperatives are, in word, *supererogatory*.

7 Conclusion: Virtues and Values in Argumentation

The concept of supererogation poses severe theoretical challenges for argumentation theory, so despite its apparent attractiveness and applicability here, it should be resisted. In ethics, the concept applies to actions that are valuable but not obligatory. It implies that there are actions that are "*good enough*" to satisfy the demands of morality even though there are better actions available. Thus, although the only actions we are under any obligation to perform are good actions, the converse fails: there are good actions we are not obligated to perform. We have to detach the ethical concepts of *good actions* from actions we *ought to do.* What we end up with is two axes for moral evaluation: one scale for those good things which *ought to be*, and another for those whose goodness does not have consequences for mandated action.

The same consequences appear in when it comes to evaluating arguments. In order to make sense of the value of such positive constructive criticism as volunteering better lines of reasoning, we would need to acknowledge two different measures. Some virtues of arguers make them better arguers, but other virtues contribute to the quality of the *argument.* And it would seem that there could be a tension between the two sets of virtues. The virtues of the noble chess player leading to his supererogatory actions may well result in better games of chess, but they do so *at the expense of* his chess prowess. Wouldn't the same situation be entirely possible in arguments?

The answer is, yes, of course, but only if one is stuck within the DAM account of argumentation that identifies good arguers with winning arguers and good arguments with winning arguments. But those are linear, impoverished concepts. Their focus is too narrowly on the product, "arguments-1" in the terminology of O'Keefe (1977). They miss the larger picture. The DAM account cannot make any sense of arguers who walk away from an argument having had their positions changed, either by winning or losing or listening and learning, and declaring it a good argument on that account.

In the case of the noble chess player, it is not easy to reconcile the qualities of character—the *virtues*—behind his supererogatory acts and the skills that make him a good chess player because the measure of final appeal in evaluating skill at chess is success at chess, and the final measure of evaluating success at chess is winning chess games. The situation is not the same when it comes to argumentation. We can still say that the measure of final appeal in evaluating skill at argumentation is success in arguments, but we do not have to acquiesce to the DAM idea that the final measure of evaluating success at arguing is winning arguments. That is something worth an argument.

References

Aikin, S. & Casey, J. (2014). Don't feed the trolls: Straw men and iron men. In D. Mohammed & M. Lewinski (Eds.), *Virtues of argumentation; Proceedings of the 10th Ossa conference*. Windsor, ONT: Centre for Research in Reasoning, Argumentation, and Rhetoric & the University of Windsor (CD-ROM).

Cohen, D. H. (2014). Commentary on van Radziewsky's virtuous arguer. In D. Mohammed & M. Lewinski (eds.), *Virtues of argumentation; Proceedings of the 10th Ossa conference*. Windsor, ONT: Centre for Research in Reasoning, Argumentation, and Rhetoric & the University of Windsor (CD-ROM).

Cohen, D. H. (2013). Virtue, in context. *Informal Logic, 33*, 471–485.

Cohen, D. H. (2008). Now THAT was a good argument: On the virtues of arguments and the virtues of arguers. International conference: Logic, argumentation, and critical thinking. Santiago, Chile: Universidad Diego Portales.

Copi, Irving, Cohen, Carl, & McMahon, Kenneth. (2011). *Introduction to Logic* (14th ed.). New York: Pearson.

van Eemeren, F. H., et al. (1996). *The fundamentals of argumentation theory*. Mahwah, New Jersey: Lawrence Erlbaum Associates, Publishers.

van Eemeren, F. H., & Grootendoorst, R. (1992). *Argumentation, communication, and fallacies: A pragma-dialectical perspective*. Hillsdale, NJ: Lawrence Erlbaum Associates, Publishers.

van Eemeren, F. H., & Grootendoorst, R. (1984). *Speech acts in argumentative discussions*. Dordrecht, Holland: Foris Publications.

Finocchiaro, M. (2013). *Meta-argumentation: An approach to logic and argumentation theory*. London: College Publications.

Govier, T. (2010). *A practical study of argument* (7th ed.). Belmont, California: Wadsworth Publishing Co.

Govier, T. (1987). *Problems in argument analysis and evaluation*. Dordrecht, Holland: Forti Publications.

Johnson, R. (2007). Anticipating objections as a way of coping with dissensus. In D. Hitchcock (Ed.). *Dissensus and the search for common ground: Proceedings of the 8th international conference of the Ontario society for the study of argumentation*. Windsor, Ontario: OSSA.

Kelley, D. (2013). *The art of reasoning* (4th ed.). New York: W.W. Norton and Company.

Kornblith, H. (1999). Distrusting reason. In P. A. French & H. K. Wettstein (Eds.), *Midwest studies in philosophy 23*. Boston, Massachusetts: Blackwell.

O'Keefe, D. J. (1977). Two concepts of argument. *Journal of the American Forensic Association, 13*, 121–128.

van Radziewsky, K. (2013). The virtuous arguer: One person, four characters. In D. Mohammed & M. Lewinski (Eds.), *Virtues of argumentation; proceedings of the 10th Ossa conference*. Windsor, ONT: Centre for Research in Reasoning, Argumentation, and Rhetoric & the University of Windsor (CD-ROM).

Wittgenstein, L. (1953). *Philosophical investigations* (G. E. M. Anscombe, Trans.). Oxford: Basil Blackwell.

Ubiquity, Ambiguity, and Metarationality: Searching for the Fallacy of Composition

Maurice A. Finocchiaro

1 Introduction

In January 2015, on more than one occasion, the President of the United States, Barack Obama, made a proposal regarding higher education at community colleges. The idea was to enable everyone to attend for two years free of tuition charges, subject only to some requirements about good grades and progress toward graduation. The proposal was applauded by some, but criticized by others. One criticism was that the thinking underlying the proposal commits the fallacy of composition:

> The spirit behind President Obama's recent proposal to make community college free is understandable, but he has fallen victim to the fallacy of composition. He has made the mistake of believing that if one person benefits from an action, then everyone else who takes the same action will also benefit (Kelly and Kelly 2015).

My aim here and now is not to discuss this particular issue or to evaluate this criticism, but rather to provide a practical motivation for scholars of logic and argumentation theory to study the fallacy of composition. That is, I firmly believe that the scholarly study of the fallacy of composition can contribute to a better understanding of such public-policy issues.

In fact, this is not an isolated example. Another illustration involves the on-going great recession affecting the whole world: on this topic, Nobel Prize economist Paul Krugman has blamed its persistence on the austerity policies that have been adopted by most countries with developed economies, and he has suggested that austerity has been the result of thinking that one can apply to a national economy the same policies that work for its constituent parts, such as households and individual firms; and this manner of thinking presumably amounts to the fallacy of composition (Krugman 2013a, b). And on the issue of global warming, an author who happens

M.A. Finocchiaro (✉)
Department of Philosophy, University of Nevada-Las Vegas, Las Vegas, USA
e-mail: maurice.finocchiaro@unlv.edu

F.H. van Eemeren and B. Garssen (eds.), *Reflections on Theoretical Issues in Argumentation Theory*, Argumentation Library 28,
DOI 10.1007/978-3-319-21103-9_10

to be a professional philosopher has claimed that arguments for global warming typically involve an aggregation of temperatures from particular regions of the world, and "to group and average in this way is to commit the fallacy of composition" (Haller 2002, p. 50).

Furthermore, lest one should think that the motivation is merely practical, let me hasten to add a theoretical one. To study the fallacy of composition is a special case of a key and well-established branch of logic and argumentation theory. In fact, with some slight but not much exaggeration, one could reconstruct the past fifty years of this field largely as a series of footnotes to Hamblin's *Fallacies* (1970), and/or as a series of developments that culminate organically with Woods's *Errors of Reasoning* (2013). And, as we shall see, the fallacy of composition is special not only in the sense of being a specific case of fallacies, but also in the sense of being especially important.

2 The Ubiquity Thesis

The fallacy of composition seems to be unique among the fallacies, insofar as its frequency and importance have been widely claimed, perhaps more than for any other fallacy. For example, in 1826, in the *Elements of Logic*, Richard Whately explicitly named and discussed this fallacy, saying among other things:

> … Fallacy of Composition. There is no Fallacy more common, or more likely to deceive, than the one now before us: the form in which it is usually employed, is, to establish some truth, separately, concerning each single member of a certain class, and thence to infer the same of the whole collectively (Whately 1826, pp. 174–175).

Moreover, at least since the epoch-making contributions of John Maynard Keynes (who died in 1946), economists tend to regard the fallacy of composition as the single worst pitfall in economic reasoning. They also consider the exposure of it to be the greatest accomplishment of the modern science of economics. They deem the avoidance of it the most important lesson one can learn from this science. And such claims are easily found in the writings of economists of both the left and right wings of the ideological spectrum, such as Paul Samuelson and Henry Hazlitt.[1]

[1]See, for example, Hazlitt 1979; Nelson 1999; Samuelson 1955, pp. 9–10, 237, 273, 350, 374, 505, 550, 693; Samuelson and Nordhaus 1989, pp. 7–8, 183–184, 399–404, 666–667, 972, 993; and Wray 2009. Cf. Woods et al. 2000, pp. 262-83; Finocchiaro 2013a. For a revealing and emblematic piece of evidence, one may view a sculpture labeled "The Fallacy of Composition": it adorns an outside wall of the building of the Faculty of Economics at the University of Groningen, and it was created in 1988 to commemorate the 50th anniversary of the foundation of that Faculty and to celebrate Keynes's epoch-making contributions to the science of economics; cf. http://www.rug.nl/science-and-society/sculpture-project/sculpture1998?lang=en, consulted on July 24, 2012; I owe my first information about this sculpture to Govier (2007, 2009).

However, despite such attention and such claims, scholars in logic and argumentation theory seem not to have done much work on the fallacy of composition, although textbooks tend to pay lip service to it.

Sometimes this scholarly neglect of the fallacy of composition is explained and partly justified in terms of its rarity or infrequency. For example, in the 1973 edition of his textbook *Logic and Philosophy*, Howard Kahane has a brief discussion of this fallacy together with its reverse twin, the fallacy of division. Here are his revealing words:

> since non-trivial real life examples of these two fallacies … are unusual, textbook examples tend to be contrived or trivial. Thus one textbook writer gives as an example of the fallacy of composition the argument that '… since every part of a certain machine is light in weight, the machine as a whole is light in weight' (Kahane 1973, p. 244; cf. Copi 1972, pp. 96–98).

Obviously, this explanation of the scholarly neglect conflicts with the ubiquity thesis reported earlier. Thus, the question arises whether the fallacy of composition is common and important, or uncommon and unimportant. This is largely an empirical question, to be resolved by following an empirical approach.

However, such an empirical investigation cannot be conducted with a *tabula rasa*, for we need to be clear about what we mean by fallacy of composition, and also we need to examine real or realistic material which typically does not come with the label 'fallacy of composition' attached to it. In other words, we need to be mindful of the fact that observation is theory-laden, and that the examination of this material must be guided by some idea of what this fallacy means, and by some idea of what to do with the material under examination so as to test it for the occurrence of this fallacy. A brief elaboration of some of these ideas is thus in order.

3 The Ambiguity of 'Fallacy of Composition'

To begin with, it is obvious that we need some understanding of what is meant by fallacy of composition. Unfortunately, historical and contemporary writings on the topic contain three notions that are prima facie distinct, but tend to be confused with each other.

First, there is reasoning from premises using a term distributively to a conclusion using the same term collectively; for example, "because a bus uses more gasoline than an automobile, therefore all buses use more gasoline than all automobiles" (Copi 1968, p. 81). Second, there is reasoning from some property of the parts to the same property for the whole; for instance, "since every part of a certain machine is light in weight, the machine 'as a whole' is light in weight" (Copi 1968, p. 80). And thirdly, there is reasoning from some property of the members of a group to the same property for the entire group; the so-called tragedy of the commons can illustrate this notion, that is, "if one farmer grazes his cattle on the commons, that will be beneficial for him; therefore if all the farmers graze their cattle on the commons, that will be beneficial for all" (Govier 2009, p. 95).

Now, the association of the second and third notions with each other is very common. For example, here is how Kahane defines this fallacy: "the fallacy of composition is committed when we reason that some property possessed by every member of a class (or every part of a whole) also is possessed by that class (or whole)" (Kahane 1973, pp. 243–244); and he is far from the only one (cf. Cohen and Nagel 1934, p. 377; Salmon 2002, p. 371). On the other hand, the association of all three is relatively rare, but does occur. One example may be found in the following textbook definition:

> The fallacy of composition consists in treating a distributed characteristic as if it were collective. It occurs when one makes the mistake of attributing to a group (or a whole) some characteristic that is true only of its individual members (or its parts), and then makes inferences based on that mistake (Halverson 1984, p. 73).

4 The Metarationality Hypothesis

Besides this three-fold distinction and the ubiquity thesis, there is a third guiding idea that needs to be at least mentioned and tentatively stated before we proceed. In a previous work, I criticized textbook accounts of fallacies, and on its basis I formulated a problem and advanced an hypothesis. The problem was formulated in terms of the following questions: "do people actually commit fallacies as usually understood? That is, do fallacies exist in practice? Or do they exist only in the mind of the interpreter who is claiming that a fallacy is being committed?" (Finocchiaro 1980, p. 334; 1981, p. 15; 2005, p. 113).

Although these were not meant to be rhetorical questions, but rather open questions that required further investigation, it is perhaps unsurprising that some readers (e.g., Govier 1982) did view them as rhetorical questions. Moreover, I did express "the suspicion that logically incorrect arguments are not that common in practice, that their existence may be largely restricted to logic textbook examples and exercises" (Finocchiaro 1980, p. 333; 1981, p. 14; 2005, p. 111). Thus, some readers thought that I was claiming that fallacies are merely figments of critics' imagination, and "are in fact an illusion" (Jason 1986, p. 92; cf. Govier 1982).

Later, I tried to be more explicit and constructive about this issue when I elaborated a general approach to the study of fallacies. One element of that approach was connected to, and extracted from, Strawson's *Introduction to Logical Theory* and his notion of "the logician's second-order vocabulary" (Strawson 1952, p. 15); that notion was extended to include 'fallacy' terminology, "since it ordinarily occurs when someone wants to comment about some logical feature of a first-order expression of reasoning. This means that the best place to begin with in the study of fallacies, or at least a crucial phenomenon to examine, is allegations that fallacies are being committed" (Finocchiaro 1987, p. 264; 2005, p. 130).

In this vein, some elaborated the idea that fallacies are more like theoretical entities such as quarks in physics, rather than like concrete objects such as buttercups in everyday life (Grootendorst 1987; Woods 1988). This elaboration was a constructive suggestion and critical appreciation, and I am far from denying its viability.

However, I now believe that the project can be articulated more clearly, incisively, and constructively in light of the notion of meta-argumentation (cf. Finocchiaro 2013b, c). That is, I distinguish a meta-argument from a ground-level argument, and define the former as an argument about one or more arguments, or about argumentation in general. Then a ground-level argument can be defined as one about such things as natural phenomena, historical events, human actions, mathematical numbers, or metaphysical entities. A prototypical case of meta-argumentation is argument analysis, in which one advances and justifies an interpretive or evaluative claim about a ground-level argument.

What I am proposing is that we search for fallacies of composition primarily in meta-argumentation rather than ground-level argumentation. However, this is not meant in the sense that we should be looking for meta-arguments that commit the fallacy of composition, but rather that we try to find meta-arguments advancing explicit conclusions that some fallacy of composition has been committed, i.e., that some ground-level argument embodies or commits a fallacy of composition. The working hypothesis is then that, at least as a first approximation, the fallacy of composition is primarily a concept of meta-argumentation, useful in the context of understanding and/or assessing ground-level argumentation.

5 Hume's Critique of a Step in the Design Argument

Let us now begin our empirical search for real or realistic material pertaining to the fallacy of composition. A memorable example of the fallacy of composition occurs in the design argument for the existence of God, at least according to the critique advanced in Hume's *Dialogues Concerning Natural Religion*. This charge is only one objection in the complex and multi-faceted criticism which Hume formulates; and correspondingly, it affects only one particular step of the design argument. Thus, even if cogent, this Humean meta-argument is not the end of the story; nevertheless, it is a crucial element of the over-all evaluation of the design argument.

It should be noted that Hume interprets the design argument primarily as inductive and empirical. In so doing, he is trying to abide by the principle of charity, for if one were to reconstruct the design argument as deductive and a priori, then according to Hume it could not even get off the ground, since it would be trying to prove a factual matter—that God exists and created the universe—from a priori considerations; and this for Hume is an inherently impossible task.

One version of the design argument is this: the universe was created by an intelligent designer (called God), because the universe is like a machine, and machines are made by (human) intelligent designers. This is, of course, an argument from analogy.

Now Hume questions the analogical premise. How could one show that the universe is like a machine? Well, in Hume's own memorable words, spoken through the character Cleanthes, the answer is this:

> look round the world, contemplate the whole and every part of it: you will find it to be nothing but one great machine, subdivided into an infinite number of lesser machines, which again admit of subdivisions to a degree beyond what human senses and faculties can trace and explain. All these various machines, and even their most minute parts, are adjusted to each other with an accuracy which ravishes into admiration all men who have ever contemplated them. The curious adapting of means to ends, throughout all nature, resembles exactly, though it much exceeds, the productions of human contrivance—of human design, thought, wisdom, and intelligence (Hume 1947, p. 143).

This does seem to provide empirical, observational support for the claim that the universe is like a machine.

However, there are problems with this reasoning. In Hume's words, spoken through the character Philo:

> But can you think, Cleanthes, that your usual phlegm and philosophy have been preserved in so wide a step as you have taken, when you compared to the universe houses, ships, furniture, machines, and, from their similarity in some circumstances, inferred a similarity in their causes? Thought, design, intelligence, such as we discover in men and other animals, is no more than one of the springs and principles of the universe, as well as heat or cold, attraction or repulsion, and a hundred others, which fall under daily observation. It is an active cause, by which some particular parts of nature, we find, produce alterations on other parts. But can a conclusion, with any propriety, be transferred from parts to the whole? Does not the great disproportion bar all comparison and inference? From observing the growth of a hair, can we learn anything concerning the generation of a man? Would the manner of a leaf's blowing, even though perfectly known, afford us any instruction concerning the vegetation of a tree? (Hume 1947, p. 147)

Here, Hume is finding two things wrong with the subargument supporting the claim that the universe is like a machine. One problem is that although many parts of the universe are like machines, produced by intelligent design, many other parts (even when orderly arranged) are produced by natural causes such as attraction and heat. That is, Hume is charging that the subargument is a hasty generalization. But this is not the only problem; for even if all parts of the universe were machine-like, we could not be sure that the same would apply to the universe as a whole. In this second criticism, Hume is charging a fallacy of composition.

Hume's criticism of this subargument of the design argument is a meta-argument, and as such it is open to analysis, interpretation, and evaluation. Note, for example, that Hume's critical conclusion is based partly on an interpretation of the subargument in question, partly on a definition of the fallacy of composition, and partly on some evaluative principle. The interpretive claim is a reconstruction of this step of the design argument as transferring to the whole universe the same property which it claims to be able to observe in all (or many) of its parts; the property is that of being caused by some intelligent design. The evaluative principle is that it is illegitimate to transfer any such property from parts to whole in this case. Hume seems to give two reasons for this evaluative principle: first, the disproportion between such parts and whole is too great, presumably because the universe is infinite or indefinitely large; second, the transference from parts to the whole universe would be like reasoning from what happens to a human hair to what happens to a whole human body, or from what happens to a leaf to what happens to a whole tree. And this second reason amounts to a meta-argument from analogy, in which Hume argues that this subargument of the design argument is illegitimate because the subargument is an argument from analogy and is as illegitimate as the analogies from hair to human body or from leaf to tree.[2]

6 Concluding Remarks

My empirical and theory-laden search has found other important historical cases, which cannot be elaborated here, but which deserve a brief mention. One of these other examples is Aristotle's geocentric argument from natural motion: that the natural motion of terrestrial bodies is straight toward the center; and therefore the natural motion of the whole earth is straight toward the center. Galileo objected by arguing that if 'center' means center of the universe, Aristotle's argument begs the question; but if 'center' means center of the earth, the premise is empirically true, but the conclusion is inherently false. And the latter is a memorable counterexample that deserves further logical analysis, because it seems to undermine the formal validity of not only Aristotle's particular argument, but also of any argument from parts to whole (Aristotle, *On the Heavens*, 296b7-297a1; Galilei 1997, pp. 83–84; cf. Finocchiaro (1980, pp. 353–356; 2014b, pp. 59–63; 2015, pp. 31–32)).

A third case involves Robert Michels's argument for the so-called "iron law of oligarchy": that political parties inevitably become oligarchic even if they claim to have democratic aims; and therefore, a democratic society inevitably becomes oligarchic. Political scientist Robert Dahl objected that such reasoning fails because there is a crucial disanalogy between such parts and such a whole: a democratic society allows competition among its parts, but a particular party does not. Similarly, sociologist Seymour Martin Lipset objected that there is another crucial difference: a democratic society has an anti-tyrannical system of checks and balances in its written or unwritten constitution, but political parties and labor unions do not (Michels 1962; Dahl 1989; Lipset 1962; cf. Finocchiaro (2013b; 2015, pp. 34–36)).

Such examples are certainly real and realistic. They are obviously also historically important. The ground-level arguments are clearly compositional; i.e., they are arguments of composition, if I may be allowed to introduce an obvious term for a

[2]There is much more to be said on this aspect of the *Dialogues*, namely Hume's employment of meta-arguments from analogy to criticize or strengthen various ground-level arguments from analogy. See Barker 1989; and Finocchiaro 2013c, pp. 201–203

type of argument that leaves open the question whether it is incorrect or fallacious; that is, an argument from premises with distributive terms or about parts or members to a conclusion with collective terms or about the whole or class. And the ground-level arguments are more or less inferentially incorrect: incontrovertibly and memorably so in the case of Aristotle's geocentric argument from natural motion; arguably and cogently so in the case of the compositional step of the theological argument from design; and arguably and plausibly so in the case of Michels's support for the iron law of oligarchy.

However, some qualifications are in order. First, even if we take these claims as acceptable, one important conceptual qualification needs to be kept in mind about such examples of the fallacy of composition. For these claims amount to saying that we have found important historical examples of arguments of composition that are inferentially incorrect. However, as Woods (2013; cf. Finocchiaro 2014a) has recently stressed, the traditional concept of fallacy is that a fallacy is a common type of reasoning that appears to be correct but is actually incorrect. This conception contains five elements: frequency, generality, reasoning, apparent correctness, and actual incorrectness. Now, in my three examples, the ground-level arguments obviously meet the condition of being reasoning; they also meet the generality condition since they are arguments from parts to whole; and they possess apparent correctness, since the exposure of the flaws of the ground-level arguments required meta-argumentation by thinkers such as Galileo, Hume, Dahl, and Lipset. But I am not sure about their common occurrence and their actual incorrectness. In fact, the same features that make these examples historically important may suggest that they are relatively uncommon; and their actual incorrectness could perhaps be questioned by questioning the critical meta-arguments of Galileo, Hume, Dahl, and Lipset. On the other hand, while such considerations would show that we have not found three examples of fallacies of compositions, they do not undermine the claim that we have found three important historical examples of seductive (i.e., apparently correct) arguments of composition. This problem required further reflection.

Another problem for future investigation concerns an issue that has received some discussion, with some promising and insightful results. The issue is that of the evaluation of the correctness of compositional arguments, and the formulation of useful evaluative principles. A key principle, which I gather from this literature (e.g., Ritola 2009), is that the evaluation of compositional arguments should not be limited to deductive evaluation, but should include inductive evaluation; for even when compositional arguments are deductively invalid, they often possess some plausibility, cogency, or inductive strength.

Another evaluative principle, advanced by van Eemeren and Grootendorst (1992, pp. 174–183; 1999), begins by urging us to distinguish between absolute and relative properties (e.g., round vs. light, i.e., light-weight); between structured or heterogeneous and unstructured or homogenous wholes or aggregates (e.g., a team of football players vs. a heap of sand grains); and between structure-dependent and structure-independent properties (e.g., round vs. white). The principle then states that properties are transferable from parts to whole (or vice versa) if and only if the properties are absolute and structure-independent. Thus, for example, it would be correct to argue that this pile of sand is white because all its grains of sand are white; for in this case the property of being white is both absolute and structure-independent. On the other hand, in the other three possible cases the arguments would be incorrect: this pile of peas is round because the peas are all round (case of structure-dependent property); this pile of sand, from several truck loads, is light because all its grains of sand are light (case of relative property); and this football team is good because its players are good (case of relative and structure-dependent property).

These considerations and this principle are useful, but are just a start. The key problem is that, aside from simple cases, it would very difficult to determine whether a given property was or was not absolute and structure-independent; and often such a determination could not be made prior to, or independently of, knowing or determining the correctness of the corresponding compositional arguments. Thus, more work is needed to find and formulate such evaluative principles.

Acknowledgements Different but overlapping versions of this paper were presented at the 2013 conference of the Ontario Society for the Study of Argumentation, held at University of Windsor, Canada; and also at the 2014 conference of the International Society for the Study of Argumentation, held at University of Amsterdam. For encouragements and comments, I am grateful to John Woods, Tony Blair, Ian Dove, Derek Allen, Michel Dufour, and Jean Goodwin.

References

Barker, S. F. (1989). Reasoning by analogy in Hume's *Dialogues. Informal Logic, 11*, 173–184.

Cohen, M. R., & Nagel, E. (1934). *An introduction to logic and scientific method.* New York: Harcourt, Brace and Company.

Copi, I. M. (1968). *Introduction to logic* (3rd ed.). New York: MacMillan.

Copi, I. M. (1972). *Introduction to logic* (4th ed.). New York: MacMillan.

Dahl, R. A. (1989). *Democracy and its critics*. New Haven: Yale University Press.

Finocchiaro, M. A. (1980). *Galileo and the art of reasoning: Rhetorical foundations of logic and scientific Method.* (Boston Studies in the Philosophy of Science, vol. 61.) Dordrecht: Reidel [now Springer].

Finocchiaro, M. A. (1981). Fallacies and the evaluation of reasoning. *American Philosophical Quarterly, 18*, 13–22. Reprinted in Finocchiaro, 2005, pp. 109–127.

Finocchiaro, M. A. (1987). Six types of fallaciousness: Toward a realistic theory of logical criticism. *Argumentation, 1*, 263–282. Reprinted in Finocchiaro, 2005, pp. 128–147.

Finocchiaro, M. A. (2005). *Arguments about arguments: Systematic, critical, and historical essays in logical theory.* New York: Cambridge University Press.

Finocchiaro, M. A. (2013a). Debts, oligarchies, and holisms: Deconstructing the fallacy of composition. *Informal Logic, 33*, 143–174.

Finocchiaro, M. A. (2013b). The fallacy of composition and meta-argumentation. In D. Mohammed & M. Lewiński (Eds.), *Virtues of argumentation: Proceedings of the 10th international conference of the Ontario society for the study of argumentation (OSSA), 22–26 May 2013* (pp. 1–8). Windsor, ON: Ontario Society for the Study of Argumentation. ISBN: 978-0-920233-66-5.

Finocchiaro, M. A. (2013c). *Meta-argumentation: An approach to logic and argumentation theory.* (Studies in Logic, vol. 42.) London: College Publications.

Finocchiaro, M. A. (2014a). Essay-review of J. Woods's *Errors of reasoning: Naturalizing the logic of inference*. *Argumentation, 28*, 231–239.
Finocchiaro, M. A. (2014b). *The Routledge guidebook to Galileo's Dialogue*. London: Routledge.
Finocchiaro, M.A. (2015). The fallacy of composition: Guiding concepts, historical cases, and research problems. *Journal of Applied Logic*, vol. 13, issue 2, part B, June 2015, pp. 24–43. Published online 20 January 2015, doi:10.1016/j.jal.2015.01.003.
Galilei, G. (1997). *Galileo on the world systems: A new abridged translation and guide*. M. A. Finocchiaro (Ed. and Trans.). Berkeley: University of California Press.
Govier, T. (1982). Who says there are no fallacies? *Informal Logic Newsletter*, *v*(i), 2–10.
Govier, T. (2007). Duets, cartoons, and tragedies: Struggles with the fallacy of composition. In F. H. van Eemeren, J. A. Blair, C. A. Willard, & B. Garssen (Eds.), *Proceedings of the sixth conference of the international society for the study of argumentation* (pp. 505–511). Amsterdam: Sic Sat.
Govier, T. (2009). Duets, cartoons, and tragedies: Struggles with the fallacy of composition. In F. H. van Eemeren & B. Garssen (Eds.), *Pondering on problems of argumentation* (pp. 91–104). Dordrecht: Springer.
Grootendorst, R. (1987). Some fallacies about fallacies. In F. H. van Eemeren, R. Grootendorst, J. A. Blair, & C. A. Willard (Eds.), *Argumentation across the lines of discipline: Proceedings of the conference on argumentation 1986* (pp. 331–342). Dordrecht: Foris Publications.
Haller, S. A. (2002). *Apocalypse soon? Wagering on warnings of global warming*. Montreal: McGill-Queens University Press.
Halverson, W. H. (1984). *Concise logic*. New York: Random House.
Hamblin, C. L. (1970). *Fallacies*. London: Methuen. Report, Newport News: Vale Press, 1986.
Hazlitt, H. (1979). *Economics in one lesson* (1st ed.) 1946. New Rochelle: Arlington House Publishers.
Hume, D. (1947). *Dialogues concerning natural religion*. N. K. Smith (Ed.). Indianapolis: Bobbs-Merrill.
Jason, G. (1986). Are fallacies common?". *Informal Logic, 8*, 81–92.
Kahane, H. (1973). *Logic and philosophy* (2nd ed.). Belmont: Wadsworth.
Kelly, W. A., & Kelly E. S. (2015). Obama and the 'fallacy of composition'. *The Wall Street Journal*, February 4. Retrieved 18 March, 2015 from http://www.wsj.com/articles/bill-kelly-and-elizabeth-sawyer-kelly-obama-and-the-fallacy-of-composition-1423095533
Krugman, P. (2013a). Austerity wrought pain, no gain. *Las Vegas Sun*, January 8, p. 3. Retrieved October 21, 2014 from http://lasvegassun.com/news/2013/jan/08/austerity-wrought-pain-no-gain/#.VHPVyW1c75E.gmail.
Krugman, P. (2013b). The punishment cure. *The New York Times*, 8 December. Retrieved October 21, 2014 from http://www.nytimes.com/2013/12/09/opinion/krugman-the-punishment-cure.html?_r=1.
Lipset, S. M. (1962). Introduction In Michels, *1962*, 15–39.
Michels, R. (1962). *Political parties: A sociological study of the oligarchical tendencies of modern democracy*. (E. Paul and C. Paul Trans.). New York: Collier.
Nelson, A. (1999). Keynes. In R. Audi (Ed.), *Cambridge dictionary of philosophy* (2nd ed., pp. 467–468). New York: Cambridge University Press.
Ritola, J. (2009). Commentary on James E. Gough and Mano Daniel's 'The fallacy of composition'. In J. Ritola (Ed.), *Argument cultures: Proceedings of the 8th Biennial conference of the Ontario society for the study of argumentation* (*OSSA, 2009*). Windsor, ON: Ontario Society for the Study of Argumentation. ISBN 978-0-920233-51-1.
Salmon, M. (2002). *Introduction to logic and critical thinking* (4th ed.). Wadsworth Thomson Learning.
Samuelson, P. A. (1955). *Economics: An introductory analysis* (3rd ed.). New York: McGraw-Hill.
Samuelson, P. A., & Nordhaus, W. D. (1989). *Economics* (13th ed.). New York: McGraw-Hill.
Strawson, P. F. (1952). *Introduction to logical theory*. London: Methuen.

van Eemeren, F. H., & Grootendorst, R. (1992). *Argumentation, communication, and fallacies*. Hillsdale: Lawrence Erlbaum Associates.

van Eemeren, F. H., & R. Grootendorst (1999). The fallacies of composition and division. In J. Gerbrandy, M. Marx, M. de Rijke & Y. Venema (Eds.), *JFAK: Essays dedicated to Johan van Benthem on the occasion of his 50th Birthday*. Amsterdam: University of Amsterdam, Institute for Logic, Language, and Computation. Retrieved June 18, 2013 from www.illc.uva.nl/j50/.

Whately, R. (1826). *Elements of logic*. London: J. Mawman. Reprint, Bologna, Italy: Editrice CLUEB, 1988.

Woods, J. (1988). Buttercups, GNP's, and quarks: Are fallacies theoretical entities? *Informal Logic*, *10*, 67–76. Reprinted in Woods, 2004, pp. 161–70.

Woods, J. (2004). *The death of argument: Fallacies in agent-based reasoning*. Dordrecht: Kluwer.

Woods, J. (2013). *Errors of reasoning: Naturalizing the logic of inference*. London: College Publications.

Woods, J., Irvine, A., & Walton, D. (2000). *Argument: Critical thinking, logic, and the fallacies*. Toronto: Prentice-Hall.

Wray, L. R. (2009). Teaching the fallacy of composition: The federal budget deficit. Retrieved 19 October 2012 from http://neweconomicperspectives.org/2009/08/teaching-fallacy-of-composition-federal.html.

Don't Feed the Trolls: Straw Men and Iron Men

Scott Aikin and John Casey

1 Introduction

Typically, philosophers consider the straw man a fallacy of relevance, inasmuch as one attacks a distorted, and hence irrelevant, version of an opponent's argument. As some of recent work has shown, however, there is more to the problem of straw manning than the *distortion* of an opponent's argument and hence more to the issue than relevance. Some forms of straw man, such as the **weak man**, rely on accurate, even *scrupulously accurate*, depictions of arguments for criticism. Other forms, such as the **hollow man** do not actually involve representations of anyone's actual argument or view. Nonetheless, these strategies, and others to be discussed here, are dialectically problematic for much of the same reasons the distortion form of straw man is, in that they, to use some metaphorical language, misrepresent the dialogical lay of the land. We will argue here that two further features complete the account of the fallaciousness of the straw man: (1) a move to close further dialogue with the straw man target (and those with similar views) and (2) a move to paint the straw man victim as unworthy of being taken seriously. This is to say: in the cases of fallacious deployments of the straw man form, the speakers perform what we call a 'closing function' on the exchange with the straw man target. The prospects of fruitful critical exchange is implicated to seem too thin for further investment, so the straw man target is left with no one interested even in his or her rebuttal. We will further argue that what makes the varieties of straw man fallacious (namely, what we'd called the 'closing function') can also be used to show that not all forms of straw men arguments ought to be considered fallacious. Finally, the considerations

S. Aikin (✉)
Department of Philosophy, Vanderbilt University, Nashville, Tennessee 37240, USA
e-mail: scott.f.aikin@vanderbilt.edu

J. Casey
Department of Philosophy, Northeastern Illinois University, 5500 N.St.Louis, Chicago, Illinois 60625, USA

F.H. van Eemeren and B. Garssen (eds.), *Reflections on Theoretical Issues in Argumentation Theory*, Argumentation Library 28,
DOI 10.1007/978-3-319-21103-9_11

that distinguish fallacious from non fallacious straw men also uncover a related phenomenon, **iron manning**, or the practice of making an opponent's argument *stronger* than it is. We will argue that there are both appropriate and fallacious versions of this tactic.

2 Varieties of the Straw Man

Our aim in this section is to show that (1) there is a variety to the straw man, (2) there's more involved in the phenomenon than the ploy of manipulating commitments, and (3) that non-fallacious, but formally identical variations of each of these forms exist.

2.1 *The Representational Form of Straw Man*

Let's call the textbook form of the straw man the "representational form." This consists in the first instance distortion of an opponent's argument, followed by a decisive refutation. We will begin with a few textbook-style examples, and then we will turn to 'real life' cases. Consider:

> APA
> *Philo*: A lot of people have suggested that the American Philosophical Association amend the practically obligatory Eastern APA interview on account of the expense, inconvenience, and stress for all involved.
> *Sophia*: Come now Philo, I hardly think that completely abandoning the system is desirable, so we ought to reject their suggestions.

APA meets the basic schematic requirements for the straw man in that we have (1) two arguers and (2) criticism of one by the other. We can also tell that the criticism here hinges on the *representation* of the first arguer's position. The first arguer maintains that the APA ought to *amend* the Eastern APA hiring process because it is expensive, inconvenient, and stressful for everyone. But the second arguer attacks a related, but substantially different claim, namely that *abandoning* the system is ridiculous. Philo not suggested that the system be *completely* abandoned; rather, she has suggested that the APA *amend* the process. Sophia has misrepresented Philo's view, and dismissed the misrepresentation as weak.

2.2 *The Weak Man*

Consider another variation of the straw man argument. Call it the *weak man*. In its broad outlines, the weak man consists in (1) *selecting* the weakest of an opponent's *actual* arguments, (2) *actually* defeating it, and (3) then drawing or implying deeper conclusions about the argument or the arguer in question. Consider the following exchange:

Locavorism

Serenity: The culinary and ecological movement known as "locavorism" maintains that favoring sustainably and ethically raised local and seasonal produce is superior to the more dominant industrial model. After all, it does not depend on petroleum-intensive fertilizer, it's not transported across the country (or the world in many cases), and it sustains local agricultural economies.

Archer: The claims of the locavorism movement are ludicrous, the alleged fuel savings in food transportation amount to very little if any overall petroleum savings. Locavorism is loco.

In this case, the locavore, Serenity, maintains that a number of different reasons independently and convergently support the single conclusion that locavorism is a wiser policy than high intensity industrial agriculture. The critic, Archer, singles out one of them, the alleged fuel savings, and refutes it as an independently and solely supporting reason, thereby implying he has dealt a blow to the argument as a whole. Archer might even have an especially decisive and sound argument, but even granted that, much would remain to consider in favor of locavorism. The weak-manner hopes to exaggerate the importance of the weak argument, but barring that, he can focus critical scrutiny on the ideological fellow travelers of the person making the weak argument.

2.3 *The Hollow Man*

In a third variation of the straw man, one invents an entirely fictitious and decisively silly position, attributes it to a purportedly real, but vaguely defined opponent, knocks it down, and thereby suggests the opposition isn't worthy of rational discussion. The "tell" for this version of the straw man, is often the infamous "some say" or "some might say" phrase that obscures the identity and therefore absolves the speaker of the charge of lying. Many readers are likely familiar with the controversy surrounding American Conservative Radio Commentator Rush Limbaugh's tendency to make jarring remarks. Unsurprisingly many have rushed to his defense. Among them was the *Wall Street Journal*'s Peggy Noonan:

Peggy Noonan

Why would the left be worse? Let me be harsh. Some left-wing men think they can talk like this because they're on the correct side on social issues such as abortion. Their attitude: I backed you on the abortions you want so much, I opposed a ban on partial birth. Hell, I'll let you kill kids at any point until they're 15, I'm cool. And that means I can call women in public life t – - – s, right? Because, you know, I think of them that way. (WSJ 3/16/2012)

Like the weak man, the hollow man does not involve *distorting* any argument so much as *inventing* an entirely new one. In this example, Noonan does not bother to identify the bearer of the view other than to say that "*some* left-wing men" think this. She provides no reference, no name, not even a hint about where she heard it or read it. She invented her dialectical opponent whole cloth, and so there is no speaker she misrepresents in terms of one or a group she just got wrong. Instead, she invents them.

3 Are There Legitimate Uses of the Straw Man?

The various schemes of straw men are defined by the way one arguer represents the views of another: badly, selectively, or falsely. The question is whether one can badly, selectively, or falsely represent someone's views without being guilty of fallacy.

Consider: it would be very hard to teach philosophy without employing some variation on the straw man scheme frequently and energetically. With regard to this reason, Brian Ribiero notes that (2008) that distortions formally identical to straw man fallacies occur frequently in the classroom from pedagogical need: (1) historical interest, (2) pedagogical ease, (3) and practical availability. There seems, in fact, to be an intuitive case for using the various schemes of the straw man pedagogically. Representational straw men might be employed to drive home particular pedagogical points. One may, in a philosophy class present an historically significant and widely anthologized version of the ontological argument, perhaps that in Anselm's *Proslogion* as representative of the argument's form and an indicator of the prospects of its quality. And so:

Ontological Argument:
Professor Gaunilo: You see, in some cases, the ontological argument proves too much. Are there really perfect islands just because their existence would be better than their non-existence? Furthermore, why is it that a quantifier can be part of a definition. Existence isn't a property! The ontological argument is looking to be in pretty bad shape.

Professor Gaunilo's argument seems to have two problems. First is the presentational version—Anselm makes it very clear that the argument cuts off contingent beings with the proof, so the 'proves too much' objection is likely not going to pay the critical dividends against Anselm's argument he takes it to. Second is the broadly Kantian critique of taking existence to not function like properties. For sure, this is a successful criticism of Anselm's version of the ontological argument, but it does not touch other versions of the argument, like the modal version of the argument. The consequence is that Professor Gaunilo may, for the purposes of an introductory philosophy course, have presented relevant challenges (and ones worth responding to, for the defender of the ontological argument), but he has not shown the argument to be in as bad shape as he has contended. One way Professor Gaunilo can go here is to elicit replies from the class defending the argument—she may run her 'proves too much' line, and those who have read carefully can come to the fore and defend Anselm. She may run the Kantian line and thereby prompt some reflection on the alternatives for the argument. What counts for the fallaciousness, we want to say, is not the form or even the representational accuracy in the argument in its presented form, but how it is used, whether it is a spur to better argument or a close to the critical exchange.

Alternately, straw-manning needn't even be critical of arguments specifically, but of performances or positions. And so in the same way that one may present an opponent as presenting a ridiculous series of reasons and criticize it as such, one may present a dialogue partner as having made a series of simple errors of practical performance. A teacher of music, for instance, might exaggerate the bad habit of her music student:

Music Teacher
Music teacher to student: you need to work on your intonation. At the moment it sounds like a tortured cat.

The teacher has distorted the student's behavior by hyperbole, but the point is to fix the student's awareness on her poor intonation. The hyperbole focuses attention on the performance—by way of a misrepresentation. A similar case might be made for the other two straw man ploys. A weak man might be used as practice.

Gay Marriage
Brad: I've heard quite a number of arguments against gay marriage in the conservative press lately.
Angelina: I have too. I heard one particularly bad one from a blogger at RedState.com he argued that if homosexuals are allowed to marry, nothing would prevent him from marrying his box turtle.
Brad: Wow, that's hilarious.

In this example, Brad signals that there are several arguments against gay marriage. We can imagine that some are better than others. Angelina responds by attacking what is likely to be weakest of them, a kind of textbook version of the slippery slope fallacy. Answering it first improves further discussion.

For a **hollow man** case, we continue our pedagogical considerations. Open just about any introductory logic text, and one will find the exercise sections full of arguments few sensible people would make (though we're often disabused of this notion). It's just easier, however, to do it this way, for the point of the fallacy exercise is to get at the form of argument, not to pin failings on specific people

Though all of these examples fit the straw man ploy in its various forms, none of them are in our view fallacious. In **Music Teacher**, the instructor attacks an exaggerated version of the student's performance to highlight a difficult to appreciate pedagogical point. In **Gay Marriage**, Angelina goes straight for the weakest of the arguments for the anti-gay marriage position, and so weak mans that view. But she does not draw the inference that this view is representative of the best of the opposition. Weak manning sometimes serves the dialectical purpose of clearing away weak arguments, which nonetheless may have a lot of adherents, and which nonetheless occupy much in demand dialectical space.

These representative, but non fallacious, straw man ploys highlight two important features about what makes most straw man arguments fallacious in the first place. The fallaciousness does not primarily consist in the distortion of someone else's argument (as in the representational straw man), in the purposeful selection of the weakest of someone's arguments (as in the weak man), or finally in the invention of weak arguments or arguers (as in the hollow man); all of these can be very useful dialectical tools. *What makes these tactics fallacious is how they are deployed.* The varieties of straw man are fallacious if they are deployed (1) to close off argument prematurely and (2) illegitimately impugn an opposing arguer's competence. So, for instance, the hollow man is fallacious when one makes up an idiotic argument, knocks it down, in order to suggest that the opposition, however vaguely defined, lacks sufficient critical skill, as in the **Peggy Noonan** example above. Such people's views are unserious and not worthy of further consideration. The other two examples show a similar tendency to tar the target with an accusation of a bad argument. In **APA**, the arguer is alleged to have made an extreme suggestion; in **Locavorism**, the arguer is alleged to be insufficiently reflective or to associate with insufficiently reflective people. Additionally, we can see how in the **Ontological Argument** case, Professor Gaunilo's performance could be either way. The argument could be taken as a final word on the argument as such, and so a (weak) criticism of Anselm's version of the argument takes the form of a criticism of the argument as a whole. Alternately, the argument performance could be taken as a challenge by her students, eliciting critical reply and development of better versions or even defenses of Anselm's own version of the argument. If the argument is deployed to close the door on critical discussion on the argument, we see the fallacy. But if it is taken as a presentation of a version of the argument that needs improvement, and so an invitation to further development, it is not fallacious but a mode of spurring critical discussion.

4 Iron Manning

If what makes the varieties of straw men fallacious is their exclusionary, or closing, function, then it is easier to distinguish fallacious cases of straw manning from non fallacious ones.

The fallaciousness of strawman arguments is indexed to context. Views or arguments that warrant careful consideration in one situation may not deserve them in another. *This means at times it may be permissible (and necessary) to exclude some views from consideration on the basis of cursory arguments.* In other words, while fallacious straw men involve the exclusion of arguments or arguers from justly deserved consideration, in light of the function of the straw man to distort over time, there is good reason to think that unreasonably or overly charitable interpretations of arguments (of arguers) can also qualify as fallacious. It's certainly fallacious, in other words, to distort a person's argument in order more easily to it knock down (and malign the person as a competent arguer); however, by parity of reasoning, a charitable distortion to present an unserious arguer as serious is equally problematic. We call this the **iron man**. Consider the following cases. Again, we will intersperse the review of cases with ones of our own devising for the sake of presentation with 'real argument' cases from the news.

4.1 *Eric Cantor*

Eric Cantor was the Republican Majority Whip in the United States House of Representatives from 2011 to 2014. In an interview with Leslie Stahl on CBS's 60 Minutes (1/1/2012), Stahl asked Cantor to square the fact that American President Ronald Reagan raised taxes during a recession with the current Republican Party view–allegedly inspired by Reagan–that taxes ought never to be raised. In response, Cantor denied that Reagan ever raised taxes. His spokesperson interrupted the interview, alleging that Stahl did not have her facts straight. She did. Coming to Cantor's defense, one blogger (Jim Hoft) made the following claim:

> Stahl, was not being honest. When Ronald Reagan took office, the top individual tax rate was 70 percent and by 1986 it was down to only 28 percent. All Americans received at least a 30 percent tax rate cut. Democrats like to play with the numbers to pretend that Reagans [sic] tax increases equalled [sic] his tax cuts. Of course, this is absurd.
> … Unfortunately, Steve Benen at the Washington Monthly continued to misrepresent Reagan's record on tax cuts. It's just soooo difficult for liberals to understand that tax cuts work. Sad.

Notice that Hoft has offered a different and (much more defensible) view on behalf of Cantor: on aggregate, taxes were lower after Reagan's years in office than before. This was not the point under consideration. The net effect of this is to distort the proper evaluation of Cantor's claim and Stahl's criticism.

4.2 *Westboro Baptist Church*

The Westboro Baptist Church is known for demonstrating at the funerals of fallen American soldiers. At their protests, they hold up signs alleging that the death of the soldier is God's punishment for the tolerance of homosexuality in America. Many people, both military and civilian, are outraged by their protests. In light of this, consider the following exchange.

> *Sally*: The Westboro Baptist Church boycotted my local synagogue, carrying signs that say "God hates fags." Their views are patently ridiculous; far from even the fringe of conservative Christianity. People should just ignore them.
> *Priscilla*: Yes, but aren't they really suggesting that our fate as a nation is bound up with the moral fibre of the American people? As we lose our sense of commitment, steadfastness, and courage, we will not realize our plans.

Priscilla raises some interesting points, but they are vaguely related to the actual content of the Westboro Church's protests and Sally's objection. The question is whether these particular arguments from the Westboroites deserve consideration. And so iron-manning can be an occasion for broader discussion, but one iron mans so that we do not have to discuss this particular argument.

4.3 Philosophy Student I

We have discussed above how teaching philosophy to undergraduates often depends on strategically employed, non-fallacious straw men. As it is necessary sometimes to straw man views, it is also necessary to iron man the student's view. With this in mind, imagine the following teacher-student exchange.

> *Alfredo*: Rawls' "Original Position" seems impossible to me. I mean, how are we to know what sorts of things we'll be interested in if we don't know anything about ourselves?
> *Professor Zoccolo*: That's an interesting point, Alfredo, you're suggesting that Rawls's Original Position does not take cognizance of how we are constituted by our social relations. Thinking them through abstractly seems problematic.

Alfredo's view certainly trends communitarian, but it would be a stretch to suggest that this is what he meant. Unlike the previous cases, however, iron-manning Alfredo shows him how to improve his contributions to the discussion.

4.4 Philosophy Student II

The norm of iron-manning student views can yield good results. It shows students how to improve their thoughts. However, it can yield classroom disaster, as it can encourage more poorly stated views. Iron-manning the student makes it such that the teacher does the work in crafting the views. Moreover, time in the classroom is too short to take all the off-the-wall views seriously. Sometimes, iron-manning undercuts a serious classroom. Consider:

> *Professor Barleycorn*: Descartes' argument in the First Meditation is that very little of what we take ourselves to know securely is certain. It may all be a dream. Or it may all be an illusion of a very powerful demon.
> *Bradley*: Dude! I had a dream like that one night—that I was in the clutches of an evil demon. And he made me do things… like terrible things… to chickens. And then, when I woke up… *it was all true*. The terrible stuff to chickens stuff, that is. That was all after I drank too much cough syrup with my beers. Did Day-Cart have a Robitussin problem?
> *Professor Barleycorn*: Ah, yes, Bradley. You've hit on something important here. Descartes's argument puts us in a position where we are not sure what we are doing, whether we've done terrible things in the past or whether we can even tell right from wrong. Yes, Bradley, you've asked a deep question here.

Bradley is way off base. For sure, his weird story deserves a moment of reply, but it is best for all involved that a lengthy analysis of Bradley's views on the matter aren't devoted class time. Some views are best left unexamined. Next time, Bradley should read. And lay off the syrup. Professor Barleycorn's reply, then, encouraging Bradley, saying he's on to something deep, polishing his badly formed question into a deep restatement of Descartes's skeptical doubts, is pedagogically abominable. Professor Barleycorn, for sure, should do her best to keep class discussion going as smoothly and as amicably as possible. But this shouldn't stand. Moreover, it is bad for Bradley. He needs to learn to get his head straight before he jumps into discussion, that not every association he has with the reading is relevant. Barleycorn has missed a teaching moment, ironically, for the sake of teaching.

5 Discussion

From these cases, the basic form of iron man argumentation can be discerned. First, as a dialectical form, the iron man requires two speakers, A and B. A proposes some argument *a* and/or some position *p*. But *a* and *p* are not defensible. B takes up with A's case with a reconstruction, a^* and p^*, that given the state of dialectical play are (comparatively more) defensible. Often this strategy is done for the sake of an onlooking audience, C, which may be interested in A's views or the issue of whether that *p*. So far, again, we can see that there is a dialectical distortion, just as there is with straw-manning, but instead of *degrading* the opponent's argument (as with the straw man), the opponent's case is *improved*. Hence our term *iron* man.

There are compelling epistemic reasons to regularly iron man one's opposition, as the truth will come out in contexts of maximally responsible and detailed argumentation. Since our epistemic objectives in argument are truth and its understanding, the most intellectually robust opponent is the best, and if one does not encounter but must construct such an opponent, then so be it. Moreover, there are ethical (and political) reasons why iron-manning may be appealing. At its core, iron-manning is a form of interpreting others communicative acts with charity. The demands of recognition, further, for underrepresented groups obtain so that their interests can be heard and have effect. Iron-manning is in the service of this. Finally, again, there are pedagogical reasons why iron-manning may be required. One sets an example, in the iron man product, for what a good contribution would look like.

So what, then, could be wrong with iron-manning? We hold that there is a fallacy of inclusion for the same reason that there is a fallacy of exclusion.

Let us return to the cases. As we saw with **Philosophy Student II**, there are pedagogical reasons why iron-manning can be objectionable, as the point of class discussion is for students to improve their own views, not having it done for them. It is here that we begin to see the trouble with some forms of iron-man: in taking some poorly articulated views seriously, improving them and submitting them to scrutiny, one makes an investment of time and intellectual energy. The trouble is that there are many investments that are unwise. Consider, further, a feature of discussion after content presentation. There is evidence now that suggests that rude or irrelevant online comments after a posting or story actually distort reading comprehension of the original piece. That is, the more comments that don't get the original point you are exposed to or the more rude comments in the discussion thread, the less likely it is that you will, afterwards, correctly recall the details of the posting. This is now being called, "The Nasty Effect." Derailed discussion not only is a waste of time, but it is miseducation.

Now consider the strategic use of iron-manning with the Eric Cantor case. The trouble is not with improving the view per se, but with the way the improvement is deployed. In this case, (a) the iron man is presented as Cantor's view, and (b) thereby it is used as evidence that Stahl is (and liberals generally are) fact challenged. But this is a distortion not only of Cantor's position, but of Stahl's, too. By iron-manning Cantor, one straw-mans Stahl, his critic. Her criticisms now seem off-target and ill-informed, when they, in fact, were not.

These two elements of iron-manning converge. When one iron mans a poorly presented view, one may encourage those who have posed the view by taking them seriously, and thereby impugn their critics. Again, sometimes this is appropriate, as some views need time and patience for their development and some speakers require maximal charity in interpreting their communicative acts. But sometimes it is inappropriate, as one can be held hostage by these speakers. On blog comment threads and chatboards, there are many who are uninformed and contribute with unhinged criticism. They are out to hijack discussion, to hold forth, to be the center of attention. These are, in internet lingo, *trolls*. Taking the trolls seriously, interpreting them with charity, and responding to them thoughtfully yields only grief. *One must not feed the trolls.*

Indeed, too often philosophers and informal logicians overlook the fact we very often find ourselves having to evaluate just *this* argument from *this* arguer, even if this argument could be stronger, or this arguer could use some help. We have argued here that even charitable alterations of arguments or arguers distort the dialectical landscape and are often unacceptable. This is for exactly the same reason why straw-manning is unacceptable. The only difference is that the straw man excludes arguments worth listening to; the iron man includes arguments not worth listening to. In all, we've identified a few rough criteria for knowing when iron-manning is fallacious:

1. When it is clear that the argument to be reconstructed is not likely to be either relevant or successful.
2. When it is clear that the improvement of and response to the argument will take more time than is allotted, and there are other, more clearly salient, issues.
3. When, even if 1 & 2 do not obtain (that is, when there may be something relevant and there is plenty of surplus time and energy), it is clear that responding to *this speaker* under *these circumstances* encourages further badly formed arguments.
4. When the positive reconstruction of the argument (iron man) in question yields mis-portrayal of the arguments prior critics as attacking a straw man.

This rough set of criteria are, in the end, an overlap of (a) issues in cognitive economy (maximizing epistemic efficiency), and (b) issues in maintenance of a properly run dialectical field. We hold 1&2 are epistometric questions, and 3&4 are dialectical questions. Hence, the basic thought that sometimes feeding the trolls is (a) a waste of time and energy, and (b) it ultimately isn't anything but bad for the way we argue.

6 Conclusion

We have argued in this paper that the dialectical phenomenon known as straw manning is much more varied than many accounts suggest. In the first place, straw manning involves more than simple distortion. It also includes forms of selection (weak manning) and invention (hollow manning). Second, not all instances of straw manning are fallacious. Finally, and somewhat ironically, charitable variations on an argument suffer from the same failings as fallacious straw men, though their mistake lies in the inclusion of arguments deserving of exclusion.

References

Aikin, S., & Casey, J. (2011). Straw men, weak men, and hollow men. *Argumentation, 25*, 87–105.

CBS News, 60 Minutes. (2012). Interview with Eric Cantor. http://www.cbsnews.com/8301-18560_162-57348499/the-majority-leader-rep-eric-cantor/?tag=contentMain;cbsCarousel.

Bizer, G. Y., Kozak, S. M., & Holterman, L. A. (2009). The Persuasiveness of the Straw Man Rhetorical Technique. *Social Influence, 4*, 216–230.

Drum, K. http://www.washingtonmonthly.com/archives/individual/2006_08/009324.php.

Elliot, D. (2011). GOP splits up for weekend conferences. NPR Weekend Edition. http://www.npr.org/2011/06/18/137265773/gop-splits-up-for-weekend-conferences.

Govier, T. (1997). *A practical study of argument, 4e*. Belmont, CA: Wadsworth.

Lewinksi, M. (2011). Towards a critique-friendly approach to straw man fallacy evaluation. *Argumentation, 25*, 469–497.

Ribeiro, B. (2008). How often do we (Philosophy Professors) commit the straw man fallacy? *Teaching Philosophy, 31*, 27–38.

Talisse, R., & Aikin, S. (2008). Two forms of the straw man. *Argumentation, 20,* 345–52.

Talisse, R., Raley, Y. (2008). Getting duped: how the media messes with your mind. Scientific American Mind. January/February.

Tindale, C. (2007). *Fallacies and argument appraisal*. Cambridge: Cambridge University Press.

van Eemeren, F. H., Grootendorst, R., Henkenmans, F. S. (2002). *Argumentation: Analysis, Evaluation, Presentation*. Mahwah, NJ: Lawrence Erlbaum.

van Eemeren, F. H., Grootendorst, R. (2004.) *A Systematic Theory of Argumentation*. Cambridge: Cambridge University Press.

van Eemeren, F. H., & Grootendorst, R.u (1992). *Argumentation, Communication, and Fallacies*. Hillsdale, NJ: Lawrence Erlbaum.

van Eemeren, F. & Houtlosser, P. (2007). The contextuality of fallacies. *Informal Logic, 27*, 59–67.

Laar, V., Albert, J. (2008). Room for Maneuver when raising critical doubt. *Philosophy and Rhetoric, 41,* 195–211.

Walton, D. (1989). *Informal logic.* Cambridge: Cambridge University Press.
Walton, Douglas (1996). The Straw Man Fallacy. *Logic and Argumentation*. Ed. Johan van.
van Bentham, J., van Eemeren, F. H., Grootendorst, R., & Veltman, F. (1996). Amsterdam: Royal Netherlands Academy of Arts and Sciences, North Holland. 115–128.
Walton, D. (1998). *Ad Hominem Arguments.* Alabama: University of Alabama Press.
Walton, D., & Macagno, F. (2010). Wrenching from context: The manipulation of commitments. *Argumentation, 24*, 283–317.
Walton, D., & Krabbe, E. (1995). *Commitment in dialogue*. Albany: State University of New York Press.
Walton, D., Reed, C., Macagno, F. (2008). *Argumentation schemes*. Cambridge: Cambridge University Press.

Story Credibility in Narrative Arguments

Paula Olmos

1 Introduction

Narrative argumentation, narration in arguments or the inherent narrativity of arguing and debating, are, no doubt, trendy topics in the field of argumentation theory. During the 10th OSSA Conference several papers were dedicated to this issue and two complete panels about "Narrative argument" have been presented at the ISSA Conference 2014. Of course, this implies a certain variety of approaches and some clarifications as to the referents and the scope of my own paper are required.

First of all, even if I take W. Fisher's narrative paradigm of rationality (1989 [1987]) as a truly attractive philosophical stance that could yield interesting insights regarding the cognitive basis of our reasoning, I claim some of its assumptions may turn our attention away from the particulars of real discourse. If we assume that:

> regardless of genre, discourse will *always* tell a story and insofar as it invites an audience to believe it or act on it, the narrative paradigm and its attendant logic, narrative rationality, are available for interpretation and assessment (Fisher 1989, p. xi),

there would be nothing specific to arguments involving explicit narratives as obvious parts or as a manifest linguistic strategy. Again, Fisher insists that "When narration is taken as the master metaphor, it subsumes the others" (1989, p. 62). So my first clarification is that here I don't mean to use "narrative" as a metaphor (however insightful) of what's happening when we argue and listen to or interpret arguments; nor as the cognitive key (however revealing) to the widespread features of our species' argumentative practices (as allegedly *Homo narrans*). I will focus, instead, on the straightforward recognition of a variety of argument types and

P. Olmos (✉)
Departamento de Lingüística, Lenguas modernas, Lógica y filosofía de la ciencia, Teoría de la literatura y literatura comparada, Universidad Autónoma de Madrid, Madrid, Spain
e-mail: paula.olmos@uam.es

F.H. van Eemeren and B. Garssen (eds.), *Reflections on Theoretical Issues in Argumentation Theory*, Argumentation Library 28,
DOI 10.1007/978-3-319-21103-9_12

argumentative discourses in which the particular linguistic features and genre-specific qualities of narration play a significant role.

2 Narrative Arguments

There are a number of widely acknowledged argument types in which narratives may be involved in significant ways. Certain explicitly "narrative-based argument schemes" have been presented and discussed in recent literature (Walton 2012; Govier and Ayers 2012) and there is also interest in pure "narrative discourse" as a possible way of arguing for a thesis in the adequate pragmatic contexts (Plumer 2011; Olmos 2014a).

Not trying at all to be exhaustive in any sense and just for the purposes of this paper, I will mention four broad categories of arguments for which an exploration of "narrative credibility" would be of interest.

(i) First of all, as it comes to everybody's mind, arguments consisting in parallel, *digressive* stories (cf.: Cic. *De inv.* I 27), i.e. stories, be they fictive or not, that are not directly related to and are causally and historically independent from the circumstances referred to in the thesis, which are presented as reasons, nevertheless, for its acceptance. They would typically include (and I refer here to Walton et al. 2008 catalogue): arguments from example (WRM 2008, p. 314), arguments from "analogy", especially "practical reasoning from analogy" (*ibid.* pp. 315–316) or arguments from precedent (*ibid.* p. 344).[1]

(ii) In second place, arguments in which the data, or part of the data are presented in narrative form; i.e. arguments which involve narrative premises which have something to do with the particulars and circumstances referred to in the thesis (they are not *digressive* but they are not *core* narratives either "which contain just the case and the whole reason for a dispute", *De inv.*, I.27). They include, for example, practical inferences from consequences (WRM 2008, p. 323), or from goal (*ibid.* p. 325), arguments from sacrifice (*ibid.* p. 322) and waste (*ibid.* p. 326), arguments from interaction of act and person (*ibid.* p. 321), pragmatic inconsistencies (*ibid.* p. 336), arguments from memory (*ibid.* p. 346).

The argument types so far mentioned do not necessarily always represent what I would call a narrative argument—especially not when they just involve a one-step consequence supported or supportable by a simple warrant. I would restrict the concept of narrative argument to cases that explicitly involve a more complex, sequential chain or compound of events that should be assessed as a whole. In any case, the credibility of the narratives endorsed as reasons or parts of reasons in these

[1]As I have pointed out elsewhere (Olmos 2014b) such argumentative digressive narratives do not have to be necessarily cast into arguments by analogy.

two categories of arguments would be essential to their interpretation and assessment. But then, we may also think of:

(iii) Arguments *about* narratives, i.e. about versions of events (these would be what I call *core* narratives, cf. Olmos 2014a), with usually partly narrative claims or conclusions (typically global assertions regarding narrative accounts of disputed facts: "what really happened is…") supported by a variety of reasons (typically involving source reliability) when facts themselves are under discussion or are unknown to the audience. Such cases would typically involve arguments from position to know (WRM 2008, p. 309) or arguments from witness testimony (*ibid.* p. 310).

These are usually *not* narrative-based arguments (the key reasons involved are not typically narrative, although they could be). However, theories about story credibility may be part of their analysis, understanding and assessment as the critical questions presented by Walton et al. (2008, p. 310) concerning "arguments from witness testimony" reveal:

CQ1: Is what the witness said internally consistent?
CQ2: Is what the witness said consistent with the known facts of the case (based on evidence apart from what the witness testified to)?
CQ3: Is what the witness said consistent with what other witnesses have (independently) testified to?
CQ4: Is there some kind of bias that can be attributed to the account given by the witness?
CQ5: How plausible is the statemente *A* asserted by the witness?

(iv) And finally, we have what we could call credible "pure narration", which I have elsewhere treated as some sort of self-standing and self-referring "argument" (Olmos 2014a), and perhaps could be better understood in terms of assuming certain argumentative qualities—rhetorical and others—in a discourse that does not explicitly present an argument. In such cases a manifestly credible narration can be interpreted as a discursive means to *implicitly* support the veracity of an account. The story's veracity is then the (usually implicit or just suggested) conclusion and its manifest narrative plausibility is its only justificatory measure. We can imagine that a particular theory or a principle of story credibility could function as such a conclusion's warrant, if challenged in subsequent interchange.

There exists, on the other hand, the rather widespread opinion that the way we go about assessing the credibility of the stories we hear is something extremely basic within our cognitive capacities. Thus, Fisher talks about our "inherent awareness of *narrative probability*" (1989, p. 5) or even our "natural capacity to recognize the coherence and fidelity of stories" (1989, p. 24). In fact, our everyday experience somewhat matches this confidence, but this doesn't mean that we cannot try to be more specific as to the way we assess such narrative *probabilitas*. In fact, there have been numerous attempts at that, and many of them from the ranks of rhetoricians, concerned with argumentative issues and the specific problems posed by argumentative settings (Olmos 2012).

3 Criterial Theories of Story Credibility

As early as in Isocrates (4th c. BCE), we may find the well-known classical triad of the virtues required by a narrative discourse to be persuasive, i.e. rhetorically effective. Narration employed in persuasive processes and rhetorical settings should be clear (*safēs*), brief (*súntomon*) and convincing (*pithanón*). In the subsequent Latin tradition this "convincing" (*pithanón*) was alternatively translated by *probabilis*, *credibilis* or *verisimilis.*[2] Fortunatianus (4th c. CE), in his *Artis rhetoricae* (II.20), supports the relevance of these three virtues by identifying the argumentative benefits expected from each one of them: "Brief, so that the audience may enjoy listening to us; clear, so that we be fully understood; verisimilar, so that our story serve as evidence" ("Brevis, ut libentius audiatur, manifesta, ut intellegatur, verisimilis, ut probetur"). According to Fortunatianus' formula, then, it is the third virtue that allows us to use narratives as supporting reasons for our claims. But how do we attain such verisimilitude that would result in the credibility or believability of our stories and, therefore, in their usefulness as assessable reasons? The main tenet of most of approaches to "story credibility" is the rough idea that a credible story should resemble "reality" or "what we know about reality". But usually this main rough idea is complemented and developed by identifying more concrete requirements. We will take a look at several of these "criterial" theories of story credibility starting with some apparently simple distinctions and advancing towards a more complicated panorama.

There has been a long-standing tradition in locating criteria for "story credibility" in, at least, two distinct realms: one *intra-diegetic* (inside the story itself), the other *extra-diegetic*. This is very clear and straightforward in Gilbert Plumer's characteristically *dyadic* account of the novel's *believability* (2011, pp. 1554–1555) which would be attained by means of its:

(1) "internal coherence": that events in the narrative be fully connected, and
(2) "external coherence": that they *also* "cohere with our widely shared assumptions about how human psychology and society [...] work".

Fisher (1989) also presented, in principle, this kind of *dyadic* approach to the evaluation of communicative discourse (which, in his view, is *always* narrative). However, while developing his criteria throughout his book, Fisher finally introduces certain ideas that point to somewhat different evaluative sources. Fisher calls "coherence" or "probability" what is roughly Plumer's "internal coherence", and

[2]This concept of the "verisimilis" is rather close to Aristotle's concept of *eikós* which is conceived as the main object of Rhetoric (for a definition of it cf. *Rhetoric* 1357 b).

"fidelity" Plumer's "external coherence". Here is a summary scheme of what Fisher says about these two testing qualities of "human communication" in different parts of his book (1989: pp. 47, 75, 88, 175).

(A) Probability/coherence: whether a story "hangs together"

A.1. Probability is assessed in three ways:

- by the story's *argumentative* or *structural coherence* (i.e. its involving a "coherent plot");
- by its *material coherence*, that is, by comparing and contrasting it to stories told in other discourses;
- and by *characterological coherence.*

A.2. Features Fisher calls *formal*, which result in the narrative satisfying the demands of a *coherence theory of truth.* The idea is that the story be "free of contradictions".

A.3. "Knowing something about the character of the speaker and his or her actual experience, one can judge whether his or her story 'hangs together' and 'rings true'." (p. 88).

(B) Fidelity: truthfulness and reliability.

B.1. Fisher calls features of fidelity *substantive* (*vs. formal*) features, which result in the narrative satisfying the demands of a *correspondence theory of truth.*

B.2. Narrative *fidelity* concerns the soundness of its internal reasoning: Does the message accurately portray the world we live in?

B.3. Narrative *fidelity* also concerns the value of its values: Does it provide a reliable guide to our beliefs, attitudes, values and actions?

This more lengthily developed and in principle more sophisticated account is ultimately only apparently *dyadic*. Considerations presented in A.1. about "material coherence" rely on a comparative approach between available stories (even, reading through the text, between available "competing" stories) which is not so much an *intra-diegetic* criterion and which may have to do with a wider assessment of the pragmatic circumstances and discursive background in which a story is uttered and interpreted—we'll see more of that later, in other authors, but as a relevantly distinct criterion, with its own weight.

More unexpected is probably the mention, in A.3., of the speaker's known or attested character as supporting the story's coherence when, for example, in Walton's considerations on "arguments by testimony" it is exactly the other way around. According to Walton, the story's apparent coherence is part of the assessment of the testifier's performance that finally supports the plausibility of an argument in which the assessable reason is that there is a reliable witness testifying for a certain claim. In any case, I suggest that this and other ethotic questions would require a better fit as they form a criterion or a set of criteria that go beyond the story's "coherence".

On the *fidelity* side, we see again the somewhat unexpected (even if fully consistent with Fisher's avowed motivations) introduction of an ethical and value-based characterization of this requirement, which has to do with its "reliable" versus its "truthful" quality. However, this very important aspect would demand, in my opinion, its own space as not immediately related to prima facie *believability* or, in any case, to a *correspondence theory of truth*. Of course the compliance of stories with values may be crucial for their usefulness in practical reasoning and so their assessment according to this criterion may be part of their acquiring the quality of "evidence" in certain contexts. But I still think it would be better to distinguish more neatly, at least in principle, between the two aspects of *fidelity* mentioned by Fisher. So Fisher's account, apparently clear, schematic and dyadic has finally proven to be rather pluralistic. This reminds us that there are still many things which could be clarified in this domain.

I will mention now the old list of requirements given by the 15th c. humanist Rudolph Agricola (ca. 1479) for a "probable account" (*probabilis expositio*), which is *triadic*, not because I intend to classify theories about story credibility according to the number of criteria they propose, but because the third criterion he adds to roughly the two equivalents of the main ones we have already seen deserves, in my opinion, some consideration. According to Agricola, in a well-known passage of his *De inventione dialectica*,[3] the kind of *probabilitas* we are after in accounting for facts is obtained by means of an exposition which should be:

(a) "rich in argumentative content" (*argumentosa*)[4]: i.e. which accounts for enough aspects of the action related;
(b) "free from contradiction" (per se *consequens*): i.e. which presents an internal coherent structure;
(c) "consistent with how things are" (*consentanea rebus*): i.e. that resembles what we know about the real world, complies with an external standard of comparison.

While (b) and (c) could be more or less equivalent to Plumer's intra- and extra-diegetic criteria, criterion (a) is, obviously, something different. It may have something to do with the "material coherence" mentioned by Fisher in the sense that the relative "degree of detail" (depth and richness) attained by a story cannot be an absolute measure, but will always be evaluated by comparison to other accounts (competing or not).

In any case, this kind of criterion, reconverted into a requirement for "coverage", reappears in modern theories regarding the testing of stories in legal settings. We find something very similar in Pennington and Hastie (1992), for example. These

[3]"Probabilis fit expositio, si sit argumentosa, si consentanea rebus, si per se consequens" (Agricola 1992 [1539], p. 350).

[4]As it has been pointed out to me by the commentator of this paper, it is interesting to note that Agricola uses the adjective with a positive connotation, in contrast with the negative connotation implied by the term "argumentosa" in Classical Latin (Cf.: Quintilian, *Institutio Oratoria* V: X, 9–11).

authors mention several factors that determine the acceptability of a story in juror's decision- making:

(a) Coherence: which sums consistency (internal criterion) and plausibility (external criterion);
(b) Coverage: of the legal evidence presented;
(c) Uniqueness: that it is the only story available.

The authors group the two most obvious principles (Plumer's internal and external coherence) under the heading "coherence" and distinguish between an internal "consistency" requirement (freedom of contradictions) and an external "plausibility" one. The second criterion (close to Agricola's "richness in argumentative content") refers not just to the particular "degree of detail" of the story but to its degree of detail relative to the data presented in trial as evidence, the idea being that the credible story should be capable of "covering", that is of explaining and situating such evidence within a global, articulate account. This I find a nice way of spelling out the pragmatic circumstances regarding the kind of criterion mentioned by Agricola when demanding an "*expositio argumentosa*" for a particular argumentative practice (in this case, juror's decision-making) and I imagine something similar could be done in other contexts as well.

Now, Penington and Hastie's criterion (c), "uniqueness", is also very interesting. It is rather akin to the "material coherence" mentioned by Fisher (although Fisher's characterization would include both coverage and uniqueness in "material coherence"), as the latter author specifies that other stories told should be compared and contrasted with the one we are testing in order to evaluate it. I would suggest, though, that this criterion should be supplemented or qualified with an additional *independence* criterion that may bring in issues about multiple-source confirmation.

It is a common rule in law that, at least, two *independent* witnesses should coincide in telling roughly "the same story" for their "joint" testimony to constitute "evidence". If there are contradictions between witnesses, this circumstance speaks against the plausibility of each of their accounts. However, the measure of the "degree of independence" of two, more or less coincident, witnesses relies precisely on their stories being at least "slightly different" so that they do not seem to have been dictated by a common source. If two people, who in principle should have seen things with their own eyes, from their own respective different positions, tell *exactly* the same story, mention the same details and qualify actions with the same vocabulary, anyone will suspect that their testimony has been unduly prearranged. I therefore suggest that Pennington and Hastie's *uniqueness* criterion should be supplemented or qualified with an *independence* criterion that may take account of such possibilities.

Let's finally mention Cicero's "multiple criteria" approach as exposed in a well-known paragraph of his *De inventione*:

> The narrative will be plausible if it seems to embody characteristics which are accustomed to appear in real life; if the proper qualities of the characters are maintained, if reasons for their actions are plain, if there seems to have been ability to do the deed, if it can be shown that the time was opportune, the space sufficient and the place suitable for the events about

> to be narrated; if the story fits in with the nature of the actors in it, the habits of the ordinary people and the beliefs of the audience. Verisimilitude can be secured by following these principles (*De inv*. I.29).[5]

This paragraph was commented by Marius Victorinus in the 4th c. CE (*Explanationum in rhetoricam M. Tullii Ciceronis*) emphasizing the opposition between the so-called "seven circumstances" (that account for the story's "coverage" and "internal coherence") and the "doxastic" standards that have to do, above all, with the "pragmatic" circumstances of discourse delivery (audience-related issues). According to Marius Victorinus (Halm 1863, p. 207) Cicero's criteria for the assessment of the plausibility of a *narratio* could thus be schematized placing, on one side, the seven circumstances that must be duly accounted for by the narrative and, on the other, the three doxastic aspects mentioned by Cicero.

Seven circumstances	Opinion
Who (person)	Nature of the agents
What (fact)	
Why (cause)	Common habits and values
Where (place)	
When (time)	
How (mode)	Audience (arbiter's) opinion
How possibly (faculty)	

This is probably an over-systematic interpretation of Cicero's paragraph, but what counts for our purposes is that *De inventione* mentions, among the extra-diegetic criteria for narrative assessment, things like the "common habits and values of the ordinary people" (in line with Fisher) and also (in an explicit rhetorical mood) the need to take into account the "audience's or arbiter's previous opinion" in analysing the "credibility in context" of a story.

4 Argumentative Assessment of Story Credibility

All the discussed proposals seem to be based on the collection and ordering of a list of different criteria that a story told in an argumentative discourse should fulfil in order to be credible and accepted as evidence of some sort. If we sum up and try to

[5]"Probabilis erit narratio, si in ea videbuntur inesse ea, quae solent apparere in veritate; si personarum dignitates servabuntur; si causae factorum exstabunt; si fuisse facultates faciundi videbuntur; si tempus idoneum, si spatii satis, si locus opportunus ad eandem rem, qua de re narrabitur, fuisse ostendetur; si res et ad eorum, qui agent, naturam et ad vulgi morem et ad eorum, qui audient, opinionem accommodabitur", Cicero, *De Inv*. I.29. (Latin and English text from Cicero 1976).

arrange what we have so far seen, starting from the most inner (intra-diegetic) to outer (extra-diegetic) criteria, we have a much more complicated framework than the dyadic theory we started with and which referred to roughly numbers 1 and 9 on our list, equivalents of which are mentioned by practically all authors:

1. Internal plot or structural coherence
2. Internal characterological coherence (Fisher, Cicero)
3. Internal degree of detail: *expositio argumentosa*, covering the seven or more circumstances: i.e. a rich enough, dense enough account (Agricola, Cicero)
4. Arguer-related, "ethotic" assessment: story/storyteller coherence (Fisher)
5. Coverage of relevant extra-diegetic evidence ("material coherence"). Relative to argumentative practice involved (Pennington and Hastie).
6. Uniqueness, situation of the story regarding other "competing" discourses (Pennington and Hastie).
7. Independence regarding other competing discourses (relative contribution to a collective reconstruction of plausibility based on multiple-source confirmation) (Olmos).
8. Audience-related, "pathotic" assessment: previous beliefs of audience. Relative to argumentative practice involved (Cicero).
9. External coherence, fidelity to the real, extra-diegetic world. Degree of realism (a complicated issue in itself).
10. Fidelity to human values: reliability and applicability of the story. Degree of humanism: ethical assessment (Fisher, Cicero).

Now, what can we do with this increasingly sophisticated list? (It could be easily extended). First of all, I see many problems in taking these criteria as a growing number of requirements that would eventually take us somehow closer to a kind of definitive list of necessary and sufficient conditions for the assessment of any story as "credible". An alternative to such an approach is provided by argumentation theory.

If we assume that the process of evaluating the credibility of a story is an argumentative practice in itself that requires arguments supporting it (or meta-arguments in case our story is already a substantial part of an argument) and further arguments if challenged, then criteria as the ones we have been reviewing (and other conceivable ones) can be interpreted as possible motives or topics, more or less combinable in argumentative structures, providing warrants for arguing for the credibility of a story or for challenging it in an argumentative interchange. I suggest to oppose the following two conceptions and usages of such criteria:

- Criteria as conditions or requirements for the *qualitative* assessment of narrative argumentative discourse. This approach implies discussions about the inclusion/exclusion of individual criteria and about their necessity/sufficiency, *vs.*
- Criteria as topical suggestions providing reasonable warrants for (meta)*argumentative* assessment, depending:

(i) on possible argument-types involved in the assessed discourse (i.e. different argument schemes would require different criteria for the assessment of the narratives making part of them);
(ii) on the discursive interactive context, possibly including competing stories (i.e. assessment would in most cases be *comparative*, Marraud 2013, p. 149ff.) or
(iii) on the goals of the particular argumentative practice in which the narrative appears.

The latter approach is coherent with my general standpoint that argument evaluation and premise assessment are, finally, argumentative practices themselves, which may involve a variety of warrants and lines of argument.

The various reviewed theorists and authors providing us with criteria for narrative credibility, coming from different traditions and interested in diverse kinds of discourse, have coherently pointed to different aspects that could be conceivably used in arguing for the correctness, reliability or truthfulness of our stories and therefore for their usefulness as evidence in argumentative discourse.

Such an approach is, in my view, applicable to any process of argument evaluation as reveal the different CQ's involved in assessing argumentation schemes which may be easily multiplied in several ways, especially if we take into account pragmatical and rhetorical issues. But in the case of our narratives, moreover, I think we must also acknowledge some rather intractable additional problems. In the next section I will concentrate on those regarding what in our summary list was criterion 9: the requirement of realism.

5 Narrative Realism

What exactly is "a realistic narrative" is not a question that we can answer in any easy way. Literature scholars have been dealing with this topic for at least the last 150 years (cf. classics as Booth [1961]1983; Stevick 1967) and the answers are multiple and historically changing. Wayne Booth in his classical *The Rhetoric of Fiction*, acknowledged that general rules fail in providing good answers: there are too many ways of being realistic and of conceiving of realism. More recently, Claudia Jünke (forthcoming), has presented a study about the three French writers Marivaux, Diderot and Stendhal, all of whom use very different literary devices (although in all three cases we are talking about explicit meta-linguistic authorial interventions) to account for the verisimilitude of their tales and novels. Jünke's study proves a certain historical variation and evolution in the conventional ways of arguing, within literary narrative, for verisimilitude. If we take in account the possibilities exploited by more contemporary novels, in which avoidance of authorial interventions becomes the norm, things get even more complicated. It is, of course an endless issue.

For the purpose of this study though I would just suggest that we take into account these two rather reasonable and relevant claims:

(a) we are not really sure of what is *plausible* in human affairs, the infinite complexity and unexpectedness of human life will always be there; it is the kind of realm where we should not look for a complete system of rules (Cf: Wittgenstein on *Menschenkenntnis* or "knowledge of human nature", PI §355–356, Wittgenstein 1999 [1953], Cf. Bouveresse 2007, pp. 80–81);
(b) storytelling is a way (one of our most basic ways) to explore what's plausible in human affairs: so the relation narration/reality is inescapably circular.

Now, regarding (a), I would say that it is part of our condition that the inconceivable, the unexpected in many cases happens in human affairs and we cannot really construe a theory that would overcome this situation, among other things because we are not allowed to make lab-experiments about what would happen if so-and-so happened regarding human life and affairs.

Krzysztof Kieślowski's film *La double vie de Véronique* (1991) is precisely about an author (a storyteller and, ironically enough, a puppeteer) who is not sure about the plausibility of a certain tale he has imagined and tries to put part of the plot into practice, inducing a girl to take certain actions just to see whether such actions are conceivable for her. The film shows how inadmissible and inhuman this "playing with others as puppets" is, even in the case of apparently inconsequential actions (as those in the film which are not really dramatic). Then, (b) is our alternative, one of our alternatives to this and Kieślowski's film is finally a piece of human life storytelling regarding the intrinsic difficulties of human life storytelling. Kieślowski uses a fiction film, a narrative, to show us that we cannot make non-narrative or real-life experiments to test stories.

This circumstance exposes the intractable circularity of the relationship between reality and narrative or storytelling. When we (in a spontaneous, natural way, in Fisher's sense) find a narrative plausible, in part we may be comparing it with what we have already experienced (it rings true because it's similar to what we know) or, alternatively, we may be partly surprised (and nevertheless convinced) by what it reveals about human nature and, from then on, apply it in our understanding of real situations. This balance is rather complex and it may be further complicated.

From the point of view of argumentation theory, we could say, with Perelman, that narratives (be them fictive or not) are partly "based on the structure of reality", partly "founding the structure of reality" (1958, pp. 351ss, 471ss). We'll have to decide in each case and depending on the characteristics of the discourses (including the particular types of argument involved) and discursive interchanges in which the narratives are inserted, which of these aspects is more relevant and should be taken into account in our analysis, evaluation or challenge.

6 Conclusion

If we assume that the evaluation of arguments or parts of arguments can be conducted in an argumentative way and become an argumentative practice in itself, we will be prepared to listen to different ways of arguing for the adequacy of the stories involved in our practices of giving reasons.

For example, Aristotle's maxim warranting the use of past stories derived from facts as evidence to be taken into account in decision-making processes, by means of arguments from example, or *paradeigmata* and which reads: "*for the most part what's coming will be similar to what's already happened*,"[6] might seem fairly reasonable. But then so it is (especially for our modern sensibility) Richard Ford's justification of the verisimilitude of the story he tells in the novel *Canada*:

> I can't make what follows next seem reasonable or logical, based on what anyone would believe they knew about the world. However, as Arthur Remlinger said, I was the son of bank robbers and desperadoes, which was his way of reminding me that no matter the evidence of your life, or who you believe you are, or what you're willing to take credit for or draw your vital strength and pride from – *anything at all can follow anything at all*. Richard Ford, *Canada* (2012).

I think both are usable (and in fact used) warrants that I personally would accept as *prima facie* good reasons supporting stories in different settings and for different purposes. They are both rather extreme though and I would certainly prefer more balanced principles for "important" or "consequential" decisions. Ironically enough, if decision-making or other serious purposes are lacking or avoided and the end of our stories is something like *frivolous entertainment*, we may always abide with Mark Twain's warning at the beginning of *Huckleberry Finn* which prevents his novel's serious use as *evidence* by precisely forbidding its narrative assessment:

> Persons attempting to find a motive in this narrative will be prosecuted; persons attempting to find a moral in it will be banished; persons attempting to find a plot in it will be shot. (Quoted by P. Stevick 1967, p. 3).

Acknowledgments This contribution has been made possible by funds provided by both the UNED Research Project's Programme (Project 2012 V/PUNED/0010, "Narrativity and Argumentation: Discursive Basis of Plausibility") and the Spanish Ministry of Economy and Competitiveness (Research Project: FFI2011-23125, "Arguing in the Public Sphere: Deliberation as a Paradigm").

References

Agricola, R. (1992 [1539]). *De inventione dialectica*, Ed. by L. Mundt. Tubinga: Max Niemeyer.
Aristotle (1959). *Ars Rhetorica*, Ed. by W. D. Ross. Oxford: Clarendon Press.

[6]"*hómoia gàr hōs epi tò polù tà méllonta toís gegónosin*", *Rhet.* 1394a7, Aristotle 1959, my translation.

Booth, W. C. (1961, 1983^2). *The Rhetoric of Fiction*. Chicago/Londres: The University of Chicago Press.
Bouveresse, J. (2013 [2007]) *El conocimiento del escritor. Sobre la literatura, la verdad y la vida*. Barcelona: Ediciones del Subsuelo.
Cicero (1976). *De inventione*, Ed. and Trans. by H. M. Hubbell. Cambridge, MS: Harvard University Press.
Fisher, W. R. (1989 [1987]). *Human Communication as Narration: Toward a Philosophy of Reason, Value, and Action*. Columbia, SC: University of South Carolina Press.
Ford, R. (2012). *Canada*. New York: Ecco Press.
Govier, T., & Ayers, L. (2012). Logic and parables: do these narratives provide arguments? *Informal Logic, 32*(2), 161–189.
Halm, K. (Ed.). (1863). *Rhetores Latini Minores*. Leipzig: Teubner.
Jünke, C. (forthcoming). Verdad y verosimilitud en la novela francesa de la ilustración al realismo. In A. Sánchez Manzano (Ed.), *Retórica y narrativa*. Madrid/León: Tecnos/Universidad de León.
Marraud, H. (2013). *¿Es logic@? Análisis y evaluación de argumentos*. Madrid: Cátedra.
Olmos, P. (2012). La preceptiva sobre la *narratio* en los rétores latinos. *Revista de Estudios Sociales 44*, 62–74. Retrieved from http://res.uniandes.edu.co/view.php/803/index.php?id=803.
Olmos, P. (2014a). Narration as argument. In D. Mohammed & M. Lewiński (Eds.), *Virtues of Argumentation. Proceedings of the 10th International Conference of the Ontario Society for the Study of Argumentation (OSSA), 22–26 May 2013*, CD edition. Windsor: University of Windsor.
Olmos, P. (2014b). Classical fables as arguments: narration and analogy. In H. Jales Ribeiro (Ed.), *Systematic Approaches to Argument by Analogy* (pp. 189–208). Amsterdam: Springer.
Pennington, N., & Hastie, R. (1992). Explaining the evidence: tests of the story model for juror decision-making. *Journal of Personality and Social Psychology, 62*(2), 189–206.
Perelman, C., & Olbrechts-Tyteca, L. (1958). *Traité de l'Argumentation. La Nouvelle Rhétorique*. Paris: PUF.
Plumer, G. (2011). Novels as arguments. In F. H. van Eemeren et al. (Eds.), *Proceedings of the 7th Conference of the International Society for the Study of Argumentation (ISSA 2010)* (pp. 1547–1558). Amsterdam: Sic Sat.
Stevick, P. (1967). *The theory of the novel*. New York/London: The fRee Pree/Collier Macmillan.
Walton, D. (2012). Story similarity in arguments from analogy. *Informal Logic, 32*, 190–221.
Walton, D., Reed, C., & Macagno, F. (2008). *Argumentation Schemes*. Cambridge: C.U.P.
Wittgenstein, L. (1999 [1953]). *Philosophical investigations*. Upper Saddle River, NJ: Prentice Hall.

Part IV
Argument Schemes

Arguments by Analogy (and What We Can Learn about Them from Aristotle)

Manfred Kraus

1 Introduction

Arguments by analogy have been a much disputed subject recently. The most controversial issues in that discussion have been whether or not there are different types of analogical arguments, whether they are to be regarded as basically inductive or deductive or as a completely distinct category of argument of their own, whether or not they involve any hidden or missing premises, and whether it is possible for analogical arguments to be deductive and yet defeasible.

Since the mid-1980s Trudy Govier has repeatedly argued in favor of a view that arguments by analogy should best be regarded as a distinct type of argument, and not as a species of either induction or deduction (Govier 1985, 1987, 1989, 2002), by denying that any universal generalizations need to be included as unstated or missing premises in such arguments. In response to her view, while basically agreeing with her distinction between 'inductive' and a priori analogies, Waller (2001) has tried to restate the case for a deductivist reconstruction of the latter, whereas Guarini (2004) attempted to show that Waller's reconstruction was unsubstantiated. Fábio Perin Shecaira, in turn, has defended Waller's deductivist analysis by introducing some modifications (2013, p. 429) and by declaring analogy arguments that do not fit Waller's schema to be "defective or sub-optimal instances of their kind" (pp. 407–408, 421). In response to the dispute between Waller, Govier, and Guarini on the possibility of 'deductive' arguments by analogy, Lilian Bermejo-Luque has recently (2012, 2014) proposed a new unitary schema for arguments by analogy as complex second-order speech acts to explain how such arguments can be 'deductive', but nonetheless defeasible. Independently from Bermejo-Luque, but in a way in some respects not dissimilar to her approach, James

M. Kraus (✉)
Philologisches Seminar, University of Tübingen, Wilhelmstraße 36,
72074 Tübingen, Germany
e-mail: manfred.kraus@uni-tuebingen.de

F.H. van Eemeren and B. Garssen (eds.), *Reflections on Theoretical Issues in Argumentation Theory*, Argumentation Library 28,
DOI 10.1007/978-3-319-21103-9_13

Freeman, in his own analysis of Govier's distinctions (2013), has insisted on the necessity of the insertion of a *ceteris paribus* clause and of qualifiers in a priori analogies and defended their status as defeasible a priori arguments.

I will propose an alternative solution. I would myself prefer to view arguments by analogy within a greater range of argument types that derive from comparisons and similarities (see also Doury 2009), including examples, or even metaphors, and analyze them as complex compound arguments that involve various different types of inferences. I further hold that Aristotle's logic and rhetoric already provides the tools needed for such an analysis of arguments by analogy.

In a first section, I will briefly analyze the main points of disagreement between scholars on arguments by analogy. I will then argue that categories such as 'deductive' and 'inductive' are structural, not normative categories, and should therefore not be used to designate argument validity ('conclusiveness'). In a next step, I will sketch the main features of Aristotle's theories on arguments involving similarities and comparisons, and will finally demonstrate how arguments from analogy can be reconstructed as complex arguments that involve inductive, abductive, and deductive components.

2 Types of Analogies

Govier, Waller and Guarini all agree that there are two types of arguments by analogy: one that operates from empirical data and yields only probable conclusions, and one that proceeds from analogies invented ad hoc and allegedly leads to conclusive inferences. The disagreement is on whether or not the latter can therefore be regarded as deductive. Govier calls those a priori analogies. Waller also adds as a third kind what he calls "figurative analogies" (2001, p. 200), that is analogies that do not actually argue for a certain claim, but simply illustrate a statement for the sake of better understanding (see also Garssen 2009). These are not to be regarded as arguments at all. Bermejo-Luque calls those "explanatory analogies" (2012, p. 6), and appears to further add also a non-discursive, "cognitive-exploratory" function of analogies, in which they act as cognitive tools in that they offer a kind of cognitive proposal for making new objects and phenomena more familiar to us. But the emphasis is on the two primarily argumentative types.

Govier's analysis of a typical 'inductive' analogy runs as follows (1989, p. 141):

(1)

1. A has features x, y, z.
2. B has features x, y, z.
3. A has feature f.
4*. Most things which have features x, y, z, have feature f.
5. Thus, probably, B has feature f.

In this reconstruction, the fourth premise "is starred because, the way most arguments by analogy are worded, it would not be explicit in the argument. It would be unstated." (p. 141). One should note the qualifier "probably" in the conclusion! While she agrees that such arguments may require some inductive generalization, what she sees involved here is "a hasty generalization—typically a generalization from a single case." (p. 142). Her example is that war and slavery have a lot in common, yet slavery was abolished by citizen action; hence it should be possible to abolish war by citizen action. Typically, in an 'inductive' analogy, "the reality and empirical detail of the analogue matter", and the conclusion "predicts a result for the primary subject" (p. 142). This is why Guarini (2004, p. 166), just as Brown (1989, p. 162), prefers to call them 'predictive'.

Govier's master example for what she calls a priori analogy is Judith Jarvis Thomson's famous example of the desperate violinist that is hooked to another human being for life support (Thomson 1971, pp. 48–49; Govier 1989, p. 142), an ad hoc example that was meant to support the claim that a woman that had gotten pregnant from rape had no moral obligation to keep the foetus alive. According to Govier, in an a priori analogy, the analogue is "constructed", it "can be entirely hypothetical and may, in fact, be positively fanciful." (1989, p. 142).

Her analysis of such an a priori analogy is slightly different from that of an 'inductive' one (p. 144):

(2)

1. A has x, y, z.
2. B has x, y, z.
3. A is W.
4'. It is in virtue of x, y, z, that A is W.
5. Therefore, B is W.

There is no qualifier such as "probably" here, as there was in 'inductive' analogy. On the contrary, Govier even suggests that from premise 4' (which seems to be presupposed in some way) it is only a short step to the universal premise:

4*. *All* things which have x, y, z are W.

This is what Govier calls a "U-claim", a universal claim. In the case of the desperate violinist, the 'U-claim' would be something like "*No-one* has an obligation to support at his or her own inconvenience the life of another human being to which he or she has been unvoluntarily linked." This premise would make the argument deductively valid. But it would also make premises 1 and 3 logically redundant and thus eliminate the analogy as superfluous. And, what is more, it is clearly an overstatement unwarranted by premises 1 and 3. Based on these considerations and on Stephen F. Barker's objections that it is often "not possible to state a suitable universal premise" and that "the universal premise […] is nearly always more dubious than the conclusion" (Govier 1989, p. 144; see Barker 1965, pp. 280–290), she is inclined to reject such a deductivist reconstruction, and to accept at best that some 'U-claim' may be implied, but not presupposed by the argument as an implicit premise (1989, p. 148). She argues that the cases are epistemologically prior to the generalization, and that hence a priori arguments by analogy work better directly from case to case rather than by way of a detour via what she calls a U-claim. In fact: "The trick about analogies—and their charm as well […]—is that we are often able to see or sense important resemblances between cases without being able to spell them out exhaustively […]." (p. 148). This is why she postulates for those analogies a special a priori, but non-deductive category.

Waller, by contrast, finds no sufficient reason "for denying the deductive status of such arguments by analogy" (2001, p. 204), just because the U-claim is hard to formulate or not immediately recognizable. He holds that analyzing an a priori analogy "is not a matter of finding the fixed and final universal principle that rightly governs the analogy" (p. 207). Rather, the analogy forces the audience to think hard and reflect upon their own principles and their implications, so that the analogy does not establish the principle, but gets the audience to recognize the principle (p. 208). In this way, while preserving the deductive status of such analogies, Waller on the other hand denies them any inductive power. According to him, "there is not a shred of induction about them." (p. 201).

In her reply to Waller, Govier criticizes this view and argues that, if the U-claim were in fact implicit as an unstated premise, as Waller claims, it would be much less required from the audience to think so hard to arrive at it (Govier 2002, p. 156). This criticism of Govier's, however, appears to underrate the cognitive capacities of audiences, which Aristotle acknowledged when emphasizing the role of the audience in supplying unstated premises in enthymemes (e.g. *Rhetoric* I 2, 1357a17-21).

To overcome this controversy, Bermejo-Luque (2012) intends to construct a unitary structural schema for both 'inductive' and a priori analogies by analyzing them as complex second-order speech acts to explain how such arguments can be 'deductive', but nonetheless defeasible. Based on a Toulminian analysis of arguments and a linguistic-pragmatic model of interpretation, by laying strong emphasis on ontological and epistemic qualifiers that qualify the inference-claim as well as the analogue and also the connecting warrant, she proposes to reduce the difference between 'inductive' and 'deductive' analogies to a matter of such qualifiers (pp. 16–22).

Likewise reducing arguments from analogy to a Toulminian warrant structure by switching the order of some of the premises in Govier's analytic schema, thus reducing differences between types of arguments from analogy to an assessment of ground adequacy and the epistemic status of the warrant, Freeman (2013) also insists on the necessity of the insertion of a *ceteris paribus* clause and of qualifiers in a priori analogies, lest they be open to counterexamples (pp. 180–183), and defends their status as defeasible a priori arguments. He shares with Shecaira (2013) the belief that synthetic a priori warrants are typical of moral arguments (Freeman 2013, pp. 179–180).

3 Deduction, Induction, Abduction

Some confusion in this controversy derives from the fact that in discussions of arguments from analogy terms such as 'deductive' and 'inductive' are more often than not applied in a normative sense, implying that a deductive argument is equivalent to a logically conclusive argument, the conclusion of which follows with necessity, whereas an inductive one yields only a plausible or probable conclusion (Bermejo-Luque 2012, pp. 2–3, 4, 21; yet apparently retracted by herself in 2014, p. 318, note 4 and pp. 320–326). In view of the fact that "there can be bad, i.e. invalid or weak, instances of each type of argument," this dichotomy, as Hitchcock points out, cannot be exhaustive unless one is willing "to label 'inductive' all arguments which are not deductively valid." (1980, p. 9). In contrast to this, *pace* Hitchcock's ultimate defence of "the distinction between deductive and inductive as a broad and exhaustive distinction between types of validity" (p. 9)—against Weddle's attempted blurring of that distinction (Weddle 1979)—in the sense of a "distinction between deductive validity and inductive strength" (Hitchcock 1980, p. 10), and his rejection of Wellman's further distinction between inductive and 'conductive' arguments (Wellman 1971) as merely "two types of inductive validity" (Hitchcock 1980, p. 9), I would strongly advocate the view that 'deduction' and 'induction' are essentially structural categories and should not be employed as normative terms.

If one adopts the stance of Aristotelian logic, a deduction (Aristotle's term for which is *syllogismós*) would be structurally defined as an inference from a universal rule and a statement about a particular case being an instance of that rule to a particular assertion about that case, as in the famous example: "All human beings are mortal; Socrates is a human being; hence Socrates is mortal." When cast in syllogistic form, in deductive arguments the middle term is always the subject in one premise, but the predicate in the other. It is easy to interpret this category in a normative sense, since, given that the premises are true, deductive arguments in standard form typically yield conclusive results, and in fact Aristotle himself reserves the term *syllogismós* to conclusive deductive arguments only (see *Posterior Analytics* I 1, 24b18-26). But by far not all formally deductive arguments are logically conclusive, as soon as negations and quantifiers get involved. Consider the following: "All human beings are mortal; Fido is not a human being; hence Fido is immortal." (It is assumed that Fido is a dog). From a structural point of view, this argument is formally deductive; but it is clearly fallacious (and would hence not count as a *syllogismós* for Aristotle).

Inductive arguments, by contrast, infer from the particular to the universal (Aristotle, *Topics* I 12, 105a13-16; *Posterior Analytics* I 1, 71a8-9; *Rhetoric* I 2, 1356b14-15: "a proof from a number of similar cases that such is the rule"). Such an inductive argument, however, can be obtained by simply switching propositions within a standard deductive argument, such as when from "Socrates is a human being" and "Socrates is mortal" it is inferred inductively (and in this case by chance correctly) that human beings in general are mortal. Aristotle lists such arguments in his taxonomy of enthymemes from signs (*Rhetoric* I 2, 1357b10-13; *Prior Analytics* II 27, 70a16-20), but explicitly remarks that this type of argument is defeasible, since it is not properly deductive (*Rhetoric* I 2, 1357b13-14). In syllogistic interpretation, the middle term takes the subject position in both premises, such as in the following example: "Socrates is a philosopher; and Socrates is bearded; hence philosophers are bearded." It is easy to see that in such an argument the conclusion will need a qualifier to make it acceptable if not even valid. For it may be perfectly reasonable to say that the argument does prove that *some* philosophers are bearded, or perhaps even that as a rule philosophers are *likely* to be bearded. Yet one single counterexample (such as Kant or Wittgenstein) will suffice to refute any general conclusion such as "*All* philosophers are bearded."[1]

This may not be how the terms 'deductive' and 'inductive' are commonly understood and used by philosophers of science and logicians these days, but the structural approach opens a path toward a more nuanced and more discriminate taxonomy of fundamental argument types and consequently a more adequate description of arguments from analogy.

For, in addition to deduction and induction, there is yet a third conceivable structural type of argument, which is generally termed 'abduction'. In an abductive argument what is inferred is the subsumption of a case under a general rule. The middle term in this case takes the position of predicate in both premises. Using again the obvious standard example, from "Socrates is mortal" and "human beings are mortal", it may be inferred that the most reasonable explanation for the observed fact will be that "Socrates is a human being". Arguments of that type are also acknowledged as enthymemes by Aristotle (*Rhetoric* I 2, 1357b17-19; *Prior Analytics* II 27, 70a20-24). Of course, as Aristotle himself remarks, even if the

---

[1]An anonymous reviewer of this paper has challenged this analysis by raising objections to the view that deductive reasoning generally proceeds from universals to particulars, and inductive reasoning vice versa, maintaining that some deductive arguments go from particular to particular, and some inductive arguments from universal to universal or from particular to particular, invoking the following two examples: (1) This pen is red; red is a color; therefore this pen is colored (deductive argument that goes from particular to particular without involving a universal). (2) This tree has leaves; this next tree has leaves; […]; this next tree has leaves; therefore probably this next tree will have leaves (inductive argument from particular to particular). To these examples I would respond in the following way: In (1), for the sake of the argument, 'red' is assumed to be a particular, not a universal. Yet in my view, if 'red' is assumed to be a particular, the formulation of this example involves a category error: Taken literally, the argument would yield: This pen is red, red is a color; therefore this pen is a color (which is obviously false). Yet, if the premises are rearranged in the following way: All red things are colored; this pen is red; therefore this pen is colored, this is most clearly an inference from a universal ('all red things') to a particular ('this pen') (see also the interpretation of the same example as "grounded on a relation of semantic inclusion between these two predicates" by Macagno et al. 2014, p. 417). Example (2), on the other hand, is not a bare induction, but actually a perfect example of a complex argument by analogy (or by example, if you will), as analyzed below: From a number of trees that have leaves it is (inductively) inferred that probably all trees in a certain area have leaves; and since still another tree is (abductively) identified as being part of the trees in the same area, it is (deductively) inferred that it will also have leaves.

premises are true, this type of inference will on no account be safe (*Rhetoric* I 2, 1357b19-21). Indeed, the Socrates in question may as well happen to be a dog or some other animal.

This trichotomy of structural argument types (as against the classical dichotomy) has notably been elaborated, based on Aristotelian syllogistic, by Charles S. Peirce in various of his writings over a span of many years, in which abduction is at first called reasoning a posteriori or hypothesis, and deduction is named reasoning a priori (Peirce 1878, see Kraus 2003). While inductive and abductive inferences are both in principle defeasible, their great advantage is that, unlike deductive inferences, they are ampliative—they 'amplify' our knowledge beyond the information contained in the premises—, which is also supposed to be a characteristic quality of arguments from analogy.

4 Aristotle on Arguments by Similarity

Aristotle, in his *Rhetoric* and *Posterior Analytics*, calls these latter two types of inferences enthymemes, since, even if all premises are true, the conclusion will only follow with a certain probability. But, as we have seen, they are at the same time quite appropriate descriptions of the structures of induction and abduction. But Aristotle says even more, namely that, just as the enthymeme is the rhetorical variant of deduction, the example (*paradeigma*) is the rhetorical variant of induction. This, I take it, is as good a description of analogy as any. Examples, like analogies, are ultimately based on similarities. And from the *Topics* onward, Aristotle develops the structure of analogy in close connection with the notion of similarity (cf. *Topics* I 17, 108a7-17; III 2, 116b27-36; Bartha 2010, p. 36; Macagno et al. 2014, p. 419). Whereas in scientific induction a maximum number of examples must be accumulated to make the induction persuasive, in rhetoric—for reasons of brevity—this is mostly reduced to one single example (or very few), but this one example has to be a particularly significant one: "[T]he example is understood as a kind of *qualitative* induction in which the fewer number of particular references is compensated by the fact that they are plausible in connection with the circumstances and the audience." (Gabrielsen 2003, p. 350; cf. Bermejo-Luque 2014, pp. 312–316, on quantitative vs. qualitative analogies).

In almost identical words, in the *Rhetoric* as well as in the *Prior Analytics*, Aristotle states that arguing by example works neither from part to whole (as induction does) nor from whole to part (as deduction does), but from part to part or from like to like, "when both come under the same genus, but one of them is better known than the other" (*Rhetoric* I 2, 1357b27-30; *Prior Analytics* II 24, 69a13-16; see Gabrielsen 2003, p. 351). This is exactly parallel to John Wisdom's description of analogy arguments as "case-by-case" reasoning (Wisdom 1957, cited in Govier 1989, p. 141). Aristotle's example is that Pisistratus, when he asked for a bodyguard, became a tyrant; hence it is inferred that when Dionysius asks for a bodyguard, he is aiming at tyranny (*Rhetoric* I 2, 1357b19). How does this example work? According to Gabrielsen's reading, "a 'part to part' example must be perceived as an unpronounced combination of an inductive and a deductive inference." (Gabrielsen 2003, p. 351). In Govier's terms, this would clearly qualify as an 'inductive' analogy, since the case adduced is taken from the experience of real life, and the generalization drawing on it ("people who ask for a bodyguard, usually aim at tyranny") would typically be used to predict another case.

Aristotle further says that examples may either be taken from reality or may simply be invented (*Rhetoric* II 20, 1393a28-31). In my view, this is basically the same distinction as Govier's between 'inductive' and a priori analogies. Invented examples, he adds, are subdivided into comparisons and fables; the examples he offers for the comparison type are in fact quite similar to the standard examples for a priori analogies: it is, he says, as if one were to say that magistrates should not be chosen by lot, since that would be similar to choosing an athlete for a sports competition by lot instead of by his strength, or to choosing by lot any of the sailors for helmsman (II 20, 1393b4-8). In these cases the examples/comparisons are clearly invented ad hoc, and in quite fanciful manner so as to highlight the paradox. Fables (also clearly a fictional genre) may be interpreted as extended forms of such a priori analogies.

Even Aristotle's theory of the metaphor in the *Poetics* can be adduced here, since it is equally based on similarities, and also in view of its cognitive and explanatory power (as Bermejo-Luque has observed, 2012, p. 8). Moreover, Aristotle notes that metaphors can be constructed from genre to species, or from species to genre (relationships we would nowadays rather categorize as synecdochae), but also directly from species to species (what we now predominantly call a metaphor). This third type strongly resembles the structure of what we now call an analogy argument. Yet Aristotle mentions a fourth kind, which he explicitly calls "by analogy", the structure of which is that A relates to X as B relates to Y; hence what Aristotle himself calls *analogía* is rather a four-term relationship of the type a : b = c : d (*Poetics* 21, 1457b7-9; cf. *Rhetoric* III 4, 1407a15-18; 6, 1408a8-9; 10, 1411a1-4; 11, 1412b36-1413a1; cf. also I 7, 1363 b 21-27; see Rapp 1992; Coenen 2002, pp. 101–113).

In a later passage of the *Rhetoric* (II 25, 1402b13-14), Aristotle states that enthymemes can be derived from four sources: probabilities, examples, infallible signs, and ordinary signs; again we find the example featuring prominently among sources for argument. And here Aristotle explicitly adds that we argue from examples, "when they are the result of induction from one or more similar cases, and when one assumes the general and then concludes the particular by an example" (1402b16-18). He thus links examples to the general realm of similarities; and he analyzes arguments by example as a two-step process, in which in a first step a general statement is established by way of induction, and then from there a particular case (the target claim) is again deduced. Hence in his view, arguments from example do argue from case to case, but they do so via a general principle.

5 Another Unitary Scheme for Arguments by Analogy

Based on what we can learn about arguments by various kinds of similarities from Aristotle, I would myself propose the following unitary analysis of arguments by analogy: I endorse the view that arguments by analogy are complex arguments that encompass at least two separate argumentative stages (cf. also the—conceptually slightly different—analysis of analogical reasoning as “a complex pattern” and “a twofold process” by Macagno et al. 2014, especially pp. 427–428). In a first stage, from the analogue case, by way of an argument from example, a general statement is inductively inferred. This is very clearly the case in so-called ‘inductive’ analogies, since in those cases one or more empirically observed examples serve as the starting point. In a subsequent stage, from this general rule another particular case (the target claim) is inferred deductively. But these two steps can’t be exhaustive. In fact, before the deduction to the target claim can be executed, it will have to be made sure beforehand that the target case is at all an instance of that general rule. This, however, will have to be done by an abductive reasoning based on some other characteristics of the target case. So we have actually a three-stage argument. But this abductive stage has mostly been overlooked in recent reconstructions.

Things may perhaps be slightly different for a priori analogy. Look at Waller’s reconstruction of the structure of such arguments (2001, p. 201):

(3)

1. We both agree with case *a*.
2. The most plausible reason for believing *a* is the acceptance of principle *C*.
3. *C* implies *b* (*b* is a case that fits under principle *C*).
4. Therefore, consistency requires the acceptance of *b*.

Shecaira observes that Waller’s schema “does not represent analogical arguments simply as deductive inferences, but rather as complexes of two inferences only one of which is deductive” (2013, p. 407; cf. also p. 424). On our account, however, his analysis in fact involves no less than three inferences. For anyone acquainted with abductive reasoning, premise 2 unmistakably evokes one of the most common standard descriptions of abduction (an “inference to the best explanation”, see Harman 1965; Lipton 2001; cf. Wellman’s “explanatory reasoning” as “reasoning from a body of data to a hypothesis that will render them intelligible”, 1971, p. 52; see Freeman 2013, p. 190). But so does premise 3 (a “case fitting under a principle”) for the target case. Shecaira comes very close to this insight, when he repeatedly speaks of principle *C* as the “most plausible (i.e., the best) reason for believing *a*” (2013, p. 429), or notes that this move “resembles an inference to the best explanation” (pp. 430; 435), but at no point he gets beyond calling it, rather vaguely, “a non-deductive sub-argument” (p. 453; cf. pp. 409; 430). Yet if Waller’s analysis is valid, it seems to suggest that in the case of a priori analogies the inductive stage is replaced by a second abductive reasoning that subordinates the ad hoc invented analogue to some principle that is already in some way part of the commitment store of the audience (cf. Waller 2001, p. 213).

This would account for the differences most analysts have observed between these two basic types of arguments by analogy. But since we learn from Aristotle that both inductive and abductive reasonings are by their very definition defeasible, because they are always open to refutation by counterexample, this means that no argument by analogy can be ultimately conclusive. This seems to be trivial for 'inductive' analogies. The general statement attained inductively in those arguments necessarily needs to be constrained by a qualifier such as 'probably' or 'presumably', which will render the ultimate conclusion only a probable or presumable one as well. Bermejo-Luque is certainly right in emphasizing the role of those qualifiers (2012, pp. 16–22). But contrary to what most analysts assume, this must equally hold for a priori analogy.

Both Waller and Guarini invoke a number of arguments that challenge the conclusiveness of Thomson's violinist analogy (Waller 2001, pp. 208–210; Guarini 2004, p. 159), to the effect that, even if the analogy as such holds, it may as well be abductively related to some different moral intuition such as that one *is* in fact morally obliged to support any other human being's life at whatever cost. Freeman's insistence on the necessity of the insertion of a *ceteris paribus* clause in such arguments, lest they be vulnerable to counterexamples, points in the same direction (2013, pp. 180–182). And both Guarini and Bermejo-Luque call attention to the fact that, since all similarities allow for a more or less, arguments by analogy must also allow for degrees of strength (Guarini 2004, pp. 159–160; Bermejo-Luque 2012, pp. 16; 23).

Freeman (2013, p. 192) ultimately argues that the *epistemic* distinction between arguments based on a priori and a posteriori warrants is more fundamental to a general theory of arguments than *structural* categories (such as inductive and deductive, which in his view mainly concern "the criteria and methods of assessing *connection adequacy*", p. 188), but that another distinction is equally fundamental, namely that between conclusive and defeasible arguments, so that the category of defeasible a priori arguments is not only not impossible, but even one out of four fundamental categories in a fourfold system of basic types of arguments (see Freeman 2014, p. 3).

If they are generally defeasible, what, then, is it that makes a priori analogies appear so compelling? There may be a number of explanations. First, there is most certainly the deductive element that comes as the last stage and makes one easily overlook the defeasible abductive or inductive parts. Second, just because in an a priori analogy the analogue is deliberately constructed ad hoc, it is of course constructed in such a way as to ideally support the claim, which makes its compelling force appear much stronger than in 'inductive' analogies from empirical data (cf. Bermejo-Luque 2014, pp. 312–316, on qualitative a priori vs. quantitative a posteriori analogies). Furthermore, since in a priori analogies both the analogue *and* the target claim are subordinated to a common general principle in a similar way, namely by an abductive move, they somehow appear to concur in supporting that general principle, so that it seems to get double support (Govier once—perhaps inadvertently—actually says that it is "from A *and* B" that we move to the U-claim, 1989, p. 148). And finally, the ontological and epistemic qualifiers that, as

Bermejo-Luque and Freeman rightly point out, would be needed in most of the propositions involved, are as a rule suppressed, which is something that frequently happens in rhetorical arguments such as enthymemes.

All this may explain why a priori analogies appear so particularly compelling that they are even sometimes interpreted as essentially deductive (in the sense of conclusive) arguments. Although Govier acknowledges the fact that her hypothetical reconstructions of a priori analogies "produce, in effect, a two-stage argument" consisting of "an inductive argument from one case to a universal statement" and "a deductive argument subsuming the subject case under that universal statement" (Govier 1989, p. 151), nonetheless, in her accompanying diagrams (pp. 150–151) the arrows emblematizing an inference all invariably point the same way downward, as if the entire argument were deductive.

6 Conclusion

In conclusion, then, we may say that a lot was to be learned about arguments by analogy and other arguments from similarities from Aristotle. Based on Aristotelian categories, a reconstruction of arguments by analogy seems possible that explains both the commonalities and the differences of 'inductive' and a priori analogies and their respective persuasive force. According to this reconstruction, arguments by analogy can be interpreted as complex compound arguments that involve inductive, abductive, and deductive elements. Since inductions are mostly, and abductions generally defeasible, the final step, although formally deductive, rests on defeasible premises and is hence in itself defeasible. On this view, both 'inductive' and a priori analogies have basically the same structure; they are invariably defeasible, but allow for degrees of strength.

Acknowledgments I would like to express my thanks to Lilian Bermejo-Luque for kindly making accessible to me her unpublished work on arguments from analogy, and for many substantial discussions on that subject.

References

Barker, S. F. (1965). *The elements of logic*. New York: McGraw-Hill.

Bartha, P. (2010). *By parallel reasoning: the construction and evaluation of analogical arguments*. Oxford: Oxford University Press.

Bermejo-Luque, L. (2012). A unitary schema for arguments by analogy. *Informal Logic, 32*(1), 1–24.

Bermejo-Luque, L. (2014). Deduction without dogmas: The case of moral analogical argumentation. *Informal Logic, 34*(3), 311–336.

Brown, W. R. (1989). Two traditions of analogy. *Informal Logic, 11*(3), 161–172.

Coenen, H. G. (2002). *Analogie und Metapher: Grundlegung einer Theorie der bildlichen Rede*. Berlin: de Gruyter.

Doury, M. (2009). Argument schemes typologies in practice: The case of comparative arguments. In F. H. van Eemeren & B. Garssen (Eds.), *Pondering on Problems of Argumentation. Twenty Essays on Theoretical Issues* (pp. 141–155, Chap. 11). Dordrecht: Springer.

Freeman, J. B. (2013). Govier's distinguishing a priori from inductive arguments by analogy: Implications for a general theory of ground adequacy. *Informal Logic, 33*(2), 175–194.

Freeman, J. B. (2014). What types of arguments are there? In D. Mohammed & M. Lewiński (Eds.), *Virtues of Argumentation: Proceedings of the 10th International Conference of the Ontario Society for the Study of Argumentation (OSSA), 22–26 May 2013* (pp. 1–15). Windsor, ON: OSSA (CD ROM).

Gabrielsen, J. (2003). Is there a topical dimension to the rhetorical example? In F. H. van Eemeren, J. A. Blair, C. A. Willard & A. F. Snoeck Henkemans (Eds.), *Proceedings of the Fifth Conference of the International Society for the Study of Argumentation* (pp. 349–353). Amsterdam: SicSat.

Garssen, B. (2009). Comparing the incomparable: Figurative analogies in a dialectical testing procedure. In F. H. van Eemeren & B. Garssen (Eds.), *Pondering on Problems of Argumentation. Twenty Essays on Theoretical Issues* (pp. 133–140, Chap. 10). Dordrecht: Springer.

Govier, T. (1985). Logical analogies. *Informal Logic, 7*(1), 27–33.

Govier, T. (1987). *Problems in argument analysis and evaluation*. Dordrecht: Foris.

Govier, T. (1989). Analogies and missing premises. *Informal Logic, 11*(3), 141–152.

Govier, T. (2002). Should *a priori* analogies be regarded as deductive arguments? *Informal Logic, 22*(2), 155–157.

Guarini, M. (2004). A defence of non-deductive reconstructions of analogical arguments. *Informal Logic, 24*(2), 153–168.

Harman, G. (1965). The inference to the best explanation. *The Philosophical Review, 74*(1), 88–95.

Hitchcock, D. (1980). Deductive and inductive: Types of validity, not types of arguments. *Informal Logic Newsletter, 2*(3), 9–10.

Kraus, M. (2003). Charles S. Peirce's theory of abduction and the Aristotelian enthymeme from signs. In F. H. van Eemeren, J. A. Blair, C. A. Willard & A. F. Snoeck Henkemans (Eds.), *Anyone Who Has a View. Theoretical Contributions to the Study of Argumentation* (Argumentation Library 8) (pp. 237–254, Chap. 19). Dordrecht: Kluwer.

Lipton, P. (2001). *Inference to the best explanation*. London: Routledge.

Macagno, F., Walton, D., & Tindale, C. W. (2014). Analogical reasoning and semantic rules of inference. *Revue Internationale de Philosophie, 270*(4), 419–432.

Peirce, C. S. (1878). Deduction, induction, and hypothesis. *Popular Science Monthly, 13*, 470–483. (1932). In C. Hartshorne, P. Weiss (Eds.), *Collected Papers of C. S. Peirce*, vol. II (pp. 372–388, Ch. 5), Cambridge: Harvard University Press.

Rapp, C. (1992). Ähnlichkeit, Analogie und Homonymie bei Aristoteles. *Zeitschrift für philosophische Forschung, 46*(4), 526–544.

Shecaira, F. P. (2013). Analogical arguments in ethics and law: A defence of a deductivist analysis. *Informal Logic, 33*(3), 406–437.

Thomson, J. J. (1971). A defense of abortion. *Philosophy & Public Affairs, 1*(1), 47–66.

Waller, B. (2001). Classifying and analyzing analogies. *Informal Logic, 21*(3), 199–218.

Wellman, C. (1971). *Challenge and response: Justification in ethics*. Carbondale, IL: Southern Illinois University Press.

Weddle, P. (1979). Inductive, deductive. *Informal Logic Newsletter, 2*(1), 1–5.

Wisdom, J. (1957). *Explanation and proof. Lectures presented at the University of Virginia* (unpublished ms.).

A Means-End Classification of Argumentation Schemes

Fabrizio Macagno

1 Introduction

Argumentation schemes have been developed in argumentation theory as stereotypical patterns of inference, abstract structures representing the material (semantic) relation and logical relation between the premises and a conclusion in an argument with a corresponding set of critical questions indicating their defeasibility conditions (Walton et al. 2008). They can be regarded as the modern interpretation and reconsideration of the ancient maxims of inference (Walton et al. 2008; Walton and Macagno 2006). Many authors in the last 50 years have proposed different sets and classifications of schemes (see Hastings 1963; Perelman and Olbrechts-Tyteca 1969; Kienpointner 1992a, b; Walton 1996; Grennan 1997; Walton et al. 2008; van Eemeren and Grootendorst 2004). These approaches raise crucial problems concerning the criteria used for distinguishing and classifying the schemes, and defining the structure of an argumentation scheme. These apparently purely philosophical questions are becoming increasingly important for practical purposes, in particular the application of the schemes to the field of education (Macagno and Konstantinidou 2013; Nussbaum 2011; Duschl 2008; Kim et al. 2012; Rapanta et al. 2013) and Artificial Intelligence (Mochales and Moens 2009, 2011).

The purpose of this paper is to address the problem of classifying the schemes, starting from the analysis of their nature and structure. The different components of the natural patterns of arguments will be distinguished, and in particular the quasi-logical and the semantic levels. These distinctions will be used to show the shortcomings of the existing classifications, and to propose a new model based on the pragmatic purpose of an argument, which is regarded as a move (speech act) in a dialogue.

F. Macagno (✉)
ArgLab, Instituto de Filosofia da Nova, Universidade Nova de Lisboa,
Av. de Berna 26C, 1069-061 Lisbon, Portugal
e-mail: fabriziomacagno@hotmail.com; fabrizio.macagno@fcsh.unl.pt

F.H. van Eemeren and B. Garssen (eds.), *Reflections on Theoretical Issues in Argumentation Theory*, Argumentation Library 28,
DOI 10.1007/978-3-319-21103-9_14

2 Existing Classifications

In the modern and contemporary theories on argumentation (or argument) schemes, several types of classification have been advanced (Walton et al. 2008, Chap. 8). The crucial problem that these theories tried to address is to manage and organize a potentially high number of patterns, so that they can be easily selected and used both for production and analytical purposes.

Perelman and Olbrechts-Tyteca conceived their system of *topoi* into two broad categories, defined based on the two purposes that they considered to be the basic ones, finding associations and dissociations between concepts (Perelman and Olbrechts-Tyteca 1969, p. 190). According to the New Rhetoric, arguments from association are divided in three main classes: Quasi-logical Arguments, Relations Establishing the Structure of Reality, and Arguments based on the Structure of Reality, while dissociation constitutes a distinct class. This classification can be represented as follows (Fig. 1):

This classification is based on several criteria, namely the conceptual-ontological structure (association-dissociation; the reference to the structure of reality), the logical structure (quasi-logical vs. non-logical arguments), and the type of relations

Quasi-Logical Arguments
▪ Contradiction and Incompatibility ▪ Identity and Definition ▪ Analyticity, Analysis and Tautology ▪ The Rule of Justice ▪ Arguments of Reciprocity ▪ Arguments of Transitivity ▪ Inclusion of the Part in the Whole ▪ Division of the Whole into its Parts ▪ Arguments by Comparison ▪ Argumentation by Sacrifice ▪ Probabilities

The Relations Establishing the Structure of Reality	
Establishment through Particular Case	*Reasoning by Analogy*
▪ Example ▪ Illustration ▪ Model and Anti-model	▪ Analogy ▪ Metaphor

Arguments based on the Structure of Reality			
Sequential Relations	*The Relations of Coexistence*	*Double Hierarchy Argument*	*Differences of Degree and Order*
▪ Causal Link ▪ Pragmatic Argument ▪ Ends and Means ▪ Argument of Waste ▪ Argument of Direction ▪ Unlimited Development	▪ Analogy ▪ The person and His Acts ▪ Argument from Authority ▪ The Speech as an Act of the Speaker ▪ The Group and its Members ▪ Act and Essence ▪ Symbolic Relation		

Fig. 1 Classification of the arguments in the New Rhetoric

between concepts (sequential vs. coexistence). However, the interrelation between all these criteria is not specified, and there is not a unique rationale linking all such different arguments.

A different approach is provided by Toulmin, Rieke and Janik in *An introduction to reasoning* (1984). The classification advanced here is based on the basic functions of the warrants on which the arguments are grounded. Their attempt was to analyse the patterns of reasoning without taking into account their purpose, or their field of use. In this fashion, nine general classes of arguments were distinguished, subdivided into subclasses (Toulmin et al. 1984, p. 199) (Fig. 2):

Also in this case, different criteria are used for the classification. Some schemes represent different types of reasoning (generalization, sign, analogy); others are characterized by logical rules of inference (dilemma, opposites), while others refer to the content of the argument (authority, classification, cause, degree). The relationship between the various criteria is not given.

The classification provided by Kienpointner in *Alltagslogik* is extremely complex and fine-grained. He analyses the scheme based on two distinct criteria, one based on the type of inference, the other on the epistemic nature of the premises and pragmatic function of the conclusion. On this view, every scheme must have either a descriptive or a normative conclusion, must be pro or contra a certain thesis, and must be real (namely based upon the truth or likeliness of the premises), or fictive (grounded upon the mere possibility) (Kienpointner 1992a; 1992b, p. 241). In this sense, all the schemes can have descriptive or normative, pro or contra, real or fictive variants. The classification provided in *Alltagslogik* groups 21 schemes in three abstract classes characterized by the typology of the inferential rule: argument schemes using a rule; argument schemes establishing a rule by means of induction; and argument schemes both using and establishing a rule. The first general class is subdivided in its turn in four content-based categories: classification, comparison, opposition, and causal schemes. The classification appears as follows (Kienpointner 1992a; 1992b, p. 246) (Fig. 3):

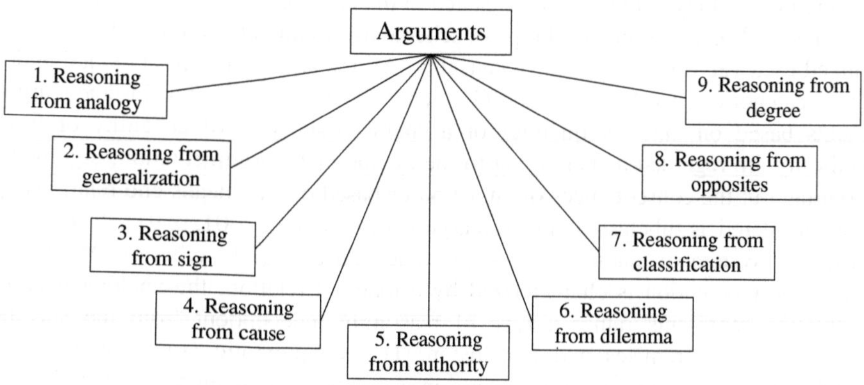

Fig. 2 Classification of the arguments in Toulmin

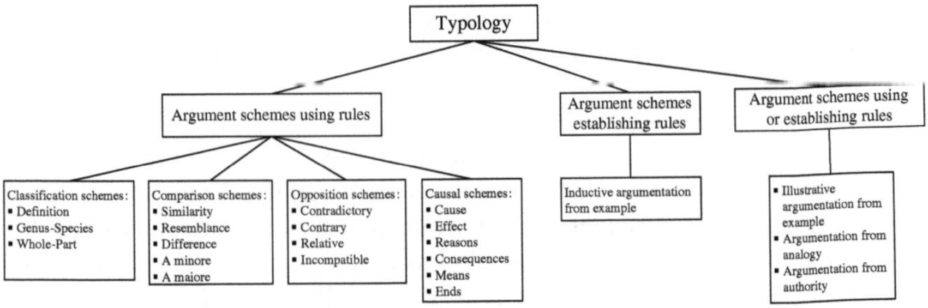

Fig. 3 Classification of the arguments in Kienpointner

Based on the aforementioned dichotomic criteria, all the argument schemes may in turn have descriptive or normative variants, different logical forms (*Modus Ponens*, *Modus Tollens*, Disjunctive Syllogism, etc.), and different word-world relation (fictive—real).

This type of classification is also based on a twofold criterion, the logical structure of the scheme (whether proceeding from a rule or establishing it inductively) and the content. However, as shown below, these two dimensions cannot be considered as matching. Moreover, reducing most of the schemes to quasi-deductively valid inferences risks overlooking the actual type of reasoning underlying an argumentation scheme (Lumer 2011, p. 3). Moreover, the pragmatic dimension taken into account as a variant of the schemes does not account for the specific type of reasoning (rule or value based) that underlies a normative conclusion.

The pragma-dialectical system of classification of schemes consists of three basic schemes (van Eemeren and Grootendorst 1992, pp. 94–102): the symptomatic argumentation, the argumentation based on similarities, and the instrumental argumentation. The first one represents types of argumentation in which the speaker tries to convince his interlocutor "by pointing out that something is symptomatic of something else," in the sense that what is stated in the argument is a sign or symptom of what is stated in the standpoint. The second scheme is grounded on a relation of analogy between what is stated in the argument and what is stated in the standpoint. Finally, in the third type of scheme the argument and the conclusion are linked by a very broad relation of causality. All the arguments are classified under these categories (van Eemeren and Grootendorst 1992, p. 97). For instance, arguments based on inherent qualities or a characteristic part of an entity or from authority are regarded as belonging to the symptomatic argumentation; arguments pointing out the consequences of an action or based on the means-end relationship are considered as subclasses of causal arguments (Garssen 2001, p. 91). Also in this case, the system of classification is grounded on a twofold criterion. While the causal argumentation is characterized by a material relation, the analogical argumentation represents rather a type of reasoning independent from the specific content of the premises and conclusion. The symptomatic argumentation is a combination of these two criteria, as a sign or a symptom presupposes an abductive pattern and a material causal relation.

The last system of classification that we can take into account is provided by Lumer (2011). He distinguishes the argumentation schemes by setting out three general classes, each including subclasses:

1. Deductive argument schemes
   a. Elementary deductive argument schemes;
   b. Analytical arguments;
   c. Definitoric arguments;
   d. Subsuming legal arguments;
2. Probabilistic argument schemes
   a. Pure probabilistic argument schemes (statistics, signs);
   b. Impure probabilistic argument schemes (best explanation);
3. Practical argument schemes
   a. Pure practical argument for pure evaluations;
   b. Impure practical argument schemes (for justification of actions; justification of instruments);
   c. Arguments for evaluations based on adequacy conditions;
   d. Arguments for welfare-ethical value judgements;
   e. Practical arguments for theoretical theses.

Also this system consists of a mix of two distinct criteria, the logical and the pragmatic one. While the first two classes are characterized by the type of reasoning on which they are based, the last one is rather a type of argument with a specific pragmatic purpose, recommending a course of action. Moreover, the subclasses are defined considering both logic-based and content-based criteria, where together to distinctions grounded on the logical form (analytic schemes; probabilistic schemes) some subclasses are based on the nature of the premises (definitoric; subsuming).

All these types of classification show how a sole criterion is not sufficient for providing a clear and comprehensive classification of schemes. In order to understand what criteria can be used and what abstract categories can be considered as the most basic ones, it is necessary to analyze the structure of the schemes. Once the common components of these heterogenic combinations of premises and conclusions are brought to light, it can be possible to find criteria for organizing them for specific purposes.

3 Types of Reasoning and Semantic-Ontological Connections

The relationship between the premises and the conclusion of an argument can be reconstructed based on generic principles. What guarantees the inferential passage is a specific major premise that includes the predicates occurring in the minor premise and the conclusion. In order to reconstruct and motivate the inferential structure, we need to distinguish the specific principle of inference from two other different levels: (1) the general rules of inference, i.e. the generic, semantic-ontological connections between the predicates of the argument, which establish the *acceptability* of an argument; and (2) the logical rules governing the formal disposition of the terms or propositions in an argument, i.e. the rules of commitment establishing the *acceptance* of an argument. These levels of abstraction will be referred to as "specific *topoi*," "generic *topoi*," and "rules of commitment" (or logical rules).

3.1 Specific Topoi

In the *Topics*, Aristotle pointed out a crucial difference between the *topoi* (or rather generic topics) and the *idia* (the specific topics) (Rubinelli 2009, pp. 59–70). According to Aristotle, the specific *topoi* represent propositions that relate to specific disciplines, such as ethics, law, or medicine, which are used to draw specific conclusions. For instance, in the third book of the *Topics* some specific principles of inference concerning the classification of "what is better" are set out (*Topics,* 116a 13–18). Specific topics can be used both as an instrument for invention, namely for generating and finding the premises of an argument, and as premises warranting the conclusion (De Pater 1965, p. 134; Stump 1989, p. 29). For instance, a specific *topos* concerning one of the possible ways of classifying an action as "better" than another can be directly used to support the conclusion. We can analyze the following case:

> Saving the money for buying a house is more desirable than spending it on expensive cars, because a house is more lasting than a car.

The reasoning can be represented as follows:

Minor premise	A house is more lasting than a car
Major premise	That which is more lasting or secure is more desirable than that which is less so
Conclusion	A house is more desirable than a car

The specific *topos* indicating one of the possible "operational" definitions of "to be better" directly warrants the conclusion. In specific domains of knowledge, specific *topoi* can be listed as instruments of invention, pre-packaged arguments that be used for supporting prototypical viewpoints. For example, ancient and modern treatises on legal topics (or rather on the specific commonly accepted principles of reasoning) indicate hundreds of topics that can be used by lawyers in certain circumstances, such as the following ones:

When a man and a woman refer to each other with the name of "spouse," marriage is not proven, but is presumable. (Everardus, *Loci Argumentorum legales*, 54, 13th paragraph).
Where a person does an act, he is presumed in so doing to have intended that the natural and legal consequences of his act shall result. (Lawson 1885, p. 262)

These propositions are used in law to support specific conclusions, i.e. *prima facie* cases that can be rebutted when additional information comes in. Such arguments, however, have the purpose of shifting the burden of production, leaving it up to the other party to provide contrary evidence.

Specific *topoi* provide relations between specific concepts ("acts"), which are abstracted from their individual occurrences (this specific act). These specific rules of inference are the subject matter of a further process of abstraction, leading from concepts to categories of concepts or meta-concepts, the generic *topoi*.

3.2 *Generic* Topoi—*Semantic-Ontological Relations*

Generic topics can be considered as the result of abstractions from the specific ones, or more correctly, from a large number of specific topics. They provide classes of both necessary and defeasible inferences. In the first class fall some maxims setting out definitional properties of meta-semantic concepts, i.e. concepts representing semantic relations between concepts, such as definition, genus, and property. For example the *locus* from definition, which establishes the convertibility between definition and *definiendum*, represents also the essential logical characteristic that a predicate needs to have in order be considered as a "discourse signifying what a thing is." Other *loci*, such as the ones based on analogy or the more and the less, are only defeasible, as they represent only commonly accepted relationships.

In the *Topics*, Aristotle focuses most of his analysis on the topics governing the meta-semantic relations between concepts, i.e. genus, property, definition, and accident. Cicero reduced the Aristotelian list of *topoi* to 20 *loci* or maxims, grouping them in generic categories (differences) and dividing them in two broad classes, the intrinsic and the extrinsic topics. While the first ones proceed directly from the subject matter at issue (for instance, its semantic properties), the external topics support the conclusion through contextual elements (for instance, the source of the speech act expressing the claim). In between are the topics that concern the relationship between a predicate and the other predicates of a linguistic system (for instance, its relations with its contraries or alternatives). We can represent Cicero's topics as follows (Fig. 4):

This classification was the model that was taken into account by several dialectical theories, of which the most important, due to its influence on the further medieval accounts, is the one developed by Boethius in *De Topicis Differentiis*.

Intrinsic		**Extrinsic**
Directly from the subject matter	***From things somehow related to the subject matter***	
1. *definitio* • By material parts (whole-part definition) • By essential parts (genus-species definition) 2. *notatio* (etymological relation)	1. *Coniugata* (inflectional relations) 2. *Genus* (genus-species relation) 3. *Forma* (species-genus relation) 4. *Similitudo* (similarity relation) 5. *Differentia* (difference relation) 6. *Contraria* (4 types of opposite relation) 7. *Adiuncta* (relation of concomitance) 8. *Antecedentia* 9. *Consequentia* 10. *Repugnantia* (incompatibles) 11. *Efficentia* (cause-effect relation) 12. *Effecta* (effect-cause relation) 13. *Ex comparatione maiorum, minorum, parium* (comparison)	Authority

Fig. 4 Cicero's classification of *generic topics*

3.3 Rules of Commitment—Logical Form

The Latin and medieval dialectical tradition analyzed in depth a type of *loci* that are not based on any semantic, metaphysical, or ontological relationship between concepts. These *loci* are not aimed at increasing the *acceptability* of a conclusion based on the *acceptability* of the content of its premises. Rather, they represent relations of *acceptance* (or commitment) between propositions. For instance, the acceptance of (or commitment to) the consequent of a conditional proposition follows from the acceptance of—or commitment to—the conditional and the antecedent thereof (Cicero, *Topica*, 53, 1–25). These "formal" topics were analyzed in particular in the dialectical theories of the 12th and 13th century. Such theories conceived the categorical syllogisms as proceeding from topics from the whole to the part, called "*dici de omni*" and "*dici de nullo*." These topics were grounded not on the semantic-ontological content of the propositions, but only on the meaning of the quantifiers (Green-Pedersen 1984, p. 256).

This distinction between semantic-ontological and formal (logical) topics suggests an analysis of the different rules of inference in which the semantic-ontological topics are combined with the logical rules. Formal topics can be thought of as representing the highest level of abstraction, which groups together more generic principles different and somehow similar argument structures (Searle 2001, p. 19). For example, the ancient topics from antecedents or "*dici de omni*" formalize the deductive pattern of *modus ponens* normally used in dialectics. However, many acceptable and reasonable arguments, such as reasoning from example or sign, follow formal patterns different from the deductive ones (see also

Blair 2007; Godden 2005). In addition to the deductive rules, also the inductive ones need to be accounted for, and the type of reasoning called "abduction" (Pierce 1992, pp. 140–141), "retroduction" (see Greenland 1998, p. 545; Poole 1988) or reasoning from best explanation (Josephson and Josephson 1996, p. 15).

The prototypical relationship between the types of argument and the logical level of abstraction can be summarized in the table below, where three most important types of reasoning (or categories of arguments of the highest level) are distinguished (Fig. 5):

This classification suggests the possibility of analyzing arguments from a multi-logical perspective, in which the logical form can be described using distinct *types of reasoning*, which in turn can include various *logical rules of inference* (*MP*, *MT*...). However, in the Latin and medieval tradition, the formal rules of inference are treated as maxims and not as distinct levels of abstraction. For this reason, the two levels of the general, semantic topics and of the logical rules were not distinguished, and the possible interconnections between them were not taken into account.

The modern theories of argument schemes or argumentation schemes inherited this model, proposing classifications essentially mirroring the ancient approach. The rules of commitment are treated at the same level as the semantic-ontological topics, and not as distinct levels of abstraction. This approach can be extremely helpful for quickly identifying common characteristics in the arguments that are frequently used, but it leads to classificatory problems. A possible solution is to acknowledge the discrepancy between logical form and semantic content as a divergence in kind, and try to show how these two levels can be interconnected. The starting point is the model that, by merging the two levels, best mirrors the multi-logical approach to natural arguments: the model of argumentation schemes (Walton et al. 2008).

Type of reasoning (abstraction - form)	Deductive axioms	Induction	Abduction
Type of argument	Argument from definition, genus...	Argument from example	Argument from (improper) signs
	Argument from cause to effect	...	Practical reasoning
	Argument from consequences	...	Argument from best explanation
	Argument from commitment	...	...

Fig. 5 Types of argument and types of reasoning

4 Argumentation Schemes as Imperfect Bridges

Argumentation schemes are stereotypical patterns of inference, combining semantic-ontological relations with types of reasoning and logical axioms and representing the abstract structure of the most common types of natural arguments. The argumentation schemes provided in (Walton et al. 2008) describe tentatively the patterns of the most typical arguments. However, the two levels of abstraction are not distinguished. For this reason, under the label of "argumentation schemes" fall indistinctly patterns of reasoning such as the abductive, analogical, or inductive ones, and types of argument such as the ones from classification or cause to effect.

In order to design a system for classifying the schemes, it is useful to understand the limits thereof, and investigate how the two distinct levels of abstraction are merged. For example the argument from cause to effect will be taken into account (Walton et al. 2008, p. 168):

Argument from cause to effect

Major premise	Generally, if A occurs, then B will (might) occur
Minor premise	In this case, A occurs (might occur)
Conclusion	Therefore in this case, B will (might) occur

This argumentation scheme is based on a defeasible *modus ponens*, which is combined with a semantic causal relation between two events. The semantic-ontological level is merged with the logical one, and this combination represents only one of the possible types of inferences that can be drawn from the same semantic-ontological connection. The actual relationship between the two levels of abstraction is much more complex. For example, we consider the classic Aristotelian causal link between "having fever" and "breathing fast," and see how this cause-effect relation can be used to draw a conclusion on the basis of different logical rules:

1. He had fever. (**Fever** causes breathing fast). Therefore, he (must have) breathed fast.
2. He did not breathe fast. (Fever causes **breathing fast**). Therefore, he had no fever.
3. He is breathing fast. (Fever causes **breathing fast**). Therefore, he might have fever.
4. He has no fever. (**Fever** causes breathing fast). Therefore, he may be not breathing fast.
5. You may have fever. When I had fever, **I** was breathing fast, and you are breathing fast.

These cases illustrate how different logical rules can be followed to draw a conclusion from the same semantic connection, in this case a causal relation. Cases (1) and (2) represent instantiations of defeasible axioms, i.e. the defeasible *modus ponens* (in 1), and the defeasible *modus tollens* (in 2). Cases 3 and 4 proceed from abductive reasoning. In (3) the conclusion is drawn by affirming the consequent, while in (4) the denial of the antecedent can be rephrased by contraposition as "not breathing fast is caused by having no fever," leading to a conclusion drawn abductively (Walton et al. 2008: 173). Finally, in (5) the conclusion is based on an inductive generalization, based on a single case. The prototypical nature of the relationship between semantic relations and logical rules (types of reasoning and axioms) hides, in this sense, the lack of correspondence between these two levels. For this reason, a classification system of the argumentation schemes based on these criteria would be inaccurate. Different criteria are needed, accounting for this twofold nature of the schemes.

5 A Means-End Classification

Argumentation schemes can be conceived as the combination of semantic (or topical) relations with logical rules of inference. A classification based on the semantic links can provide an instrument for bringing to light the material relations between premises and conclusion. However, the same semantic relation can be combined with various logical rules, and lead to various types of conclusion. For example, causal relations are the ground of the argument from cause to effect, but also of arguments from sign and practical reasoning. A classification based only on the semantic content would blur these fundamental differences. For this reason, it is necessary to find an overarching classificatory principle.

Argumentation schemes can be thought of as instruments for reconstructing and building arguments (intended as discourse moves), i.e. analytical or invention tools. For this reason, in order to provide a classificatory system to retrieve and detect the needed scheme it can be useful to start from the intended purpose of an argumentation scheme. From an analytical point of view, the analysis of an argument in a discourse, a text, or dialogue presupposes a previous understanding of the communicative goal (and, therefore, the "pragmatic" meaning) of the argument and the components thereof. For example, an argument can be aimed at classifying a state of affairs, supporting the existence of a state of affairs, or influencing a decision-making process.

This teleological classification needs to be combined with a practical one, as the generic purposes of a move need to be achieved by means of an inferential passage. In this sense, the classificatory system needs to account for the possible means to achieve the pragmatic purpose of an argument. Not all the semantic (material) relations that are at the basis of the schemes can support all the possible conclusions or purposes of an argument. Definitional schemes are aimed at supporting the classification of a state of affairs, and are unlikely to lead to the prediction or retrodiction of an event. Similarly, a pattern of reasoning based on the evaluation of the consequences of an action or an event can be used to establish the desirability of a course of action bringing it about, but cannot reasonably lead to the truth or falsity (or acceptability) of a proposition. For this reason, the analysis of the pragmatic meaning (i.e. the purpose) of an argument provides a criterion for restricting the paradigm of the possible means to achieve it. The crucial problem is to find categories of argument purposes that can establish criteria for distinguishing among classes of semantic relations, which in turn can be specified further according to the means to achieve such goals.

The first distinction to be made is based on the nature of the subject matter, which can be a course of action or a state of affairs. In the first case, the goal is to support the desirability or non-desirability of an action, while in the second one the schemes are aimed at providing grounds for the acceptability of a judgment on a state of affairs. The ancient dialectical accounts (see Cicero, *Topica* and Boethius, *De Topicis Differentiis*) distinguished between two types of argumentative "means" to bear out a conclusion, i.e. the "internal" and the "external" arguments. The first ones are based on the characteristics of the subject matter (such as arguments from definition or cause), while the others derive their force from the source of the statement, i.e. from the authority of who advances the judgment or the proposal (arguments from authority). This first distinction can be represented as follows (Fig. 6):

The acceptability of a conclusion can be supported externally in two ways. If the argument is aimed at establishing the desirability of a course of action, the authority can correspond to the role of the source needed for recommending or imposing a choice ("You should do it because he told you that!"). Otherwise, the popular practice can be a reason for pursuing a course of action ("We should buy a bigger car. Everyone drives big cars here!"). When external arguments are used to support also a judgment on a state of affairs, the relevant quality of the source is not the

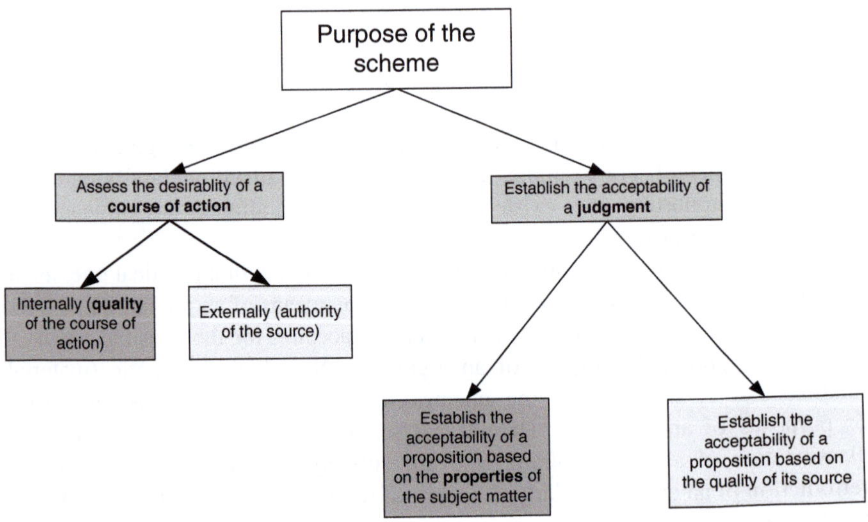

Fig. 6 Basic purposes of an argument

speaker's authority (which is connected with the consequences of not complying with the orders/conforming to common behavior) but rather with his superior knowledge. The quality of the source can be also used negatively to show that a source is not reliable (it is not a good source), and that consequently the conclusion itself should be considered as doubtful (*ad hominem* arguments). The external arguments can be represented as follows (Fig. 7):

Internal arguments need to be divided into the two categories of arguments aimed at assessing the desirability of a course of action, and the ones supporting the acceptability of a judgment. Courses of action can be classified as desirable or not depending on the quality of their consequences (the course of action is a condition of a resulting positive or negative state of affairs) or their function in bringing about a desired goal (an action is productive of a desired state of affairs) (Fig. 8):

The arguments used to provide grounds for a judgment on a state of affairs can be divided according to the nature of the predicate that is to be attributed. The most basic differentiation can be traced between the predicates that attribute the existence of a state of affairs (the occurrence of an event or the existence of an entity in the present, the past, or the future), and the ones representing factual or evaluative properties. The arguments supporting a prediction or a retrodiction are aimed at establishing whether or not an event has occurred or will occur, or whether an entity was or will be present (existent). The arguments proceeding from casual relations (in particular from material and efficient causes) bear out this type of conclusion. The other type of predicates can be divided in two categories: factual judgments and value judgments. The first type of predicates can be attributed by means of

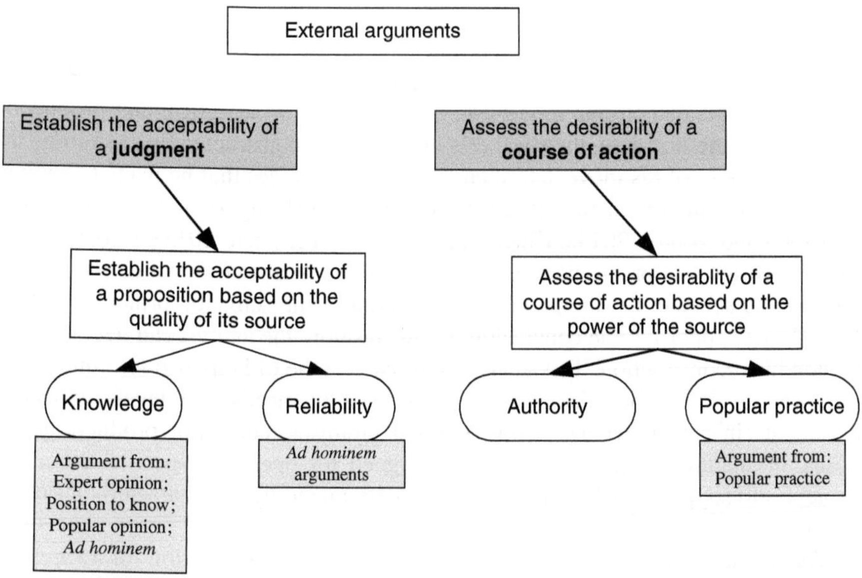

Fig. 7 External arguments

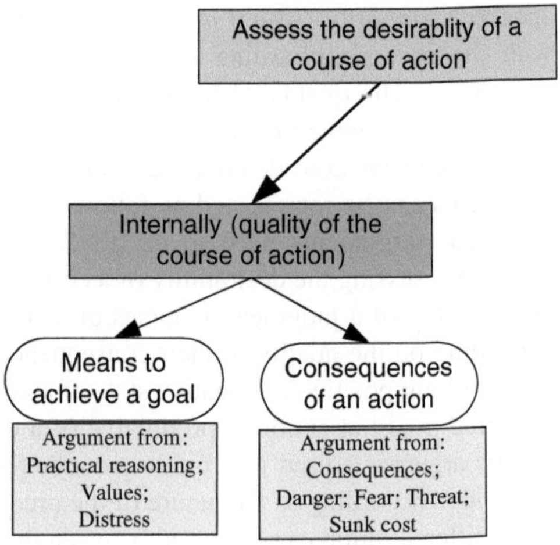

Fig. 8 Internal practical arguments

reasoning from classification, grounded on descriptive (definitional) features and supporting the attribution of a categorization to an entity or an event (Bob is a man; Tom is a cat). Value judgments are classifications that are not based on definitions of categorical concepts (to be a cat) but on values, or rather hierarchies of values. Such judgments proceed from criteria for classifying what is commonly considered to be "good" or "bad." Also the reasoning underlying the attribution of evaluative predicates, such as "to be a criminal," can be considered as belonging (also) to this group of arguments. These latter patterns are grounded on signs of an internal disposition of character, which in its turn is evaluated. The distinctions discussed above are summarized in Fig. 9 below.

This system of classification of argumentation schemes is based on the interplay between two criteria, the (pragmatic) purpose of an argument and the means to achieve it. This dichotomic model can be used both for analytical and production purposes. In the first case, the speaker's intention is reconstructed by examining the generic purpose of his move, and then the possible choices that he made to support it, based on the linguistic elements of the text (Macagno and Zavatta 2014; Macagno and Walton 2014a, Chap. 5; Macagno and Damele 2013). Depending on the desired level of preciseness, the analysis can be narrowed down until detecting the specific scheme, i.e. the precise combination of the semantic principle and the logical rule supporting the conclusion. In this fashion, the analyst can decide where to stop his reconstruction. This analytical model can be of help also for educational purposes, as it can be adapted to various teaching needs and levels (detecting arguments in a text; reconstructing implicit premises, etc.). For production purposes, the nature of the viewpoint to be argued for opens up specific alternative strategies to support it, which in turn can be determined by the characteristics of the conclusion.

This model relies on the analyst's or the speaker's reconstruction (or awareness) of the purpose of a move, which can be partially identified by taking into

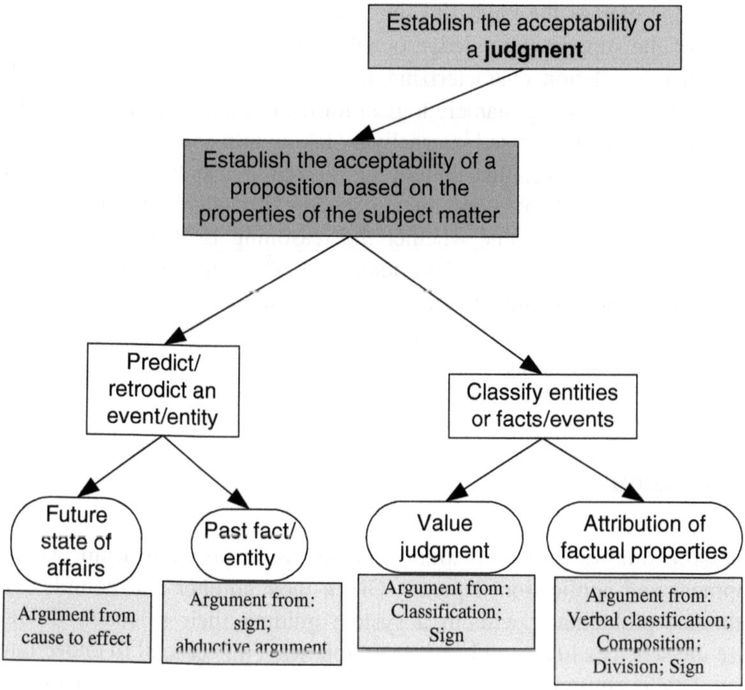

Fig. 9 Establishing the acceptability of a judgment on a state of affairs

consideration the nature of the subject matter (whether it is a decision or a judgment). The purpose then opens up possible choices according to the generic goal of the communicative act. The speaker's intention can be further specified by detecting the most generic strategy chosen to provide a basis for the acceptability of the conclusion. In this case, in order to reconstruct the move or provide an argument, the analyst or the speaker can choose whether to use some properties of the subject matter or to appeal to an external source. In the first case, the means used to achieve the goal are determined by the nature of the subject matter. In particular, the crucial distinction is between the classification and the prediction or retrodiction of an entity or state of affairs. This choice leads to a further specification of the nature of the viewpoint that the speaker intends to support with his argument (is the event a future or a past one? is the classification a value judgment or does it consist in the attribution of factual properties?), and then to the specific means that can be used to achieve this precise purpose (argument from values, from definition, etc.). In case of decision-making, the argumentation schemes are classified according to the same interrelation between goals and generic strategies. The internal arguments can be divided between reasoning from consequence and reasoning from means to goal.

An alternative to the internal, more complex arguments, is provided by external arguments, where the choice of backing the conclusion by means of the opinion of a knowledgeable and reliable source can be further made more specific by distinguishing between the kinds of sources (experts or the majority of people) and the nature of the support (knowledge or reliability).

The semantic relation characterizing a scheme can be "shaped" according to different types of reasoning, namely logical forms. For instance, the desirability of a course of action can be assessed internally by taking into consideration the means to achieve a goal. However, this pattern of reasoning can be stronger or weaker depending on whether there is only one or several alternatives. The paradigm of the possible means will determine whether the reasoning is abductive or deductive, resulting in a conclusion more or less defeasible. The same principle applies to the other semantic relations, such as the ones proceeding from cause or classification, which can be shaped logically according to inductive (or analogical), deductive, or abductive types of reasoning.

6 Conclusion

The classification of argumentation schemes is a problem from which their development and application depends. Given their number and complexity, their use becomes problematic without a system guiding their selection. In order to organize the schemes in a useful and accessible way, it is crucial to understand their nature and their components. Argumentation schemes are the result of a combination of two levels of abstraction: semantic (or topical) relations, and logical forms. Semantic relations provide a criterion of classifying the arguments based on the content of their major premise, and represent what makes a conclusion more *acceptable* than the premises. The logical forms (the types of reasoning and rules of inference) instantiate the rules of *acceptance*, namely how a premise supports a conclusion based on the relation between the antecedent and consequent, or between the quantification of the predicates in the premises and the conclusion. The possible combinations between them are extremely complex. Argumentation schemes are imperfect bridges between these two levels. They are the most frequent and common combinations that characterize the fundamental arguments used in everyday argumentation. They are incomplete abstractions, simplified and prototypical patterns that cannot be organized according to the aforesaid semantic and logical levels.

In order to classify the schemes, it is necessary to find a criterion of classification transcending both levels of abstraction, and leading to a dichotomic system, which can be used proceeding both from the affirmation of a disjunct, and from exclusion of the alternative. The classificatory system proposed in this paper is not based on what an argument is, but rather on how it is understood and interpreted, i.e. on its communicative purpose. In this fashion, a classification system can mirror the actual practices of reconstructing and using arguments. The pragmatic purpose of an argument is connected with the means to achieve it, which are determined by the ontological structure of its conclusion and premises. On this view, it is possible to suggest a course of action, to predict an event, or to classify an entity, depending on the nature of the predicate(s) attributed in the premises that support or can be used to support the conclusion. The system of classification becomes a tree of dichotomic choices aimed at reconstructing or achieving a communicative goal.

This proposal presupposes a strict interaction between the pragmatic and the reasoning dimension of discourse. An argument is regarded as a speech act, whose meaning depends on how it can be reasonably interpreted in a specific context by a specific interlocutor (Macagno and Zavatta 2014; Macagno and Douglas 2015; Macagno and Walton 2014b). For this reason, pragmatically ambiguous messages reveal different argumentative structures, and correspond to distinct or more or less complete arguments. For example, we consider the following communication between a lawyer of a Mafia boss and a judge, which is aimed at different goals depending on the actual interlocutor or the potential audience:[1]

> In your interest, my client complains about the fact that you are too strict. You should be more careful.

This speech act is clearly aimed at different purposes, and depending on the background information shared with the interlocutor, the message can be interpreted differently. This reported classification of the judge as "too strict" can be considered apparently (by a bystander or general audience) as a friendly advice, leading to an implicit invitation to comply with the softer, commonly attitude of judges in general (popular practice). The only problem is that it is told indirectly by an accused party to a judge in charge of judging him, and that the classification is not neutral, but strongly negatively evaluated by the speaker (my client "complains"). By adding the tacit information concerning the common practices used by the mafia, the purpose of the speech act becomes a threat (namely an argument from negative consequences that are brought about by the speaker unless some conditions are complied with), based on a value judgment on the judge's behavior. On the one hand, this speech act is intended to communicate a neutral piece of information, a classification that cannot be regarded as threatening by a third party (the police). On the other hand, the lawyer conveys a clear message and a clear instruction to the judge on how to behave, by threatening him. The background information concerning the conveyance of threats by mafia leads the hearer to adding further tacit premises and reconstructing the actual purpose of the "classification" or "advice." In this sense, the pragmatic dimension of communication, namely the relevance of a speech act in a specific context, becomes the starting point for analyzing its argumentative structure.

[1]"Un avvertimento indiretto una volta mi fu recapitato tramite un avvocato, nel corso di uno dei miei primi procedimenti di mafia a Palermo. Mi riferì, «nel mio interesse» (così disse …), che il suo cliente mafioso si lamentava di me perché io ero un po' troppo «rigido», e quindi era meglio che stessi «più attento». Anche in quel caso feci la mia segnalazione per iscritto al capufficio e alla Procura di Caltanissetta." (Ingroia 2010, p. 47).

References

Aristotle (1984). *Topics* (W. A. Pickard-Cambridge, Trans.). In J. Barnes (Ed.), *The works of Aristotle*. Princeton: Princeton University Press.

Blair, J. A. (2007). The "logic" informal logic. In H. V. Hansen, et al. (Eds.), *Dissensus and the search for common ground CD-ROM* (pp. 1–16). Windsor, ON: OSSA.

Boethius, S. (1978). *De Topicis Differentiis* (edited with a translation, introduction and commentary by E. Stump). Ithaca, NY: Cornell University Press.

Cicero, M. T. (2003). *Topica* (edited with a translation, introduction and commentary by T. Reinhardt). Oxford: Oxford University Press.

De Pater, W. (1965). *Les Topiques d'Aristote et la Dialectique Platonicienne*. Fribourg, Germany: Éditions de St. Paul.

Duschl, R. (2008). Science education in three-part harmony: Balancing conceptual, epistemic, and social learning goals. *Review of Research in Education, 32*, 268–291.

Everardus, N. (1607). *Loci Argumentorum legales*. Venetiis: apud Matthaeum Valentinum.

Garssen, B. (2001). Argumentation schemes. In F. van Eemeren (Ed.), *Crucial concepts in argumentation theory* (pp. 81–99). Amsterdam: Amsterdam University Press.

Godden, D. (2005). Deductivism as an interpretive strategy: A reply to Groarke's defense of reconstructive deductivism. *Argumentation and Advocacy, 41*(3), 168–183.

Greenland, S. (1998). Probability logic and probabilistic induction. *Epidemiology, 9*, 322–332.

Green-Pedersen, N. J. (1984). *The tradition of topics in the middle age*. Munich, Germany: Philosophia Verlag.

Grennan, W. (1997). *Informal logic*. Montreal, QC: McGill-Queen's University Press.

Hastings, A. (1963). *A reformulation of the modes of reasoning in argumentation*. Evanston, Illinois: Ph.D. dissertation, Northwestern University.

Ingroia, A. (2010). *Nel labirinto degli dèi*. Milano: Il Saggiatore.

Josephson, J., & Josephson, S. (1996). *Abductive inference. computation, philosophy, technology*. New York: Cambridge University Press.

Kienpointner, M. (1992a). *Alltagslogik: Struktur und Funktion von Argumentationsmustern*. Stuttgart, Germany: Fromman-Holzboog.

Kienpointner, M. (1992b). How to classify arguments. In F. H. van Eemeren, R. Grootendorst, J. A. Blair, & C. A. Willard (Eds.), *Argumentation illuminated* (pp. 178–188). Amsterdam: Amsterdam University Press.

Kim, M., Anthony, R., & Blades, D. (2012). Argumentation as a tool to understand complexity of knowledge integration. In *Proceedings of the 2nd International STEM in Education Conference—Beijing, China—24–27 November 2012* (pp. 154–160). Beijing: Beijing Normal University.

Lawson, J. (1885). *The law of presumptive evidence*. San Francisco: Bancroft & Co.

Lumer, C. (2011). Argument schemes—an epistemological approach. In F. Zenker (Ed.), *Argumentation: Cognition and Community. Proceedings of the 9th International Conference of the Ontario Society for the Study of Argumentation (OSSA), May 18–21, 2011* (pp. 1–32). Windsor, ON (CD ROM).

Macagno, F., & Damele, G. (2013). The dialogical force of implicit premises: Presumptions in enthymemes. *Informal Logic, 33*, 365–393.

Macagno, F., & Douglas, W. (2015). Classifying the patterns of natural arguments. *Philosophy & Rhetoric, 48*(1), 26–53.

Macagno, F., & Konstantinidou, A. (2013). What students' arguments can tell us: Using argumentation schemes in science education. *Argumentation, 27*, 225–243.

Macagno, F., & Walton, D. (2014a). *Emotive language in argumentation*. New York: Cambridge University Press.

Macagno, F., & Walton, D. (2014b). Argumentation schemes and topical relations. In G. Gobber & A. Rocci (Eds.), *Language, reason and education* (pp. 185–216). Bern: Peter Lang.

Macagno, F., & Zavatta, B. (2014). Reconstructing metaphorical meaning. *Argumentation, 28*, 453–488.

Mochales, R., & Moens, M. F. (2009). Argumentation mining: The detection, classification and structuring of arguments in text. In *Proceedings of the Twelfth International Conference on Artificial Intelligence and Law (ICAIL), June 8–12. Universitat Autonoma de Barcelona, Barcelona* (pp. 98–107). New York: ACM.

Mochales, R., & Moens, M. F. (2011). Argumentation mining. *Artificial Intelligence and Law, 19*, 1–22.

Nussbaum, M. (2011). Argumentation, dialogue theory and probability modeling: An alternative framework for argumentation research in education. *Educational Psychology, 46*, 84–106.

Peirce, C. S. (1992). *Reasoning and the logic of things: The Cambridge conferences lectures of 1898*. Edited by K.L. Ketner. Cambridge, MA: Harvard University Press.

Perelman, C. & Olbrechts-Tyteca, L. (1969). *The new rhetoric: A treatise on argumentation* (J. Wilkinson & P. Weaver Trans.). Notre Dame, IN: University of Notre Dame Press.

Poole, C. (1988). Induction does not exist in epidemiology, either. In K. J. Rothman (Ed.), *Causal inference* (pp. 153–161). Chestnut Hill, MA: E.R.I.

Rapanta, C., Garcia-Mila, M., & Gilabert, S. (2013). What is meant by argumentative competence? An integrative review of methods of analysis and assessment in education. *Review of Educational Research, 83*, 483–520.

Rubinelli, S. (2009). *Ars Topica. The classical technique of constructing arguments*. Dordrecht: Springer.

Searle, J. (2001). *Rationality in action*. Cambridge, MA: MIT Press.

Stump, E. (1989). *Dialectic and its place in the development of medieval logic*. Ithaca: Cornell University Press.

Toulmin, S., Rieke, R., & Janik, A. (1984). *An introduction to reasoning*. New York: Macmillan.

van Eemeren, F., & Grootendorst, R. (1992). *Argumentation, communication and fallacies*. Hillsdale, NJ: Erlbaum.

van Eemeren, F., & Grootendorst, R. (2004). *A systematic theory of argumentation: The pragma dialectical approach*. Cambridge: Cambridge University Press.

Walton, D. (1996). *Argumentation schemes for presumptive reasoning*. Mahwah: Lawrence Erlbaum Publishers.

Walton, D., & Macagno, F. (2006). Argumentative reasoning patterns. In *Proceedings of 6th CMNA (Computational Models of Natural Argument) Workshop, ECAI (European Conference on Artificial Intelligence), Riva del Garda, Italy, August 28–September 1* (pp. 48–51). Trento: University of Trento Italy.

Walton, D., Reed, C., & Macagno, F. (2008). *Argumentation schemes*. New York: Cambridge University Press.

Part V
Contextual Embedding of Argumentation

Argumentative Norms: How Contextual Can They Be? A Cautionary Tale

Harvey Siegel

1 The Case for and Limits of Contextualism

> Argumentation is always situated: it always occurs in context.
>
> (van Eemeren and Garssen 2012b, p. xiii)

It is true, as van Eemeren and Garssen say, that argumentation always occurs in context: to engage in argumentation, an arguer must be in some context or other. But are *argument norms* similarly contextual? That is, are the norms governing argument quality relative to or dependent upon the context in which the argument is either asserted or evaluated? Let *contextualism*[1] be the view that *criteria of argument quality vary by context*: According to contextualists, whether an argument is good or not, and how good it is, depends upon the context in which it is either uttered or evaluated. Many authors have urged that contextualism, or something like it, is true.[2]

There is an obvious *prima facie* case for contextualism which rests on the fact that the 'good-making' features of arguments seem to vary by context: What makes

[1]The questions pursued here do not concern the view called 'contextualism' in epistemology and philosophy of language. There 'contextualism' is understood as a response to skepticism, according to which in ordinary, 'low-stakes' contexts we know, e.g., that we have hands, but in 'high stakes' contexts we don't know this because we can't rule out the possibility that we're being deceived by an evil demon. For an overview of the literature and a defense of this sort of contextualism, cf. DeRose 2009.

[2]Among many others, in addition to those authors discussed below, cf. Fogelin 1985/2005and Battersby and Bailin 2011. Battersby and Bailin helpfully distinguish dialectical, historical, intellectual, political, social and disciplinary contexts; I strongly recommend their discussion.

H. Siegel (✉)
Department of Philosophy, University of Miami, P.O. Box 248054, Coral Gables, FL 33124-4670, USA
e-mail: hsiegel@miami.edu

F.H. van Eemeren and B. Garssen (eds.), *Reflections on Theoretical Issues in Argumentation Theory*, Argumentation Library 28,
DOI 10.1007/978-3-319-21103-9_15

an argument good in a scientific context seems to differ in some respects from what makes an argument good in a court of law, a conversation among friends, or a marketing strategy discussion in the corporate boardroom. That is, it seems to be the case that the quality of arguments sometimes depends upon criteria that are context-relative. For example, scientific arguments at least often have to meet criteria of explanatory adequacy; legal arguments often have to meet criteria of evidence admissibility; etc. So it seems that the norms of argument quality are relative to context: an argument can be good although it doesn't meet legal criteria of evidence admissibility if it is offered or evaluated in a scientific or corporate boardroom context; an argument can be good although it doesn't meet criteria of explanatory adequacy if it is offered or evaluated in the context of a court of law or a conversation around the dinner table.

However, it would be too quick to conclude on the basis of this *prima facie* case that argument norms are indeed contextual. For we should distinguish between differences in argumentative context entailing differences in criteria of argument quality, on the one hand, and differences in the *purposes* of argumentation entailing such differences, on the other. We should agree that people argue for different purposes, a point generally agreed among argumentation scholars and reflected in the range of approaches reflected in their scholarship. Three important such purposes are: the *persuading* of one's audience of a particular claim, thesis, or standpoint (reflected in *rhetorical* approaches to the study of argument); the achieving of *consensus* (reflected in *dialectical* approaches); and the enhancement of the epistemic status of claims or conclusions argued for (reflected in *epistemic* approaches). Argument norms do differ across these: an effective persuasive argument may be less successful at fostering consensus or supporting a conclusion, etc. But these are differences of *purpose*, not context.[3]

More importantly, and the main point argued for here: *contextualism, if correct, depends upon an underlying non-contextualism*. Suppose there is a genuine contextual dimension of argumentative norms, such that (C):

> (C): What makes a good argument good in a particular context, say, a scientific one, differs at least in part from what makes an argument good in contexts such as corporate boardrooms, conversations among friends, or courts of law.

From what context might (C) itself be established by argument? If (C) is worthy of belief, as asserted by contextualists, there must be a good argument that supports it; good reasons that render it so worthy. But that argument's quality can't itself be limited to some particular context, because if it is so limited, (C)'s epistemic status will itself be relative to context. That is, the argument that establishes (C) will itself be good in some contexts but not in others. And this seems to undercut the

[3]Notice that I am *not* claiming that argument purpose differs systematically across context— this I would deny—but rather asking whether the criteria that arguments must meet in order to be good differ in this way. Here I am indebted to the good advice of John Biro and Jan Steutel. It is uncontroversial that arguments are advanced for a variety of purposes. For a typical acknowledgement of this, see Toulmin 1958, p. 12.

argument for (C): if it supports (C), it will do so only in some contexts, and will fail to do so in others. And this sounds like the familiar problem with (epistemological) relativism.[4]

2 The Problem with Relativism

What is relativism, and what is the problem with it? Let relativism be understood as:

> *ER*: For any knowledge-claim *p*, *p* can be evaluated (assessed, established, etc.) only according to (with reference to) one or another set of background principles and standards of evaluation $s_1,\ldots s_n$; and, given a different set (or sets) of background principles and standards $s'_1,\ldots s'_n$, there is no neutral (that is, neutral with respect to the two (or more) alternative sets of principles and standards) way of choosing between the two (or more) alternative sets in evaluating *p* with respect to truth or rational justification. *p*'s truth and rational justifiability are relative to the standards used in evaluating *p*. (Siegel 1987, p. 6)

If this is relativism, what is the problem with it? The problem, familiar since Plato's *Theatetus*, is that it is *self-referentially incoherent* or *self-refuting*, in that defending the doctrine requires one to give it up. Why?

Insofar as she is taking issue with her non-relativist philosophical opponent, the relativist wants both (a) to offer a general, non-relative view of knowledge (and/or truth or justification), and assert that that general view—i.e., that knowledge is relative—is epistemically superior and preferable to its rivals; and also (b) to deny that such a general, non-relative view is possible or defensible. The relativist needs to embrace *both* (a), in order to see her position both as a rival to, and, further, as epistemically superior to, the position of her non-relativist opponent; and (b), in order to honor the fundamental requirements of relativism. But the mutual embrace of (a) and (b) is logically incoherent. For the embrace of (a) forces the rejection of (b): if relativism is the epistemically superior view of knowledge (i.e., (a)), then one general view of knowledge is both possible and defensible as epistemically superior to its rivals (contrary to (b)). Similarly, the embrace of (b) forces the rejection of (a): if no general, non-relative view of knowledge is possible or defensible (i.e., (b)), then it cannot be that relativism is itself epistemically superior to its rivals (contrary to (a)). This argument strongly suggests that the assertion and defense of relativism is incoherent.[5]

[4]I am speaking throughout only of *epistemological* relativism.

[5]For a more precise and detailed analysis of relativism and its vicissitudes, cf. Siegel 1987, 2004, and 2011, from which the version of the argument just given in the text is adapted.

3 Relativism and Contextualism

Of course, contextualism is not the same as relativism. Can the contextualist escape this incoherence problem? The key question is: From what context might the contextuality of argument norms be established? The worry is this: It appears that any argument for contextuality will itself necessarily be made from some context or other. Consequently the contextualist appears to be committed to the claim that the norms governing its quality will be forceful only contextually. If its quality is context-dependent, its normative force is equally so, thus rendering it unable to stand against or compete effectively with parallel arguments for the contrary conclusion launched from alternative contexts. The problem for the contextualist can be illustrated by drawing explicitly the analogy between the self-referential argument against relativism just rehearsed and the analogous argument against contextualism with respect to argument norms:

> *CAN*: For any argument *A* purporting to establish (C), *A* can be evaluated (assessed, established, etc.) only according to (with reference to) one or another set of contextually bound argument norms $n_1,\ldots n_n$; and, given a different set (or sets) of argument norms $n'_1,\ldots n'_n$, there is no neutral (that is, neutral with respect to the two (or more) alternative sets of principles and standards) way of choosing between the two (or more) alternative sets in evaluating *A* with respect to its ability to establish the truth or rational justification of (C). (C)'s truth and justificatory status are relative to the contextual norms used in evaluating *A*.

The problem with *CAN* can now be spelled out on analogy with the problem with *ER*: Contextualism appears to be *self-referentially incoherent* or *self-refuting*, in that defending the doctrine requires one to give it up. Why?

Insofar as she is taking issue with her non-contextualist philosophical opponent, the contextualist wants both (a′) to offer a general, non-contextual view of argument norms, and assert that that general view—i.e., that argument norms are contextual—is epistemically superior and preferable to its rivals; and also (b′) to deny that such a general, non-contextual view is possible or defensible. The contextualist needs to embrace *both* (a′), in order to see her position both as a rival to, and, further, as epistemically superior to, the position of her non-contextualist opponent; and (b′), in order to honor the fundamental requirements of contextualism. But the mutual embrace of (a′) and (b′) is logically incoherent. For the embrace of (a′) forces the rejection of (b′): if contextualism is the epistemically superior view of argument norms (i.e., (a′)), then one general, non-contextual account of argument norms is both possible and defensible as epistemically superior to its rivals (contrary to (b′)). Similarly, the embrace of (b′) forces the rejection of (a′): if no general, non-contextual account of argument norms is possible or defensible (i.e., (b′)), then it cannot be that contextualism is itself non-contextually superior to its rivals (contrary to (a′)). This argument strongly suggests that the assertion and defense of contextualism is incoherent.

4 The Fate of Contextualism

Thus the contextualization of argument norms is capable of being established only from a 'universal,' 'a-contextual'[6] context. How should we make sense of this situation?

The threat of incoherence establishes a strong, in-principle limit on the degree to which argument norms can be rightly regarded as contextual. As we saw earlier, arguments can be offered for different purposes. Can the norms governing their quality be relativized to context more generally, such that argument *A* can be good in (e.g.) a scientific journal but bad in a court of law or a casual conversation among friends? Yes, but only in so far as those contextualized norms —e.g., that scientific arguments can be good/bad in so far as they meet (or not) norms of explanatory adequacy—are *themselves established by arguments whose quality is not itself contextual or contextually bound.* The argument constitutes an incoherence proof[7] of a thoroughgoing contextualism concerning argument norms—such a thoroughgoing contextualism is incoherent—and establishes the limits of a defensible contextualism. We can coherently be *pluralists* about argument norms,[8] allowing that there are multiple legitimate argument norms, and that some of them are operative only in particular contexts. We should be pluralists in this sense. But we cannot, on pain of incoherence, be so thoroughgoingly contextualist as to hold that the case for this view is itself sanctioned by norms whose force is itself limited to particular contexts.

5 Are Prominent Theorists Problematically Contextualist?

Let us now briefly consider some prominent argumentation theorists who embrace one or another sort of contextualism to see whether their contextualisms violate the limits of a defensible contextualism just adduced.

6There is of course no 'view from nowhere' or 'a-contextual context'—hence the scare quotes. All our arguments are offered and evaluated in some context or other and from some conceptual scheme, perspective or point of view. The point on the table is just that the quality of arguments used to establish this very point is not itself dependent on the context in which the argument is offered or evaluated, and acknowledging it does not commit one to either relativism or contextualism. It is central to philosophical discussions of relativism; for systematic treatments of it in that context, cf. Siegel 1987, 1997, 2004, and 2011. Thanks to Derek Allen and Geoff Goddu for pressing me on this.

7Thanks to Christoph Lumer for this felicitous expression.

8A similar pluralism is endorsed by Godden (2005)

5.1 Stephen Toulmin

Toulmin famously held that "the merits of our arguments…are *field-dependent*" (1958, p. 15, emphasis in original):

> [A]ll the *canons* for the criticism and assessment of arguments…are in practice field-dependent, while all our terms of assessment are field-invariant in their *force*. We can ask, 'How strong a case can be made out?' [for arguments in three different fields] and the question we ask will be how strong each case is when tested against its own appropriate standard. We may even ask, if we please, how the three cases compare in strength, and produce an order of merit…But in doing so we are not asking how far the cases for the three conclusions measure up to a common standard: only, how far each of them comes up to the standards appropriate to things of its kind. The form of the question, 'How strong is the case?', has the same force or implications each time: the standards we work with in the three cases are different. (1958, p. 38, emphases in original)

It is unclear whether a Toulminian 'field' is the same sort of thing as that which other writers refer to as a 'context'. If these are not the same, then Toulmin should not count as the sort of contextualist we are concerned with here. But assuming for the sake of argument that he should so count, it is clear that he does not face the incoherence worry laid out earlier. He does not argue or suggest that his case for the field-dependence of argument quality[9] is itself launched from any particular field or context; he seems clearly enough to hold that the field-dependence of argument quality he advances is not itself dependent on any particular field or context. He does not suggest, for example, that judged from the context of argumentation theory argument quality is field-dependent, but judged from the context of physics, formal logic or history argument quality is field-independent. Rather, he urges that it is a field-independent truth that argument quality is field-dependent. So he does not embrace or endorse the problematic (b′) above. So he cannot fairly be charged with a problematic incoherence.

Toulmin makes an important point: some criteria of argument quality apply in some contexts but not others—e.g., a good inductive argument will not be good in most logico-mathematical contexts, in which deductive soundness is required[10]—and this is one example of the way in which argument norms are contextual. That said, I am not here endorsing Toulmin's overall views concerning argument quality; those views are not my present concern. I am arguing only that, insofar as his view is rightly thought of as contextualist, it is not such as to run the risk of incoherence set out above.[11]

---

[9]In his discussion Toulmin uses the words 'canons', 'criteria' and 'standards' to pick out those things in accordance with which argument quality is determined or assessed. These are not synonymous but I won't tarry on this point here.

[10]Although we must be careful here, for these criteria do not vary systematically by field. The variation is messier than one might expect. Cf. Siegel 1997, pp. 29–33.

[11]I think the same can be said of the prominent Toulminians Mark Weinstein and John Woods. Cf. Weinstein 2013 and, e.g., Woods 2005, p. 497.

5.2 *Douglas Walton*

Walton has long defended a version of contextualism. Consider, from among many such passages in his writings:

> [T]he validity or correctness of an argumentation scheme, as used in a given case, depends on the context of dialogue appropriate for that case. (1996, p. 13)
> [A]ny claim that a fallacy has been committed must be evaluated in relation to the text of discourse available in a given case... [A]n argument will always occur in a context of dialogue...Much of the work of analysis and evaluation of the allegedly fallacious argument will involve placing that argument in a context of dialogue. (1996, p. 14).
> [A]rguments are evaluated as correct or incorrect [on Walton's proposed pragmatic standard of argument evaluation] insofar as they are used either to contribute to or to impede the goals of dialogue. (1998, p. 3)
> [A] presumptive argument based on an argumentation scheme should always be evaluated in a context of the dialogue of which it is a part. (2001, p. 159)
> This pragmatic dimension [of justifying schematic arguments] requires that such arguments need to be examined within the context of an ongoing investigation in dialogue in which questions are being asked and answered. (2005, p. 8)

Like Toulmin's, Walton's contextualism is not guilty of the sort of incoherence illustrated above. He makes the important points that instances of argumentation take place in the context of particular dialogues, that particular argumentation schemes are suitable (or not) for such contexts, and that the evaluation of particular argumentative moves and exchanges depends upon the schemes appropriate for the context in question. He does not suggest that his own (pragmatic, dialogical) theory of argument evaluation is itself justified only contextually. That is, he does not assert (b′) above. So there is no incoherence here. (Whether or not his pragmatic, dialogical approach is a good one I do not take up here.)

5.3 *Geoff Goddu*

Goddu argues compellingly that "the correct evaluation of an argument is context dependent." (2003b, p. 381) The most important reason he offers for thinking so is that "when evaluating an argument...we must take into account not only the actual support that the premises provide, but the degree of support the premises *need* to provide as well. We need to know if the actual degree of support is *enough* and what support is enough will change from context to context." (2004, p. 30, emphases in original, note deleted; cf. also p. 33) He illustrates his claim with several suggestive examples. The most straightforward is that of the same argument, utilizing the same evidence, put forward by the prosecution in both civil and criminal trials: in the former the argument is adequate if it establishes the defendant's guilt by a preponderance of the evidence; in the latter the evidence must establish guilt beyond a reasonable doubt. If the argument establishes that the probability of the defendant's guilt is .6, it is adequate in the context of the civil trial but not in that of the criminal trial.[12]

As with Toulmin and Walton, Goddu's contextualism does not involve the sort of incoherence we are concerned with here. His correct point concerning the context dependence of argument adequacy is not itself true only in some contexts and not in others; he does not suggest either that his argument for context dependence is itself context dependent or that that argument is adequate in some contexts and not others. Rather, he establishes the context-independent conclusion that argument evaluation is contextual. Like Toulmin and Walton, he does not assert (b′) above. So there is no incoherence here.

5.4 Frans van Eemeren

The final author to be considered is Frans van Eemeren. Van Eemeren (in collaboration with several of his co-authors) embraces a substantial but constrained version of contextualism. He acknowledges both general, context-independent and context-dependent criteria "for the fulfilment of norms of reasonableness", which norms are "incorporated in the rules of critical discussion" at the heart of the Pragma-Dialectical approach:

> Because the application of the critical norms of reasonableness is partially dependent on the requirements that result from the exact circumstances in which the argumentation occurs, such that these norms can be implemented in slightly different ways, the content of these criteria can sometimes be context dependent. This means that the context in which the argumentative exchange takes place has to be, in principle, taken into account explicitly in determining the fallaciousness [of a given argumentative move/strategic maneuver].
> Besides the general criteria which are context independent, specific criteria which are context-dependent will also play a role in the evaluation of [such moves/maneuvers]… (van Eemeren 2011b, p. 40)
>
> When reflecting upon the criteria that can be brought to bear to distinguish between sound and fallacious strategic maneuvering, I make a distinction between general criteria for judging fallaciousness that are context-independent and more specific criteria that may be dependent on the macro-context in which the strategic maneuvering takes place. (van Eemeren 2011a, p. 154)

As these citations make clear, van Eemeren's contextualism is not so thoroughgoing as to run into the incoherence problem described above. It explicitly acknowledges context-independent criteria for the satisfaction of the pragma-dialectical norms of reasonableness. Moreover, those norms, incorporated in the pragma-dialectical rules governing critical discussions, are themselves

[12]For this and other examples see Goddu 2003b, p. 380, 2004, pp. 27–30; cf. Goddu 2001 for an early articulation of his view of argument evaluation and Goddu 2003a, 2005 for systematic discussions of the difficulties of specifying 'the context of an argument' and 'context dependence' respectively. A closely related point concerning the context-dependence of the evaluation of some scientific arguments is made in Rudner 1953.

context-independent: whatever the context, if one violates a rule one violates the associated norm. Most importantly for present purposes, van Eemeren's argument for contextualism is not itself contextually bound. Like our other authors, he does not assert (b′) above. Once again, there is no incoherence here.[13]

6 Conclusion: Contextualism, but Only Within Limits

If the argument offered here is successful, argument norms can be established only by arguments/reasons that are non-contextual in character and epistemic force. This leaves room for a healthy *pluralism* concerning argument norms. There are important contextual dimensions of argument quality and important things concerning contextually specific aspects of argument quality for argumentation theorists to study and say.[14] There are multiple legitimate argument norms, and some of them are operative only in particular contexts. But that any particular argument norm is a legitimate norm in a particular argument context cannot itself be established contextually.

Is this really a problem worth worrying about? After all, as we've just seen, none of the theorists considered above go over the line; their contextualisms are all sufficiently bounded so as to not risk the incoherence worry I have been belaboring. That these theorists stay clear of the difficulty is of course a good thing. The lesson to be learned from this discussion, if there is one, is a cautionary one: in theorizing about the contextual character of argument norms, don't go over the line. Contextualism defended non-contextually is, or at least might be, OK; contextualism that extends to the defense of that view itself, not so much. As with other such topics, self-referential incoherence is a worry to take seriously when theorizing about argument norms.

Acknowledgments I presented an ancestor of this paper as a powerpoint talk at the 'Argumentation and Philosophy: Different Issues or Productive Tensions?' symposium at the Universidad Nacional Autónoma de México in Mexico City in 2009 and at the 7th ISSA conference in Amsterdam in 2010 but never wrote it up for publication. I presented a revised and

[13]Van Eemeren's general approach, like Walton's, is both pragmatic and dialectical. For a very helpful comparison of the two views, especially with respect to contextualism, cf. van Eemeren et al. 2010. I should note once again (but not pursue here) a widespread ambiguity in the argumentation literature: dialogical/dialectical approaches, like those of Walton and van Eemeren, focus on norms governing particular argumentative moves in dialogue, while other approaches, and in particular Goddu's and epistemic theorists such as Lumer and Biro and me, focus not on the norms governing such moves but rather on those governing the evaluations of particular arguments conceived as abstract objects. Cf. Goddu's papers cited above, Lumer (2005), Biro and Siegel (2006) and Siegel and Biro (2010).

[14]Some of which are said in such venues as van Eemeren and Garssen 2012a and the series in which this volume appears, as well as the work of Walton and van Eemeren cited above.

expanded talk at the 8th ISSA conference in July 2014. I am grateful to Jan Steutel and to the audiences at the several presentations, especially Derek Allen, John Biro, Geoff Goddu, Cristoph Lumer, Mark Weinstein and John Woods for insightful comments, criticisms and suggestions.

References

Battersby, M., & Bailin, S. (2011). Critical inquiry: Considering the context. *Argumentation, 25* (2), 243–253.

Biro, J., & Siegel, H. (2006). Pragma-dialectic versus epistemic theories of arguing and arguments: Rivals or partners? In P. Houtlosser, & A. van Rees (Eds.), Considering pragma-dialectics: A festshrift for Frans H. van Eemeren on the occasion of his 60th birthday (pp. 1–10). Mahuah, NJ: Erlbaum.

DeRose, K. (2009). *The case for contextualism: Knowledge, skepticism, and context* (Vol. 1). Oxford: Oxford University Press.

Fogelin, R. J. (2005). The logic of deep disagreements. *Informal Logic, 25*(1), 3–11 (Originally published in *Informal Logic* (1985), *7*(1), 1–8).

Godden, D. (2005). Deductivism as an interpretive strategy: A reply to Groarke's recent defense of reconstructive deductivism. *Argumentation and Advocacy, 41*, 168–183.

Goddu, G. C. (2001). The 'most important and fundamental' distinction in logic. *Informal Logic, 22*(1), 1–17.

Goddu, G. C (2003a). The context of an argument. In J. A. Blair, et al. (Eds.), *Informal logic at 25: Proceedings of the Windsor conference*, CD-ROM (pp. 1–14). Windsor, ON: OSSA.

Goddu, G. C. (2003b). Context and argument evaluation. In F. H. van Eemeren, et al. (Eds.), *Proceedings of the fifth conference of the International Society for the Study of Argumentation* (pp. 377–381). Amsterdam: Sic Sat.

Goddu, G. C. (2004). Cogency and the validation of induction. *Argumentation, 18*(1), 25–41.

Goddu, G. C. (2005). Epistemic contextualism and the context of an argument. In D. Hitchcock (Ed.), *The uses of argument: Proceedings of a conference at McMaster University, 18–21 May 2005* (pp. 148–155). Windsor, ON: The Ontario Society for the Study of Argumentation.

Lumer, C. (2005). The epistemological theory of argument—how and why? *Informal Logic, 25*(3), 213–243.

Rudner, R. (1953). The scientist *qua* scientist makes value judgments. *Philosophy of Science, 20* (1), 1–6.

Siegel, H. (1987). *Relativism refuted: A critique of contemporary epistemological relativism*. Dordrecht: Springer.

Siegel, H. (1997). *Rationality redeemed?: Further dialogues on an educational ideal*. New York: Routledge.

Siegel, H. (2004). Relativism. In I. Niiniluoto, M. Sintonen, & J. Woleński (Eds.), *Handbook of epistemology* (pp. 747–780). Dordrecht: Kluwer.

Siegel, H. (2011). Epistemological relativism: Arguments pro and con. In S. D. Hales (Ed.), *A companion to relativism*. Malden, MA: Blackwell.

Siegel, H., & Biro, J. (2010). The Pragma-dialectitian's dilemma: Reply to Garssen and van Laar. *Informal Logic, 30*(4), 457–480.

Toulmin, S. E. (1958). *The uses of argument*. Cambridge: Cambridge University Press.

van Eemeren, F. H. (2011a). In context: Giving contextualization its rightful place in the study of argumentation. *Argumentation, 25*(2), 141–161.

van Eemeren, F. H. (2011b). *In alle redelijkheid/In reasonableness*. Amsterdam: Rozenberg and Sic Sat Publishers.

van Eemeren, F. H., & Garssen, B. (Eds.). (2012a). *Exploring argumentative contexts*. Amsterdam: John Benjamins Publishing Company.

van Eemeren, F. H., & Garssen, B. (2012b). Introduction. In van Eemeren and Garsssen (Eds.), *Exploring argumentative contexts* (pp. xiii–xx). Amsterdam: John Benjamins Publishing Company.

Van Eemeren, F. H., Houtlosser, P., Ihnen, C., & Lewiński, M. (2010). Contextual considerations in the evaluation of argumentation. In C. Reed, & C. W. Tindale (Eds.), *Dialectics, dialogue and argumentation: An examination of Douglas Walton's theories of reasoning and argument* (pp. 115–132). London: King's College.

Walton, D. N. (1996). *Argumentation schemes for presumptive reasoning*. Mahwah, NJ: Lawrence Erlbaum Associates Publishers.

Walton, D. N. (1998). *The new dialectic*. Toronto: University of Toronto Press.

Walton, D. N. (2001). Abductive, presumptive and plausible arguments. *Informal Logic, 21*(2), 141–169.

Walton, D. N. (2005). Justification of argument schemes. *Australasian Journal of Logic, 3*, 1–13.

Weinstein, M. (2013). *Logic, truth and inquiry*. London: King's College.

Woods, J. (2005). Eight theses reflecting on Stephen Toulmin. In D. Hitchcock (Ed.), *The uses of argument: Proceedings of a conference at McMaster University, 18–21 May 2005* (pp. 495–504). Windsor, ON: The Ontario Society for the Study of Argumentation.

Reasonableness in Context: Taking into Account Institutional Conventions in the Pragma-Dialectical Evaluation of Argumentative Discourse

A.F. Snoeck Henkemans and J.H.M. Wagemans

1 Introduction

Over the last couple of years, the pragma-dialectical research program has focused on the development of tools for the analysis and evaluation of argumentative discourse in specific institutional contexts, such as the domains of legal, political, medical, and academic communication. In developing these tools, the aims and conventions pertaining to the particular context of argumentative activity play an important role. Knowledge of these aims and conventions is indispensable for providing an adequate analysis of the argumentation put forward in that particular context. Moreover, this type of knowledge helps formulating the criteria for evaluating the reasonableness of the argumentation.

The use of institutional aims and conventions in the evaluation of argumentative discourse has led to much debate among argumentation scholars on how exactly context may influence fallacy judgments. Some scholars take it as a starting point that in different contexts, different standards for the reasonableness of the discourse apply. According to Walton, for instance, an argument that is reasonable in one

This article is an amended version of the paper we presented at the ISSA 2014 International Conference on Argumentation. We would like to thank Bart Garssen and Frans van Eemeren for their helpful comments. For a short overview of the pragma-dialectical research program and its collaborators, see van Eemeren et al. (2014, pp. 517–519).

A.F. Snoeck Henkemans (✉) · J.H.M. Wagemans
Department of Speech Communication, Argumentation Theory, and Rhetoric,
University of Amsterdam, Amsterdam, The Netherlands
e-mail: a.f.snoeckhenkemans@uva.nl

J.H.M. Wagemans
e-mail: j.h.m.wagemans@uva.nl

F.H. van Eemeren and B. Garssen (eds.), *Reflections on Theoretical Issues in Argumentation Theory*, Argumentation Library 28,
DOI 10.1007/978-3-319-21103-9_16

context may be fallacious in a different context, because the norms to be applied by the evaluator depend on the goal of the type of dialogue at hand:

> In order to evaluate whether an argument in a particular case is relevant or irrelevant, reasonable or fallacious, and so forth, it is necessary to determine whether the argument has been put forward in a deliberation, for example, as opposed to a negotiation or persuasion dialogue or other type of dialogue. For the goals and the rules for each type of dialogue are quite different (Walton 1998, p. 254).

In contrast to Walton, pragma-dialecticians regard the norms laid down in their 'model of a critical discussion' as context-independent standards of argumentative reasonableness:

> Although we agree […] that fallacy judgments are in the end always contextual judgments that depend on the specific circumstances of situated argumentative acting, we do not agree that the norms underlying these judgments are context-dependent. In our view, the norms expressed in the rules for critical discussion are general – who knows even universal – norms for sound argumentation that are not limited to one particular type of argumentative activity. […] Using the rules for critical discussion as a context-*in*dependent standard, we take the peculiarities of the various argumentative activity types into account when we start evaluating whether these rules have been obeyed or violated (van Eemeren and Houtlosser 2007, p. 65, original italics).

In order to determine whether the rules for critical discussion have been violated or not, in pragma-dialectics 'criteria' are used (van Eemeren and Grootendorst 1992, pp. 104–106). The contextuality of fallacy judgments, as becomes clear from the remarks below, has to be situated on the level of these criteria:

> The context-dependency of judgments of argumentative discourse lies in the way in which the conduct of argumentative discourse is conventionally disciplined in a certain activity type by specific criteria for determining whether or not a certain type of maneuvering agrees with the relevant norm, which criteria may vary to some extent per argumentative activity type – in a law case, for instance, different criteria apply to making a legitimate appeal to authority, e.g. by referring to a certain law code, than in a political debate (van Eemeren and Houtlosser 2007, p. 64).

Some institutional norms, however, seem to be irreconcilable with the general rules for critical discussion. An example is to be found in Feteris's analysis of argumentation in the legal setting, where she notes that 'to safeguard legal rights, there are time limits within which an appeal must be taken. Otherwise the party who has won the trial can never be sure about his rights' (1990 p. 113). The existence of this time limit is not completely in accordance with the pragma-dialectical 'freedom rule,' according to which discussants have the *unconditional* right to put forward a standpoint or call into question the standpoint of the other party in the discussion (van Eemeren and Grootendorst 2004, pp. 136, 190–191).[1]

[1]Another example is the medical consultation, where, according to Snoeck Henkemans and Mohammed, an institutional burden of proof is imposed on doctors 'to justify treatment options without patients having to express any disagreement about these options' (2012, p. 30, note 3).

This kind of examples raises the question whether the abovementioned starting-point that the contextuality of fallacy judgements has to be situated at the level of the criteria for rule violation instead of at the level of the rules themselves can be maintained. And if it cannot be maintained, what would be the consequences of the existence of a discrepancy between an institutional convention and a pragma-dialectical rule for the evaluation of the argumentation in the institutional context concerned?

To answer these questions it should first become clear what the main difference is between 'rules' and 'criteria'. To this end, we investigate in Sect. 2 what types of norms are distinguished within pragma-dialectics and what role they play in the evaluation of argumentation. In Sect. 3, we then discuss in what ways institutional conventions may relate to the different types of pragma-dialectical norms. By means of a number of examples, we describe the consequences of possible discrepancies between both systems of norms for the evaluation of the argumentation put forward in the context concerned.

2 Rules and Criteria

For a pragma-dialectical evaluation, first, standards need to be available that specify what it means to discuss reasonably. A proposal for such standards is expressed in the so-called 'code of conduct for reasonable discussants', a set of ten rules (or 'commandments') that is derived from a larger set of fifteen rules that constitute the 'procedure of a critical discussion', which is an integral part of the 'model of a critical discussion' (van Eemeren and Grootendorst 2004, pp. 123–186).

In order to determine the reasonableness of a contribution to the discussion, however, it does not suffice, as we have seen, to know which rule of the code of conduct is at issue. The evaluator also needs to dispose of criteria that can be used to decide whether the contribution is in accordance with the rule or not (van Eemeren and Grootendorst 1992, p. 106). With respect to the nature of such criteria, van Eemeren makes a distinction between 'general' and 'specific' criteria:

> I make a distinction between general criteria for judging fallaciousness that are context-independent and more specific criteria that may be dependent on the macro-context in which the strategic maneuvering takes place, because this specific context requires a well-adapted implementation of the general criteria (van Eemeren 2010, p. 201).

When justifying a particular fallacy judgment, the evaluator therefore refers to two types of norms: to the general rule that has been violated and to the (general or specific) criterion that is used to establish that the rule is violated.

How do the conventions that are at force within a specific institutional context relate to these pragma-dialectical norms? From what we have discussed until now, it can be concluded that institutional conventions can, in principle, play a role at two different levels in the evaluation of argumentation: the level of the rules and the level of the criteria. But how can the evaluator determine on which of these two levels a given institutional convention is operative? To answer this question, we will now turn to analyzing the nature of the pragma-dialectical norms for the evaluation in more detail.[2]

The norms specified in the code of conduct for reasonable discussants can be characterized as rules that specify the rights and obligations of the discussants. In abstract terms, such rules are formulated as 'X should do Y' or negatively as 'X should refrain from doing Y'. An example is the so-called 'freedom rule', which is listed as Commandment 1 of the code of conduct: 'Discussants may not prevent each other from advancing standpoints or from calling standpoints into question' (van Eemeren and Grootendorst 2004, p. 190). Some of the rules of the code of conduct specify conditional obligations. In abstract terms, such conditional deontic rules are formulated as 'if Z is the case, X should do Y' or negatively as 'if Z is the case, X should refrain from doing Y'. An example is the so-called 'obligation-to-defend rule,' (Commandment 2 of the code of conduct): 'Discussants who advance a standpoint may not refuse to defend this standpoint when requested to do so' (van Eemeren and Grootendorst 2004, p. 191). In the literature, different names are used for this type of rule: they are called normative rules, regulative rules (Grossi et al. 2006, p. 1) and 'deontic' rules (Wagemans 2009, p. 41). Since this type of rules prescribes what discussants should do or should refrain from doing, we have chosen to refer to this kind of rules as 'prescriptive' rules.

The norms constituting the procedure of a critical discussion can only partly be characterized as prescriptive rules, because some of the rules belonging to this procedure are of a different nature: They contain definitions of terms or specifications of when a certain state of affairs may be said to obtain. Such rules take the abstract form of 'X counts as Y'.[3] An example is the rule that defines what counts as a conclusive attack on a standpoint, which is listed as Rule 9b of the procedure: 'The antagonist has conclusively attacked the standpoint of the protagonist if he has successfully attacked either the propositional content or the force of justification of the complex speech act of argumentation' (van Eemeren and Grootendorst 2004, p. 151). The need for specifying what is meant by the 'conclusiveness' of an attack follows from the occurrence of the term in Rule 14a, which specifies when the protagonist should withdraw his standpoint: 'The protagonist is obliged to retract the initial standpoint if the antagonist has conclusively attacked it [...] in the argumentation stage [...]' (van Eemeren and Grootendorst 2004, p. 154).[4] In the literature, such rules are known as 'constitutive' rules, 'classificatory' rules, 'conceptual' rules (Grossi et al. 2006, p. 1), 'non-deontic eidetic-constitutive' rules

[2]We summarize here the account of the nature of the pragma-dialectical rules as provided by Wagemans (2009, pp. 36–37, 41–42).

[3]Like some rules of the code of conduct, some rules of the procedure specify *conditional* obligations. This is for instance the case in Rules 3, 4, and 14.

[4]Other examples of such definitional rules are Rules 7, 8, and 9a of the procedure, which define terms that play a crucial role in Rules 10, 11, and 14b of the procedure.

(Ritter et al. 1971-2007, vol. 8, pp. 448–449) or just ‘adeontic’ rules (Wagemans 2009, p. 41). Since the main function of such rules is to define the meaning of certain terms, we shall call them ‘definitional’ rules.

Generally speaking, an evaluator is only able to decide whether a discussant complied with a prescriptive rule if he knows how to interpret the terms that are used in that rule. This knowledge may come from three different sources: (1) the definitional rules mentioned in the procedure of a critical discussion; (2) the general criteria mentioned in the pragma-dialectical literature (an example given by van Eemeren (2010, pp. 203–204) of a context-independent general soundness criterion for assessing whether the argumentation scheme rule has been violated in the case of an argument from authority, is the critical question whether the authoritative source is quoted correctly); and (3) the specific criteria mentioned in the pragma-dialectical literature (van Eemeren (2010, p. 197), for instance, mentions several specific criteria for fallaciousness, which may vary depending on the macro-context).

What the general and specific criteria have in common is that they are all definitional in character. They do not concern rights or obligations but specify which conditions have to be fulfilled in order for a discussion move to count as a violation of a particular prescriptive rule. The difference between the two types of criteria lies in their scope: general criteria are of the form ‘X counts as Y’ and specific criteria are of the form ‘X counts as Y in context Z’.

Summarizing, the rules of the code of conduct for reasonable discussants and part of the rules of the procedure for critical discussion can be characterized as ‘prescriptive’, while another part of the procedural rules can be seen as definitional rules. Since the latter rules in fact function as context-independent criteria, the pragma-dialectical terminology would be more consistent if they were called ‘general criteria’ instead of ‘rules’. In Fig. 1 we present an overview of our analysis of the different types of norms that play a part in the pragma-dialectical evaluation of argumentative discourse in institutional contexts.

NORMS	NATURE	TERM
Rules of the ‘code of conduct for reasonable discussants’	prescriptive	‘RULES’
Rules of the ‘procedure for a critical discussion’	prescriptive definitional	‘RULES’ ‘GENERAL CRITERIA’
Criteria applicable to all contexts	definitional	‘GENERAL CRITERIA’
Criteria applicable to specific contexts	definitional	‘SPECIFIC CRITERIA’

Fig. 1 Pragma-dialectical norms for the evaluation of argumentative discourse

3 Justifying a Rule Adaptation

Now that we have clarified the distinction between rules and criteria, we shall analyze by means of a number of examples at which of these two normative levels institutional conventions are operative and how this influences the evaluation of the reasonableness of the argumentation put forward in the context concerned. We thereby assume that institutional conventions, just like pragma-dialectical norms, may either be prescriptive or definitional in nature.[5]

Whenever the evaluator faces a definitional convention, he may use it in order to formulate a specific criterion for rule violation. In this case, the pragma-dialectical starting point that the rules for critical discussion are generally applicable in all contexts of argumentative activity can be maintained. For it is not the general rule but the context-specific criterion that renders a certain discussion reasonable in the one context and fallacious in the other.

An example of such a convention can be found in the activity type of Prime Minister's Question Time in the British House of Commons. As Mohammed points out, as representatives of a certain party, politicians may be held accountable not just for the standpoints they have put forward personally, but also for the standpoints their political party has made public in one way or another:

> In principle, it is necessary, in order to hold political parties to account, to consider that the commitments that can be attributed to a certain MP are not restricted to those deriving from his own positions. It should be possible, to different degrees of justifiability, to attribute to MPs from a certain political party commitments deriving from positions that have been assumed by the leaders of their parties, election manifestos, or other public expressions of opinion made in the name of the Party (Mohammed 2009, p. 132).

By virtue of their party political obligations, politicians may therefore be required to account for a standpoint they have not put forward themselves, but that belongs to their political party's official points of view. In such a case, an attack on a standpoint ascribed to the politician does not necessarily constitute a violation of the so called 'standpoint rule', which forbids attacks on a standpoint 'that has not actually been put forward by the other party' (van Eemeren and Grootendorst 2004, p. 191).[6] Whereas in a different context, someone who carries out such an attack may be accused of having committed the straw man fallacy, in the context of Prime

---

[5]Although it is theoretically possible to convert a definitional rule into a prescriptive one, such a conversion always results in the description of an obligation that the arguer is free to take upon himself or not. For instance, the abovementioned definitional rule 9b concerning the requirements for a conclusive attack may be rewritten as the following conditional prescriptive rule: 'If the antagonist wants his attack to count as a conclusive attack, he is obliged to successfully attack either the propositional content or the force of justification of the complex speech act of argumentation'. Conversely, rewriting a prescriptive rule as a definitional rule requires a formulation of the form 'X counts as obligation Y'. Such conversions therefore show that the distinction between 'rules' and 'criteria' still holds.

[6]In fact, the rule does not forbid attacks on a standpoint that has not actually been put forward by the other party, but rather on a standpoint that the other party cannot be held committed to.

Minister's Question Time, such an accusation would not hold if the attack concerns a standpoint belonging to the MP's political party's official points of view.

From the example it becomes clear that the general obligation expressed by the prescriptive rule, namely that discussants have to account for the standpoints they can be held committed to, remains in force. The institutional convention only gives rise to a specification of the criterion for determining when exactly this general rule is violated in the specific context concerned.

The evaluator may also encounter cases in which institutional conventions are prescriptive in nature and express rights or obligations that differ from the ones expressed in the pragma-dialectical rules for critical discussion, for instance because they are restricted or extended. This raises the question as to how the existence of such discrepancies relates to the pragma-dialectical starting point that the rules for critical discussion are generally applicable to all contexts of argumentative activity.

In case of a discrepancy between an institutional convention and a pragma-dialectical rule, the consequences for the evaluation of a discussion move made within the context concerned depend on what the rationale for this discrepancy is. Sometimes, the convention can be related to the so-called 'higher-order conditions' for critical discussion.[7] These are conditions that need to be fulfilled in order to enable the discussants to comply with the 'first-order' discussion rules:[8]

> The 'internal' mental states that are a precondition to a reasonable discussion attitude can be regarded as 'second-order' conditions for a critical discussion, while the presupposed 'external' circumstances in which the argumentation takes place apply as 'third-order' conditions (van Eemeren and Grootendorst 2004, pp. 36–37).

If an institutional convention can be interpreted as a way of compensating for the non-fulfillment of one or more higher-order conditions, discussion moves that are in accordance with that convention but not with one of the rules for critical discussion may still be judged as reasonable. For the point of the convention is to further the reasonable resolution of the dispute by compensating for the restrictions that follow from the non-fulfillment of particular higher-order conditions.

An example of an institutional context in which such a deviating prescriptive convention applies is the medical consultation. As Goodnight (2006) and Snoeck Henkemans and Mohammed (2012) have pointed out, in doctor-patient consultations, the doctor has an institutional obligation with respect to the burden-of-proof. Ideally, a physician needs to present all the available treatment options and provide evidence for and against each of these options (Snoeck Henkemans and

[7]Feteris (1990, p. 111) mentions this as one of the reasons why some rules in the legal process deviate from the pragma-dialectical rules: 'The distinction between the rules for discussion and the conditions which have to be fulfilled in order to conduct a rational discussion, forms an analytical distinction which makes it possible to explain why legal proceedings differ on one level in certain respects from a critical discussion and why these differences are compensated on a higher level in order to make the procedure a rational one.'

[8]For a description of these conditions, see also van Eemeren and Grootendorst (2004, pp. 189–190) and van Eemeren et al. 1993, pp. 30–34).

Mohammed 2012, p. 22). The main reason to impose this burden of proof upon the physician is that in medical consultations there usually is an 'asymmetric' relationship between the discussants: In most cases, the physician is an expert and the patient is a layman.

According to van Eemeren, Grootendorst, Jackson and Jacobs, 'the ideal model assumes skill and competence in the subject matter under discussion and on the issues raised' (1993, p. 32). In the context of a medical consultation, it cannot be assumed right away that this second-order condition is fulfilled, for patients cannot be expected to possess the knowledge and skills to engage in a discussion about what would be the best treatment option for a medical problem. The institutional burden of proof that is imposed on the doctor can therefore be seen as compensating for the non-fulfillment of a second-order condition for resolving a difference of opinion on the merits. Although this institutional convention is not in line with the pragma-dialectical burden-of-proof rule, the resulting extension of the physician's obligations does not endanger the resolution of a dispute, but, on the contrary, promotes it. In this case, therefore, it is justified to change the pragma-dialectical rule that is used for making fallacy judgments in accordance with the institutional convention.

There are, however, also cases in which the discrepancy between institutional conventions and the pragma-dialectical rules cannot be explained as a way of creating the conditions for reasonable discussion, but only as a means of achieving specific other institutional goals. An example of such a convention is to be found in the legal civil process. According to the pragma-dialectical 'obligation-to-defend rule', as van Eemeren and Grootendorst state, 'discussants who advance a standpoint may not refuse to defend this standpoint when requested to do so' (2004, p. 191). As a consequence, 'unlike a legal dispute, an argumentative dispute can in principle never be settled once and for all. The discussion can always be reopened' (2004, p. 138). In the civil process, as we already noted in the introduction, the right to reopen the discussion is limited in order to guarantee that specific legal aims can be achieved. The legal rules limit the obligations of the party who has won the trial to defend his point of view to a certain time span.[9]

Now if the evaluator on the basis of observing this discrepancy would attempt at formulating a context-specific criterion that leaves the general applicability of the rule intact, he would create a contradictory evaluation standard. For the unlimited right to criticize a standpoint would then in the legal context be defined as a right that expires after a certain period of time has elapsed, which is a nonsensical definition of 'unlimited'.

The only conclusion the evaluator can draw from the existence of this discrepancy is that within the legal context, 'legal certainty' is considered to be of greater importance than 'critical testing'. Imposing time limits on the moves of discussion parties furthers the aim of safeguarding parties' legal rights but is,

[9]At the same time, this means that the rights of the party who has lost the trial to challenge his opponent's standpoint (Rule 1, Freedom rule) are also limited to a certain period of time.

strictly speaking, not conducive for critically testing the acceptability of a standpoint. Therefore, although the convention is defensible from a legal perspective, it should be considered fallacious from a pragma-dialectical perspective.

4 Conclusion

In this chapter we first of all provided an account of the nature of the pragma-dialectical evaluation standards. The reasonableness of argumentative discourse is judged on the basis of general prescriptive rules that specify the rights and obligations of the parties involved in the discussion. Apart from these rules, in order to establish whether a particular discussion move is fallacious or not, general and specific criteria may have to be applied. These criteria are definitional in nature, because they specify the meaning (or scope) of the terms occurring in the prescriptive rules.

We then turned to analyzing the influence of institutional conventions on the pragma-dialectical evaluation of argumentation. Several parameters determine the influence. First of all, the evaluator should establish whether a particular convention is prescriptive or definitional in nature and, in case it is prescriptive, whether the rights and obligations deviate from those expressed in the rules of the code of conduct for reasonable discussants. Then, there are three possibilities:

(1) If the convention is definitional in nature, it may be of help in (further) specifying the context-dependent criteria the evaluator uses to determine whether or not a rule violation has occurred.
(2) If the convention is prescriptive in nature and deviates from the rules for critical discussion in a certain respect, the evaluator may have to adapt the rules on which his fallacy judgments are based. Such a rule adaptation can only be justified by showing that the adaptation compensates for the non-fulfillment of certain higher-order conditions for resolving a difference of opinion on the merits. For only in this way can it be maintained that the norms that are used in the evaluation further the realization of an argumentative aim.
(3) If in the case of such a discrepancy it is not possible to justify a rule adaptation in the manner described above, the original pragma-dialectical rule should be used for the evaluation. If rules are only adapted to do justice to the specific institutional aims of the activity type concerned, the norms used in the evaluation are not necessarily conducive to a reasonable resolution of a dispute. An evaluator who decides to let the reasonableness of argumentation in institutional contexts depend on conventions that are not or only partly conducive for critically testing the acceptability of a standpoint, confuses argumentative reasonableness and institutional efficacy.

All in all, we may conclude that the pragma-dialectical starting point that the contextuality of fallacy judgments is to be situated at the level of the criteria, cannot be maintained in all cases. If a prescriptive convention deviates from the pragma-dialectical rules in such a way that this compensates the non-fulfillment of a higher-order condition for conducting a critical discussion, the contextuality of fallacy judgments is to be situated at the level of the rules. It is in this case justified to adapt the pragma-dialectical rule on which fallacy judgments are based in such a way that it is in accordance with the institutional convention.

References

van Eemeren, F. H., & Grootendorst, R. (1992). *Argumentation, communication and fallacies: A pragma-dialectical perspective*. Hillsdale, NJ: Erlbaum.

van Eemeren, F. H., Grootendorst, R., Jackson, S., & Jacobs, S. (1993). *Reconstructing argumentative discourse*. Tuscaloosa: The University of Alabama Press.

van Eemeren, F. H., & Grootendorst, R. (2004). *A systematic theory of argumentation: The pragma-dialectical approach*. Hillsdale, NJ: Erlbaum.

van Eemeren, F. H., & Houtlosser, P. (2007). The contextuality of fallacies. *Informal Logic, 27*(1), 59–67.

van Eemeren, F. H. (2010). *Strategic maneuvering in argumentative discourse*. Amsterdam: Benjamins.

van Eemeren, F. H., Garssen, B. J., Krabbe, E. C. W., Snoeck Henkemans, A. F., Verheij, B., & Wagemans, J. H. M. (2014). *Handbook of Argumentation Theory*. Dordrecht: Springer.

Feteris, E. T. (1990). Conditions and rules for rational discussion in a legal process: A pragma-dialectical perspective. *Argumentation and Advocacy, 3*, 108–117.

Goodnight, T. G. (2006). When reasons matter most: Pragma-dialectics and the problem of informed consent. In P. Houtlosser & M. A. van Rees (Eds.), *Considering pragma-dialectics: A festschrift for Frans H. van Eemeren on the occasion of his 60th birthday* (pp. 75–85). Mahwah, NJ: Erlbaum.

Grossi, D., Meyer, J. -J. Ch., & Dignum, F. (2006). Counts-as: Classification or constitution? An answer using modal logic. In L. Goble & J. -J.Ch. Meyer (Eds.), *Deontic logic and artificial normative systems: 8th International Workshop on Deontic Logic in Computer Science, DEON 2006, Utrecht, The Netherlands, July 12–14, 2006. Proceedings*. Heidelberg: Springer.

Mohammed, D. (2009). *'The honourable gentleman should make up his mind': Strategic manoeuvring with accusations of inconsistency in Prime Minister's Question Time*. Unpublished doctoral dissertation, University of Amsterdam.

Ritter, J., Gründer, K., & Gabriel, G. (red.) (1971–2007). *Historisches Wörterbuch der Philosophie*. 13 Vols. Basel: Schwabe.

Snoeck Henkemans, A. F., & Mohammed, D. (2012). Institutional constraints on strategic maneuvering in shared medical decision-making. *Journal of Argumentation in Context, 1*(1), 19–32.

Wagemans, J. H. M. (2009). *Redelijkheid en overredingskracht van argumentatie: Een historisch-filosofische studie over de combinatie van het dialectische en het retorische perspectief op argumentatie in de pragma-dialectische argumentatietheorie* [Reasonableness and persuasiveness of argumentation: A historical-philosophical study concerning the combination of the dialectical and the rhetorical perspective on argumentation in the pragma-dialectical theory of argumentation]. Unpublished doctoral dissertation, University of Amsterdam.

Walton, D. (1998). *The new dialectic: Conversational contexts of argument*. Toronto: University of Toronto Press.

Deference, Distrust, and Delegation: Three Design Hypotheses

Sally Jackson

1 Introduction

A central premise of a design theory of argumentation (Jackson 2015) is that argumentation is a set of invented cultural practices that change over time to adjust to material circumstances, including the emergence of new communication technologies. A design perspective suggests that societies try out ideas about how to reach conclusions and agreements, embodying them in techniques and technical systems, some of which accrete to a durable set of reasoning practices, even though these ideas and practices may not be consistent with other ideas and practices that have already been added to the set. The result at any point in time is some collection of practices carried forward from the past, plus new, emerging ideas that must somehow co-exist with the old.

I have argued elsewhere (Jackson 2012; Jackson and Aakhus 2014) that design is becoming much more important to our understanding of argumentation. In part, this is because in reviewing the achievements of the past, it has become important to see how something that improved on the practice of argumentation at one point in time can itself be improved on as the surrounding cultural context changes. But even more significantly, design thinking applied to contemporary problems allows theorists to test the practice of argumentation against *what it could be*, not just against legacy ideas about what it means to be reasonable.

S. Jackson (✉)
Department of Communication, University of Illinois at Urbana-Champaign, Champaign, USA
e-mail: sallyj@illinois.edu

F.H. van Eemeren and B. Garssen (eds.), *Reflections on Theoretical Issues in Argumentation Theory*, Argumentation Library 28,
DOI 10.1007/978-3-319-21103-9_17

2 The Nature of Design Thinking, in General, and in Argumentation

Design thinking is an intellectual stance that cuts across disciplines. It is sometimes heavily theorized (in fields like architecture and software engineering) to support an associated professional practice of design. In recent decades, though, many fields with no tradition of actually designing have appropriated this way of thinking, and sometimes also appropriated designers' ways of working. In chemistry (chosen for its distance from argumentation), "rational design" of molecules has emerged as a widely recognized path to discovery just since around the 1980s, as the powerful ideas of Nobelist Paul Ehlich converged with rapid technological advances of the late twentieth century (Strebhardt and Ullrich 2008). This involved a shift from seeing chemistry as experimentation with molecules existing in nature to seeing chemistry as intentional design of new substances. The shift is so pronounced that it has become utterly commonplace, even outside the discipline, to talk about drug design, materials design, and more.

Argumentation theory appears to be poised to make a similar shift. Design thinking in argumentation might or might not support an associated professional practice of argumentation design. At a minimum, design thinking in argumentation would involve speculative inquiry into alternative ways of carrying out the broad human project of becoming more reasonable. Engaging in intentional design of argumentation, or even just thinking about doing so, flips a perceptual switch that allows us to see many achievements of the past as exercises in design. For argumentation, this perceptual switch makes it possible to think of the development of logic systems as a long series of experiments in whether we can improve on whatever is natural in human capacity for reasoning.

Already, there are indications that argumentation theory is well able to support design practice. Most obviously, a large body of work on software-based argument support systems has already begun to emerge. Aakhus et al. (2013) review technical developments in this area and outline a set of design requirements for "developing socially intelligent systems to augment human reasoning and interaction" (p. 10). But even absent specific technological artifacts like software systems, argumentation scholars are increasingly involved in interventions that they describe as design problems. For example, Sprain et al. (2014) offer an excellent case study of an effort to design deliberation formats that carefully structure and limit the contributions of experts during citizen deliberation over complex societal choices.

Design inquiry is not just applied research, but an intellectual stance with its own preferred methods that can generate new theory and findings. Nelson and Stolterman (2012) describe design inquiry as a "third way of knowing," complementary to scientific and humanistic inquiry. What they mean by this is that when humans engage in design, they do not merely produce artifacts, but also learn new things about the natural and social world. An example may help to clarify this rather abstract point. The quite convincing evidence that people are not very good at evaluating their own reasoning is an empirical finding, part of a scientific enterprise;

the exposure of consequences of this for argument is a critical task; and the invention of effective ways to de-bias our reasoning is a creative task, part of a design enterprise. Designing de-biasing strategies and checking how well they work generates knowledge that would not be generated through other forms of argumentation scholarship.

In communication, a general class of things learned through design has to do with what is achievable through use of language—and this includes some things that have become achievable only through some historically and culturally situated invention (such as the invention of logic as a formal system). Acknowledging a deep connection to Craig's (1999) constitutive view of communication, Jackson and Aakhus (2014, p. 126) explain how design can be a path to discovery:

> The design of something new in communication reconstitutes the practice of communication, occasionally changing it profoundly and irreversibly. As in other domains, the design of something new cannot violate laws of nature, but it *can* contradict something that has always been believed about the nature of communication. It is in this sense that design can be seen as a way of knowing for communication; the most important thing that can be learned from really creative design is *how else communication can be constituted.*

To put this slightly differently, societies have been coming up with ways to improve the practice of argumentation for thousands of years, each time exposing some new set of possibilities for how to be more reasonable. When we (as theorists) choose to look at these achievements as improvements in the design of argumentation, our attention is drawn both to the malleability of human reason and to the possibility of indefinite future improvement.

My purpose in this paper is to take a familiar kind of problem in argumentation and use it to explore what this third way of knowing might add to argumentation theory.

3 A Practical Problem for Argumentation: Weighing Expert Opinion

Given that there are experts and non-experts, and that both are often parties to a controversy, what should happen when most experts line up on one side of the controversy? This is an open question for argumentation theory. John (2011) suggests that in such cases, people behaving rationally should defer to experts, and in some cases they may have a moral obligation to do so. Mizrahi (2013) argues, to the contrary, that expert opinion is a poor basis for deciding what to believe or do, because experts, notwithstanding knowledge superior to that of non-experts, still do not demonstrate a high enough correlation between truth and expert belief. In other words, relying on experts does not yield a high enough proportion of good decisions. Responding to Mizrahi, Seidel (2014) argues that to forego expert advice is "self-undermining," recommending instead a policy of "reasonable scrutiny" that would help differentiate between reliable expert judgments and unreliable ones.

These three very recent papers give contemporary interpretations of ideas that have waxed and waned throughout Western intellectual history. Different times and circumstances have favored any of three competing ideas: (a) that rational people should defer to authority greater than their own; (b) that they should distrust all authority and attempt direct examination of any question of importance; and (c) that they should trust authority once it has been adequately tested for reliability. Each of these postures may be considered to be a mid-range epistemic policy–a preference for reasoning of some particular kind, or a disdain for that kind of reasoning. Each of these epistemic policies has been considered a way of being rational, and each has also been subject to sustained critique. As uniformly applied policy, these postures are mutually incompatible, and all have vulnerabilities. Hence, what to do with authority in general, and expert opinion in particular, has been and remains challenging for argumentation theory.

But changing theoretical ideas about appeal to authority also reflect change in argumentation as a practice. Appeal to authority has actually been a different kind of argument over the centuries–depending on many factors, but especially on what at each time and place has been considered the source of authority. Nowadays, appeal to authority mostly means reliance on experts, and this requires entirely different argument evaluation strategies than those employed before there was such a thing as an expert in a specific field—expertise being a modern notion, not an ancient one. Asking about a speaker's character made sense in Aristotle's time, leading him to reflect deeply on ethos as a resource. Asking whether a speaker is an authority "in X" would have made little sense until perhaps the middle of the 19th century, even though it is certainly also the case that there have been people with extraordinary knowledge and skill, meriting others' deference in some specific domain but not in others, throughout human history. Nor has appeal to authority remained static in the post-WWII era, as it has become increasingly difficult to differentiate scientific authority from government policy (especially as expressed in funding for science).

Structurally, appeal to authority may have had very similar characteristics across the ages. But if the environment changes, the strengths and weaknesses of this argument form may also change. In some contexts, appeal to authority may be the best available basis for a conclusion; in others, it may be only a shortcut; in still others, it may represent a refusal to engage in deeper thinking about a topic. In other words, argumentation practice is sensitive to surrounding cultural context, and our theoretical assessments of particular argument forms may need constant updating.

4 Design Implications of Postures Toward Expertise

If we understand argumentation as a changeable practice that is constantly being redesigned to meet the needs of its practitioners, all ideas about argumentation are liable to affect the practice. A design hypothesis is any notion, theoretical or intuitive, about how argumentation might be conducted to better achieve its purpose. Like an empirical hypothesis, a design hypothesis must conform with facts, but its real test is its ability to support particular human purposes in particular circumstances: its ability to satisfy something like the "design requirements" outlined by Aakhus et al. (2013). Design hypotheses do not compete with one another in the way empirical hypotheses do; each new design hypothesis may add to our overall rationality in some circumstance. New problems, or new contexts for old problems, may need new design ideas. Design theory builds by adding options.

In a design theory of argumentation, normative components can take the form of design hypotheses, and these may concern not only standards for appraisal but also procedures to follow or resources to provide or anything else that may improve the outcomes of argumentation. Both a posture of deference and a posture of skepticism can be reframed as design hypotheses. This shift is accomplished when the general posture is used to rationalize a particular way of incorporating expertise into argumentative discourse. And other design hypotheses beyond these two can be imagined. One of these is the idea of making a deliberate prior choice to delegate a difficult question to someone who may not know the answer at present, but who can be trusted to find the best possible answer. Deference, distrust, and delegation are three distinct ideas about how to integrate expert opinion into a discussion; each of these ideas is capable of supporting innovation in the design of argumentation.

4.1 Deference

A posture of deference is based on the idea that people should accept conclusions that are accepted by those most knowledgeable about a topic. In some places and times, this has been not just an epistemic policy, but a sort of social obligation involving the giving of respect to people who have in some sense earned that respect. If deference is built into the rules of a kind of interaction, the only reasonable question to ask of an authority is what they believe or what they recommend.

A strong contemporary defense of deference as a general posture can be found in the work of the Third Wave science studies group led by Collins and Evans (2007). Based on careful examination of what is involved in becoming an expert in anything, Collins and Evans aim for a philosophical defense of deference to experts. Within their framework, expertise is defined primarily in relation to expert communities. Individuals may have various kinds of expertise depending on how they stand with respect to an expert community. Collins and Evans have distinguished several forms of expertise, of which the most relevant to my topic are contributory expertise, interactional expertise, and primary source knowledge.

Contributory expertise, interpreted within a wide range of enterprises other than science, consists in having the capacity to move a discussion forward, toward a resolution of disagreement among experts themselves. People who publish original research in the specialized literature of a field are contributory experts. The contributory expert helps to build the expert field through direct extension of what an expert in that field knows. According to Collins and Evans, contributory expertise can only be acquired by immersion in the expert community and direct practice in contributing.

Interactional expertise is an understanding of the field sufficient to be in conversation with experts even if unable to contribute anything new. This form of expertise involves understanding the methods of the field, and even being able to critique the application of these methods to scientific problems, but it is expertise developed toward an end other than contributing new knowledge. Interactional expertise is not just a diminished version of contributory expertise but an acquired ability to do a different job. Interactional expertise is partly generalizable across fields, but it must also be developed in interaction with contributory experts.

Primary source knowledge is a form of expertise that is acquired at a distance from the expert community. A person can acquire primary source knowledge by reading the expert literature. However, this is a very different kind of knowledge than the knowledge possessed by even a novice contributor. The relationship to the expert field is completely unidirectional in this case and lacks the tacit knowledge that contributory experts possess but do not (and maybe cannot) communicate in writing. As Collins and Weinel (2011, p. 402) point out:

> [T]o become an expert in a technical domain means acquiring the tacit knowledge pertaining to the domain. As far as is known, there is only one way to acquire tacit knowledge and that is through some form of 'socialisation'; tacit knowledge cannot be transferred via written or other symbolic form so some form of sustained social contact with the group that has the tacit knowledge is necessary.

This is extremely important; it means that no matter how diligently a person studies what has been written about a topic, that person will still lack important components of expert judgment.

In short, the argument for deference is that to really understand an expert's judgment requires prolonged immersion in the material and social world of the expert–in other words, altering one's life course to become an expert. Attempting to retrace an expert's reasoning or to evaluate the same evidence the expert had available will not replicate expert judgment, because tacit knowledge and experience are indispensable ingredients in such judgments. Except in special conditions where experts' trustworthiness is compromised, our most rational posture toward expert fields, according to Collins and Evans, is to believe what they say.

As a design hypothesis, deference works by formally acknowledging true gaps between what an expert knows and what can be fully defended to skeptical non-experts. In sustained questioning of experts by non-experts, a point must always be reached where the expert "just knows" something that cannot be known in the same way by anyone who has not been socialized into the expert community. If experts are part of a discussion, they must be allowed their expertise, even if what they see when they look at evidence is uninterpretable to non-experts looking at the same evidence.

Collins and Evans describe their own aim as a normative theory of expertise that includes an "approach to the question of who should and who should not be contributing to decision-making in virtue of their expertise" (p. 52). Notice how this normative theory of expertise might underwrite the design of social systems for managing the use of expert opinion in deliberation and decision-making. Designing around deference generally means differentiating among the participants in a discourse and assigning special communication privileges to some but not others; it may involve forms of compulsion (such as rules and laws) that take matters out of the realm of individual reasoning. It can mean limiting the kinds of questions that can be asked of experts or the kinds of arguments that can be raised against their conclusions. But it is the overall performance of the designed system, not the quality of the individual appeals to expertise, that may be appraised from a design perspective.

4.2 (Dis)Trust

A posture of distrust is based on the idea that accepting anything without question is dangerous and that authority is most dangerous when it is most difficult or most costly to question. In some places and times, this posture has been accompanied by the assumption that all citizens are capable of making independent assessments of facts and reasoning if they are willing to inform themselves–and that they have a duty to do so. In contemporary practice, this notion leads motivated citizens to conduct exhaustive "primary source" research on topics of interest to them. The challenge for this posture is the tenuousness of the assumption that ordinary citizens, sufficiently motivated, can reach independent conclusions of a quality equal to the conclusions of experts. If Collins and Evans are correct about what expertise really consists of, no amount of exposure to "primary sources" of expert fields will allow the consumer of those sources to develop expert judgment. However, even those who agree with Collins and Evans on the nature of expert communities do not always give up on the idea that non-experts should withhold trust until experts themselves have been tested. The idea of retracing and directly evaluating an expert's reasoning has not completely disappeared within the general public, but among theorists it has given way to the idea that what can be interrogated is whether the experts themselves should be trusted. To competently interrogate experts requires a different, potentially generalizable set of skills, possibly included in what Collins and Evans call "interactional expertise."

Theoretically, distrust of authority can co-exist nicely with trust in expert opinion, so long as expert opinion can be evaluated through non-expert questioning. This is demonstrated in Walton's (1997, 2002) very detailed analyses of arguments from expertise, which include explorations of how institutions (e.g., courts of law) design procedures for rigorous testing of whether to admit expert testimony and for specifying what can be concluded from any particular piece of expert testimony. Distrust is a starting position from which non-experts can arrive at confidence in experts, but only after those experts have been thoroughly scrutinized.

As a design hypothesis, distrust tends to generate audit-like procedures that check for anything being hidden, anything that might incentivize experts to prefer one judgment over another, anything that experts might be missing or ignoring, any change in meaning as an assertion passes from context to context, and so on. This has design implications both for citizens and for experts, including implications for how to design participation formats to fit particular controversies: formats that adjust to differing degrees of citizen trust in expert communities and public bureaucracies. For example, in "post-trust societies" (as described by Löfstedt 2005), there may be greater public calls for openness of information and transparency in how information is used. It can also mean regulating the experts themselves, for example, through oversight boards composed either of peers or of ordinary citizens.

4.3 Delegation

A third design hypothesis, less visible within argumentation theory because it has no associated epistemic posture, is delegation of a decision through implicit or explicit bilateral agreement. The core idea behind delegation is that some issues require such sustained analytic effort that the only feasible way to make progress toward resolution is to transfer responsibility to some trusted person or group that willingly accepts this responsibility. Where deference and critical trust may be seen either as epistemic policies or as design hypotheses, delegation really only makes sense as something designed into a broader framework for making decisions. Retrospectively, accepting a result from a delegated inquiry may look like any other argument from expert opinion. Procedurally, it is quite different.

Delegating responsibility for a question implies that the answer will be accepted once it has been returned from the delegation process, so it is tempting to see this as a version of the deference posture. But delegation is not just deference, and indeed, sometimes it involves nothing that could be mistaken for deference to authority. For example, delegation is the design principle behind the use of trial juries, where a judgment that any citizen is capable of making is handed over to arbitrarily selected individuals who agree to invest time, attention, and effort in arriving at their judgment.

But delegation is different from deference in another very important respect. Deference is an acknowledgement that some individual possesses superior knowledge that others are not, and cannot be, in a position to question. Delegation involves a sort of agreement between the community as a whole and the individuals (who may be selected arbitrarily) to whom the community assigns responsibility for answering the community's questions about a domain. When important matters are delegated to experts, it is assumed and often explicitly stated that the experts owe a duty of care to anyone who depends on their expertise. Delegation may require someone to become an expert on the question at hand–for example, as a juror–but that expertise does not merit deference unless understood as part of an implicit contract in which acting in good faith is as important as being knowledgeable. In other words, deference does not involve any accountability, while delegation does.

As a design hypothesis, delegation works through a kind of bargain in which deference to a judgment is promised in exchange for dutiful performance. Without some form of accountability to ordinary citizens, experts and expert communities may feel that they deserve deference, but ordinary citizens often do not agree to this. In such cases, experts must make their way in argumentation just as any other arguer would.

Scientific fields sometimes behave as though they hold delegated responsibility for society's knowledge about a domain, and other times behave as though they are completely autonomous. Because it is not always clear to everyone involved whether responsibility has been accepted, using delegation as a tool to understand the role of expertise in public affairs remains complex. The best contemporary examples of delegation as a design principle involve explicit bilateral agreements. One model is the practice associated with "informed consent" for both acceptance of medical procedures and participation in experimental research. Informed consent specifically acknowledges the autonomy of the recipient's decision and the obligation of an expert to fully inform the recipient of benefits and risks associated with each possible decision.

But nothing like informed consent qualifies many of the efforts scientific fields make to influence public policy. Occasionally, experts demand deference without acknowledging any duty of care, without manifesting this duty of care in their behavior, and, frequently, with explicit disavowal of any duty of care. Scientific communities desire autonomy from public accountability, and research literatures reflect interests (and viewpoints regarding those interests) that acknowledge no duty beyond various forms of research ethics. But unilateral assertions of authority by experts are not at all the same as the voluntary delegation of authority to experts– and it should come as no surprise when members of the public refuse to defer to such unilateral assertions.

The motivation behind delegation is the belief that a problem is of sufficient complexity to require a great deal of diligence for a good solution. This diligence takes at least two forms: preparation for attempting the solution (for example through professional training), and prolonged consideration of the problem from all possible angles. What makes delegation safer than generalized deference is the assurance that the expert community will in fact do due diligence on behalf of the public. Deferring to expertise is dangerous when an individual expert or a community of experts refuse to accept a duty of care (Jackson 2012). Delegation as a design principle is about structuring a system in which it is understood that specific people or institutions are responsible, to everyone else with a stake in the conclusion, for exercising the due diligence needed to understand an issue and make good decisions as needed.

4.4 *Mixed Messages*

Design hypotheses in argumentation are ideas about how reasoning might be improved. These ideas circulate within a culture partly through direct restatement (e.g., "Question authority"), but partly through their incorporation into ways of doing things that embody the ideas in procedures that accumulate track records of outcomes that people regard as either reasonable or unreasonable. Design hypotheses with good track records get embedded in invented practices that can achieve surprising levels of permanence as other practices are built over them. So, within any society, we can find institutionalized practices that "make sense" by assuming that we should generally defer to a certain kind of expertise, other institutionalized practices that make sense by assuming that we should regard expert opinion with great caution applied in every individual case, and still other institutional arrangements that depend on the sort of bilateral agreement I have labelled delegation. Running through all of these practices, there may be no one coherent set of standards for argument appraisal.

In any given controversy, this mixed bag of practices, each well-established and well-understood by practitioners, can create contradictory intuitions among participants as to what it means to behave reasonably in any given situation. A controversy in which these (and possibly other) design hypotheses are all operating at once can seem quite discordant, and may erupt into direct comparative assessment of the design hypotheses themselves.

5 Design Hypotheses in Action: Health Advice

To try to present more clearly what is meant by a design hypothesis and to illustrate how contrasting design hypotheses may look in practice, consider the extreme complexity exhibited in the making of health advice and in controversies related to that advice. One such controversy is over childhood vaccination, or more precisely, over whether parents should be required to vaccinate their children against infectious diseases. The combined Measles/Mumps/Rubella (MMR) vaccine has been a special site for controversy, especially in the US and UK. Public health officials in both countries are overwhelmingly supportive of vaccinating children against these highly infectious diseases. Within the public, however, a significant minority of parents refuse to vaccinate their children, justifying this refusal on a variety of grounds, but mostly on the suspicion that MMR vaccine may cause dangerous and irreversible side effects such as autism.

5.1 The Vaccination Controversy Viewed from Critical and Empirical Perspectives

Anti-vaccination movements have often accompanied a change in public health policy. Jones (2010) documents one of the earliest, a protest against smallpox immunization that spread from Muncie, Indiana, to other localities within the state. Many of the themes seen in the current controversy over MMR are identical to those documented by Jones. In the 1893 protests against mandatory smallpox vaccination, as in today's resistance to the MMR vaccine, citizens questioned the safety and efficacy of the vaccine, but also objected to health officials denying them a free choice in whether to be vaccinated; and as is happening today, these citizens were represented as irrational in their refusal to defer to expert opinion. Then and now, the controversy was as much about individual responsibility for choice as about the safety and effectiveness of the vaccine.

But the environment for argumentation changed in the hundred years between the outbreak of protest over smallpox vaccination and the outbreak of protest against MMR vaccination. In Muncie, print journalism controlled the pace of the controversy and eventually throttled the ability of dissenters to publish their views. In the communication platforms that define the current media ecology, people move in and out of the active discussion as its relevance for their own lives shifts. At every moment there are participants who are absolutely new to the discussion (wondering whether to vaccinate their child) and long-time participants who have grown jaded by seeing the same arguments recycled over and over. The controversy seems to pulse as interested participants enter, make their decisions, and exit. Various kinds of uninvolved commentators are part of the discourse too, including academics introducing new concepts like "argument enclaves." It is an unsettled discourse that does not appear to be moving toward a single resolution of the central question for parents (whether they should vaccinate their babies) or for communities (whether vaccination should be required by law for all babies).

John (2011) characterizes the controversy as "an instance of a general phenomenon: non-expert failure to defer to expert testimony." He continues: "It seems intuitive that something has gone wrong in such cases, and that non-experts ought, in some objective sense, to have deferred to expert testimony" (p. 497).

But when non-experts "fail to defer," is it really the non-experts who have failed? An important element of the public resistance to vaccination, especially the MMR vaccine, is the suspicion that this vaccine is linked to the onset of autism, a suspicion grounded in parents' own firsthand observations. Offit and Coffin (2003) fault the press (especially the television news program *60 Minutes*) for presenting emotionally affecting content without scientifically meaningful interrogation of that content. Parents' direct observations of symptoms of autism in their own children, appearing soon after vaccination, are a continuing source of evidence for the link. Offit and Coffin explain how *60 Minutes* might have presented observational evidence of this kind within a context that would have helped parents and viewers to reason more clearly about causality.

Burgess et al. (2006) apply a general framework for understanding "public outrage" to the MMR vaccine controversy. This framework specifies a dozen situational factors–for example, perceived coercion–that amplify outrage. All of these factors were present to some degree in the way the public health establishment reacted to a conjecture, published in the medical journal *The Lancet*, that MMR vaccination might trigger autism through other immediate physiological reactions to the vaccine (Wakefield et al. 1998; retracted by the journal's editors in 2010). One factor of special significance was the unresponsiveness of the public health establishment to parental fears–a dismissiveness that eroded trust in the expert community. Tindale (2012) makes a similar point from an entirely different set of background assumptions: What happened here was not citizens' failure to defer but experts' failure to win trust. So against John's characterization of this as a case of failure to defer, we have a number of other analyses of failure to inform and failure to persuade.

Note that all of these accounts assume that citizen and parental resistance to vaccination really should have been overcome in the end. But two empirical studies, Hobson-West (2007) and Hample (2012), raise doubts about whether it is useful, or even accurate, to see this controversy as a failure of anything. Both examined groups critical of mandatory vaccination. Hobson-West's data came from face-to-face interviews with leaders of 10 groups organized around a range of issues spanning decades of debate in the UK over vaccination. Hample's data came from online discussions within a virtual community formed around resistance to required vaccination in the US. The picture of citizen reasoning emerging from these analyses is complex and multi-faceted, not reducible to a matter of deferring to expertise or refusing to do so. Hobson-West's qualitative analysis of interviews with group leaders exposed a number of themes having nothing to do with questions of expertise. One important theme (of five) was the notion that vaccination is a governmental strategy used in place of more fundamental improvement in living conditions, especially for the poor; against this notion, the safety and efficacy of vaccines are beside the point. Hample's detailed qualitative content analysis of an online discussion group identified several additional themes of interest: suspicion of government/industry conspiracy, feelings of guilt associated with both vaccinating and not vaccinating, and supporting community members in their off-line confrontations with "pro-vaxxers." Both studies contradict any simple characterization of vaccine resistance as an irrational refusal to defer to expert authority.

Very importantly, both of these empirical studies also portray contemporary resistance to vaccination as a difficult and socially costly choice that involves active search for information beyond what is typically received from the family physician. Parents who resist medical advice on vaccination do not simply reject expert opinion but engage in serious and sustained inquiry. In some cases, resistance to vaccination also involves active search for physicians who will provide the kind of treatment judged best by the parent. Empirically, this controversy is not about argument from expert testimony, nor about general epistemic postures such as deference to expertise. For most participants, the controversy is simply about whether to vaccinate their children. Much is at stake in this decision, and the resources available for making the decision are extraordinarily difficult to evaluate.

5.2 Design Hypotheses Operating in the Vaccination Controversy

Empirical and critical perspectives on health controversies like this one are both theoretically and practically important. They can help practitioners such as public health officials to better understand the reasoning of ordinary citizens and to construct more effective arguments to try to win public compliance. A design perspective contributes something different, but also important: a point of entry for thinking about the systems within which argumentation takes place and about how seemingly unreasonable behavior may have an important function within these systems. Specifically, the backdrop for this controversy includes a complex deference system to which the vast majority of citizens subscribe and a set of trust safeguards to which the vast majority of experts subscribe. Small minorities of dissenters do not undermine the systems; they may, in fact, be essential to maintain the integrity of the systems.

Although the idea of deferring to disciplinary expertise (that is, to medical research rather than to the judgment of individual doctors) is still relatively new in human history, it has become deeply embedded in technical practices such as randomized clinical trials for proposed treatments, peer reviewed publication, and evidence based medicine. A variety of durable institutional arrangements, including laws requiring certain vaccinations, reflect a decision that society has already made to defer to medical expertise on matters of public health. This decision can be revisited–for example, to consider other kinds of expertise that might guide thinking about public health, such as sociology or economics–but the scale on which this re-evaluation takes place is not the individual argument from expertise but the design of these durable institutional arrangements and the highly elaborated technical practices that represent our current best ideas about how to reason our way to good decisions. In the vaccination controversy, laws that require vaccination for enrolment in school enforce deference to medical science, at least in the US. An individual has options for avoiding compliance with specific laws, but not for escaping the societal deference that is paid to medical research.

Public health authorities, legally empowered to decide for all of us which treatments are safest and most effective, willingly defer to upstream medical research; downstream, they expect deference from citizens, and they get it from the vast majority. Most citizens acknowledge that they are in no position to seriously review the conclusions of experts, and they willingly defer both to public health officials and to their own health care providers. Monitoring by the US Centers for Disease Control shows that more than 90 % of children receive the MMR vaccine as they reach the recommended age for vaccination, despite persistent anti-vaccination advocacy and despite the availability of exemptions in many states.

Caution with respect to expert authority is similarly built into the environment in which the anti-vaccination controversy thrives. Even if citizens acknowledge the value of expertise, they may doubt or question anyone claiming to possess expertise. Snoeck Henkemans and Wagemans (2012) pointed out that one protection that makes it reasonable for patients to trust their physicians is a Dutch law that requires physicians to cooperate in patients' efforts to get a second medical opinion when they do have doubts. There is also danger in deferring without question to an expert field: The members of the field may become socialized into a common disregard for the values of the surrounding society. Our designed systems for managing this danger have the flavor of Walton-ish tests for scrutinizing expert performance, adapted to inspecting the taken-for-granted practices of the expert field. Despite the high levels of deference afforded to medical research as an aggregate, researchers themselves operate under increasing levels of oversight and scrutiny, mandated by law in many countries (including the US and throughout the EU). Independent ethics committees that review and approve the conduct of research differ from scientific peer review in having members who are not from the researcher's own field, and even in some cases members who are not scientists of any kind. These safeguards are built into the environment, and, besides their direct effects as regulatory mechanisms, they also keep alive the idea that experts must continue to earn our trust, even after we have made decisions to defer to them routinely.

The vaccination controversy occurs within a framework that institutionalizes deference to a kind of expertise and continued trust-checking of the experts themselves. But nothing has been said yet about delegation and the designed systems it might generate. Here, as in many similar controversies, the responsibility of expert communities to the public remains contested; experts' due diligence is typically aimed not at responding to public concerns and questions, but at satisfying the standards of other experts. The suspicion that MMR vaccine might have a link to autism originated with parents observing symptoms of autism in recently vaccinated children, and the dismissiveness of many experts continues to inflame anti-vaccination feeling (as was noted in 2006 by Burgess, Burgess and Leask). One way to make sense of the persistent opposition to public health advice on vaccination is to see it as an effort to enforce due diligence on the part of all expert communities involved: for example, to reshape the medical research agenda to include investigations of public concerns or to object to the special arrangement that exempts pharmaceutical companies in the US from certain kinds of legal liability. Lacking the bilateral compact that defines delegation, a committed few continue to question whether medical research has taken seriously the possibility of a link between vaccination and autism.

An important final point is that a certain incoherence results from arguing within a context in which several competing ideas about reasonableness have each been institutionalized in different ways. In recent months, following an outbreak of measles among visitors to Disneyland, public attacks on the "anti-vaxxers" have become frequent and fierce. Jimmy Kimmel, a late-night talk show host, mocked anti-vaxxers (e.g., as "being more afraid of gluten than of smallpox") and aired a 5-min PSA-style video showing a series of "real doctors" ridiculing parents who refuse to vaccinate. The broadcast provoked a deluge of counter-attacks, including a twitter campaign for a boycott of the talk show and the network that produces it.

In the back-and-forth of the controversy, the various possible postures toward expertise get thoroughly aired, and charges of inconsistency are frequent. But no one arguing today can enact only one of these postures; when these postures function as design ideas and generate durable systems, we assume each posture in turn as we act within these systems.

6 Conclusion

Ordinary people do not think of themselves as trying out design hypotheses as they consider whether to try to reason through an issue autonomously or to delegate this task to someone else, just as they do not think of themselves as selecting an argumentation scheme or other abstraction. But every design hypothesis that has been advanced throughout human history can find its way into individual instances of reasoning. In fact, one very interesting feature of designed systems for argumentation is that as people operate within these systems, the core ideas behind the system can work their way into commonsense reasoning, becoming "naturalized." Systems that have been designed for generating, evaluating, and using expertise naturalize deference to expert fields—though not necessarily to individual experts.

In academic research on the controversy over MMR vaccination, critical attention has been divided among the small minority of individual parents who resist mandatory or recommended vaccination, the journalists who amplify fears about vaccination, and the public health authorities who fail to be responsive to public fears. No doubt some of these players are performing incompetently. No doubt some of the arguments made on each side are terribly defective.

A design approach to the problem of expert opinion does not aim to evaluate particular arguments from expert opinion; rather, it asks what resources we have in any situation, or in any homogeneous class of situations, for improving on even the general form of such arguments. Improvement means the same thing for a design approach as for any other contemporary argumentation theory: broadly, a higher proportion of defensible conclusions reached voluntarily. Recall that Mizrahi (2013) characterized argument from expertise as weak, based on evidence that experts are very often wrong. If we were to discover a poor rate of good conclusions from any existing or proposed design for the conduct of argumentation, we would certainly regard that design as flawed. But in a design-centered approach, the question is not whether a particular argument form is strong or weak but what we can do to improve the overall contribution of argumentation, across many occasions in which argumentation may lead to a belief or an action. Our interest centers on how best to work with what we have available. Without a superior alternative, we might well institutionalize a fallible form of argument, if it improves our overall reasonableness.

So design thinking about argumentation draws attention to a distinct class of questions: for example, questions about how an innovation like peer review affects a whole society's capacity for reasonableness, both positively and negatively. If we zoom out to examine the impact of designed systems for producing, evaluating, and deploying expertise, our attention is drawn to the overall behavior of these systems —their track records. Most importantly, a design perspective on argumentation draws attention to the features of the communication environment that are changeable and to what can be done to make individuals and societies more or less reasonable.

Acknowledgments The author wishes to acknowledge many helpful comments from Scott Jacobs.

References

Aakhus, M., Muresan, & Walcholder, N. (2013). In Mohammed, D., & M. Lewiński (Eds.), *Virtues of Argumentation. Proceedings of the 10th international conference of the Ontario Society for the Study of Argumentation (OSSA)* (pp. 1–12). 22–26 May 2013. Windsor, ON: OSSA.

Burgess, D. C., Burgess, M. A., & Leask, J. (2006). The MMR vaccination and autism controversy in United Kingdom 1998–2005: Inevitable community outrage or a failure of risk communication? *Vaccine, 24*, 3921–3928. doi:10.1016/j.vaccine.2006.02

Collins, H., & Evans, R. (2007). *Rethinking expertise*. Chicago: University of Chicago Press.

Collins, H., & Weinel, M. (2011). Transmuted expertise: How technical non-experts can assess experts and expertise. *Argumentation, 25*(3), 401–413. doi:10.1007/s10503-011-9217-8

Craig, R. T. (1999). Communication theory as a field. *Communication Theory, 9*(2), 119–161. doi:10.1111/j.1468-2885.1999.tb00355.x

Hample, J. M. (2012). Analysis of arguments favoring vaccine resistance. In J. Goodwin (Ed.), *Between citizens & scientists: Proceedings of a conference at Iowa State University* (pp. 183–193). Great Plains Society for the Study of Argumentation.

Hobson-West, P. (2007). 'Trusting blindly can be the biggest risk of all': Organized resistance to childhood vaccination in the UK. *Sociology of Health & Illness, 29*, 198–215. doi:10.1111/j.1467-9566.2007.00544.x

Jackson, S. (2012). Black box arguments and accountability of experts to the public. In J. Goodwin (Ed.), *Between citizens & scientists: Proceedings of a conference at Iowa State University* (pp. 1–18). Great Plains Society for the Study of Argumentation.

Jackson, S. (2015). Design thinking in argumentation theory and practice. *Argumentation, 29*, 243–263. doi:10.1007/s10503-015-9353-7

Jackson, S., & Aakhus, M. (2014). Becoming more reflective about the role of design in communication. *Journal of Applied Communication Research, 42*, 125–134. doi:10.1080/00909882.2014.882009

John, S. (2011). Expert testimony and epistemological free-riding: The MMR controversy. *Philosophical Quarterly, 61*, 496–517. doi:10.111/j.1467-9213.2010.687.x

Jones, K. H. (2010). Rebelling against lawful authority? The vaccination controversy during the smallpox epidemic at Muncie, Indiana, 1893. *Journal of the Indiana Academy of the Social Sciences, 14*, 74–87.

Löfstedt, R. E. (2005). *Risk management in post-trust societies*. New York: Palgrave MacMillan.
Mizrahi, M. (2013). Why arguments from expert opinion are weak arguments. *Informal Logic, 33*, 57–79.
Nelson, H., & Stolterman, E. (2012). *The design way: Intentional change in an unpredictable world* (2nd ed.). Cambridge, MA: MIT Press.
Offit, P., & Coffin, S. (2003). Communicating science to the public: The MMR vaccine and autism. *Vaccine, 22*, 1–6. doi:10.1016/S0264-410X(03)00532-2
Seidel, M. (2014). Throwing the baby out with the bathwater: From reasonably scrutinizing authorities to rampant scepticism about expertise. *Informal Logic, 34*, 192–218.
Snoeck Henkemans, A. F., & Wagemans, J. H. M. (2012). The reasonableness of argumentation from expert opinion in medical discussions: Institutional safeguards for the quality of shared decision making. In J. Goodwin (Ed.), *Between citizens & scientists: Proceedings of a conference at Iowa State University* (pp. 345-354). Great Plains Society for the Study of Argumentation.
Sprain, L., Carcasson, M., & Merolla, A. J. (2014). Utilizing "on tap" experts in deliberative forums: Implications for design. *Journal of Applied Communication Research, 42*(2), 150–167. doi:10.1080/00909882.2013.859292
Strebhardt, K., & Ullrich, A. (2008). Paul Ehrlich's magic bullet concept: 100 years of progress. *Nature Reviews Cancer, 8*(6), 473–480. doi:10.1038/nrc2394
Tindale, C. W. (2012). Dismantling expertise: Disproof, retraction, and the persistence of belief. In J. Goodwin (Ed.), *Between citizens & scientists: Proceedings of a conference at Iowa State University* (pp. 393–402). Great Plains Society for the Study of Argumentation.
Wakefield, A. J., Murch, S. H., Anthony, A., Linnell, J., Casson, D. M., Malik, M., et al. (1998/Retracted 2010). Ileal-lymphoid-nodular hyperplasia, non-specific colitis, and pervasive developmental disorder in children. *The Lancet, 351*(9103), 637–641. doi:10.1016/S0140-6736(97)11096-0 (Retraction published February 2010, *The Lancet, 375*[9713], p. 445).
Walton, D. N. (1997). *Appeal to expert opinion: Arguments from authority*. University Park, PA: Pennsylvania State University Press.
Walton, D. N. (2002). *Legal argumentation and evidence*. University Park, PA: Pennsylvania State U. Press.

Part VI
Linguistic Approaches to Argumentation

A Plea for a Linguistic Distinction Between Explanation and Argument

Thierry Herman

1 Introduction

The aim of this paper is to offer a slightly new point of view on a very old and common problem: how to distinguish between explanation and argumentation? I will offer here a linguist's point of view on this problem, which is often tackled by philosophers and critical thinkers. After explaining the linguistic clues I use to distinguish explanation and argument, I will discuss rhetorical strategies that take the appearance of an explanation to fulfil argumentative purposes. During this examination, I will point out uses of the French connectives "car" and "parce que", but non-French speakers will be able to understand what I would like to underline.

Broadly speaking, two points of view on the difference between explanation and argumentation can be found in literature. The first one is more philosophical, dealing mainly with informal logic and critical thinking and the second one is dealing with linguistics, which is perhaps less known outside French tradition on argumentation. There are problems within each of these approaches: the old issue of differences between explanation and argumentation is still not resolved. Recently, McKeon (2013) argued for example that explanations should be considered as arguments. On the other side, Govier (2005) has written that explanations and arguments are different, but some explanations can nevertheless be seen as arguments within different contexts.

For his part, the French linguist Jean-Michel Adam considers that explanations and arguments adopt different patterns, called sequences. He argued in a seminal book that an argumentative sequence (inspired from Toulmin's model) differs from an explicative sequence by the explicit presence in the latter of a problem and a solution. Thus, example 1 must be seen as an explanation:

T. Herman (✉)
EFLE and Institute of Language Sciences and Communication,
Universities of Lausanne and Neuchâtel, Lausanne and Neuchâtel, Switzerland
e-mail: Thierry.Herman@unil.ch

F.H. van Eemeren and B. Garssen (eds.), *Reflections on Theoretical Issues in Argumentation Theory*, Argumentation Library 28,
DOI 10.1007/978-3-319-21103-9_18

(1) Why should I stop smoking? Because, as soon as I run, I get breathless.

An explanation, according to Adam (2011), ties together four "propositions" (not in the logical sense of the term): Proposition exp. 0: Introduction; P. exp. 1: Problem or Question (Why P? How P?); P. exp. 2: Solution or Answer (Because Q) and P. exp. 3: Conclusion—Evaluation. The presence of an explicit question and its immediate answer introduced by because (P. exp. 2 and P. exp. 3) seems to be the criteria to distinguish explanation from argumentation. The problem is that example (2) would probably be seen as an argumentative sequence in Adam's viewpoint.

(2) I should stop smoking, because as soon as I run, I get breathless.

The problem of these two similar examples is that a conclusion can be an *explanandum* and that premises can function as an *explanans*, just because of the presence of a why-question. This sudden change of nature of the sequence seems unsatisfactory, since the semantic point of view within these clauses appears untouched.

In the philosophical approach, problems arise because of several difficulties rightfully underlined by Govier (1987):

1. […] 'thus' [may be] used in the paradigmatic logical role, preceding the conclusion in an argument. But in other cases, 'thus' functions just as naturally in an explanation.
2. According to the classic deductive-nomological account, explanation is one type of argument. Although this account is now widely criticized, it was dominant in the philosophy of science for several decades and still enjoys influence.
3. As many informal logic teachers have observed for their displeasure, it is very difficult to teach students the distinction between explanation and argument. They find it hard to grasp in theory and still more difficult to apply in practice.
4. Even when the distinction is grasped in theory, many passages, real or invented, can be interpreted as either explanation or argument (Govier 1987, pp. 159–160).

The first quotation illustrates that the same connectives can be used in argumentation and explanation; this is also the case in French. The second one points out that, historically, explanation was just an argument scheme; thus explanation was seen as a category inside argument. The third one illustrates a very common pedagogical problem: a lot of people, including students but not excluding teachers, do not understand the difference between explanation and argumentation. The last one, finally, emphasizes either an empirical problem of some unclassified examples or an insufficiency of theory that prevents from distinguishing between explanation and argument. Why is it so difficult to grasp the difference between these two types of discursive patterns? Answering this question requires to understand first how they are both defined.

To sum up the general frame in which explanations and arguments are distinguished, one could start by stating that: "Arguments offer justifications; explanations offer understanding" (Govier 2005, p. 21). In other words:

> In order for a collection C of propositions to represent one's evidential reasons for a proposition P, one must be more certain of the propositions in C than one is of P. (2) In

order for a collection C of propositions to represent one's explanatory reasons for a proposition P, one needn't be more certain of the propositions in C than one is of P (McKeon 2013, pp. 286–287).

This leads to consider that "(P) Carole is the best math student in the class, (Q) because she is the only student in the class who is going to a special program for gifted students" (Govier 2005, p. 22) may be interpreted as an explanation if everyone knows (P) but as an argument if the addressee must be convinced that (P) is true. Hence, the difference between argumentation and explanation depends on the addressee's knowledge.

But this view, which is unstable—as Govier's example of Carole reveals—may also be unsatisfactory. I would like to highlight three problems related to this kind of philosophical account in the next sections.

2 Problems with the Philosophical Account

The first problem is that certainty is viewed as an evaluation by the addressee. McKeon argues against Govier's premise that "one must be more certain of the propositions in C than one is of P" (McKeon 2013, p. 286), writing: "[Govier's premise] is false. […] I am certain of A and B, but not of C. I come to see that A and B are evidential reasons for C and as a consequence I become equally certain of C […]" (McKeon 2013, p. 287). This counter-argument highlights the pronoun "I", which is clearly the addressee's epistemic evaluation of C, between uncertainty and certainty. Thus, certainty appears to be a cognitive reality and not a linguistic feature. It raises the problem of the accessibility of an evaluation of certainty for any analyst. This lack of a clear-cut criterion about addressee's evaluation prevents any analyst from settling between explanation and argument in ambiguous cases.

As a linguist, my solution is not to evaluate cognitive certainty but to describe how it is linguistically encoded. Works on epistemic modality[1] epitomize this view on certainty to the extent that "manually annotate and consequently automate identification of statements with an explicitly expressed certainty or doubt, or shades of epistemic qualifications in between" (Rubin 2010, p. 535) can now be done. It means that a discourse analyst interested in evaluating whether a statement is an explanation or an argument should focus on certainty encoded by the speaker's rather than the addressee's evaluation. Within this frame, only absolute certainty (the highest of the five levels described by Rubin et al. (2006), Rubin (2010)) is a relevant category for explanation.

[1]"Epistemic modality, or certainty, concerns a linguistic expression of an estimation of the likelihood that a certain hypothetical state of affairs is, has been, or will be true (Nuyts 2001). Subtle linguistic clues, or markers, contribute toward the user's understanding of how much credibility can be attached to individual propositions and whether the information comes from the first-hand or second-hand sources" (Rubin 2010, p. 535).

The second problem with the—broadly considered—philosophical account is also tied with cognitive contingencies. Context-dependency is quite a hurdle in this case. These two quotations illustrate the problem [italics are mine]:

> Passages that appear to be arguments are sometimes not arguments but explanations. The appearance of words that are common indicators […] cannot settle the matter, because those words are used in both explanations and arguments. *We need to know the intention of the author* (Copi and Cohen 2008, p. 19).
> In such a context, there would be no point in arguing for that claim, because there is no need to try to rationally persuade anyone that it is true; the people *spoken to already believe it* (Govier 1987, p. 23).

My view, as a linguist and discourse analyst, is that we can only infer relevant intentions from what is said and make assumptions about the addressee's mental states (beliefs, desires, intentions, etc.) from a contextual point of view. Works by Grice (1975) or Sperber (1996) are typically used to calculate meaning from what has been said. On the other side, rhetoric is first defined by making adjustments with the addressees' beliefs and desires (Herman and Oswald 2014). Knowing intentions and beliefs is quite an impossible task, but a discourse analyst should make assumptions or hypotheses about these mental states and estimate their probability within a given context of communication.

The third philosophical problem is linked with a strong vision of truth. "Explaining why C [I should stop smoking] is true is the very same thing as giving a reason to think C is true" (Wright 2002, p. 37) is a typical quotation that illustrates how truth evaluation is unavoidable in these matters or in order to settle the question. Linguists, on the other side, aren't generally interested in knowing the truth, but rather in showing how reality is represented.

(3) (P) Joe took the time machine, (A) because he needed digital pictures of Napoleon during the battle of Waterloo.

(3) will be seen as an explanation even if (P) is very likely to be false in 2014 and because (P) is represented as real. Linguistic markers underline it: use of the simple past; act of an assertion; no doubt mentioned on an epistemic level. This utterance appears to be true and is intended to appear so for the addressee independently of our knowledge of the state of the world.

So, if we accept to get around these problems as I do with the linguist's points of view I've just underlined, we can define explanation as follows:

> Explanation of a proposition (P) by a proposition or a set of propositions (Q) implies that (P) is linguistically presented as indisputable, i.e. represented as true or as certain.

This leads of course to another difficulty: what is linguistically indisputable? The key criterion I shall use here is *linguistic modalities*.

3 Using Linguistic Modalities

I will rely here on the most thorough book on the subject in French, Laurent Gosselin's book published in 2010 (Gosselin 2010), in which he details six types of linguistic modalities: alethic, epistemic, appreciative, axiological, boulomaïc and deontic modalities (logical modalities like necessity is treated within this system of modalities). Of course, the modalities that are tied to the question of explanation are essentially alethic modality (truth represented) and epistemic modality on certitude (and degrees of certitude). Let's examine these two cases.

"Alethic modality characterizes fundamentally descriptive judgments [it supposes preexisting facts and reports them] that refer to an existing reality, independently of judgments passed on it" (Gosselin 2010, p. 314, my translation). Statements expressing alethic modality are not considered as *standpoints*, but as facts which cannot start with "I guess that" or "I find that"—see example 4. This is quite a good test to distinguish alethic modalities from epistemic ones.

(4) Albert is a widower → ??[2] I guess that Albert is a widower

Conversely, epistemic modalities are linked with subjectivity. Gosselin talked about "subjective truth". It is difficult to insert a circumlocution like "No one could deny" before an epistemic utterance—see example 5—without a sort of power grab on this utterance. Thus, epistemic modalities are always linked with a kind of evaluation. It could be a highly shared and quite obvious evaluation in certain contexts or a more personal one that appears to be generally admitted. There's no problem however to insert "I guess that" or "I find that" before the epistemic utterance.

(5) "Our economy is weakened" → I find that our economy is weakened versus ? No one can deny that our economy is weakened
(6) "My computer is old" → I guess that my computer is old versus ? No one could deny that my computer is old[3]

Alethic modality is quite clear: it is the only modality that necessarily leads to an explanation. Such statements are linguistically represented as true. Hence, any causal conjunction following an alethic statement A is designed to offer an explanation of it (why A? or How A?).

Dealing with epistemic modality is a bit more complex and confusing. Epistemic modality concerns "subjective truths", *beliefs* on objects of this world, "descriptive

[2]By convention, quotation marks signal not impossible utterances, but highly improbable (??) or strange (?) ones without a clearer context.

[3]This example is echoing the problem of "language" and "speech" (Ferdinand de Saussure). "Old" in language in intrinsically evaluative and subjected to a point of view (I judge this as old), but its evaluative features can be irrelevant in certain contexts. If the computer mentioned in (6) is 2 years old, the personal evaluation will probably be very salient and probably challenged, but if it is an 18 years old computer, it is highly probable that, in this context, no one will deny its old age (see point 4 below).

judgments which do not constitute value judgments, but which do not either put back to an autonomous reality" (Gosselin 2010, p. 325). With epistemic modality, what is represented is not a matter of truth but a matter of certainty and a matter of degrees of certainty.

In principle, epistemic modality expressed in (7) leads to argumentation, since the conclusion is a subjective standpoint underlined by the modal verb (may) and provided that following arguments give reasons to justify beliefs.

(7) My computer may be too old now.

But there is a major problem with epistemic modality when the epistemic value is absolute certainty (e.g.: "My computer is old"). Here, the subjective part of the clause, which was inherent in the modal verb "may", seems erased by the certitude of the modal verb "to be". It remains, though, that "old" is an inherently subjective adjective, even if the evaluation seems shared or obvious. But it is not always the case and when epistemic modalities are rephrased as alethic ones, the result can have a powerful rhetorical effect—see the move between (8) and (9).

(8) "It is estimated that there are 2 million weapons in Switzerland" → (9) "There are 2 million weapons in Switzerland"

With this kind of move, an evaluation of reality (8) is encoded as an alethic sentence (9) which is imposed (and counted) as a true fact. In this case, when reasons are provided, they appear as explanations. (9) is not expected to be contradicted or called into question by the addressee. This strategy offers a crucial advantage to the speaker, which is pointed out by Aristotle in Topics:

> Not every problem, nor every thesis, should be examined, but *only one which might puzzle one of those who need argument* [...]. For people who are puzzled to know whether snow is white or not need perception (Aristotle, Topics, I, part 11).

This move—transforming epistemic clauses into truly alethic utterances—uses what Danblon (2001) calls obviousness effect. A consequence of this effect is to let some premises or conclusions appear as not open to discussion or to justification or not expecting to be discussed—as some linguistic presuppositions do. Hence, it prevents the opening of a confrontation stage and, consequently, an argumentative dialogue—according to the pragma-dialectical view on argumentation (Eemeren and Grootendorst 2004).

4 Pseudo-Explanations

There are also moves in which the speaker can exploit the blurring lines between explanation and argument without transforming modalities. In order to analyze such moves, one must decide if the conclusion of an argument or an explanation is represented as admitted. In other words, the analyst must evaluate if the speaker commits the audience to believe the reality described in the conclusive clause. This evaluation, based on linguistic clues, leads me to conclude that we need a third category between argument and explanation: a kind of *pseudo-explanation* where (P) is considered as admitted and takes advantage of the certainty expressed to appear as explicative but can also be disputed as an argument, since it *remains* non-alethic.

Here are some cases of apparent explanations or pseudo-explanations:

The first case exploits the "invisible" epistemicity of non-axiologic evaluative terms: "Philip is tall", "Taxis are expensive". This move counts clearly on a supposed common ground, or a *doxa*, between speaker and audience. Language isn't sufficient per se and context is essential. If Philip is a classic European basketball player, probably no one will contest (P) "Philip is tall"; if he is a grown-up French man whose height is about 1m80 (5.91 feet), (P) will probably be more disputable. If, finally, his height is about 1m55 with the same contextual data, (P) will probably be considered as ironic. Because the speaker counts on a collective acceptance on his/her claim, "Philip is tall, because he ate a lot of soup" can be counted as an explanation. Still, the "conclusion" part of it remains intrinsically epistemic and cannot be considered as "pure" explanation. Example (6) illustrates this case.

The second case is an echo of the first one. *Doxa*, general beliefs and stereotypes taken for granted—e.g. "French people eat cheese after the main course, because…"—also offer apparent explanations. In this example, the speaker gives no linguistic clue that "the French eat cheese after the main course" is a disputable generalization. It is assessed as a monolithic truth. Hence, the audience is invited to consider it as true and non-disputable. Present tenses, iterative truths, generalities are some of the linguistic clues which point out taken for granted opinions. It must be underlined here that this case implies an absence of axiological and appreciative modalities in language (see *infra*). For example, "French people are disgusting frog-eaters" is clearly stereotypical, but the adjective "disgusting" is appreciative—implies (strong) speaker's subjectivity—and is not a pseudo-explanation for this reason.

The third and last case I can think of—without aiming at completeness in these observations—can be called an easy gamble on certainty. The future tense, even if it is inherently unknown and disputable, may encode a virtual certainty. "John will arrive at noon: he told me that he caught the 11:00 am train" offers an example where future can be taken for granted and represented as certain, provided that no unexpected incident appears. The weather forecast frequently offers this kind of prediction for the next day: "rain will fall tomorrow" is offered as certain and may be understood as a pseudo-explanation. In this context, it is interesting to underline that many weather forecasts mention a degree of probability in their previsions, recalling here that predictions are not as certain as they appear.

These cases have one common trait: they count on audience's acceptance. Now, in contrast, we may find alethic clauses that are in fact "an argument" without being explanation or pseudo-explanation. Inference to best explanation is, despite its name, an argumentative move. If (9) is alethic without further context, (P), in example (10), becomes epistemic, because (Q) is used to establish the truth represented in (P).

(9) John has left the party
(10) (P) John has left the party (I guess that John has left the party), (Q) because no one has seen him for an hour

Yet, the alethic form of (P) hides the intrinsic uncertainty of the conclusion—only (Q) reveals that the truth of (P) is not presupposed, but inferred. Note that "I am certain that John has left the party" is completely epistemic and appears paradoxically less certain than (9). In such cases, the process of establishing a conclusion implies in retrospect that (P) cannot be considered as true or certain. Hence, it cannot be an explanation. It is important to see that the alethic nature of (P) disappears when it becomes clear that (P) is inferred and not stated.

Apart from alethic and epistemic modalities, Gosselin defines axiological and appreciative modalities which are linked with an evaluative point of view. Both modalities are used when a speaker expresses not objects of belief, but objects of desire and value judgments, whether these value judgments are validated by the subjective view of the speaker (appreciative modality: "I love this movie") or by the collective view of an institution (axiological modality: "It is wrong to act like that"). In these two cases, utterances imply a complete commitment of the speaker to his point of view. These modalities are not represented as true or indisputable: speaker's commitment is intrinsically tied with a possible disagreement. Even when appreciative modalities are generalized, for instance in "This is a great movie", the subjective adjective "great" is intrinsically representing a subjective evaluative standpoint that isn't cancelled in generalization. Even if a lot of people can agree with axiological modalities—because they imply communities through institutions, norms, ethics—the fact that the speaker is committing him or herself to the value-based evaluation implies a possible (but often improbable) disputation. Hence, using these modalities in utterances that are followed by justifications is always an act of *arguing* in favour of a standpoint.[4]

Let's sum up our position, before examining how connectives can interact with Table 1.

[4]I won't speak here about deontic ("you must go!") and boulomaïc ("I want to eat pizza") modalities. They are often linked with commitments from the speaker, for example when the speaker is delivering a piece of advice ("You *should* lose weight")—hence, it is clearly open to argumentation; but, the problem addressed in this paper concerns only a part of deontic and boulomaïc modalities that are open to justification. Some deontic modalities, giving orders for example, are not even supposed to be questioned or explained.

Table 1 Explanation, apparent explanation and argumentation

Linguistic representation	Nature of (P) because (Q)	Expectations
A. (P) is represented as a true fact	Explanation	(P) will probably not be called into question
B. (P) is represented as already admitted	Pseudo-explanation	
C. (P) is represented as disputable	Argument	(P) may be called into question

5 French Connectives in Interaction with Explanation and Argument

"Because" can be translated in French either by "parce que" or "car". The main difference is the following one: "Parce que" is generally and quite often connected to an explicative move:

> "Affirmation that P has a cause Q, in the phrase P parce que Q always takes for granted truth of P. We start with P, considered as undisputed and then we present its origin Q" (Groupe Lambda-l 1975, p. 59, my translation)

This quotation of the seminal article on differences between those French connectives highlights that P can be taken for granted, even if Q is open to discussion. Hence, using "parce que" is a possible rhetorical strategy in order to make an argument appear as an explanation:

(11) According to Samy Chaar, who has met her some time ago, this nomination "is good news, because [parce que] we have avoided a war of succession" (Le Temps, October 10 2013, my translation).

Example (11) illustrates that the speaker seems to "forget" the evaluative (appreciative) modality contained in "good news" and offers this argumentative move as an explanation. The obviousness effect of "good news" included in an explicative move is an interesting power grab: the audience is supposed to accept the idea of "good news". This strategic move can be illustrated in Table 1 as moving from case C to appear like case A or B.

Unlike "parce que", "car" is exclusively argumentative:

> Enunciation of Q is represented as being intended for justification of the enunciation of P (Groupe Lambda-l 1975, p. 259, my translation)

"Car" illustrates in fact a double meta-discursive move: "I've said P and I justify P by saying Q". "Car" doesn't directly provide a cause for P but a reason that justifies *saying* P. This presupposes that P can be or is disputed. Therefore, "car" is strictly an argumentative indicator. Hence, when "car" is used with apparent explanations, it reveals inherently greater expectations to be called into question than with "parce que" and gives up "explicative appearance" to exhibit an argumentative nature. This move from case B in Table 1 to case C can be illustrated by example 12:

(12) (P) The conference fee is expensive, (Q) because [CAR] the organizing committee must pay many students to do the job

The use of "car" instead of "parce que" reveals in fact that P may already be a disputed issue in a community which leads the speaker to a justification. The speaker acknowledges that P is a matter of concern or may lead to an open debate. Thus, the pseudo-explanation is in fact embedded in a real or potential argumentative situation.

Some examples are even stranger. In principle, if "car" is strictly argumentative, one shouldn't find "car" with alethic modality. It's not the case, as shown by examples (13) and (14):

(13) (P) Noël Mamère : "I'm leaving the Green Party, (Q) because [car] the party is captive of its factions" (Le Monde, September 26, 2013, p. 10, my translation).

(14) (P) Nelson Mandela's agony goes on (Q) because [car] "his soul isn't in peace", according to traditional chiefs who estimate that Mandela's ancestors are irritated by family quarrels (Tribune de Genève, June 30, 2013, my translation).

In these examples, (P) are undisputed statements of fact. So, what are the effects of this "move" that leaves case A in Table 1 to appear like case C?

From a contextual point of view, Noël Mamère's and Nelson Mandela's cases are clearly moving from a non-polemic linguistic explanation which is taking place in a polemic context. Even if the truth of (P) isn't called into question, the causes in (Q) are expected to be disputed. "Car", in these situations, reveals the speaker's self-consciousness that his/her explanation will almost certainly create a dispute or arouse an opposition: disagreements about offered causes or about the link between (P) and (Q) are now expected.

This… explanation may enable us to understand an empirical test led by Sandrine Zufferey (2012). In this test, participants were asked to fill a blank within two clauses with either "parce que", "car" or "puisque" (since). Example (15) has delivered rather unexpected results.

(15) John laughed ____ Peter stumbled

Indeed, 72.5 % of participants put "parce que" (72.5 %) as a connective between these clauses whereas 27.5 % participants prefer "car" (27.5 %). It is perfectly standard and expected to see a massive preference for "parce que" because of the alethic nature of "John laughed". But how is it possible to explain that more than a quarter of the respondents preferred "car"? It is difficult to answer, because there wasn't any situational context in this test. But in order to understand why "car" is still perceived as possible, one must probably admit that "car" shows a readiness for discussion. To be more specific, "car" indicates that "Peter stumbled" may be disputed as the true or the only cause of John's laughter.

6 Conclusion

We wanted to highlight in this paper that, in a linguistic perspective, two criteria must be used to make fruitful distinction between explanation and argument: one is a semantico-enunciative analysis of proposition (P) which may be done with linguistic modalities; the second one is contextual expectation to be eventually called into question. These two criteria lead to distinguish in fact three categories: explanations, apparent explanations and arguments. We defined apparent or pseudo-explanations as non-alethic clauses explained or justified by some reason when these non-alethic clauses are expressed with an absolute certainty, i.e. taken for granted by the speaker, and do not contain appreciative or axiological modalities.

Strategic moves to open or to close a possible disputation must be analysed within this frame. We may find at least two cases: non-certainty bound modalities (appreciative modalities for example) may be linguistically encoded as generalized ("This is a wonderful movie"). In this case, it seems that the evaluative nature of this clause will remain as argumentative. But in the second case ("John is rich"), erasing the epistemic nature of this clause ("I think that John is rich") leads in fact to turn an argumentative move into an explanation.

Finally, the dynamics of some connectives (at least in French) is a way to analyse rhetorical and strategic moves: adding a layer of explanation on some intrinsic argument (some uses of "parce que") may be a way to impose as indisputable an argument; expressing in an explanation an expectation of plausible future argument (some rare cases of "car") leads to understand that the speaker is self-conscious of a potential disagreement either about the cause advanced or about the uniqueness of the presented cause.

Acknowledgements Thanks to Steve Oswald for the precious help in Amsterdam, to Jérôme Jacquin for the motivating moral support and to Thierry Raeber for his enthusiasm and nice ideas of linguistic tests.

References

Adam, J.-M. (2011). *Les textes types et prototypes: séquences descriptives, narratives, argumentatives, explicatives, dialogales et genres de l'injonction-instruction* (Nouv. éd. entièrement rev. et augm). Paris: A. Colin.

Aristotle. (2014). *Complete works of Aristotle, volume 1: The revised Oxford translation*. Princeton: Princeton University Press.

Copi, I. M., & Cohen, C. (2008). *Introduction to logic* (13th ed.). Upper Saddle River, N.J.: Prentice Hall.

Danblon, E. (2001). La rationalité du discours épidictique. In M. Dominicy & J.-M. Adam (Eds.), *La mise en scène des valeurs: la rhétorique de l'éloge et du blâme* (pp. 19–47). Lausanne: Delachaux et Niestlé.

Gosselin, L. (2010). *Les modalités en français: la validation des représentations*. Amsterdam: Ed. Rodopi.

Govier, T. (1987). *Problems in argument analysis and evaluation*. Foris: Dordrecht.
Govier, T. (2005). *A practical study of argument* (6th ed.). Belmont [etc.]: Thomson Wadsworth.
Grice, H. P. (1975). Logic and conversation. In D. Davidson & G. Harman (Eds.), *The logic of grammar* (pp. 64–75). Encino, Calif: Dickenson Pub. Co.
Groupe Lambda-l. (1975). Car, parce que, puisque. *Revue Romane, 10*, 248–280.
Herman, T., & Oswald, S. (Eds.). (2014). *Rhétorique et cognition: perspectives théoriques et stratégies persuasives/Rhetoric and cognition: theorical perspectives and persuasive strategies*. Bern: P. Lang.
McKeon, M. W. (2013). On the rationale for distinguishing arguments from explanations. *Argumentation, 27*(3), 283–303. http://doi.org/10.1007/s10503-012-9288-1.
Nuyts, J. (2001). *Epistemic modality, language, and conceptualization: A cognitive-pragmatic perspective*. Amsterdam: John Benjamins Publishing Company.
Rubin, V. L. (2010). Epistemic modality: From uncertainty to certainty in the context of information seeking as interactions with texts. *Information Processing & Management, 46*(5), 533–540. http://doi.org/10.1016/j.ipm.2010.02.006.
Rubin, V. L., Liddy, E. D., & Kando, N. (2006). Certainty identification in texts: Categorization model and manual tagging results. In J. G. Shanahan, Y. Qu, & J. Wiebe (Eds.), *Computing attitude and affect in text: Theory and applications* (pp. 61–76). New York: Springer. Retrieved from http://link.springer.com/chapter/10.1007/1-4020-4102-0_7.
Sperber, D. (1996). *Relevance: communication and cognition* (2nd ed.). Oxford: Wiley-Blackwell.
van Eemeren, F. H., & Grootendorst, R. (2004). *A systematic theory of argumentation: The pragma-dialectical approach*. Cambridge: Cambridge University Press.
Wright, L. (2002). Reasoning and explaining. *Argumentation, 16*(1), 33–46. http://doi.org/10.1023/A:1014940822482.
Zufferey, S. (2012). "Car, parce que, puisque" revisited: Three empirical studies on French causal connectives. *Journal of Pragmatics, 44*(2), 138–153. http://doi.org/10.1016/j.pragma.2011.09.018.

Verbs of Appearance and Argument Schemes: Italian *Sembrare* as an Argumentative Indicator

Johanna Miecznikowski and Elena Musi

1 Introduction

This paper addresses the relations between verbs of appearance and argument schemes, taking as an example the Italian verb *sembrare* ('to seem') in its function as an argumentative indicator.[1] In the framework of Pragma-Dialectics, the notion of argumentative indicators has been defined as including "all words and expressions that refer to any of the moves that are significant to the argumentation process" (van Eemeren et al. 2007, p. 2). Such argumentative clues can belong to different classes of linguistic items, ranging from verbs to conjunctions and to various kinds of discourse markers.[2] Within Pragma-Dialectics, argumentative indicators have been considered, above all, from the point of view of the analyst facing the task of argumentative reconstruction. In this perspective, it has been underlined that indicators may work at different levels, signaling, for example, the

---

[1]The study presented is part of a research on the relationship between inferential uses of perception verbs and argumentation conducted at the Università della Svizzera italiana ("From perception to inference. Evidential, argumentative and textual aspects of perception predicates in Italian", SNF grant n.141350, direction: Johanna Miecznikowski and Andrea Rocci, cf. http://www.perc-inferenza.ch).

[2]Discourse markers are particles, connectives, sentence adverbs or more complex lexical expressions that do not contribute to the propositional content of their host utterance, are syntactically poorly integrated and whose primary function is to relate utterances to their co- and context at the textual, inferential or interactional level. See Bazzanella (2006) for a more detailed discussion of the category and Miecznikowski et al. (2009), for a corpus based analysis focussed on argumentative functions of the discourse connective *allora* in Italian.

J. Miecznikowski (✉) · E. Musi
Istituto di studi italiani, Università della Svizzera italiana, Lugano, Switzerland
e-mail: johanna.miecznikowskifuenfschilling@usi.ch

E. Musi
e-mail: elena.musi@usi.ch

F.H. van Eemeren and B. Garssen (eds.), *Reflections on Theoretical Issues in Argumentation Theory*, Argumentation Library 28,
DOI 10.1007/978-3-319-21103-9_19

commitment of the interactants in a particular stage of a critical discussion,[3] argumentative moves or the presence of a particular argumentation scheme. From a linguistic point of view, it is crucial to acknowledge that the usefulness of indicators for the analyst depends on their usefulness for the participants engaged in an argumentative interaction. Like in the case of other aspects of textual or conversational structure, the construction of argumentative relations at the different levels mentioned above is, in the first place, the participants' task; functional categories are emic, not etic (Pike 1954). What justifies the attribution of an indicator function to a linguistic expression is, then, the potential of the expression to guide interlocutors and readers in this task. In any particular context, this potential will depend both on the expression's functions coded in a relatively stable manner in the linguistic system (e.g. in the lexicon or in the domain of recurrent syntactic constructions and discourse routines) and on the specific pragmatic configuration (Bazzanella and Miecznikowski 2009) the expression is used in. As we will argue in our paper, corpus-based linguistic analysis, focused on single expressions and their contexts of occurrence, can fruitfully contribute to a better understanding of argumentative indicators in this sense.

Like other verbs of appearance interlinguistically (e.g. English *to seem*, Spanish *parecer*), the verb *sembrare* has been attributed an evidential function in the linguistic literature when occurring in certain syntactic and pragmatic contexts.[4]

In language typology, the notion of evidentiality has been defined a grammatical category encompassing those grammatical elements (clitics, particles, bound morphemes) "marking how someone knows something" (Aikhenvald 2004, p. 6). The communicative function of indicating *information sources* or *modes of knowing* is to contextualize the propositional content of an assertion or weak assertion (guiding its interpretation) and to justify and modulate the speech act in question (evidentials specify "the kind of justification for a factual claim which is available to the person making that claim [...]", Anderson 1986, p. 274). The most commonly grammaticalized types of information sources are direct experience (eventually distinguished according to perceptual modality), inference, and report/hearsay (cf. Willett 1988).

Research on lexical evidentials (e.g. Squartini 2007) has underlined that those types of information sources are relevant also in languages that do not

[3]According to the Pragma-Dialectical framework (e.g. van Eemeren and Grootendorst 1992), argumentation takes place within the context of a critical discussion involving protagonists and antagonists that critically test standpoints in order to reduce a difference of opinion. According to that model, the subtasks, or stages, defining a critical discussion are the confrontation stage (a difference of opinion is made explicit), the opening stage (the interactants commit themselves to resolve the difference of opinion and agree upon some basic assumptions and rules), the argumentation stage (arguments are put forward to justify or refute standpoints), and the concluding stage.

[4]Appearance verbs and evidential uses of perception verbs have been studied in Romance and Germanic languages by Usoniene (2001), Pietrandrea (2005), Cornillie (2007, 2009), Aijmer (2009), Diewald and Smirnova (2010), Strik Lievers (2012), Musi (in press a, b). For a diachronic perspective cf. Gisborne and Holmes (2007) and Whitt (2011) on English and Musi (2014) on Italian *sembrare*.

grammaticalize evidentiality—which is the case of Italian and of the majority of European languages. In these linguistic systems, evidentiality has been investigated as a functional rather than as a grammatical domain. The category of information source may be indicated using sentence adverbs, verbal tenses and modes as well as verbal constructions that acquire an evidential function in specific contexts. It is in this line of thinking that the notion of evidentiality is currently used to analyze the semantics of appearance verbs.

Evidentiality and argumentation are related because the justification of claims is, of course, the defining feature of one of the central moves in argumentative discourse. An important difference between evidentially marked utterances and full-fledged argumentative moves is that, in the former case, the speaker signals the presence of evidence in favor of his or her assertion and categorizes that evidence in a generic fashion, whereas in the latter case, the speaker establishes a discourse relation between the assertion and one or more specific arguments given in the text. Accordingly, speakers can use evidentials both to support argumentation (contributing to establish argument-conclusion relations present in a critical discussion), and as an alternative to argumentation (merely suggesting the existence of evidence without actually formulating any arguments). Recent studies at the semantic-pragmatic interface have concentrated on the argumentation supporting function of modal and evidential expressions (Rocci 2008, 2012, 2013; Miecznikowski 2011). It has been argued that, in argumentative discourse, these expressions function as indicators strengthening and categorizing argument-conclusion relations that are spelled out textually.

An example is the Italian modal verb *dovere* 'must', which has been analyzed as an evidential qualifying the utterance's content as inferred (cf. Dendale 1994 on French *devoir* and, more recently, Squartini 2004 and Pietrandrea 2005 on Italian *dovere*). As underlined by Rocci (2013), *dovere*'s function as an argumentative indicator becomes apparent when compared with other epistemic expressions that lack this function:

a. *È andato a casa presto. Doveva essere stanco.*
'He went home early. He must have been tired.'
b. *È andato a casa presto. Sono sicuro che era stanco.*
'He went home early. I'm sure he was tired.'
(Rocci 2013, p. 130)

In a. the *imperfetto* form of the modal verb marks the propositional content of the second utterance (p: 'He was tired') as inferred. It thus instructs the addressee to reconstruct the speaker's path of reasoning leading to conclude p, looking for premises in the context and in the surrounding co-text. Since the content of the first utterance ('he went home early') is a good premise candidate, and provided that no better candidates are available, this instruction encourages the addressee to infer a discourse relation between the two adjacent utterances, interpreting the preceding sentence as an argument supporting p. In b., in contrast, the belief expression "sono sicuro" is not an inferential evidential, but mainly expresses a high degree of subjective certainty. Hence, its presence does neither trigger the reconstruction of a path of reasoning, nor does it favor relevance implicatures establishing an argumentative discourse relation between the two utterances. The sources of the speaker's certainty are not specified in any way and may or may not include the content of the preceding utterance.

One of the ideas put forward in the research on evidential modals as argumentative indicators is that the categorization of modes of knowing in an utterance restricts the range of argument schemes with which the utterance is compatible in argumentative discourse. An example is the modal-evidential verb *dovere* in its conditional form *dovrebbe* ('should'). As claimed by Rocci (2012), this form is incompatible with argument schemes from the effect to the cause, while it can signal causal relations proceeding from the cause to the effect:

a. *Giovanni ha lavorato molto. Dovrebbe essere stanco.*
'John worked a lot. He should be tired'
b. *Giovanni è stanco. *Dovrebbe aver lavorato molto.*
'John is tired. He should have worked a lot'
(Rocci 2012, p. 2134)

In a., an argument-conclusion relation based on reasoning from the cause ('having worked a lot') to the effect ('being tired') can be inferred between the two utterances, a relevance implicature supported by the inferential marker *dovrebbe*. Also in the short text b., the presence of the inferential *dovrebbe* in the second utterance encourages the interpretation of the first utterance as an argument. The construction of an argument-conclusion relation is pragmatically plausible, moreover, for a suitable inference scheme is available: reasoning from the effect ('being tired') to the cause ('having worked a lot'). Nevertheless, *dovrebbe* sounds odd in this context. The author convincingly explains this effect by pointing out that this inferential marker not only generically signals that the speaker's information source is reasoning, but has a more specific evidential function. The contrast between a. and b. indicates that in the domain of causal reasoning *dovrebbe* prefers one direction of causality over the other.

In the present analysis, we will develop this idea, showing that *sembrare* constructions preferentially occur with certain argument schemes and insisting in the role of the verb's lexical meaning at this regard. After presenting our data (Sect. 2), we will provide an overview of the syntactic constructions of *sembrare* associated with evidential meanings (Sect. 3). The remaining sections will focus on argumentation. Existing research on copulative constructions with appearance verbs as indicators of argument schemes will be discussed (Sect. 4). In Sect. 5, we will introduce the Argumentum Model of Topics (Rigotti and Greco Morasso 2010), an approach providing tools for the analysis of the inferential configuration of arguments, and present the results of our corpus study conducted using this approach. The main points of our paper will be summed up in a short conclusion (Sect. 6).

2 Data

The data considered in this paper consist of 40 texts taken from a mixed corpus of reviews, editorials and posts published in the comment spaces associated with reviews and editorials.[5] The texts in our corpus have been collected from the Italian daily newspapers *La Stampa* and *La Repubblica* and from four thematic websites about art exhibitions (www.mostreinmostra.it), music (www.fullsong.it), haute cuisine (www.passionegourmet.it) and consumer electronics (www.digital.it).

The choice of these text genres is motivated by the important role argumentation plays in them and by the variety of activity fields they cover. In editorials, journalists express an opinion, mostly on a political matter, backing it up by arguments. In reviews, experts or consumers evaluate an object on the basis of first-hand experience as well as field-specific knowledge and values (Miecznikowski 2015). Comment spaces allow for a lot of variation in terms of text genres; argumentation is common in most types of posts, however. On one hand, users react to the standpoints and arguments put forward in the text they comment on; on the other hand, on the metacommunicative level, users formulate opinions about the text as such, usually backing up their judgment by at least one argument.[6]

3 *Sembrare* Constructions

The verb *sembrare* semantically presupposes two participants, namely an experiencer and an experienced. The experience in question can be entirely mental or involve perception.

The mental/perceptual process undergone by the experiencer is expressed by various syntactic constructions in which the experiencer role is either expressed by an indirect object NP or left implicit.

The main form-function patterns attested with *sembrare* are the following:

I. Copula constructions asserting similarity between two entities *a* and *b* (both expressed by referential NPs), the first having a set of properties identical to a set of properties of the second ("comparison meaning", cf. Kratschmer 2013):

(1) *[Marco]$_a$ sembra [suo padre]$_b$* .
'Marco looks like his father'.

[5]The corpus has been compiled within the project *From perception to inference* (cf. footnote 1). We would like to thank Martina Cameroni, Maria Chiara Pasinetti and Francesca Saltamacchia for their contribution to data collection.

[6]See Miecznikowski and Musi (in press), who adopt a genre perspective to investigate the relationship between reviews published online and the posts published in the corresponding comment spaces.

In (1), *sembrare* indicates that Marco resembles his father (physically, if not specified otherwise in the context).[7] In this example, as is usually the case in type I contexts, the experiencer coincides with the speaker and is left implicit.

II. Copula constructions and personal constructions with an embedded infinitive asserting the existence of clues to attribute a property *B* to an individual *a* and warranting the implicature, under certain circumstances, that the speaker indeed attributes *B* to *a*. *B* can be expressed by various types of complements, e.g. by adjectives (2), predicative NPs (3) or infinitives (2):

(2) *[Marco]$_a$ (mi) sembra [affamato/aver fame]$_B$.*
'Marco seems hungry/to be hungry (to me)'.
(3) *Da come parla, [Marco]$_a$ (mi) sembra [un esperto]$_B$*
(3) 'Judging from the way he speaks, Marco seems an expert (to me)'.

In example (2), the speaker states that some (unspecified) clues exist which normally warrant the predication that Marco is hungry. In (3), a property attributed to Marco ('the way he speaks') matches a typical feature of experts and functions as evidence in support of the categorization of Marco as an expert.

Differently from context (1), in which a relation of identity or inclusion is excluded (Marco cannot be considered to be his father), in (2) and (3) *a* and *B* are semantically and ontologically compatible, and it is conceivable that Marco is hungry/an expert. Kratschmer (2013) has termed "categorization meaning" the meaning of *sembrare* exemplified by (2)–(3). According to this author, the comparison meaning of *sembrare* indicates the speaker's intention to make two entities closer in some respects (Kratschmer 2013, pp. 296–297), whereas the categorization meaning indicates the speaker's attempt to determine the nature of the entity in subject position. In the examples above, if no contextual clues point to the contrary, the hearer may indeed infer that the experiencer (here: the speaker) holds the weak belief that Marco is hungry (2) and that Marco is an expert (3).

It is interesting to note that, in type II constructions, the presence of an overt first person experiencer (*mi/a me* 'to me') actually explicitly indicates that the speaker attributes *B* to *a*. In contrast, type II constructions that leave the experiencer unspecified are semantically indeterminate as to the speaker's commitment at this regard. An argument in favor of this analysis is that it is possible to combine the latter with a coordinate adversative proposition negating the attribution of *B* to *a* (e.g. "Marco sembra affamato, ma non lo è" 'Marco seems hungry, but he is not'),

[7]The verb *sembrare*, which here has been translated by *look like,* can be used to express physical similarity. In this respect, *sembrare* differs from its English correspondent *to seem,* but also from French *sembler,* with which it shares the etymological origin (Late Latin *similare*). It has to be noticed, though, that construction I uses of Italian *sembrare* are quite rare; more frequently, physical similarity is referred to using the more specific verb *assomigliare* (a rough semantic equivalent of French *ressembler*).

while the same configuration of utterances containing *sembrare* + *mi/a me* sounds odd.

III. Constructions with a propositional complement clause in subject function. These directly and explicitly attribute a belief to the experiencer, presupposing that this belief is based on available evidence:

(4) *(Mi) sembra [che Marco sia stanco]$_{p}$.*
'It seems (to me) that Marco is tired'.

In type III constructions, the attribution of a belief to the experiencer is favored by the presence of the complement clause. This syntactic constituent usually denotes a proposition, i.e. a third order entity that can be attributed a truth value and thus become a term of a belief relation.[8]

When used in its comparison reading, *sembrare* does not have any evidential function.[9] The construction types II and III, in contrast, can fulfill evidential functions under two conditions. The first condition is that the experiencer holds the (albeit weak) belief that B can be predicated of *a* (context II) or that *p* is the case (context III). As has been pointed out above, if this is the case depends on the presence of *mi/a me* and on the wider context in II, whereas the experiencer's holding a belief is encoded grammatically in III. When this condition is fulfilled, *sembrare* denotes a complex situation in which someone holds a belief on the basis of some available evidence. The second condition is that the experiencer coincides with the speaker and that the experience takes place in the moment of speech. In that case, exemplified by (2) and (3) above, the verb has a performative character (Faller 2002), i.e. knowledge acquisition is not reported, but presented as achieved in the moment of speech, and the relation between the proposition and the available evidence is mapped onto the ongoing speech event.

When *sembrare* is used evidentially, it always signals an indirect mode of knowing, i.e. either inference or hearsay/report. In this paper, we will be concerned especially with the verb's inferential uses. Example (2) above is a typical case: if the speaker holds the belief that Marco is hungry, this belief is based on a reasoning

---

[8]According to Lyons' classification of ontological entities (1977, pp. 438–452), taken up also in Functional Discourse Grammar (Dik 1997), propositions are third order entities which can be judged in terms of truth value, whereas (differently from second order entities, i.e. states of affairs) they cannot be located in space and time.

[9]It could be objected that the process of comparison presupposed by construction type I is a kind of information source: the information that is required to state a relation of similarity stems from a process of comparison. However, true evidential operators differ from presupposition triggers such as construction I *sembrare* by the fact that they are not part of the asserted propositional content, but are external to it. Their meanings are quite general and can be combined with a large range of propositions independently of their content. By the way, in (1), the speaker, while committing herself to asserting the results of the comparison process, leaves the mode of knowing proper unspecified: (1) is both compatible with a situation in which the speaker has actually seen Marco and Marco's father and has inferred the similarity relation on that basis and with a situation in which the speaker has come to know about the resemblance between father and son by hearsay.

process that takes into account a set of Marco's properties in combination with further, more general, premises. In what follows, we will take a closer look at the type of reasoning *sembrare* is compatible with. We will hypothesize that *sembrare*, like other modal and evidential verbs in Italian (see the examples of *dovere* discussed in the introduction), fulfils an argumentative function by supporting the construction of argument-conclusion relations and by restricting the range of argumentative schemes on which these can be based.

4 Symptomatic Argumentation

In the pragma-dialectic approach, three main types of argument schemes are distinguished, namely those based on a symptomatic relation, those based on a relation of analogy and those based on a causal relation (van Eemeren and Grootendorst 1992, pp. 98–99; Hitchcock and Wagemans 2011). In symptomatic argumentation, the argument (minor premise) and the standpoint have a common referent (X) but different predicates, as visualized in the following scheme:

Y is true of X
Because Z is true of X
AND Z is typical (characteristic/symptomatic) of Y.
(van Eemeren and Grootendorst 1992, p. 98)

The property Z attributed to the referent X in the minor premise is a "symptom" of the property Y ascribed to it in the standpoint. The major premise states the association between entities or situations which justifies the relation between the argument and the standpoint. The critical questions underlying symptomatic argumentation are the following:

- Is Z indeed typical of Y?
- Is Z not also typical of somethingelse (Y')?
  (van Eemeren and Grootendorst 1992, p. 99)

According to Garssen (1997, pp. 77–101) the category of symptomatic argumentation encompasses different subtypes of arguments such as those based on a classification, on genus-species relations, on definition and on evaluation criteria.

Van Eemeren et al. (2007, p. 160) identify copulative constructions in which the predicative is an adjective or noun containing the copula *to be*, or its modal variants *to seem/appear*, as particularly suitable to form the standpoint or the minor premise in a symptomatic argumentation. According to these scholars, the above-mentioned copulative constructions are likely to signal symptomatic argumentation because the copula normally refers to states rather than to events or processes, mirroring the nature of symptomatic argumentation, which is about qualities and features rather than about events or processes.

In analogy with van Eemeren's et al. (2007) proposal, also Italian *sembrare* can be hypothesized to be associated with symptomatic argument schemes, when used evidentially. Lexical semantic arguments lend further support to this hypothesis. One of the core elements of the meaning of *sembrare* is the idea of matching properties. In construction type I, the properties of two different referents are compared and a match of properties is stated (similarity). In many instances of construction type II, the clues that warrant the attribution of category *B* to *a* are properties *Z* of *a* that match salient features typically associated with instances of category *B* (in example 2 discussed above, for instance, some of Marco's properties match those of tired people; in example 3, the way Marco talks is similar to the way experts typically talk). It is in such instances of construction type II that one observes a clear semantic affinity with symptomatic argumentation, since they involve a single referent (*a*, corresponding to X in the symptomatic scheme), a category (*B*, corresponding to Y) and one or more properties Z shared by the referent and typical instances of the category. Consider the following example taken from a *La Repubblica* editorial:

(6) *Sembra una beffa la conclusione del processo Mills-Berlusconi. Dopo anni di preparazione, mesi di udienze, non abbiamo neanche un verdetto sulla colpevolezza o meno dell'ex premier Berlusconi.*
'The conclusion of the Mills-Berlusconi trial seems mockery. After years of preparation, months of hearings, we do not even have a verdict on the guiltiness or innocence of the former Prime Minister Berlusconi'.
(*La Repubblica*, editorial, February 2012)

In example (6), the speaker categorizes the long-awaited conclusion of an important trial as mockery. The "referent" (*a*, X) is, in this case, an event that the journalist topicalizes using an event noun (*conclusione*). The main argument supporting the categorization of this event as an instance of mockery is given in the next utterance, which caracterizes the result of the trial as utterly deluding. *Non... neanche* 'not even' situates the result on an scale below an expected minimal level; the contrast with long-lasting and probably effortful preparations ("anni […]" 'years […]', "mesi […]" 'months […]' further downscales the result. Rephrasing the example, we can say that a complex property Z is predicated of the trial and of its conclusion, namely to have raised and deluded expectations. This property arguably corresponds to a technique that people frequently use to mock others. If a confident categorization as mockery would require referring to the intentions of the institutional agents in question, the journalist here prefers to just identify a "symptom" of mockery, underlining a certain characteristic unfolding of events:

The conclusion of the Mills-Berlusconi trial (X) *seems* mockery (Y)
Because the conclusion of the trial (X) has utterly deluded the Italian people ('we'), producing a result far below the expectations created (Z)
(*and* raising and deluding expectations (Z) is typical of mockery (Y).

In conclusion of this section, we would like to point out that, despite the relevance of a certain kind of similarity relation, type II constructions of *sembrare* are not compatible with argumentation from analogy (in which "the argumentation is presented as if there were a resemblance, an agreement, a likeness, a parallel, a correspondence or some other kind of similarity between that which is stated in the argument and that which is stated in the standpoint", van Eemeren and Grootendorst 1992, p. 138). According to Van Eemeren et al. (2007, p. 160), the schematic structure of argumentation from analogy is as follows:

Y is true of X
because Y is true of Z
and Z is comparable to X.

In reasoning from analogy the argument (minor premise) and the standpoint share a common predicate (Y in the scheme above), which is attributed to different referents. This contrasts with *sembrare*'s categorization reading, where the minor premise and the standpoint share the same referent.

5 *Sembrare* and Argument Schemes in Editorials, Reviews and Comments

5.1 *Analytical Approach*

Sembrare occurs 52 times in our corpus. 39 occurrences are performative; among these, 2 are of type I construction, 17 of type II and 20 of type III. In order to find out which are the argument schemes compatible with *sembrare*, we have analyzed the local co- and context of all tokens in order to determine plausible implicit premises and have reconstructed the inferential relations applying the Argumentum Model of Topics (Rigotti 2006, 2009a; Rigotti and Greco-Morasso 2010).

Compared to the pragma-dialectical approach to argument schemes illustrated in the preceding section, AMT allows for a more detailed analysis of implicit premises. According to AMT, the inferential structure of any argumentation presupposes the presence of both procedural and material premises. Procedural premises have the form of maxims that define the inferential connections at issue. They are based on *loci*, pieces of an ontology shared by the speech community which "bind the truth value of the standpoint to the acceptance by the considered public of propositions referring to specified aspects of the ontology of the standpoint" (Rigotti 2006, p. 527). Material premises are of two types: the *endoxon*, a major premise that refers to shared general knowledge and is often left implicit, and the *datum*, a factual (minor) premise that is often (but not necessarily) made explicit. In order to generate relevant arguments, as represented in the schema in Fig. 1, procedural and material components must be combined in a double syllogistic structure:

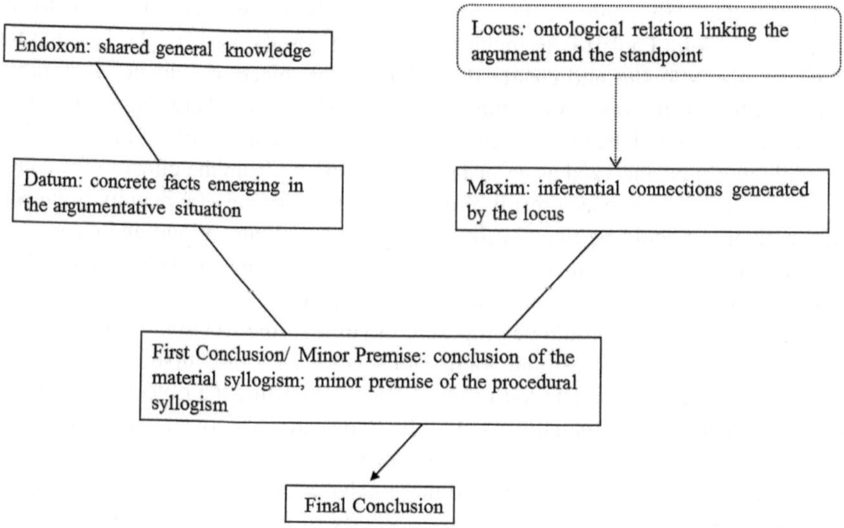

Fig. 1 The Argumentum Model of Topics

5.2 *Sembrare* as an Indicator of Symptomatic Argumentation

Our data confirm the role of *sembrare* as an indicator of symptomatic relations. The verb is indeed compatible with symptomatic argumentation in each of its evidential constructions. More specifically, the attested subtypes of argument schemes exploit ontological relations from definition, from the parts to the whole and from other extensional implications, from implications and from concomitances.

To illustrate this group of argument schemes, we will reconstruct an example taken from an editorial of the Italian daily newspaper *La Stampa* about a speech in support of democracy as a prerequisite for peace, which Pope Wojtyła delivered in occasion of the disorders in Iraq during 2003:

(5) *Dunque siamo grati dal profondo del cuore a Giovanni Paolo II per la costanza e la determinazione con cui ha levato la voce (una voce anche fisicamente piu' alta e chiara, sembra che stia assai meglio ed è questo un altro motivo di consolazione).*
'Therefore we are deeply grateful to John Paul II for the persistence and the determinacy with which he has raised his voice (a voice also physically louder and clearer, it seems that he is in much better health and this comforts us even more).'
(*La Stampa*, editorial, April 2003)

In (5), the verb *sembrare* indicates that that the speaker is committed to the proposition "John Paul II is in much better health" on the basis of the fact that the Pope's voice is louder and clearer than before. This piece of evidence is a *datum* made explicit in the text. As to the ontological relationship between a loud voice and a state of good health, it can be conceptualized in different manners. The example might be analyzed as an instance of reasoning from the effect to the cause, if we view a loud voice as a result of the proper functioning of a healthy organism. Alternatively, it could be hypothesized that good health and a loud and clear voice are properties that are frequently associated in the experience of the speaker and the hearer, giving rise to argumentation by concomitance.

Yet another solution could be proposed, in virtue of the fact that the journalist, in this text, has chosen to institute John Paul's voice as a discourse referent and to attribute a property to it. The journalist seems to underline the object-like status of the Pope's voice, rather than the event of the Pope using his voice. For this reason, a part-whole relationship might be relevant in this example. If we assume that the voice is a relevant part of a person and that loudness and clearness are synonyms of healthiness when applied to a voice, the property of healthiness can be transferred from the voice to the entire person, through a maxim like the one proposed in the following reconstruction (Fig. 2):

The validity of the transfer is, of course, questionable. As underlined by van Eemeren and Garssen (2009), only absolute structure-dependent properties, such as those expressing colours or materials, are always transferrable. The choice of *sembrare*, which signals weak commitment, is congruent with such a context.

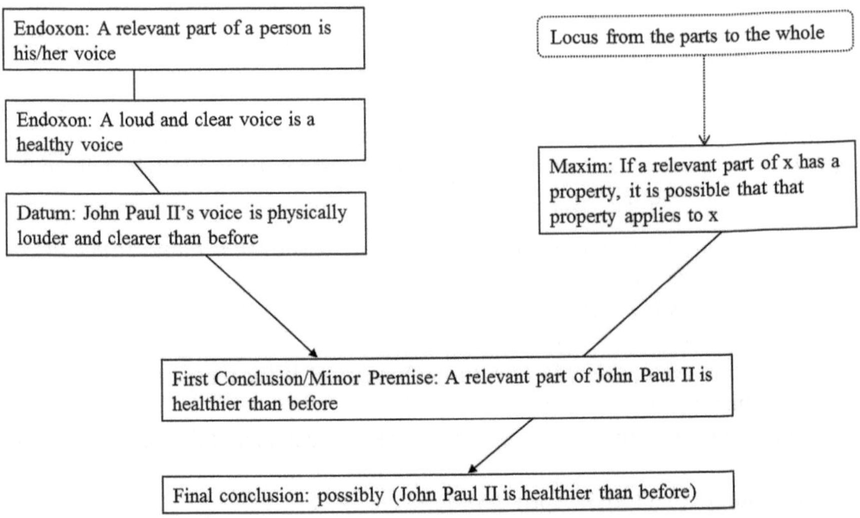

Fig. 2 Argumentative reconstruction exploiting a *locus* from the parts to the whole

5.3 *Sembrare* as an Indicator of Causal Argumentation

As we have seen discussing the preceding example, symptomatic argumentation does not exclude causal schemes (from the effect to the cause). In a number of contexts, however, causality—be it from the effect to the cause or from the final cause (Rigotti 2009b)—is even the most prominent ontological relation warranting the inferential transition from argument to conclusion. We have found cases of this type mostly in contexts in which speakers refer to the field of human action. In this use of *sembrare*, the preferred syntactic construction in the corpus is the complement clause construction.

The example we propose is taken from a post published on the website of the Italian daily newspaper *La Repubblica*, which comments on an editorial about Silvio Berlusconi's defeat in the 2011 elections:

(6) *La saga SB [Silvio Berlusconi] è stata una tragedia italiana che ha fatto rivivere atteggiamenti machisti ed incolti che ci hanno riportato indietro di decenni quando il nostro Paese nuotava ancora nell'analfabetismo e le nonne si stupivano della nuova invenzione della televisione.*
Fortunatamente sembra che il Paese sia uscito dallo stato ipnotico in cui i vari programmi televisivi lo avevano affogato.
Napolitano sciogli le Camere! Questo è il momento.
'The SB [Silvio Berlusconi] saga has been an Italian tragedy that has renewed machist and uncultivated attitudes, taking us decades back, when our country was still swimming in illiteracy and astonished grandmothers admired the new invention of television.
Luckily, it seems that the country has woken up from the hypnotic state in which the various television programs had drowned it.
Napolitano, dissolve the Parliament! This is the moment.'
(*La Repubblica*, post commenting on an editorial, June 2011)

In an utterance marked by *sembra* + complement clause, the author of this post claims that the country has got out of "the hypnotic state in which the various television programs had drowned it". The mentioned hypnotic state temporally coincides with Berlusconi's government ("la saga SB" 'the SB saga'), as the allusion to the status of television during that "Italian tragedy" suggests. The metaphor of waking up from hypnosis stresses the citizens' regaining consciousness and agency and conveys a positive connotation, which is made explicit by the evaluative propositional adverb *fortunatamente* 'luckily'.

In the context of this comment space dedicated to Silvio Berlusconi's defeat at the 2011 elections, it is evident that the *datum* on which the author bases the inference marked by *sembra* is the voters' verdict. It is from this collective act that the author infers that Italian citizens have "woken up" from "hypnosis". We think a plausible way to reconstruct the underlying reasoning is to assume two *loci*, one from the effect to the cause and one from extensional implications.

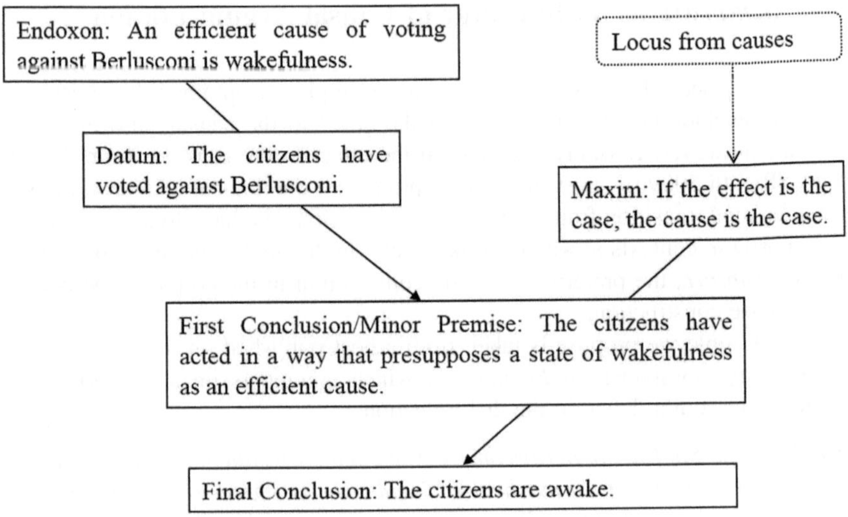

Fig. 3 Argumentative reconstruction exploiting a locus from causes

By this two-step reasoning, it is possible to causally infer an agent's state of mind from his/her acts (Fig. 3) and, taking for granted a certain prior state, to infer that the agent has undergone a change (Fig. 4).

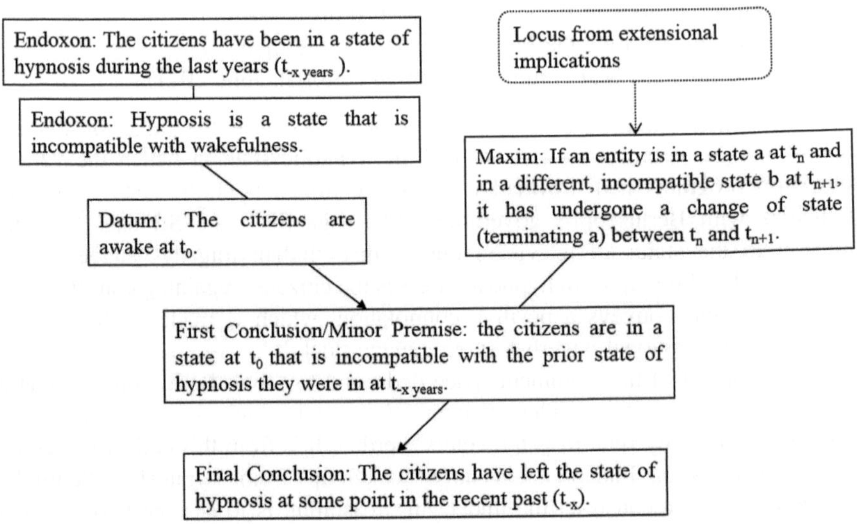

Fig. 4 Argumentative reconstruction exploiting a locus from extensional implications

5.4 Discussion

The data we have examined show that *sembrare* can indicate symptomatic argumentation in any of its evidential constructions, while it tends to be associated to causal relations only in the most pragmaticalized one (the one in which *sembrare* functions most clearly as a propositional operator, rather than as a predicate attributed to a specific subject[10]). Moreover, the semantic relationship between causal reasoning and the lexical meaning feature /matching properties/ is rather weak. Both observations lead to the hypothesis that the possibility to express causal reasoning might be mediated by the dominant evidential function of the complement clause construction, which shifts language users' attention from the lexeme's core meaning to the pragmatic operation of indicating an indirect mode of knowing.

Nevertheless, that functional generalization is not complete. Even in complement clause constructions, *sembrare* is not compatible with any argument scheme. In fact, symptomatic and causal arguments share some relevant features. One of these is that the various argument schemes of this group are based on loci that we can define "syntagmatic", following Rigotti (2006):

> We speak of syntagmatic loci to indicate all the classes of arguments that refer to aspects that are ontologically linked to the standpoint, either directly or indirectly, such as [..] the relationship between the whole and its constituent parts; included in this group of loci are also the classes of arguments which assume as their hooking point those pieces of world, traditionally called causes, effects, circumstances and concomitances, that condition the state of affairs the standpoint refers to.
>
> (Rigotti 2006, p. 528)

The term *syntagmatic loci* has been adopted in the AMT framework (e.g. Rigotti 2007) to oppose these to the paradigmatic ones, in which the argument and the standpoint refer to ontologically independent states of affairs and are rather linked by relations *in absentia* such as opposition or analogy. The AMT model distinguishes, moreover, the intermediate class of complex loci encompassing those cases which present features of both syntagmatic and paradigmatic argument schemes. A typical example of a complex locus is the locus from authority. This locus establishes a causal (and hence syntagmatic) relation between the qualities of an author and the truth of his or her discourse, while the relation between the state of affairs referred to in the standpoint and the communicative situation in which the

[10]Predicates are propositional operators when they take a proposition as one of their arguments, remaining outside the proposition itself and not contributing to its content, but operating on it (for an analysis of modals and evidentials as propositional operators see Hengeveld 1990).

authoritative discourse is uttered is no direct ontological one (and hence of a paradigmatic kind).[11]

Sembrare appears to be compatible with syntagmatic loci and, in the hearsay reading of the complement clause construction, with the complex locus of authority as well (e.g. *A quanto dicono, sembra che la sinistra vincerà le elezioni*, 'According to what they say, the right wing will win the elections'). On the contrary, it is not compatible with paradigmatic loci.

Another restriction, which regards causality, is that *sembrare* is not equally compatible with any causal argument scheme. We have found several instances of argumentation from the effect to the cause, but none from the cause to the effect, neither in inferences concerning the past or present nor in predictions. The following set of constructed examples illustrates this tendency. Whereas the conclusion introduced by *sembra* in (7a) can easily be derived from the premise expressed in the preceding statement, this is not the case in (7b), where *sembra* (in contrast to other solutions such as *deve* 'must') is acceptable only if additional perceptual or hearsay evidence is assumed to be available in the context:

(7a) *Marco ha una faccia stanchissima. Sembra che abbia fatto tardi ieri sera.*
'Marco has a very tired face. It seems he went to bed late, yesterday night.'

(7b) ?*Marco ha fatto tardi ieri sera. Sembra che sia stanchissimo*. [perceptual or hearsay evidence required].
'?Marco went to bed late yesterday night. It seems that he is really tired'.

In predictions, inferential *sembrare* seems to be less acceptable with the future tense than when it is combined with a periphrasis such as *stare per,* which indicates a phase immediately prior to an event, or with alethic *dovere* 'must' with future reference, which indicates a situation that will cause an event:

(8a) *(Mi) sembra che stia per/debba cadere.* '(To me), it looks as if he/she/it is about to fall.'

(8b) ?*(Mi) sembra che cadrà.* '(To me), it looks as if he/she/it will fall.'

A possible explanation of these patterns is a temporal one: by choosing inferential *sembrare* speakers typically signal that the available datum allows to infer a simultaneous state of affairs. This is compatible with the basic scheme of symptomatic argumentation (cf. Section 4) and is evident in the cases illustrated by the examples (1) to (5) discussed in previous sections; but this analysis applies also to (8a). The extension to causal inferences about the past illustrated by (6) and (7) could be mediated by the *passato prossimo*, since one of the functions of this tense is to denote a resultant state. The resultant state is, by the way, communicatively highly

[11]Cicero proposes, in his *Topica* (see Riposati 1947, pp. 34–35), a distinction between intrinsic loci (*alii in eo ipso de quo agitur haerent*, 'some [loci] are linked to the subject of the discussion'), and extrinsic loci (*alii assumuntur extrinsecus*, 'other [loci] are derived from outside'). This topical taxonomy has been further elaborated by Boethius in his *De Topiciis Differentiis* (see Stump 2004), who also suggests a third category of *loci medii* situated between the intrinsic and the extrinsic *loci.*

relevant in our example (6). We are aware of apparent exceptions to this generalization such as the use of *sembrare* in weather forecasts or with the passato remoto:

(9) (observing the sky): *Sembra che pioverà.* 'It seems it will rain.'
(10) *Mi sembra che il centro commerciale fu costruito negli anni '70.*
'As far as I know, the shopping mall was built in the Seventies'.

However, these examples may be considered instances of mixed loci that share less properties with inferential uses of *sembrare* than with the verb's hearsay uses, which, according to our data, are not subject to any temporal restriction. In (10), a context type that is not attested in our corpus, the knowledge source is recall from memory, whereas (9), for cultural reasons, may be framed as a semiotic practice of sign reading rather than being an instance of genuine causal reasoning.[12] Further research on appearance verbs expressing inferences about the past and the future is needed to corroborate this hypothesis.

6 Conclusion

The empirical study presented in this paper has shown that evidential uses of Italian *sembrare* can be used to introduce a standpoint and that they constrain the set of relevant argument schemes. The lexical meaning of *sembrare* makes this verb compatible with symptomatic as well as certain causal argument schemes which may be subsumed under the wider category of syntagmatic or mixed argument schemes. According to a hypothesis that has to be checked against a larger and more varied set of data, inferential uses (a) show a preference to express a temporal relation of simultaneity between the datum and the conclusion, which (b) can be extended to reasonings about non simultaneous causes and effects, especially when the verb is combined with temporal and modal markers that encode a posteriority or anteriority relation between an event and a state.[13]

Lexical semantic analysis, syntactic analysis and the argumentative reconstruction of texts are all necessary to understand which inferential processes are encoded by evidential constructions and to define their function as argumentative indicators in discourse. Perception and appearance verbs combine epistemic stance marking and evidential meanings and often occur in contexts in which the justifications at the basis of the uttered proposition are left implicit. Their polysemy and dependance on syntactic constructions calls for a fine-grained, context-sensitive semantic analysis.

[12] It may be relevant, at this regard, that Italian modal verbs behave atypically as well in meteorological contexts, as shows the use of *deve* in *Deve piovere* 'it will rain', discussed by Squartini (2004) and Rocci (2013), p. 143.

[13] As far as future reference is concerned, the role played by lexical and modal verbs implying posteriority relations has been examined by Miecznikowski (in press), on the basis of an Italian corpus of economic predictions.

The investigation of evidential and modal verbs usefully completes the growing body of research on discourse markers as argumentative indicators. Discourse markers, for example conclusion introducing connectives or concessive markers are useful to the analyst to recognize stance and argumentative moves, while evidentials and modals appear to be particularly relevant to argumentative analysis with regard to stance-taking and argument schemes.

Acknowledgments We would like to thank the participants to the 8th Conference of the International Society for the Study of Argumentation (ISSA) for their very helpful comments and suggestions.

References

Aikhenvald, A. (2004). *Evidentiality*. Oxford: Oxford University Press.

Aijmer, K. (2009). Seem and evidentiality. *Functions of Language, 16*(1), 63–88.

Anderson, L. B. (1986). Evidentials, paths of change, and mental maps: Typologically regular asymmetries. In W. Chafe & J. Nichols (Eds.), *Evidentiality: The linguistic coding of epistemology* (pp. 273–312). Norwood, NJ: Ablex.

Bazzanella, C. (2006). Discourse markers in Italian: Towards a 'compositional' meaning. In K. Fischer (Ed.), *Approaches to discourse particles* (pp. 449–464). Amsterdam: Elsevier.

Bazzanella, C., & Miecznikowski, J. (2009). Central/peripheral functions of allora and 'overall pragmatic configuration'. In M. B. Mosegaard Hansen & J. Visconti (Eds.), *Current trends in diachronic semantics and pragmatics* (pp. 107–121). Oxford: Emerald.

Cornillie, B. (2007). *Evidentiality and epistemic modality in Spanish (Semi-)auxiliaries: A cognitive-functional approach*. Berlin/New York: Mouton de Gruyter.

Cornillie, B. (2009). Evidentiality and epistemic modality: on the close relationship between two different categories. *Functions of Language, 16*(1), 44–62.

Dendale, P. (1994). Devoir: marqueur modal ou évidentiel? *Langue française, 102*, 24–40.

Diewald, G., & Smirnova, E. (2010). *Evidentiality in German: Linguistic realization and regularities in grammaticalization*. Berlin/New York: Mouton de Gruyter.

Dik, S. (1997). *The theory of functional grammar*. Berlin/New York: Mouton de Gruyter.

Faller, M. T. (2002). *Semantics and pragmatics of evidentials in Cuzco Quechua*. PhD Thesis, Stanford.University, Stanford.

Garssen, B. (1997). *Argumentatieschema's in pragma-dialectisch perspectif. Een theoretisch en empirisch onderzoek*. Amsterdam: IFOTT.

Gisborne, N., & Holmes, J. (2007). A history of English evidential verbs of appearance. *English Language and Linguistics, 11*(1), 1–29.

Hengeveld, K. (1990). The hierarchical structure of utterances. In J. Nuyts, A. M. Bolkestein, & C. Vet (Eds.), *Layers and levels of representation in language theory* (pp. 1–24). Amsterdam/Philadelphia: John Benjamins.

Hitchcock, D. and Wagemans, J. (2011). The pragma-dialectical account of argument schemes. In E. T. Feteris, B. Garssen and A. F. Snoeck Henkemans (Eds.), *Keeping in touch with Pragma-Dialectics: In honor of Frans H. van Eemeren* (pp. 185–206), Amsterdam, John Benjamins.

Kratschmer, A. (2013). Modèle interprétatif sémantico-pragmatique modulaire des constructions italiennes avec *sembrare / parere*. In W. De Mulder, J. Mortelmans, T. Mortelmans (Eds.), *Marqueurs temporels et modaux en usage, Cahiers Chronos* 26, pp. 293–314.

Lyons, J. (1977). *Semantics*. Cambridge: Cambridge University Press.

Miecznikowski J., Gili Fivela, B., & Bazzanella C. (2009). Words in context. Agreeing and disagreeing with *allora*. In G. Gobber et al. (Eds.), *Word meaning in argumentative dialogue*, Special Issue of *L'analisi linguistica e letteraria* (Vol. 1, pp. 205–218).

Miecznikowski, J. (2011). Construction types and argumentative functions of possibility modals: Evidence from Italian. In F. H. van Eemeren, B. Garssen, D. Godden, & G. Mitchell (Eds.), *Proceedings of the 7th Conference of the International Society for the Study of Argumentation* (pp. 1284–1297). Amsterdam: Rozenberg/SicSat.

Miecznikowski, J. (2015). L'argomentazione nelle recensioni on-line. In B. G. Fivela, E. Pistolesi & R. Pugliese (Eds.), *Parole, gesti, interpretazioni. Studi linguistici per Carla Bazzanella* (pp. 57–78). Roma: Aracne.

Miecznikowski, J. (in press). Envisager le futur dans les prévisions économiques. In L. Baranzini, J. Sánchez Méndez & L. de Saussure (Eds.), *Le futur dans les langues romanes*. Frankfurt am Aim: Peter Lang.

Miecznikowski, J. & Musi, E. (in press). Text genres adapted to new contexts: the case of online reviews. In J. Miecznikowski, M. Casoni, S. Christopher, A. Kamber, E. Pandolfi & A. Rocci (Eds.), *Proceedings of the Vals-Asla meeting "Language norms in context"*, 12th–14th February 2014, Special Issue of *Bulletin suisse de linguistique appliquée.*

Musi, E. (2014).Verbi d'apparenza tra semantica e sintassi: il caso di *sembrare* in italiano antico. *AION Linguistica* (Vol. 3).

Musi, E. (in press a). Evidential modals at the semantic-argumentative interface: appearance verbs as indicators of defeasible argumentation. *Informal Logic*, *34*(3).

Musi, E. (in press b). *Sembrare* tra semantica e sintassi. Proposta di un'annotazione multilivello. In *Proceedings of the XLVIII International SLI (Società linguistica italiana) Conference "Livelli di analisi e fenomeni d'interfaccia"*, 26th–28th September 2013.

Pietrandrea, P. (2005). *Epistemic modality: Functional properties and the Italian system.* Amsterdam/Philadelphia: John Benjamins.

Pike, K. L. (1954). Emic and etic standpoints for the description of behavior. In K. L. Pike (Ed.), *Language in relation to a unified theory of the structure of human behavior* (pp. 8–28). Glendale: Summer Institute of Linguistics.

Rigotti, E. (2006). Relevance of context-bound loci to topical potential in the argumentation stage. *Argumentation, 20*, 519–540.

Rigotti, E. (2007). Can classical topics be revived within the contemporary theory of argumentation? In F. H. van Eemeren, A.J. Blair, F. Snoeck Henkemans & C. Willards (Eds.), *Proceedings of the Sixth Conference of the International Society for the Study of Argumentation* (pp. 1155–1164). Amsterdam: Rozenberg/SicSat.

Rigotti, E. (2009a). Whether and how classical topics can be revived within contemporary argumentation theory. In F. H. van Eemeren & B. Garssen (Eds.), *Pondering on problems of argumentation* (pp. 157–178). Amsterdam: Springer.

Rigotti, E. (2009b). Locus a causa finali. Special Issue of *L'analisi linguistica e letteraria* (pp. 559–576).

Rigotti, E., & Greco Morasso, S. (2010). Comparing the Argumentum Model of Topics to other contemporary approaches to argument schemes: the procedural and material components. *Argumentation, 24*(4), 489–512.

Riposati, B. (1947). *Studi sui Topica di Cicerone*. Milano: Vita e Pensiero.

Rocci, A. (2008). Modality and its conversational backgrounds in the reconstruction of argumentation. *Argumentation, 22*(2), 165–189.

Rocci, A. (2012). Modality and argumentative discourse relations: a study of the Italian necessity modal dovere. *Journal of Pragmatics, 44*(15), 2129–2149.

Rocci, A. (2013). Modal conversational backgrounds and evidential bases in predictions: the view from the Italian modals. In K. Jaszczolt & L. de Saussure (Eds.), *Time: language, cognition and reality*. Oxford: Oxford University Press.

Squartini, M. (2004). Disentangling evidentiality and epistemic modality in Romance. *Lingua, 114*, 873–895.

Squartini, M. (Ed.). (2007). *Evidentiality between lexicon and grammar*. Special Issue of *Italian Journal of Linguistics, 19*(1).

Strik Lievers, F. (2012). *Sembra, ma non è. Studio semantico-lessicale sui verbi con complemento predicativo.*. Accademia della Crusca: Firenze.

Stump, E. (2004). *Boethius's 'De Topiciis Differentiis'*. Ithaca, NY: Cornell University Press.

Usoniene, A. (2001). On direct/indirect Perception with verbs of seeing and seeming in English and Lithuanian. *Working Papers, 48*, 163–182.

van Eemeren, F. H., & Grootendorst, R. (1992). *Argumentation communication and fallacies. A pragma-dialectical perspective*. Hillsdale: Lawrence Erlbaum.

van Eemeren, F. H., Houtlosser, P., & Snoeck Henkemans, F. (2007). *Argumentative indicators in discourse. A Pragma-dialectical study*. Amsterdam: Springer.

van Eemeren, F. H., & Garssen, B. (2009). The fallacies of composition and division revisited. *Cogency, 1*(1), 23–42.

Whitt, R. J. (2011). (Inter)subjectivity and evidential perception verbs in English and German. *Journal of Pragmatics, 43*(1), 347–360.

Willett, T. (1988). A cross-linguistic survey of the grammaticization of evidentiality. *Studies in language, 12*, 51–97.

Linguistic Argumentation as a Shortcut for the Empirical Study of Argumentative Strategies

Pierre-Yves Raccah

1 Introduction

Research in argumentation has acknowledged the important role of discourse in the study of argumentative strategies and manoeuvring. This acknowledgement is not recent; however, more recent is the inclusion, within the possible objects of research on argumentation, of the relationship between institutional contexts and argumentative discourse, via conventionalized institutional practices. The recent interest for the empirical observation of argumentation through institutional practices was underlined by van Eemeren (2010, p. 129) in these terms:

> … the term *argumentation* [… also refers to] an empirical phenomenon that can be observed in a multitude of communicative practices which are recognized as such by the arguers. Because these communicative practices are generally connected with specific kinds of institutional contexts […] they have become conventionalized. Due to this context-dependency of communicative practices, the possibilities for strategic manoeuvring in argumentative discourse in such practices are in some respects determined by the institutional *preconditions* prevailing in the communicative practice concerned.

This new interest for an empirical approach to the relationship between institutional contexts and argumentative strategies, via communicative practices linked to institutional preconditions, opens a wide and important field of research, as van Eemeren convincingly shows in his 2010 book.

As van Eemeren pointed out, the empirical study of this multidimensional space is possible because, among other reasons, all the terms of these relations are, at least partially, observable through discourse. Since discourse gives empirical hints to grasp the different facets of this space, it may be argued that there may be a way of describing meaning, a way which would allow to account, at least partially, for the dynamics of those relations: this would provide a sort of shortcut to the description

P.-Y. Raccah (✉)
CNRS LLL—UMR 7270, University of Orléans, Orléans, France
e-mail: pyr@linguistes.fr

F.H. van Eemeren and B. Garssen (eds.), *Reflections on Theoretical Issues in Argumentation Theory*, Argumentation Library 28,
DOI 10.1007/978-3-319-21103-9_20

of argumentative strategies, as they are partially in-formed by the institutions. Obviously, such a shortcut lives aside an enormous part of the field opened by the abovementioned remarks. Nevertheless, for one who is 'only' interested in a better description of the semantics of natural languages, it offers interesting and rich perspectives.

This is what this paper is intended to show. We will also see that this shortcut is not a completely new idea in semantics: I will examine how several ideas borrowed from the paradigm of *Argumentation Within Language* can be adapted to an empirical study of the relationship between argumentation and the institutional constraints. Finally, I defend the idea that this shortcut is useful also for those who are engaged in the complete study of strategic manoeuvring: since most of what is observable in that field is discourse, it may be useful to make explicit the reasoning which compels to describe the institutional conventions the way we do. A rigorous semantic description is more than useful for this purpose.

Among the various ways of describing meaning that might meet those requirements, I emphasize the interest of several aspects of the so called "View-Point Semantics" (*VPS*), partially inspired by Mikhaïl Bakhtin's work on the "inhabited" character of natural language words (see, for instance, Bakhtin (1929, p. 279), as well as by Oswald Ducrot's work on the semantic constraints on argumentative orientation and strength (see, for instance, Ducrot (1988)). In particular, I focus on the technique it provides for, so to speak, extracting ideological and cultural preconditions from discourses, which inform the observer on the institutional conventionalized practices.

2 From Strategic Manoeuvring to Semantics (Through the Route of Empiricity …)

The field of research opened by van Eemeren and Houtlosser (2009) and further investigated by van Eemeren (2010) includes, among other, the study of the multi-dimensional space of relationships between the different kinds of institutional contexts, the different types of institutionalized purposes, the different aspects of conventionalized communicative practices, the different aspects of communicative activities, and the different types of argumentative strategies. As for the parameters that must be taken into account in order to investigate that field, van Eemeren and Houtlosser (2009, p. 11) circumscribe them in this way:

In analyzing the strategic function of the maneuvering that is carried out by making a particular argumentative move, the following parameters need to be considered:

1. the results that can be achieved by the manoeuvring;
2. the routes that can be taken to achieve these results;
3. the constraints imposed by the institutional context;
4. the commitments defining the argumentative situation

Following van Eemeren and Houtlosser (and one really wants to follow them—at least on those points), what we have to observe are things like *results*, *routes*, *constraints* and *commitments*. Moreover, in agreement with one of the cornerstones of pragma-dialectical theories, the empirical study of that field is possible because those 'ingredients' are observable through discourse. Obviously—and fortunately—the discourses through which these parameters can be observed are not necessarily the same discourses as those which are analyzed for their strategic manoeuvring: the institutional constraints are, in many cases, laid down in laws, rules, procedures and other linguistic productions, so that the discourse that is being studied for its strategic manoeuvring is not the only source for determining those constraints. This is fortunate because if the source of observation of the institutional constraints involved with strategic manoeuvring were exactly the ones which inform on strategic manoeuvring, the risk of circularity would be enormous…

Finally, as van Eemeren insisted in his introductory lecture at ISSA 2014, the study of strategic manoeuvring must be *contextualized, empirical* and as *formal* as possible.

We will see how an empirical semantics of human languages can do the job and collect and organize observational data for a study of strategic manoeuvring that would meet the requirements proposed by van Eemeren and Houtlosser (2009). In a first step (2.1), I will give reasons to accept that discourses give empirical cues which allow to access the four parameters mentioned above; in a second step (2.2), I will carefully explicate what can be counted as an *empirical cue*, through a discussion of what can be a real empirical observation in human and social sciences. Such a discussion is necessary in order to make a clear sense of what an *empirical cue* may be where subjectivity is inherent to observation and causality is not observable. This, in turn, will help better understand why and how discourses are necessary input in order to get acquainted with institutional information (3.1) and why traditional corpora are not sufficient to collect the necessary empirical material for semantic or pragmatic studies.

2.1 Empirical Observation for Strategic Manoeuvring and Semantics

From the three theses I underlined (the ingredients, the observability through discourse, and the three desired properties of the study) it follows there *must* be a way of describing meaning which accounts for how utterances inform with respect to *results*, *routes*, *constraints* and *commitments.*

The claim is stronger than what it first appears: the term *meaning* is used here in a technical sense, where it refers to *the semantic value of languages units*, independently of the situation in which they are used; as opposed to the term *sense*, (utterance meaning), which we use to refer to *the semantic value of utterances in situations*.

The reason why that claim has to be acceptable is that the only observable facts that lead a hearer, in a given situation, to reach a particular *result*, *route*, *constraint* or *commitment*, rather than others, are the linguistic units used in the utterance. Obviously, in other situations, the same linguistic units might (and will) lead the hearer to reach other *results*, etc., so that the study of strategic manoeuvring really has to be contextualized, in spite of that claim. But, given that in each particular situation, it is the choice of some linguistic unit rather than some other that produces some effect rather than some other, in order to carry out an empirical study, it must be acknowledged that a set of instructions which is stable with respect to situations, must be given by the language units which are used in the discourse. Acknowledging this allows to meet the last requirement underlined by van Eemeren: having the study of strategic manoeuvring supported by semantic descriptions (i.e. independent of context), is a necessary (though not sufficient) condition for a possible formal study.

Having seen why there *must* be something empirical about semantic observation, we have to understand how there *can* be something empirical about observation in semantics, in spite of the necessary role of interpretation and its necessary subjectivity, and in spite of the fact that causal relations are not empirically observable.

2.2 Empirical Observation in General

In order to achieve this goal, I will now address, from a more general perspective, two essential aspects of empirical observation: causality and subjectivity. This will help understand (a) why and how, in spite of the fact that causal relations are not accessible to our sensorial system, they play an essential role in empirical sciences, and (b) why and how, in spite of the necessary radical subjectivity of individual observation, a certain degree of constructed objectivity can be achieved within a community.

(a) Causality

Empirical observation concerning the parameters underlined by van Eemeren and Houtlosser can be expressed by (meta-)statements of the form:
The linguistic segment ***X*** used in the institutional situation ***S***
produced the effect ***R***, with respect to parameter ***P***.
As can be seen by the reference to *produced effects*, these (meta-)statements convey implicit causal attributions. This is not specific to the field of strategic manoeuvring, nor to that of argumentation, and not even to linguistics or any human or social science: indeed, any scientific observational statement, like, for instance, “water boils at 100 °C”, carries implicit causal attributions; in our last example, if we try to substitute “43 years old” for “100 °C”, we immediately understand that the original statement conveys the implicit causal assumption according to which the cause of the boiling is the temperature (and not the age of the technician…).

Now, no scientist and no thinking human being in general would ever pretend they have observed some causal relation *with their sensorial apparatus*: causal relations are not observable through our sensorial apparatus and causality is always *only* a hypothesis. Obviously, some causal attributions are more plausible than others, but *plausibility* is not a proof…

Acknowledging that causal relations are not directly observable through our sensorial apparatus does not imply believing that *causality doesn't exist,* but only understanding that *causal statements cannot be used as empirical evidence.*

And, since we have just seen that all scientific empirical observational statements convey an implicit causal attribution, it follows that no scientific empirical observational statement can be directly used as evidence for some theoretical standpoint. This may seem paradoxical, but it is not. The same idea can be reformulated in another way, which shows a way out from that apparent paradox: 'any statement about the world, which evokes a causal relation between facts of the world, refers to non directly observable facts'. The apparent paradox dissolves itself as soon as we abandon the naïve belief that only material things *really* exist for science, a belief which entails that only direct observation can count as evidence. In order to comply both with the necessity of non material entities, and with the requirement that they be empirically grounded, sciences, and especially 'hard' sciences have developed a very sophisticated system of indirect observation, including criteria of validity for the causal attributions supposed by that indirect observation.

(b) Objectivity and intersubjectivity

Since scientific statements suppose previous causal attribution hypotheses, our perception of the world is significantly influenced by our theoretical biases.

Again, acknowledging that our beliefs about the existence of what we perceive cannot be invoked as a proof of its existence *is something different from* believing that those beliefs are false. And, in the same way, acknowledging that the way we perceive the world is influenced by our theoretical biases *is something different from* believing that the world plays no role in the way we perceive it.

Roughly, the essential reason for that difference is that, though we cannot directly access the world (we can only access it through the individual interpretation of what our sensorial apparatus gives), the world accesses our actions and reacts to them. Thus, analyzing what is stable in different selected human actions and in the world's reactions to them *may* give us collective stable elements to make hypotheses about how the world is within that zone of stability.

In Raccah (2005), I showed that an essential scientificity requirement, valid for any kind of science, is that it should provide descriptions of a class of phenomena, in such a way that the descriptions of some of those phenomena provided *de dicto* explanations for the descriptions of other ones. I also pointed out that fulfilling empiricity requirements could not lead to believe that science describes the phenomena 'the way they are', since one cannot seriously believe that there is a possibility, for any human being, to *know* the way things are. Though scientific observers cannot prevail themselves of *knowing* how the world *is*, they have access to the world through their interpretation of the states of their sensorial apparatus: that interpretation often relies on previously admitted scientific—or non scientific—theories.

If we want to apply these requirements to semantic theories, we have to find observable semantic facts, which can be accessed through our senses. As we will see in the next section, it seems that we are faced with a big difficulty, which might force us to admit that there cannot be such a thing as an empirical semantic theory: we will see that semantic facts are abstract and thus not directly accessible to our sensorial apparatus. We seem to be in a situation in which the very object about which we want to construct an empirical science prevents its study from being an empirical study…

However, if we admit that physics is a good example of empirical sciences, we should realize that we are not in such a dramatic situation. For what the physicist can observe through her/his senses, say, the actual movements of the pendulum (s)he just built, is not what her/his theory is about (in that case, the virtual movements of *any*—existing or non existing—pendulum): the object of physical theories is not more directly accessible to the observers' sensorial apparatus than the object of semantic theories. Physicists use different tricks in order to overcome that difficulty, one of which is the use of *indirect observation*: some directly observable[1] entities are considered to be traces of non directly observable objects or events, which, in some cases, are seen as one of their causes, and, in other cases, as one of their effects.

If we are willing to keep considering physics as an empirical science, we are bound to consider that that *indirect observation* strategy is not misleading; we only have to see how it could be applied to the study of meaning. In order to illustrate how this could be done, I will examine an example and will abstract from it.

2.3 *Empiricity in What Concerns the Study of Human Languages Semantics*

Now that we have been reminded that (i) causality is not directly observable, (ii) scientific empirical statements of observations suppose causal attributions,

[1]Though I have shown (Raccah 2005) that nothing can be *directly observable* by a human being (since anything requires the interpretation of the state of our sensorial apparatus), I will use that expression to refer to objects or events whose access is granted by the interpretation of the effect they directly produce on our sensorial apparatus. This terminological sloppiness is introduced for the sake of legibility….

(iii) sciences speak of indirectly observable entities embedding relations between directly observable entities, I would like to elaborate on a few interesting properties of the causal attributions used within the sciences of language(s), and, in particular, semantics. This will help understand why semantics can be a shortcut for strategic manoeuvring.

2.3.1 A Few Conceptual Distinctions

The concepts I resort to for this study are not all used in a normalized way: in the intent to be understood by different trends of thoughts, I will first focus on several conceptual differences (it should be noted that the terms I used to refer to these concepts may very well not be the ones some or other reader would use. I do not mean to compel them to use the same terms I use rather than the ones they prefer: I only aim at characterizing the concepts and insist on their differences.

(a) Several concepts of language
Though it is unavoidable that notions which are deeply related to our ways of thinking are grasped in different manners, according to the differences in those ways of thinking, it *is* possible, and highly desirable (see Pascal 1655, pp. 523–535) to ascertain that these *conceptions* are about the same *concept*. In the case of *language*, the differences in *conceptions* are frequently altered by an incorrect assimilation of three distinct *concepts*:

(i) something that human beings speak (or write) in, that is usually acquired by all human beings between birth and 24 months, that may serve to communicate, to think, to deceive, etc., that may be different from one group of human beings to another, that may be learnt, taught, etc.; English, French, Spanish, etc. are different instances of this *something*, which is called "idioma" in Spanish, "langue" in French; the noun referring to it may be pluralized;

(ii) the faculty that human beings have (some people may believe that it is also the case for some animals, robots, gods, etc.), and that enables them to learn, use and possibly forget the *something* I coined as the first concept; this second *object* is called "lenguaje" in Spanish, "langage", in French; the noun referring to it cannot be pluralized;

(iii) an abstract system, consciously and deliberately built by a human being, or by a team of human beings, in order to achieve a specific goal or set of goals.
The fact that these three different concepts happen to be called, in English, by the same name is not an evidence for their being the same concept… To avoid such confusions, I will use the term *human languages* for concept (i), *Language Faculty*, for concept (ii), and *artificial language*, for concept (iii).

(b) Several concepts of meaning
The difference between a sign and its use in a particular situation is acknowledged by most linguists. However, one of its consequences on the study of semantics and pragmatics, namely the essential difference in nature

between *utterance meaning* and *sentence meaning*, is not so often taken into account.[2]

In order to fully understand the rest of this paper, it will be necessary to keep this difference in mind: I will speak of *utterance meaning* in order to refer to the result of some interpretation of a discourse or of an utterance in a particular situation; in contrast, I will speak of *sentence meaning* in order to refer to the contribution of language units (not only grammatical sentences) to the interpretation of their different possible utterances.

Note that this apparently 'neutral' terminology presupposes that each unit of any language has something stable which is partially responsible for the infinitely many possible interpretations its use may lead to.[3]

2.3.2 Instructional Semantics

Semantics can thus be conceived of as the discipline which empirically and scientifically studies the contribution of language units (simple or complex) to the construction of the meanings of their utterances in each situation. The contribution of the situations to the construction of utterance-meanings is studied, according to that conception, by pragmatics.

According to that conception of semantics, *utterance-meaning* is, clearly, the result of a construction achieved by some hearer, construction influenced by the *linguistic meaning* (*sentence-meaning*, *phrase-meaning*) of the language units used in the utterance and by the elements of situation taken into account by the hearer. Diagram 1 illustrates this conception:

Diagram 1 The determination of utterance-meaning by sentence-meaning and situation

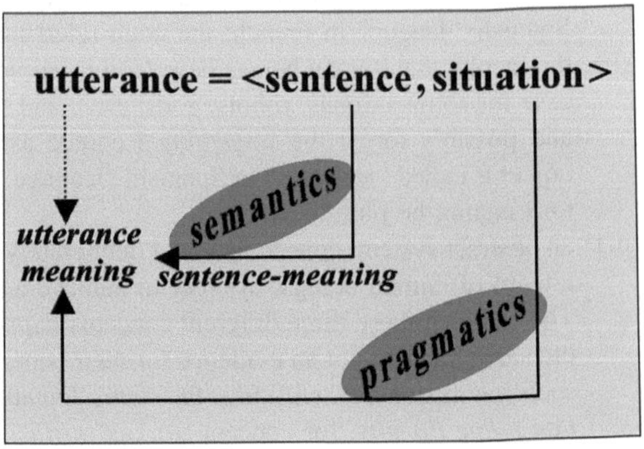

[2]As far as I know, one of the first explicit modern presentation of the conceptual difference between *utterance meaning* and *sentence meaning* is due to Dascal (1983).

[3]This very strong claim is evidenced by the fact that any dunce can acquire, *and does acquire*, a human language in 18-24 months, being exposed only to speech and human attitudes.

This pre-theoretic way of understanding the canvas of utterance-meaning construction belongs to the *instructional semantics* trend, as presented, for instance, in Harder (1990, p. 41):

> the emphasis is on meaning as something the speaker tells the addressee to do. If A (the addressee) does as he is told (follows the instructions), he will work out the interpretation that is the product of an act of communication

2.3.3 Causal Attributions in Semantics, and Their Essential Properties

Suppose an extra-terrestrial intelligence, ETI, wanted to study the semantics of English and, for that purpose, decided to observe speech situations. Suppose ETI hides in a room where several—supposedly English speaking—human beings are gathered, a classroom, for instance. Suppose now that ETI perceives that John pronounces "It is cold in here". If all of ETI's observations are of that kind, there is no chance that it can formulate grounded hypotheses about the meaning of the sequence it heard. For what can be perceived of John's utterance is only a series of vibrations, which, in themselves, do not give cues of any kind as to what it can mean (except for those who understand English and interpret the utterance using their private know-how). If ETI wants to do its job correctly, it will have to use, in addition, observations of another kind. Intentional states are ruled out since they are not directly accessible to the observers' sensorial apparatus. It follows that we will have to reject any statement of the kind: "the speaker meant so and so", or "normally when someone says XYZ, he or she wants to convey this or that idea" or even (in case the observer understands English) "I, observer, interpret XYZ in such and such a way and therefore, *that* is the meaning of XYZ". ETI will have to observe the audience's behaviour and see whether, in that behaviour, it can find a plausible *effect* of John's utterance: it will have to use indirect observation. The fact that it may be the case that no observable reaction followed John's utterance does not constitute an objection to the indirect observation method: it would simply mean that ETI would have to plan other experiments. After all, even in physics, many experiments do not inform the theorists until they find the experimental constraints that work.

Before we go further, let me insist and emphasize that we have just seen that the different 'popular learned conceptions'[4] of semantics are wrong. Indeed, the observable phenomena of semantics (i) cannot be directly *meanings*, since these are not accessible to our sensorial apparatus; (ii) they are not just *utterances*, since that would not be enough to describe meaning phenomena; (iii) they are not pairs consisting of *utterances* and '*intended meanings*', since such intentional things are

[4]That is, the conception an educated person could have about semantics without having learnt and reflected about it previously… This is, it must be admitted, the conception held by many people who speak or write about language!.

not accessible to empirical observation. In our extra-terrestrial example, we suggested that they are pairs consisting of utterances and behaviours.

I will take that suggestion as seriously as possible: in the rest of this section, I examine how to constrain the relationship between utterances and behaviours, and sketch some of the consequences of this choice.

(a) The causal attribution hypothesis

Suppose that, in our example, ETI notices that, after John's utterance, the following three actions take place: (i) Peter scratches his head, (ii) Paul closes the window and (iii) Mary writes something on a piece of paper. We all know (actually, we think we know, but we only believe…) that the correct answer to the question "what action was caused by John's utterance?" is most probably "Paul's". However, ETI has no grounds to *know* it and, in addition, it may be the case that Paul closed the window not because of John's utterance (which he may even not have heard), but because *he* was cold, or because there was too much noise outside to hear what John was saying… Obviously, the most plausible hypothesis, in normal situations, is the one according to which Paul's action was caused by John's utterance; but the fact that it is plausible does not make it cease to be a hypothesis…

Thus, before ETI can continue its study, it must admit the following general hypothesis

H_0: *Utterances may cause behaviours*

Moreover, in each experimental situation *s*, ETI must make specific hypotheses h_s which particularise H_0 in the situation *s*, and relate particular actions with the utterance under study (an aspect of van Eemeren's *contextualization*). It is important to remind that H_0 and the different h_s are not facts about the world but hypotheses: they do not characterise the way things *are* but rather the way things *are conceived of* in our rationality.

(b) The *non materiality* hypothesis

Let us suppose that ETI shares with us the aspects of our contemporary occidental rationality expressed by H_0. This would not prevent it from believing that the way John's utterance caused Paul's action is that the vibrations emitted by John during his utterance physically caused Paul to get up and close the window. Though it hurts our contemporary occidental rationality, this idea is not absurd: the fact that we simply cannot take it seriously does not *make* it false.[5] Moreover, utterances do have observable physical effects: a loud voice can hurt the hearers' ears, specific frequencies can break crystal, etc. What our rationality cannot accept is the idea that the *linguistic* effects of the utterances could be reduced to material causality. In

[5]Some Buddhist sects seek the "language of nature" in which the words emit the exact vibrations which correspond to the objects they refer to… Even though most of us, occidental thinkers, reject the belief underlying that quest, there is no ground to profess that the belief is silly independently of our set of beliefs.

order to rule out this idea, we need another hypothesis, which is also characteristic of our rationality rather than of the state of the world:

H_1: *The linguistic effects of an utterance are not due to material causes*

As a consequence of H_1, if we cannot believe that the observable actions caused by an utterance are due to its materiality, we are bound to admit that they are due to its form. In our rationality, the causal attribution requested by H_0 is constrained to be a formal causality.

(c) The non immediateness hypothesis

If we use the term *sentence* to refer to a category of form of utterances, we start to be in the position to fill the gap between what we can observe (utterances and behaviours) and what we want semantics to talk about (sentences and meanings). However, there is yet another option that our rationality compels us to rule out: ETI could accept H_1 and yet believe that though the causality that links John's utterance to Paul's action is not material, it directly determined Paul's action. That is, one could believe that John's utterance directly caused Paul to close the window, without leaving him room for a choice. This sort of belief corresponds to what we can call a 'magic thinking'; indeed, in Ali Baba's tail, for instance, there would be no magic if the "sesame" formula were recognised by a captor which would send an "open" instruction to a mechanism conceived in such a way that it could open the cave. The magical effect is due to the directedness of the effect of the formula. It is interesting to note that this feature of our rationality, which compels us to reject direct causality of forms, is rather recent and probably not completely 'installed' in our cognitive systems: there are many traces in human behaviour and in human languages of the 'magic thinking'. From some uses of expressions like "Please" or "Excuse me" to greetings such as "Happy new year!", an impressing series of linguistic expressions and social behaviours suggests that, though a part of our mind has abandoned the 'magic thinking', another part still lives with it. Think, for instance, about the effects of insults on normal contemporary human beings…

However, for scientific purposes, we definitely abandoned the 'magic thinking' and, again, since it is a characteristic of our rationality and not a matter of knowledge about the world, no observation can prove that it has to be abandoned: we need another hypothesis, which could be stated as follows:

H_2: *The directly observable effects of utterances are not directly caused by them*

The acceptance of that "anti-magic" hypothesis has at least two types of consequences on the conception one can have of human being.

The first type of consequences pertains to ethics: if utterances do not directly cause observable effects on human actions, no human being can justify a reprehensible action arguing that they have been told or even ordered to accomplish them. If a war criminal tries to do so, he or she will give the justified impression that he or she is not behaving like a human being, but rather like a kind of animal or robot. As human beings, we are supposed to be responsible for our actions; which does not mean that we are free, since a reprehensible decision could be the only way of serving vital interests. Though this type of consequences of H_2 are serious and important, they do not directly belong to the subject matter of this paper and we will have to end the discussion here. However, we think they were worth mentioning…

The second type of consequences of H_2 concern the relationship between semantics and cognitive science. Indeed, H_2, combined with H_0 and H_1, can be seen as a way of setting the foundations of a science of human cognition and of picturing its relationship with related disciplines. If we admit, in agreement with H_0, H_1 and H_2, that an utterance may indirectly and non materially cause an action, we are bound to accept the existence of a non physical causal chain linking the utterance to the action, part of that chain being inaccessible to our sensorial apparatus. The object of semantics is the first link of the chain; the first internal state can be seen as the *utterance meaning*. The action is determined by a causal lattice of which the utterance meaning is a part, and which includes many other elements and links; none of these elements or links are directly observable, though indirect observation can suggest more or less plausible hypotheses about them. Different theoretical frameworks in cognitive science construe that causal lattice in different ways; they also use the variations of different observable parameters in order to form these hypotheses. In our example, the only two directly observable parameters were utterances and actions, for the part of the lattice that we are interested in is the chain that links utterances to actions. However, other kinds of cognitive science experiments could be devoted to studying the variations of other directly observable parameters, such as electrical excitation, visual input, outside temperature, etc. for the beginning of the chain and movement characteristics, body temperature, attention, etc. for the end of the chain.[6]

Note that the fact that cognitive science and semantics may share experimental devices is not sufficient to adhere to the present fashion and suggest that there can be a "cognitive semantics": the object of semantics (the link between utterances and utterance meanings, as it is inscribed in languages units) does not belong to the causal lattice which constitutes the object of cognitive science.[7]

[6]I obviously didn't choose realistic nor very interesting parameters… but my purpose is only illustrative.

[7]See Raccah (2011) for more about this subject.

3 Strategic Manoeuvring, Human Languages & Argumentation

From the necessity of devising experiments providing indirect observation for semantics, as analyzed above, many consequences follow, from many different points of view. For the purpose of this paper, I would like to restrict myself to discussing two of them, which are related to the connection between strategic manoeuvring and semantic approaches to argumentation: namely the essential role of discourses analysis, and the essential insufficiency of ordinary corpora.

3.1 The Essential Role of Discourses Analysis in Semantics

As acknowledged by the pragma-dialectical approach to strategic manoeuvring, most, if not all, of what we know about results, routes, constraints and commitments involved in the strategy that is carried out by making an argumentative move, is the result of the interpretation of texts or discourses. It follows that, if we don't use an empirically grounded formal model in order to account for how this knowledge is built out of these texts and discourses, the essential knowledge used for describing argumentative strategies will remain intuitive.

In order to account for how this knowledge is built, out of the interpretation of texts and discourses, the semantic models that can be used must enable to describe how languages units impose the construction of the particular senses (utterance meanings), in the situations in which they are uttered, senses which constitute the different pieces of that knowledge. And, in order to allow for such descriptions, the language units have to crystallize some aspects of the socialized world which constitute the institutional situation. Diagram 2 illustrates this point.

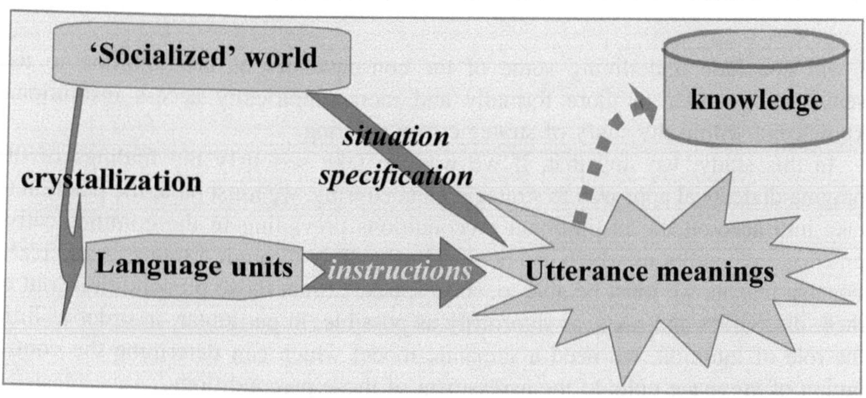

Diagram 2 From situations and language units to knowledge concerning strategic manoeuvring

3.2 About Corpora

The second consequence of this causal study which I would like to emphasize concerns the kind of corpora that can be useful for an empirical study of strategic maneuvering through semantics. The requirements for such corpora are limited to the ones for semantic corpora, since any discourse and any text refers to the institutional constraints on its own interpretation. However, these 'limited' requirements that must meet a corpus in order to be usable for an empirical study of semantics are not so weak and, actually, very seldom met in the corpora used in the literature.

Indeed, ordinary corpora provide only (in the best cases) one half of the empirical data required to study semantics: they usually only provide the linguistic units that have been used (the *signifier*), but do not give cues for the utterance meanings that have been actually constructed in the real situation in which they have been used. This leaves the second half of the necessary data to the observer's intuition. The fact that observer's intuitions are usually rather good does not help: on the contrary, it makes the observer rely on these intuitions without even noticing it. In order to illustrate this point, one only needs to imagine a physicist's reaction to another physicist claiming "I know where the cannon ball will fall, so I don't have to tire myself out by examining what is happening in the field"...

Obviously, the actual interpretation that a reader or a hearer made in the actual situation in which those linguistic units were used (like any interpretation whatsoever) is not accessible through our sensorial apparatus. Therefore, no corpus could possibly provide it. However, it is the burden of the observers to justify the interpretations they assign to those texts and discourse. Again, indirect observation is necessary: a useful corpus for semantics should contain cues for assessing the correctness or, at least, the plausibility of hypotheses on what has been understood.

4 Provisional Conclusions, and Perspectives

I will conclude underlining some of the consequences of the ambition to use semantics in order to more formally and more empirically access institutional knowledge within the study of strategic manoeuvring.

In this study, we saw that, if we want to take seriously the findings of the pragma-dialectical approach to strategic manoeuvring, we must be in the position to take into account the institutional preconditions prevailing in the communicative practice, preconditions which can be observed mainly through discourses and texts. For that reason, we must be able to, so to speak, extract those preconditions out of these discourses and texts, as rigorously as possible; in particular, in order to limit the role of intuition, we need a semantic model which can determine the contribution of language units to the assessment of those preconditions.

Neither cognitive semantics nor truth-conditional semantics can do the job because the descriptions they provide have nothing to do with socialized ways of understanding the institutions: what is needed is an instructional semantics that accounts for how the language units influence the hearer's way of seeing the role of institutions, or, from a complementary point of view, how the language units reveal the speakers' ways of understanding the impact of institutions. As a consequence, what is needed is a semantics that assigns socialized points of view to language units, constraints on points of view to connectors and operators, in order to allow to compute the points of view suggested by more complex language units. Given that causal relations are not observable though our sensorial apparatus, particular attention must be paid to the refutability of each observational statement. Moreover, given that the interpretation that was actually built out of a discourse or a text is not directly accessible to observation, particular attention must also be paid to the justification of the interpretation assigned to the triple < language unit, situation, addressee > .

Such semantic models, called *ViewPoint Semantics* (VPS), have been developed and are mainly used to extract knowledge and/or ideologies from texts and discourses. Their use for assessing institutional preconditions prevailing in the communicative practice, in order to study strategic manoeuvring, is promising, from a practical point of view, and inspiring, from a theoretical point of view.

References

Bakhtin, M. M. (1929). Bakhtine Mikhail Mikhaïlovitch (1929). *Problemy tvorchestva Dostoevskogo.* Leningrad 1929. 2nd edn: *Probemy poetiki Dostoevskogo.* Moscow, 1963. Translated to French by Kolitcheff, Isabelle. *La poétique de Dostoievski.* Paris, 1970–1998; Le Seuil.

Dascal, Marcelo. (1983). *Pragmatics and the philosophy of mind 1: Thought in language.* Amsterdam: John Benjamins.

Ducrot, O. (1988). Topoï et formes topiques. *Bulletin d'études de linguistique française de Tokyo, 22,* 1–14.

Harder, Peter. (1990). The pragmatics and semantics of reference. *Copenhagen Studies in Language, 13,* 41–78.

Pascal, B. (1655). De l'esprit géométrique. Fragments edited by Ernest Havet in *Pensées de Pascal publiées dans leur texte authentique.* Paris, 1883; Delagrave.

Raccah, P.-Y. (2005). What is an empirical theory of linguistic meaning a theory of? In Z. Frajzyngier, et al. (Eds.), *Diversity and language theory. Studies in language companion series.* Amsterdam: John Benjamins.

Raccah, P.-Y. (2011). Linguistique critique : Une exploration cognitive. *Intellectica 56*: 305-314. Special issue: *Linguistique cognitive: une exploration critique*, dir.: Jean-Baptiste Guignard.

van Eemeren, F. H. (2010). *Strategic maneuvering in argumentative discourse. Extending the pragma-dialectical theory of argumentation.* Amsterdam: John Benjamins.

van Eemeren, F. H., & Houtlosser, P. (2009). Strategic manoeuvring. Examining argumentation in context. In F. H. van Eemeren (Ed.), *Examining argumentation in context. Fifteen Studies on strategic maneuvering.* Amsterdam: John Benjamins.

MIX
Papier aus verantwortungsvollen Quellen
Paper from responsible sources
FSC® C105338

If you have any concerns about our products,
you can contact us on
ProductSafety@springernature.com

In case Publisher is established outside the EU,
the EU authorized representative is:
Springer Nature Customer Service Center GmbH
Europaplatz 3, 69115 Heidelberg, Germany

Printed by Libri Plureos GmbH
in Hamburg, Germany